R. Gupta's®

Popular Master Guide

Staff Selection Commission (SSC)

Delhi Police

Head Constable

(Ministerial)

Recruitment Exam

by

RPH Editorial Board

2026
EDITION

RAMESH PUBLISHING HOUSE, NEW DELHI

Published by
O.P. Gupta *for* Ramesh Publishing House

Admin. Office
12-H, New Daryaganj Road, Opp. Officers' Mess,
New Delhi-110002 ✆ 23275224, 23245124

E-mail: info@rameshpublishinghouse.com
For Online Shopping: www.rameshpublishinghouse.com

Showroom
• Balaji Market, Nai Sarak, Delhi-6 ✆ 23253720, 23282525
• 4457, Nai Sarak, Delhi-6, ✆ 23918938

Book Code: R-1702

ISBN: 978-93-5012-487-1

Price: ₹ 360

Printed at: Deepak Offset, Delhi

CONTENTS

Scheme of Examination

The selection process shall consist of the following compulsory tests in the given order:

Tests/Exams	Maximum Marks/Qualifying
(i) Computer Based Examination by SSC	100 Marks
(ii) Physical Endurance & Measurement Tests (PE&MT) by Delhi Police	Qualifying
(iii) Typing Test on Computer by Delhi Police	25 Marks
(iv) Computer (Formatting) Test by Delhi Police	Qualifying

COMPUTER BASED EXAMINATION-OBJECTIVE TYPE:

All candidates (Male & Female) shall be put through a Computer Based Examination of one and half hour **(90 minutes)** duration to be conducted at different Centres. The Computer Based Examination will consist of one objective type paper containing **100 Questions** carrying **100 Marks**. There will be **negative marking** of 0.50 marks for each wrong answer. The question paper for Computer Based Examination will cover the foilowing subjects and will be conducted in **HINDI and ENGLISH only.**

	Subject	No. of Questions	Max. Marks
Part-A	General Awareness	20	20
Part-B	Quantitative Aptitude (Basic Arithmetic Skill)	20	20
Part-C	General Intelligence	25	25
Part-D	English Language (Basic Knowledge)	25	25
Part-E	Computer Fundamentals, MS Excel, MS Word, Communication, Internet, WWW and Web Browsers etc.	10	10
	Total	**100**	**100**

TYPING TEST ON COMPUTER (MAXIMUM 25 MARKS)

Candidates who qualify in the Physical Endurance & Measurement Tests (PE&MT) as well as Persons with Disabilities (PwD) who qualify in Computer Based Examination will be called for Typing Test on Computer. The test shall be of 10 minutes duration. The marks will be taken into account while preparing the final result. The candidates will be allotted marks according to speed achieved in the typing test.

COMPUTER (FORMATTING) TEST (QUALIFYING)

The candidates who qualify in the Typing Test on Computer shall be called for Computer (Formatting) Test and will be tested on MS-Word, MS-PowerPoint and MS-Excel which will be of qualifying nature. The candidates will be given 10 minutes time for each tests separately. The candidates shall have to format in the same way as it is in the supplied handout and to print the same in the printer.

Previous Years' Paper

Staff Selection Commission (SSC)

Delhi Police—Head Constable (Ministerial)

Recruitment Examination, 2022

(Exam held on 10-10-2022)

GENERAL AWARENESS

1. Union Education Minister and Skill Development Minister Dharmendra Pradhan launched ...., a single platform to provide the best-developed ed-tech solutions and courses to students of the country.
A. NEAT 2.0 B. NEAT 3.0
C. AICTE 3.0 D. AICTE 2.0

2. Which of the following IITs has developed a Solar-powered Unmanned Autonomous Survey Craft for Indian Ports and Inland Waterways?
A. IIT Bangalore B. IIT Roorkee
C. IIT Delhi D. IIT Madras

3. Who has been appointed as the chairperson of the National Human Rights Commission (NHRC) in April 2021?
A. Dipak Mishra
B. J.S. Verma
C. Arun Kumar Mishra
D. H.L. Dattu

4. This state of matter is made up of ionised gas, which consists of a balanced mix of electrons, positive ions and neutral particles. What is it?
A. Liquid B. Plasma
C. Gas D. Fog

5. Which place in India is famed for the celebration of Dev Deepawali?
A. Haridwar B. Ganganagar
C. Patna D. Varanasi

6. Which of the following is NOT an objective of micro finance institutions in India?
A. Promotion of financial inclusion
B. Improvement of the credit score of the poor
C. Poverty alleviation
D. Improvement of living standards

7. Kalyani Amma is famously associated with:
A. Kathak B. Manipuri
C. Mohiniyattam D. Kathakali

8. When was the Microfinance Institutions Network (MFIN) recognised by the Reserve Bank of India (RBI) as India's first Self-Regulatory Organisation (SRO) for the Nonbank Financial Company – Microfinance Institutions (NBFC-MFIs)?
A. 2009 B. 2014
C. 2012 D. 2016

1. B	2. D	3. C	4. B	5. D	6. B	7. C	8. B

9. When, for the first time in independent India, did the government announce three annual plans called Plan Holidays?
A. 1967 to 1970
B. 1965 to 1968
C. 1966 to 1969
D. 1968 to 1971

10. Social forestry means the management and protection of forests. Which of the following is NOT a category of social forestry?
A. Rural forestry
B. Tribal forestry
C. Urban forestry
D. Farm forestry

11. Where was the Supreme Court established under the Charter of 1774?
A. Bombay B. Calcutta
C. Shimla D. Madras

12. What is the percentage of the source of lighting through electricity for households in India as per the 2011 Census?
A. 67.2% B. 66.2%
C. 62.7% D. 69.8%

13. The total literacy rate of the state of .... was the lowest, according to the 2011 census.
A. Jharkhand B. Rajasthan
C. Bihar D. Uttar Pradesh

14. As per CMIE data, in March 2022, what is the urban unemployment rate in India?
A. 8.28% B. 8.88%
C. 8.22% D. 8.27%

15. Which organisation conducted the Young Scientist Programme 'YUVIKA-2022' for students?
A. Indian Space Research Organisation (ISRO)
B. Council of Scientific and Industrial Research (CSIR)
C. Indian Council of Medical Research (ICMR)
D. Defence Research and Development Organisation (DRDO)

16. Who among the following became the first President of the Indian National Congress in 1885?
A. Dadabhai Naoriji
B. Pherozeshah Mehta
C. Womesh Chandra Bonnerjee
D. Gopal Krishna Gokhale

17. Jahaz Mahal, built by Sultan Ghiyas-ud-din Khilji, is located in ....
A. Madhya Pradesh
B. Rajasthan
C. Telangana
D. Gujarat

18. Babur wrote Tuzuk-i-Baburi in which of the following language?
A. Persian B. Turkish
C. Afghani D. Urdu

19. The 11th edition of the Khel Mahakumbh was inaugurated at the Sardar Patel Stadium in Ahmedabad in March 2022, by ....
A. Kirit Kumar Parmar
B. Narendra Modi
C. Acharya Devvrat
D. Harsh Sanghvi

20. Which of the following is NOT correct about the Constitution of India?
A. It suits the requirement of India
B. It reflects the historical, social, political and economic conditions of the Indian people
C. It is a document of social relevance
D. The original Constitution contained 395 Articles in 25 parts and 12 schedules

9. C	10. B	11. B	12. A	13. C	14. A	15. A	16. C	17. A	18. B	19. B	20. D

QUANTITATIVE APTITUDE

21. Choose the INCORRECT statement.
A. LCM of 12 and 15 is 60
B. LCM of 14 and 7 is 14
C. LCM of 8 and 7 is 1
D. LCM of 3 and 5 is 15

22. Find the fourth proportional to 19, 23 and 38.
A. 46 B. 28
C. 42 D. 24

23. A cylindrical tank having an internal radius 14 m, contains water up to the depth of 10 m. What is the total area of the wet surface?
$\left(\text{Use } \pi = \frac{22}{7}\right)$
A. 1496 m^2
B. 1492 m^2
C. 1494 m^2
D. 1498 m^2

24. In how many years will ₹1,900 produce an interest of ₹798 at the rate of 7% simple interest per annum?
A. 6 B. 8
C. 9 D. 5

25. Ranjan purchased a bicycle for ₹5,000 and paid ₹250 for its transportation. If he sells the bicycle for ₹5,075, find his profit or loss percentage.
A. Loss of 3.33%
B. Loss of 33.3%
C. Loss of 1.75%
D. Profit of 3.33%

26. The value of $2.\overline{13} \div 3.\overline{12}$ is:
A. $\frac{211}{309}$ B. $\frac{301}{309}$
C. $\frac{249}{309}$ D. $\frac{239}{309}$

27. What is the value of the expression
$(1 + y)(1 + y^2)(1 + y^4)(1 + y^8)(1 - y)$?
A. $1 - y^{16}$ B. $1 - y^{40}$
C. $1 - y^{32}$ D. $1 - y^{42}$

28. A sum of money after a period of 2 years becomes ₹34,560, and it becomes ₹41,472 after a period of three years, being compounded at 'R' rate of interest. What is the value of R?
A. 25% B. 20%
C. 12% D. 10%

29. Find the average of the first 20 multiples of 9.
A. 180 B. 94.5
C. 189 D. 21.5

30. Annual production of four different types of chocolates has been tabulated in the following table. Which of these chocolates has encountered minimum percentage increment in production?

Chocolates	2010	2011
A	720000	780000
B	850000	880000
C	690000	740000
D	580000	670000

A. D B. C
C. A D. B

21. C	22. A	23. A	24. A	25. A	26. A	27. A	28. B	29. B	30. D

31. In a race, a cyclist covers a distance of 500 m in 625 sec in the first lap. He covers the second lap of the same length in 375 sec. What is the average speed (in m/sec) of the cyclist?

A. 5 B. 10
C. 3 D. 1

32. A conical shaped cup, when filled with ice-cream, forms into the shape of a hemisphere at its open end. What is the volume of the ice cream, if the radius of the base of the cone is 3 cm and the vertical height of the cone is 7 cm?

A. $\frac{2574}{21}$ cm^3

B. $\frac{2754}{21}$ cm^3

C. $\frac{2504}{21}$ cm^3

D. $\frac{2547}{21}$ cm^3

33. Kiran, Vishal and Dinesh work in a juice factory. Kiran takes 2 hours to extract as much juice as Vishal can in 3 hours. Dinesh takes 5 hours to extract as much juice that Kiran extracts in 4 hours. A tank can be filled with juice in 48 hours, if all of them work together. How long will it take to fill the tank, if Dinesh alone is trying to fill the tank?

A. 140 hours B. 135 hours
C. 132 hours D. 148 hours

34. A dealer purchased a water cooler for ₹5,800. He allows a discount of 12% on its marked price and still gains 10%. Find the marked price of the water cooler.

A. ₹7,220 B. ₹6,880
C. ₹7,250 D. ₹7,280

35. One boy and one girl together can complete a piece of work in 12 days. A boy alone can complete the work in 15 days. In how many days can one girl alone complete the work?

A. 70 days B. 50 days
C. 60 days D. 44 days

36. If the price of a leather bag is increased by 15%, and then decreased by 15%, what will be the net percentage decrease in its price?

A. 3.25% B. 2.25%
C. 3.30% D. 2.30%

37. If sec A + tan A = 5, then sec A − tan A = ?

A. $\frac{5}{2}$ B. $\frac{1}{5}$

C. 5 D. $\frac{2}{5}$

38. If $\frac{1}{x}+\frac{1}{y}+\frac{1}{z}=1$, then $\left(\frac{1}{z-1}\right)\left(\frac{1}{x}+\frac{1}{y}\right)+\left(\frac{1}{y-1}\right)\left(\frac{1}{x}+\frac{1}{z}\right)+\left(\frac{1}{x-1}\right)\left(\frac{1}{y}+\frac{1}{z}\right)=?$

A. 1 B. −1
C. 2 D. 0

39. Simplify the following:

$6\frac{2}{7}$ of $2\frac{6}{11}\times\frac{1}{4}+\left\{25\div5\times\frac{3}{5}\right\}$

A. 10 B. 7
C. 9 D. 5

40. In a ΔPQR, PQ = PR, and S is a point on PQ, such that PS = RS = QR. Then what is the measure of ∠QPR?

A. 72° B. 60°
C. 36° D. 23°

31. D	32. A	33. D	34. C	35. C	36. B	37. B	38. A	39. B	40. C

GENERAL INTELLIGENCE

41. Select the set in which the numbers are related in the same way as are the numbers of the following sets.

(NOTE: Operations should be performed on the whole numbers, without breaking down the numbers into its constituent digits. E.g. 13 – Operations on 13 such as adding/deleting/multiplying etc. to 13 can be performed. Breaking down 13 into 1 and 3 and then performing mathematical operations on 1 and 3 is not allowed)

(64, 12, 4)

(128, 19, 3)

A. (70, 21, 12)
B. (72, 21, 12)
C. (72, 21, 11)
D. (72, 20, 12)

42. Read the given statements and conclusions carefully. Assuming that the information given in the statements is true, even if it appears to be at variance with commonly known facts, decide which of the given conclusions logically follow(s) from the statements.

Statements:

I. All ladders are tables.
II. Some tables are chairs.
III. All chairs are furniture.

Conclusions:

I. Some furniture are ladders.
II. All tables are furniture.

A. Only conclusion II follows
B. Only conclusion I follows
C. Neither conclusion I nor II follows
D. Both conclusions I and II follow

43. In a code language, 'WRITE' is coded as D60X and 'APPLE' is coded as D35B. How will 'BASIS' be coded in the same language?

A. R37C B. T35A
C. R35C D. T37A

44. Which letter-cluster will replace the question mark (?) to complete the given series?

WFCI, PAZH, IVWG, ?

A. CQTF B. CQTE
C. BQTF D. BQTE

45. Select the correct combination of mathematical signs to sequentially replace the * signs and to balance the given equation.

572 * 4 * 64 * 365 * 41 * 27 = 441 * 380

A. ÷, +, −, ×, +, −
B. ÷, −, −, +, ×, +
C. +, ÷, −, ×, −, +
D. ÷, −, +, −, ×, +

46. Select the number from among the given options that can replace the question mark (?) in the following series.

51, 46, 40, 33, 25, ?

A. 20 B. 11
C. 16 D. 10

47. Select the numbers from among the given options that can replace the question marks (?) in the following series.

27, 41, 55, 73, ?, ?, 135

A. 91, 113
B. 87, 114
C. 91, 115
D. 89, 112

41. B	42. C	43. C	44. C	45. B	46. C	47. A

48. Study the given diagram carefully and answer the question. The numbers in different sections indicate the number of persons.

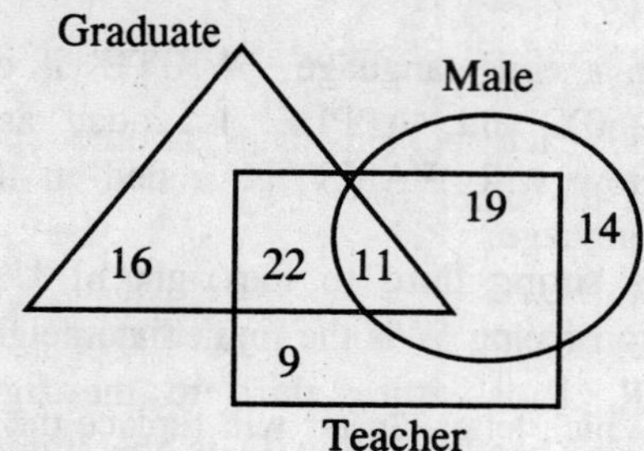

How many such teachers are there who are NEITHER male NOR graduate?

A. 22 B. 11
C. 9 D. 19

49. Select the combination of letters that when sequentially placed in the blanks of the given series, will complete the series.

DEFD _ F _ DEFD _ DE _ DEFD

A. EDEF B. EFDF
C. DEDE D. EEFF

50. Which of the following options represents the correct order of the given words as they would appear in the English dictionary?

1. Pickle 2. Picador
3. Picnic 4. Pickaxe
5. Piccolo

A. 5, 2, 1, 4, 3
B. 2, 4, 5, 1, 3
C. 2, 5, 4, 1, 3
D. 5, 2, 4, 3, 1

51. Select the option that is related to the fifth letter cluster in the same way as the second letter cluster is related to the first letter cluster and the fourth letter cluster is related to the third letter cluster.

GBC : UPQ :: DSX : RGL :: PEN : ?

A. DGF B. DSB
C. BRY D. LSU

52. Select the figure that will come next in the following figure series.

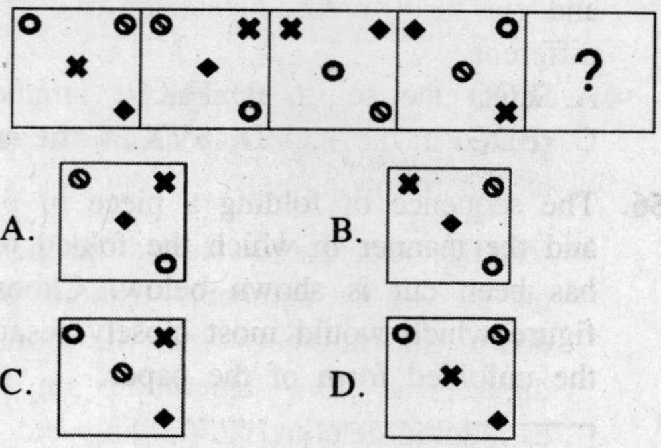

53. Select the option that is related to the fifth word in the same way as the second word is related to the first word and the fourth word is related to the third word. (The words must be considered as meaningful English words and must not be related to each other based on the number of letters/ number of consonants/vowels in the word)

Horse: Stable :: Bee: Beehive :: Lion: ?

A. Sty B. Farm
C. Cage D. Den

54. The sequence of folding a piece of paper and the manner in which the folded paper has been cut is shown below. Choose the figure that would most closely resemble the unfolded form of the paper.

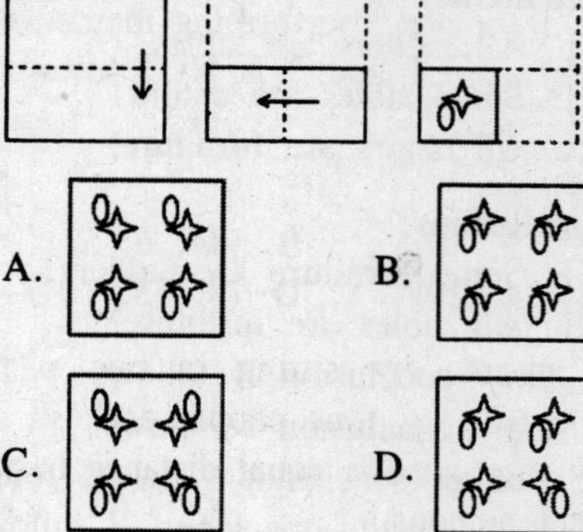

48. C	49. A	50. C	51. B	52. D	53. D	54. C

55. Four letter-clusters have been given out of which three are alike in some manner and one is different. Select the one that is different.

A. LOQ B. FIK
C. BDG D. SVX

56. The sequence of folding a piece of paper and the manner in which the folded paper has been cut is shown below. Choose a figure which would most closely resemble the unfolded form of the paper.

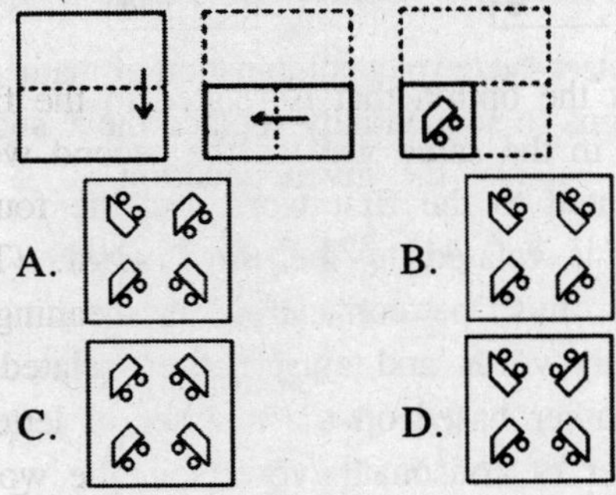

57. Select the set in which the numbers are related in the same way as are the numbers of the following set.

(NOTE: Operations should be performed on the whole numbers, without breaking down the numbers into its constituent digits. E.g., 13 – Operations on 13 such as adding /deleting /multiplying etc. to 13 can be performed. Breaking down 13 into 1 and 3 and then performing mathematical operations on 1 and 3 is NOT allowed).

(6, 15, 18)

(7, 35, 49)

A. (25, 7, 40) B. (44, 6, 51)
C. (4, 34, 29) D. (8, 65, 104)

58. Eight people are sitting in two parallel rows containing four people each in such a way that there is equal distance between adjacent persons.

In the first row, P, Q, R and S are seated and all of them are facing the south.

In the second row, U, V, W and X are seated and all of them are facing the north.

Thus, each person faces another person from the other row.

X is sitting third to the right of U. The person facing W is the immediate neighbour of R. P is sitting third to the right of R. The person facing Q is the immediate neighbour of U. S is sitting second to the left of P.

Who amongst the following faces U?

A. P B. S
C. R D. Q

59. 'P @ Q' means 'P is the husband of Q'

'P & Q' means 'P is the mother of Q'

'P # Q' means 'P is the wife of Q'

'P × Q' means 'P is the brother of Q'

If 'A @ B & C × D # E', then how is E related to A?

A. Wife's father
B. Son
C. Daughter's husband
D. Wife's brother

60. Select the correct mirror image of the given figure when the mirror is placed at MN as shown below.

A. ɘbƨ7rGh
B. ɘpƨ⅃ɿGɥ
C. ɘbƧ7ɹGɥ
D. ɘbƧ7ɿGh

55. C	56. D	57. D	58. A	59. C	60. D

61. In a certain code language, 'BIKE' is written as '23' and 'RIDE' is written as '32'. How will 'NICE' be written in that language?

A. 27 B. 25
C. 28 D. 26

62. Six friends - P,Q,R,S,T and U - are sitting around a circular table, facing towards the centre of the table. S is an immediate neighbour of P and T. Q is second to the left of S. If R is an immediate neighbour of P, where is U sitting?

A. Immediate left of R
B. Second to the left of T
C. Immediate right of Q
D. Third to the right of P

63. Select the figure that will replace the question mark (?) in the following figure series.

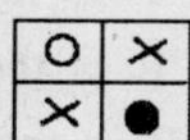 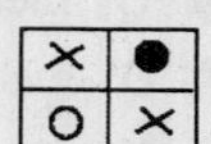  ?

A. B.
C. D.

64. Pointing to the photo, Neha said, "This woman is the wife of my father's paternal grandfather's only son." How is girl in the photo related to the Neha?

A. Mother B. Sister
C. Father's Mother D. Father's Sister

65. Select the correct combination of mathematical signs to sequentially replace the * signs and to balance the given equation.

23 * 8 * 4 * 321 * 87 * 280

A. ×, +, −, ÷, =
B. +, ×, −, ÷, =
C. ×, ÷, +, −, =
D. +, −, ×, ÷, =

ENGLISH LANGUAGE

66. Select the most appropriate synonym of the given word.

Diligent

A. Intelligent B. Handsome
C. Industrious D. Lazy

67. Sentences of a paragraph are given below in jumbled order. Arrange the sentences in the correct order to form a meaningful and coherent paragraph.

(*a*) The average person has about one to one and a half gallons of a liquid inside his or her body called blood.
(*b*) The circulatory system is responsible for the movement of blood throughout the body through blood vessels.
(*c*) Blood is the most essential and important part of the body's circulatory system.
(*d*) The heart is the pump that makes it all happen

A. (*a*) (*b*) (*d*) (*c*) B. (*a*) (*c*) (*b*) (*d*)
C. (*c*) (*a*) (*b*) (*d*) D. (*a*) (*d*) (*c*) (*b*)

68. Select the most appropriate ANTONYM of the given word.

Expel

A. Eulogise B. Accept
C. Deport D. Adulate

69. Select the option that can be used as a one-word substitute for the underlined group of words.

Advertisements on television for soaps promise <u>younger looking</u> skin.

A. Rejuvenated B. Smarter
C. Lighter D. Brighter

61. A	62. B	63. C	64. C	65. C	66. C	67. B	68. B	69. A

70. Select the option that can be used as a one-word substitute for the given group of words.

A disorder that involve difficulty in reading, interpret words

A. Dyslexia B. Dysgraphia
B. Delusion B. Disability

71. Select the most appropriate homonym to fill in the blank.

He is not a ...... Don't misunderstand him.

A. chit B. cheat
B. sheath B. chid

72. Select the most appropriate option to fill in the blank.

A human being requires a .... intake of nutrients and protein for keeping a fit and healthy body.

A. certain B. similar
C. hygienic D. balanced

73. The following sentence has been divided into parts. One of them may contain an error. Select the part that contains the error from the given options. If you don't find any error, mark 'No error' as your answer.

Sam slowly poured / the juice / inside the glass.

A. the juice B. No error
C. inside the glass D. Sam slowly poured

74. Select the most appropriate option that can substitute the underlined segment in the given sentence.

The teacher told him strictly that he <u>hadn't ought to do</u> that in the class.

A. ought not to have done
B. ought not has done
C. ought not done
D. hadn't ought to have done

75. Select the most appropriate meaning of the underlined idiom in the given sentence.

He <u>backed up</u> his friend's claim.

A. collected B. added to
C. withdrew D. supported

76. Select the most appropriate meaning of the given idiom.

Better late than never

A. Timely and efficient
B. Better to arrive late than not to come at all
C. Better to equip yourselves to be quick
D. Always be on time

77. Select the most appropriate synonym of the underlined word in the given sentence.

The care, affection, and guidance which I have got from my teachers <u>inspired</u> me to become a teacher.

A. infused B. compelled
C. motivated D. quickened

78. Select the most appropriate synonym of the given word.

Accrue

A. Fetter B. Spank
C. Reject D. Gather

79. Select the most appropriate option to fill in the blank.

The steady progress of military technology has brought weapons of ever-increasing .... power.

A. destructive B. super
C. world-ending D. killer

80. Select the INCORRECTLY spelt word.

A. Etarnel B. Supreme
C. Ultimate D. Perfect

81. Select the most appropriate synonym of the given word.

Vagrant

A. Trader B. Fighter
C. Drifter D. Loser

70. A	71. B	72. D	73. C	74. A	75. D	76. B	77. C	78. D	79. A	80. A	81. C

82. Select the INCORRECTLY spelt word in the following sentence.

Early rising enables us to get a long day ahead of us, permitting us to wrap up all of our work eficiently.

A. permitting B. enables
C. eficiently D. wrap up

83. Select the most appropriate option that can substitute the underlined segment in the given sentence.

My mother always loves to spend her leisure time on our <u>piece of enclosed land planted with fruit trees</u>.

A. orchard B. garden
C. lawn D. farm

84. The following sentence has been divided into parts. One of them may contain an error. Select the part that contains the error from the given options. If you don't find any error, mark 'No error' as your answer.

His whole life, he wrote music, / played the piano, / and was a singer

A. and was a singer
B. No error
C. played the piano
D. His whole life he wrote music

85. Sentences of a paragraph are given below in jumbled order. Arrange the sentences in the correct order to form a meaningful and coherent paragraph.

(*a*) It accounts for the adaptation and evolution of organisms, those innumerable features that so wonderfully equip them for survival and reproduction.

(*b*) It is by way of this passive choosing, this natural selection, that the physical features of an entire population come to change over time.

(*c*) Furthermore, it accounts for the divergence of species from common ancestors and thus for the endless diversity of life.

(*d*) The theory of natural selection is the centerpiece of On the Origin of Species and of evolutionary theory.

A. (*a*) (*b*) (*d*) (*c*) B. (*b*) (*a*) (*c*) (*d*)
C. (*d*) (*c*) (*a*) (*b*) D. (*d*) (*a*) (*c*) (*b*)

Directions (Q.No. 86-90): *In the following passage, some words have been deleted. Read the passage carefully and select the most appropriate option to fill in each blank.*

The room was decorated with a number of (1) .... objects, difficult to be seen around, small items of antique statuary and clay pots. (2) .... the wall hung a stick, (3) .... about with ivy leaves. It was (4) .... with a small chaise longue. The wooden boards (5) .... beneath the feet of the boy present.

86. Select the most appropriate option to fill in blank number 1.

A. absolute B. unusual
C. frequent D. creaky

87. Select the most appropriate option to fill in blank number 2.

A. Upon B. Above
C. On D. Beside

88. Select the most appropriate option to fill in blank number 3.

A. scattered B. wound
C. held D. tied

89. Select the most appropriate option to fill in blank number 4.

A. furnished B. fissured
C. famished D. featured

90. Select the most appropriate option to fill in blank number 5.

A. snapped B. crumbled
C. swiped D. creaked

82. C	83. A	84. A	85. D	86. B	87. C	88. B	89. A	90. D

COMPUTER FUNDAMENTALS

91. .... function in MS-Excel 2010 returns the total number of characters in a string.
A. LEN B. COUNTIF
C. SUM D. COUNTA

92. Which of the following is not a document processing software?
A. Open Office Impress
B. Microsoft Word
C. Notepad
D. WordPad

93. Which of the following is the symbol that must be used in email address?
A. # B. @
C. % D. $

94. In MS-Excel 2010 .... function provides only the current system date.
A. TODAY B. CURRENT
C. YEAR D. NOW

95. Hide option is present in .... tab in MS-Excel 2010 ribbon bar.
A. Data B. File
C. Insert D. View

96. A markup language and file format used for storing, transmitting, and reconstructing arbitrary data is known as ....
A. HTML B. XML
C. EML D. SGML

97. Mozilla is a web browsing software developed in the year ...., by the Mozilla Foundation.
A. 2001 B. 2002
C. 2003 D. 2000

98. In MS-Excel 2010 .... is used for hiding columns within the sheet.
A. Ctrl + 0
B. Ctrl + 9
C. Alt + 0
D. Alt + 9

99. The .... is a name for the lower edge of the worksheet window, which displays various information about an excel worksheet in MS-Excel 2010.
A. Status bar B. Ribbon
C. Task bar D. Title bar

100. In MS-Excel 2010 .... are named from A onwards and .... are named from 1 onwards.
A. table, pivot table
B. chart, graph
C. columns, rows
D. rows, columns

EXPLANATORY ANSWERS

1. (B): Union Education Minister and Skill Development Minister Shri Dharmendra Pradhan launched NEAT 3.0, a single platform to provide the best-developed ed-tech solutions and courses to students of the country. NEAT is a game-changer in bridging the digital divide, especially among the economically disadvantaged students and also in fulfilling the knowledge-based requirement of India and the world.

2. (D): Researchers at IIT-Madras have created a solar-powered Unmanned Autonomous Survey Craft. It is developed for Indian ports and inland waterways. Its objective

91. A	92. A	93. B	94. A	95. D	96. B	97. B	98. A	99. A	100. C

is to carry out autonomous oceanographic and hydrographic surveys and to enable real-time data transfer over great distances. These craft can be used to ease maritime traffic even in shallow water.

3. **(C):** Justice Arun Kumar Mishra was appointed as the chairperson of the National Human Rights Commission (NHRC) of India on February 6, 2021. He is a former judge of the Supreme Court of India. The President of India appoints the chairperson and members of the NHRC based on recommendations from a six-member committee. The NHRC is a statutory public body that was established on October 12, 1993, under the Protection of Human Rights Ordinance of 1993.

4. **(B):** Plasma is the state of matter made up of ionized gas, which is a balanced mix of electrons, positive ions, and neutral particles. Plasma is often called the "fourth state of matter" along with solid, liquid, and gas. Plasma is created by heating a gas, which forms a soup of positively charged particles (ions) and negatively charged particles (electrons).

5. **(D):** Varanasi, Uttar Pradesh is famous for celebrating Dev Deepawali, also known as the festival of Kartik Poornima. The festival is celebrated on the 15th day of Shukla Paksha in the month of Kartik, which is the full moon in the Hindu month of Kartika (November–December). Dev Deepawali is celebrated in the ghats of Varanasi and includes cultural programs and a dance performance called "Nritya Ganga".

6. **(B):** Microfinance institutions primarily focus on promoting financial inclusion, poverty alleviation, and improvement of living standards by providing financial services such as credit, savings, and insurance to low-income individuals who lack access to traditional banking services. The direct improvement of credit scores specifically is not typically a primary objective of microfinance institutions, although their services can indirectly contribute to this by providing opportunities for financial stability and growth among borrowers.

7. **(C):** Kalyani Amma, also known as Kalamandalam Kalyanikutty Amma, is famous for her contributions to the development and popularization of Mohiniyattam, a classical dance form that originated in Kerala, India. She was one of the first students at Kerala Kalamandalam, the first institute for training in art forms, and was established as one of the first formal teachers of Mohiniyattam along with Guru Krishna Panikker.

8. **(B):** The Reserve Bank of India (RBI) recognized the Microfinance Institutions Network (MFIN) as India's first Self-Regulatory Organization (SRO) for Non-Banking Financial Company-Microfinance Institutions (NBFC-MFIs) in 2014. As an SRO, MFIN plays a crucial role in supporting adherence to RBI regulations and industry standards among its member NBFC-MFIs. It ensures compliance with specific guidelines tailored for microfinance activities, fostering a level playing field and safeguarding borrowers' interests.

9. **(C):** During this period of 1966 to 1969, the Indian government faced challenges in implementing the Five-Year Plan due to external factors like wars and internal issues like drought. As a result, they opted for a temporary break from the traditional five-year planning cycle and focused on formulating annual plans with a stronger emphasis on agriculture and industry. This period is referred to as the "Plan Holidays."

10. (B): Tribal forestry, or community forestry involving indigenous or tribal communities, often has its own distinct focus and approaches separate from traditional social forestry programs. Social forestry generally includes rural forestry, urban forestry, and farm forestry, which all involve engaging different sectors of society in tree planting, conservation, and sustainable forest management for environmental and social benefits.

11. (B): The Charter of 1774 established the Supreme Court of Judicature at Fort William in Calcutta. This court was the highest court of law in British India at that time and played a significant role in administering justice and upholding British law in the region. The court was located at Fort William and was British India's highest court until 1862. The court had both civil and criminal jurisdiction, and its jurisdiction included admiralty, ecclesiastical, and appellate jurisdiction.

12. (A): According to the 2011 Census, 67.2% of households in India used electricity as their primary source of lighting. This was an increase of 11 percentage points from 2001, and reduced the rural-urban gap by 7 percentage points from 44% to 37%.

13. (C): The state with the lowest overall literacy rate in the 2011 Indian census was Bihar. This highlights the significant disparity in literacy levels across different regions of the country. While Kerala boasted the highest literacy rate at over 93%, Bihar fell short at around 61.8%. This gap reflects the challenges faced by certain states in prioritizing education and ensuring access to learning opportunities for all residents.

14. (A): The urban unemployment rate in India for March 2022 was 8.28%, as reported by the Centre for Monitoring Indian Economy (CMIE). This data point offers a snapshot of the job market situation in urban areas specifically. It's important to consider trends over time and compare this figure to national and rural unemployment rates to get a more comprehensive understanding of the Indian labour market.

15. (A): The Young Scientist Programme 'YUVIKA-2022' for students was conducted by the Indian Space Research Organization (ISRO). ISRO organizes this program specifically to introduce young students, particularly those in rural areas, to the exciting world of space science, technology, and applications. By providing a glimpse into these captivating fields, ISRO hopes to nurture the next generation of scientists and engineers who will shape the future of India's space program.

16. (C): Womesh Chandra Bonnerjee served as the inaugural President of the Indian National Congress when it was founded in 1885. He was a prominent figure in the early Indian nationalist movement and played a key role in shaping the Congress party during its formative years.

17. (A): Jahaz Mahal, also known as the "Ship Palace," is a magnificent monument located in the Mandu Fort complex in Mandu, Madhya Pradesh, India. It was built by Sultan Ghiyas-ud-din Khilji of the Malwa Sultanate in the 15th century. The palace is aptly named for its unique shape, which resembles a ship sailing through the two artificial lakes that surround it.

18. (B): Babur wrote his autobiography, Tuzuk-i-Baburi, in Turkish, also known as Chagatai or Türkish. In 1589, one of Babur's nobles, Mirza Abdur-Rahim, translated Tuzuk-i-Baburi into Persian at the request of Akbar, Babur's grandson. The Persian translation is called Baburnamah. Babur's writing style is straightforward and clear, and he records events with great respect for truth.

19. (B): Prime Minister Narendra Modi inaugurated the 11th Khel Mahakumbh at Ahmedabad's Sardar Patel Stadium. 36 general sports and 26 para-sports are currently part of the khel Mahakumbh. It started in Gujarat in 2010 with 16 sports and 13 lakh participants. More than 45 lakh people registered themselves for the 11th Khel Mahakumbh.

20. (D): The statement "The original Constitution contained 395 Articles in 25 parts and 12 schedules" is not correct about the Constitution of India. The original Constitution of India had 395 articles in 22 parts and 8 schedules when it came into effect on January 26, 1950. Later, three parts were added as amendments, making the total 25 parts. The Constitution of India is the world's longest-written national constitution and India's highest law.

21. (C): Checking options:

(A) LCM of 12 and 15

$$\begin{array}{c|cc} 3 & 12, & 15 \\ \hline & 4, & 5 \end{array}$$

LCM = 3 × 4 × 5 = 60 (correct)

(B) LCM of 14 and 7

$$\begin{array}{c|cc} 7 & 14, & 7 \\ \hline & 2, & 1 \end{array}$$

LCM = 7 × 2 × 1 = 14 (correct)

(C) LCM of 8 and 7
= 8 × 7 = 56 ≠ 1 (incorrect)

(D) LCM of 3 and 5
= 3 × 5 = 15 (correct)

Hence, option (C) is incorrect.

22. (A): Let fourth proportional = x

∵ 19, 23, 38 and x are in proportion

Then, $\frac{19}{23} = \frac{38}{x}$

$\Rightarrow 19x = 23 \times 38$

$\Rightarrow x = \frac{23 \times 38}{19} = 46$

Hence, fourth proportional = 46.

23. (A): Total surface area of cylinder

$= 2\pi r\ (h + r)$

$= 2 \times \frac{22}{7} \times 14(10 + 14)$

$= 88 \times 24$

$= 2112\ m^2$

Area of circle $= \pi r^2$

$= \frac{22}{7} \times 14 \times 14$

$= 22 \times 28$

$= 616\ m^2$

∴ Total area of the wet surface

$= 2112 - 616$

$= 1496\ m^2$.

24. (A): $T = \frac{SI \times 100}{p \times r}$

$= \frac{798 \times 100}{1900 \times 7}$

= 6 years.

25. (A): CP = ₹ 5000 + 250 = ₹ 5250

SP = ₹ 5075

Loss = 5250 - 5075 = ₹ 175

$\text{Loss\%} = \frac{175}{5250} \times 100$

$= \frac{10}{3}\%$

= 3.33%.

26. (A): The value of $2.\overline{13} \div 3.\overline{12}$

$$= \frac{\frac{213-2}{990}}{\frac{312-3}{990}} = \frac{211}{990} \times \frac{990}{309}$$

$$= \frac{211}{309}$$

27. (A): The value of the expression

$(1 + y)(1 + y^2)(1 + y^4)(1 + y^8)(1 - y)$

$= (1 - y^2)(1 + y^2)(1 + y^4)(1 + y^8)$

$= (1 - y^4)(1 + y^4)(1 + y^8)$

$= (1 - y^8)(1 + y^8)$

$= 1 - y^{16}$.

28. (B): SI for 1 year = 41472 − 34560

= ₹ 6912

$$\text{Rate of interest} = \frac{\text{SI} \times 100}{p \times t}$$

$$= \frac{6912 \times 100}{34560 \times 1}$$

= 20%.

29. (B): 9, 18, 27, ... 180 are in AP

Here, $a = 9$, $d = 9$, $n = 20$

$$S_n = \frac{n}{2}\{2a+(n-1)d\}$$

$$= \frac{20}{2}\{2 \times 9 + (19) \times 9\}$$

= 10 × (18 + 171)

= 10 × 189

$$\therefore \quad \text{Average} = \frac{10 \times 189}{20}$$

$$= \frac{189}{2}$$

= 94.5

30. (D): $A : \% = \frac{6}{72} \times 100 = \frac{25}{3} = 8.33\%$

$B : \% = \frac{3}{85} \times 100 = \frac{60}{17} = 3.5\%$

$C : \% = \frac{5}{69} \times 100 = \frac{500}{69} = 7.2\%$

$D : \% = \frac{9}{58} \times 100 = \frac{900}{58} = 15.5\%$

Hence, chocolate B has minimum increment in production.

31. (D): $\text{Average speed} = \frac{\text{Total Distance}}{\text{Total Time}}$

$$= \left(\frac{500+500}{625+375}\right) \text{ m/s}$$

$$= \left(\frac{1000}{1000}\right) \text{ m/s}$$

= 1 m/s

32. (A): Volume of ice-cream

= Volume of cone + volume of hemisphere

$$= \frac{1}{3}\pi r^2 h + \frac{2}{3}\pi r^3$$

$$= \frac{1}{3}\pi r^2 [h + 2r]$$

$$= \frac{1}{3} \times \frac{22}{7} \times 3 \times 3[7+6]$$

$$= \frac{198 \times 13}{21}$$

$$= \frac{2574}{21} \text{ cm}^3.$$

33. (D): According to the question,

The ratio of efficiency of Kiran and Vishal = 3 : 2

Ratio of efficiency of Dinesh and Kiran = 4 : 5

The efficiency of Vishal : Kiran : Dinesh

= 10 : 15 : 12

1 hour work done = 10 + 15 + 12 = 37

They together complete the work in 48 hrs.

Total work = 37 × 48 = 1776

Work done by Dinesh alone

$= \frac{1776}{12}$

= 148 hrs.

34. (C): Let MP = 100

$\text{Discount} = \frac{12}{100} \times 100 = ₹\,12$

SP = 100 - 12 = ₹ 88

100 + 10 = 110

When SP is ₹ 110, then CP = ₹ 100

When SP is ₹ 88, then CP = $\frac{100}{110} \times 88 = ₹\,80$

When CP is ₹ 80, then SP = ₹ 88

When CP is ₹ 5800, then SP

$= \frac{88}{80} \times 5800$

= ₹ 6380

When SP is ₹ 88, then MP = ₹ 100

When SP is ₹ 6380, then MP

$= \frac{100}{88} \times 6380$

= 25 × 290

= ₹ 7250

35. (C): (Boy + Girl)'s 1 day work = $\frac{1}{12}$

Boy's 1 day work = $\frac{1}{15}$

∴ Girl's 1 day work = $\frac{1}{12} - \frac{1}{15}$

$= \frac{5-4}{60}$

$= \frac{1}{60}$

Hence, Girl alone can do this work in 60 days.

36. (B): Let CP = ₹ 100

After increased 15%, then CP = ₹ 115

Now decreased 15%

100 - 15 = ₹ 85

When CP is ₹ 100, then SP = ₹ 85

When CP is ₹ 115, then SP = $\frac{85}{100} \times 115$

$= \frac{391}{4}$

= 97.75

Hence, % decrease in price

= 100 - 97.75

= 2.25%.

37. (B): $\because \sec^2 A - \tan^2 A = 1$

$\Rightarrow (\sec A + \tan A)(\sec A - \tan A) = 1$

$\Rightarrow 5(\sec A - \tan A) = 1$

$\Rightarrow \sec A - \tan A = \frac{1}{5}$

38. (A): $\because \frac{1}{x} + \frac{1}{y} + \frac{1}{z} = 1$

$\therefore \frac{1}{x} + \frac{1}{y} = 1 - \frac{1}{z} = \frac{z-1}{z}$

$\frac{1}{x} + \frac{1}{z} = 1 - \frac{1}{y} = \frac{y-1}{y}$

$$\frac{1}{y}+\frac{1}{z}=1-\frac{1}{x}=\frac{x-1}{x}$$

$$\therefore \left(\frac{1}{z-1}\right)\left(\frac{1}{x}+\frac{1}{y}\right)+\frac{1}{y-1}\left(\frac{1}{x}+\frac{1}{z}\right)+\frac{1}{x-1}\left(\frac{1}{y}+\frac{1}{z}\right)$$

$$=\left(\frac{1}{z-1}\right)\left(\frac{z-1}{z}\right)+\left(\frac{1}{y-1}\right)\left(\frac{y-1}{y}\right)+\left(\frac{1}{x-1}\right)\left(\frac{x-1}{x}\right)$$

$$=\frac{1}{z}+\frac{1}{y}+\frac{1}{x}$$

$= 1.$

39. (B): $\frac{44}{7}$ of $\frac{28}{11}\times\frac{1}{4}+\left\{25\div 5\times\frac{3}{5}\right\}$

$$=\frac{4\times 28}{7}\times\frac{1}{4}+\left\{5\times\frac{3}{5}\right\}$$

$$=\frac{28}{7}+3$$

$= 4 + 3$
$= 7$

40. (C):

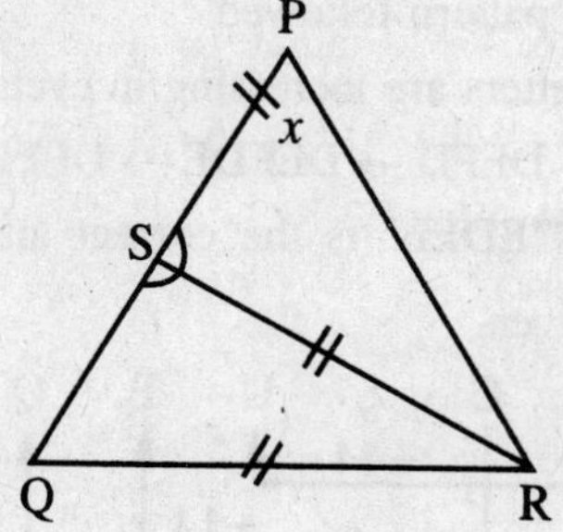

In Δ PQR, PQ = PR

$\Rightarrow \angle PQR = \angle PRQ$

Let $\angle QPR = x$

In ΔPSR, PS = SR

$\Rightarrow \angle SPR = \angle SRP$

$\therefore \angle SRP = x$

$\angle PSR + x + x = 180°$

$\Rightarrow \angle PSR = 180° - 2x$

$\Rightarrow \angle PSR + \angle RSQ = 180°$ (linear pair)

$\Rightarrow \angle RSQ = 180° - (180 - 2x) = 2x$

Similarly, In Δ SQR, QR = RS

$\Rightarrow \angle RSQ = \angle SQR$

$\Rightarrow \angle SQR = 2x$

$\Rightarrow \angle PQR = \angle SQR = 2x$

In Δ PQR, PR = PQ

$\Rightarrow \angle PQR = \angle PRQ$

$\Rightarrow 2x = (180° - 4x + x)$

$\Rightarrow 2x = 180° - 3x$

$\Rightarrow 5x = 180°$

$$\Rightarrow x=\frac{180}{5}=36°$$

Hence, the measure of angle QPR = 36°.

43. (C): Code of number

= the sum of the positional values of all the letters – 15

The last letter in the word is decreased to 1 positional value to make the first letter of the code.

The first letter in the word is increased to 1 positional value to make the last letter of the code.

Given,

W R I T E
+1 –1
D X

Code of number

= (23 + 18 + 9 + 20 + 5) – 15

= 75 – 15 = 60

and

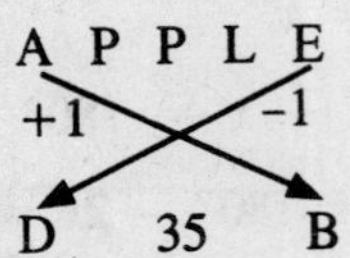

Code of number

= (1 + 16 + 16 + 12 + 5) − 50

= 50 − 15 = 35

Similarly,

B A S I S

+1 −1

R 35 C

Code of number

= (2 + 1 + 19 + 9 + 19) − 50

= 50 − 15 = 35.

44. (C):

W	F	C	I
−7↓	−5↓	−3↓	−1↓
P	A	Z	H
−7↓	−5↓	−3↓	−1↓
I	V	W	G
−7↓	−5↓	−3↓	−1↓
B	Q	T	F

Hence, BQTF will come at the place of question mark.

45. (B): 572 ÷ 4 − 64 − 365 + 41 × 27 = 441 + 380

⇒ 143 − 429 + 1107 = 821

⇒ 1250 − 429 = 821

⇒ 821 = 821

Hence, the combination of ÷, −, −, +, ×, + mathematical signs will sequentially replace the * signs to balance the given equation.

46. (C): 51 46 40 33 25 [16]

−5 −6 −7 −8 −9

Hence, 16 will come at the place of question mark.

47. (B):

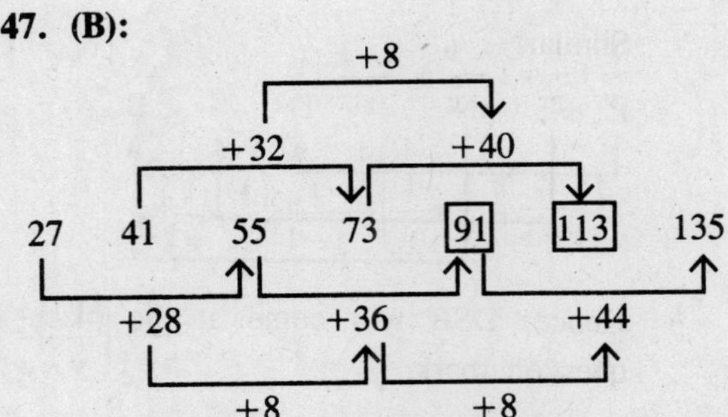

Hence, 91 and 113 will replace the question marks in the series.

49. (A): Given,

DEFD _ F _ DEFD _ DE _ DEFD

Let's check each option:

(A) EDEF

DEF - DEFD - DEFDE - DEFDEF - D

Pattern followed

(B) EFDF

DEF - DEFE - DEFDD - DEFDEF - D

No pattern followed

(C) DEDE

DEF - DDFE - DEFDD - DEEDEF - D

No pattern followed

(D) EEFF

DEF - DEFE - DEFDF - DEFDEF - D

No pattern followed

Here, letters are increasing in cyclic manner

DEF → DEFD → DEFDE → DEFDEF → D

Hence, 'EDEF' is the correct answer.

51. (B): Given,

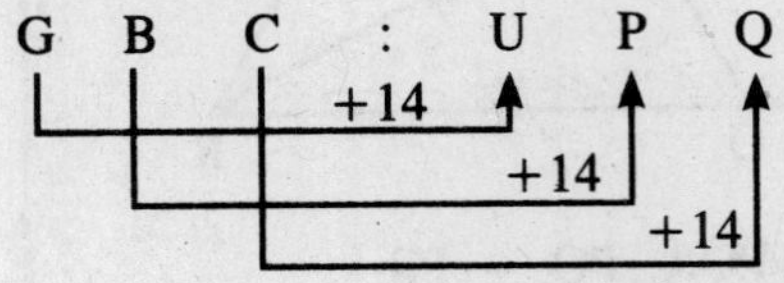

and

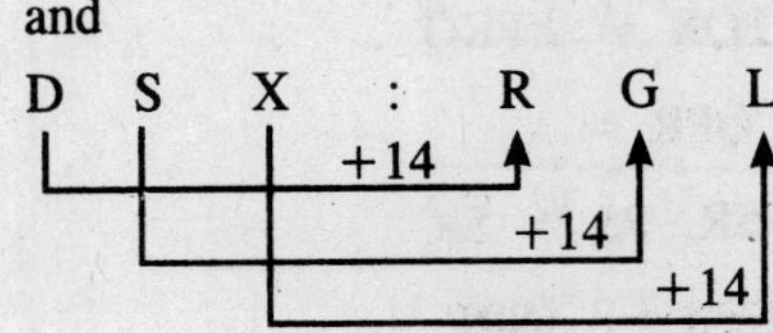

Similarly,

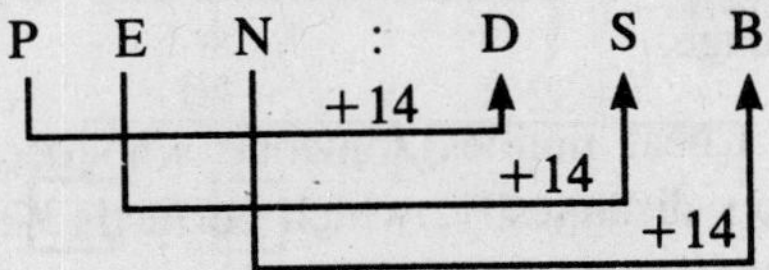

Hence, DSB will come at the place of question mark.

55. (C): Checking option:

(A) L O Q
+3 +2

(B) F I K
+3 +2

(C) B D G
+2 +3

(D) S V X
+3 +2

Hence, option (C) is different.

57. (D): Given,

$(6, 15, 18) \Rightarrow \frac{6\times15}{18}=5$

$(7, 35, 49) \Rightarrow \frac{7\times35}{49}=5$

Similarly,

$(8, 65, 104) \Rightarrow \frac{8\times65}{104}=5$

58. (A): Given,

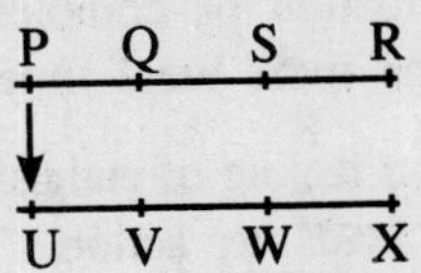

Hence, P faces U.

59. (C): Given expression:

A @ B & C × D # E

B → A: Husband
A → D: Daughter
A → E: Daughter's husband
C → B: Mother
D → C: Brother
E → D: Wife

Hence, E is the daughter's husband of A.

61. (A): The pattern followed in the given code is:

Sum of positional values of all the letters − 4

Given,

B	I	K	E
↓	↓	↓	↓
2	9	11	5

= 2 + 9 + 11 + 5 − 4

= 27 − 4

= 23

and

R	I	D	E
↓	↓	↓	↓
18	9	4	5

= 18 + 9 + 4 + 5 − 4

= 36 − 4

= 32

Similarly,

N	I	C	E
↓	↓	↓	↓
14	9	3	5

= 14 + 9 + 3 + 5 − 4

= 31 − 4

= 27.

62. **(B):**

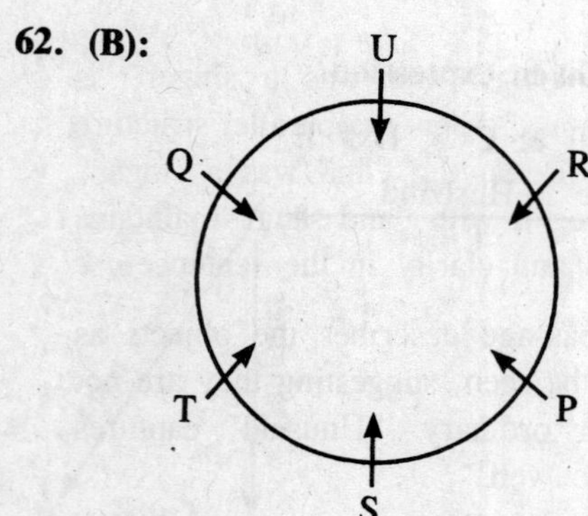

Clearly, U is sitting second to the left of T.

65. **(C):** $23 \times 8 \div 4 + 321 - 87 = 280$

$\Rightarrow 23 \times 2 + 321 - 87 = 280$

$\Rightarrow 46 + 321 - 87 = 280$

$\Rightarrow 280 = 280$

Hence, $\times$, $\div$, $+$, $-$ and $=$ signs will replace the * signs to make the given equation balanced.

66. **(C):** The most appropriate synonym of the word diligent is Industrious. Diligent and industrious both refer to someone who is hardworking, meticulous, and conscientious in their efforts and work ethic.

68. **(B):** The most appropriate antonym of the word Expel is Accept. Expel means to force someone to leave or eject from a place, while Accept means to receive willingly or agree to something. These two words are opposite in meaning.

69. **(A):** "Rejuvenated" means to make something look or feel younger, fresher, or more lively. In the context of advertisements promising younger-looking skin, the word "rejuvenated" conveys the idea of skin appearing refreshed and more youthful.

70. **(A):** Dyslexia is a specific learning disability characterized by difficulties with accurate and/or fluent word recognition and by poor spelling and decoding abilities. It is associated with difficulties in reading, interpreting, and understanding written language.

71. **(B):** Cheat implies someone who deceives or acts dishonestly, which perfectly fits the sentence's meaning. "He is not a cheat" clarifies that the person shouldn't be judged as someone who deceives.

72. **(D):** Balanced signifies a proper proportion of different elements. In the context of diet, a balanced intake refers to getting the right amount of various nutrients and protein for optimal health. This aligns perfectly with the sentence's meaning.

73. **(C):** The preposition inside is not the most appropriate choice in this context. A more natural way to express pouring something into a container is to use "into." "Pour" implies moving a liquid from one place to another, and "into" specifies the destination – in this case, the glass.

74. **(A):** Ought not to have done is the grammatically correct way to express a past situation where someone shouldn't have acted in a particular way. It combines "ought not to" (expressing disapproval of a past action) with the past participle "have done" to indicate a completed action.

75. **(D):** Supported perfectly captures the essence of the idiom "backed up" in this context. It means to offer evidence, confirmation, or agreement to someone's statement.

76. **(B):** Better to arrive late than not to come at all emphasizes that it's preferable to arrive or do something later than planned, rather than not doing it altogether. It highlights the importance of participation or completion, even if it's not at the most ideal time.

77. **(C):** Inspired suggests a feeling of enthusiasm and motivation that leads to action. This perfectly aligns with the context of the

sentence, where the care and affection from teachers motivated her to become a teacher themselves.

78. (D): Accrue means to accumulate or gather over time, typically referring to the gradual buildup of something such as interest, benefits, or resources. Therefore, gather is a suitable synonym for "accrue," as it also implies the process of collecting or accumulating.

79. (A): Destructive emphasizes the capability of causing damage or destruction. This aligns perfectly with the idea of weapons and their increasing potential to cause harm. Therefore, destructive is the most precise and impactful word that highlights the negative consequences of the progress in military technology.

80. (A): The incorrectly spelled word is Etarnel.

Eternal is the correct spelling for this word, meaning everlasting or infinite. Supreme, Ultimate, and Perfect are all spelled correctly.

81. (C): The most appropriate synonym for the word vagrant is drifter. A vagrant is someone who moves around a lot because they don't have a permanent home or job, and they have to steal or ask for things to survive.

82. (C): The incorrectly spelled word is eficiently. The correct spelling is "efficiently," which means performing a task or function in a way that minimizes waste and time.

83. (A): Orchard refers specifically to an intentional plantation of fruit trees, typically maintained for commercial production or personal enjoyment. An orchard can be a small, enclosed space like the one described in the sentence, or it can encompass a larger area with rows of fruit trees.

84. (A): The phrase "and was a singer" is redundant and disrupts the parallel structure of the list. Removing "and was a singer" and replacing it with "and sang" maintains consistency and clarity in the sentence.

86. (B): The passage describes the objects as difficult to be seen, suggesting they are not common or ordinary. "Unusual" captures this essence well.

87. (C): "On" is a common preposition used to indicate position on a surface. It's a natural choice for describing a stick hanging on a wall.

88. (B): "Wound" suggests that the ivy leaves are wrapped or twined around the stick in a decorative way.

89. (A): The sentence describes how the room was equipped with a chaise longue. "Furnished" signifies equipping a place with furniture.

90. (D): The context suggests the wooden boards made a sound as the boy walked on them. "Creaked" is the most suitable word to describe this sound as it implies a characteristic sound of old wooden floorboards under pressure.

91. (A): LEN is a versatile function that can be used to count all characters within a text string, regardless of their type. This includes letters (uppercase and lowercase), numbers, symbols (e.g., punctuation marks, mathematical symbols), and even spaces.

92. (A): Open Office Impress is not a document processing software, but a presentation program. Microsoft Word, Notepad, and WordPad are all examples of document processing software. Open Office Impress is a presentation program that is part of the OpenOffice office suite package. It is similar to Microsoft PowerPoint and allows users to create slides with text, lists, tables, charts, clip art, and other graphic objects.

93. (B): The @ symbol is required in an email address. It separates the user's name from their internet address. For example, in the email address example@mail.com, "example" is the email prefix and "mail.com" is the email domain.

94. (A): In MS-Excel 2010, the TODAY function displays the current date in a worksheet, regardless of when the workbook is opened. The syntax for the TODAY function is =TODAY() and it takes no arguments. Excel automatically updates the date whenever the workbook is opened or the worksheet recalculates.

95. (D): The Hide option is in the View tab in the MS-Excel 2010 ribbon bar. The View tab allows users to change views in Excel, including viewing sheets, windows, and worksheet size. It also allows users to hide and show elements in the Excel window.

96. (B): Extensible Markup Language (XML) is a markup language and file format used to store, transmit, and reconstruct arbitrary data. XML is similar to HTML, but without a pre-set tag system, allowing users to create their own tags. XML is designed to be simple, general, and usable across the internet, and is a textual data format that supports different human languages.

97. (B): The Mozilla Foundation and its subsidiary, the Mozilla Corporation, developed the free and open-source web browser in 2002. The browser was originally codenamed "Phoenix" and was created by Mozilla community members who wanted a standalone browser instead of the Mozilla Application Suite bundle.

98. (A): In MS-Excel 2010, the keyboard shortcut for hiding columns within the sheet is Ctrl + 0 (zero). The selected columns will disappear from your view. You can use the same shortcut on any visible column next to the hidden columns to unhide them.

99. (A): The status bar is the name for the lower edge of the worksheet window in MS-Excel 2010 that displays information about the worksheet. It can show information such as the sum, count, and average of the current sheets, and the status of the worksheet modes. The status bar can also show information about the spreadsheet data, and the on/off status of keyboard keys like Caps Lock, Scroll Lock, and Num Lock.

100. (C): Columns are named from A onwards (A, B, C, D, etc.).

Rows are named from 1 onwards (1, 2, 3, 4, etc.).

This naming system creates a grid-like reference for each cell in your worksheet. By combining a column letter and a row number, you can uniquely identify any cell (e.g., cell A1, cell B3, cell C10). This cell referencing system is fundamental for data entry, selecting ranges of cells, and using formulas in Excel.

YOUR SPACE

YOUR SPACE

Previous Paper (Solved)

Delhi Police–Head Constable (Ministerial) Exam-2012

1. Pick out the most appropriate pair to fill in the blanks in the same order, to complete the sentence meaningfully:

He had managed to ______ several times, but was finally ______ by the police.

A. escape, arrested
B. defend, acquitted
C. deceive, cheated
D. cheat, robbed

2. A sentence has been broken into different parts. The parts have been scrambled and numbered as given below. Choose the correct order of these parts from the given alternatives.

(1) keeper of the
(2) guardian of
(3) as well as
(4) The U.N.O. is supposed to be the
(5) the morally conceived
(6) political conscience
(7) expressly defined rights and duties of sovereign states
(8) and

A. 4, 1, 6, 8, 2, 5, 3, 7
B. 4, 2, 6, 8, 1, 3, 5, 7
C. 4, 2, 7, 3, 1, 5, 8, 6
D. 4, 1, 7, 3, 2, 5, 8, 6

Directions (Q. Nos. 3 to 7) : *Read the following passage carefully and answer the questions that follow :*

The Rajputs occupy an honoured place in the history of India. They were a war-like people, proud and patriotic. They were zealous of their honour, and would lay down their lives to uphold it. They loved their homes and fought bravely to defend the honour of their women folk. Nothing would tame their spirits. Perils only called forth their courage and poverty only increased their power of resistance. None could fight like them. Their motto was 'Better death than dishonour.'

3. Which of the following represents the central theme of the passage?

A. The pride of the Rajputs
B. Rajputs and their sacrifices
C. The rise and fall of the Rajputs
D. Rajputs – the spirited heroes of Indian history

4. Which of the following is opposite in meaning to the word **'proud'** in the passage?

A. courteous
B. humble
C. kind
D. cowardly

5. The expression **"tame their spirits"** in the passage means

A. Suppress their ambitions
B. Arouse their enthusiasm
C. Develop their courage
D. Curb their enthusiasm

6. Which of the following statements is not true in the context of this passage?

A. The Rajputs achieved eminence in history due to their great bravery.
B. They would fight for upholding women's honour.
C. In moment of danger they would exhibit great courage.
D. They could not face the challenge of poverty.

7. According to the writer, the Rajputs occupy an honoured place in history, because
   A. they were fond of wars.
   B. they were proud of their war.
   C. they were jealous of people's honour.
   D. they lived and died upholding their self-respect.

8. Select the word which is opposite in meaning to **"JUVENILE"**
   A. Blind B. Mature
   C. Youthful D. Control

9. Which of the words is spelt correctly?
   A. Accommodation
   B. Accomodation
   C. Acomodation
   D. Acommodation

10. Choose the phrase which can correctly substitute the italicised part of the following sentence:

    The police ***broke away*** the meeting as it turned violent.

    A. broke through B. broke off
    C. broken with D. broke up

11. Choose the correct option with reference to the following two sentences:
    I. This is the best ***stationary*** shop in our locality.
    II. I saw a ***stationery*** van there.
    A. Both I and II are correct
    B. Both I and II are incorrect
    C. Only sentence I is correct
    D. Only sentence II is correct.

12. In the following sentence choose the word opposite in meaning to the italicised word to fill in the blanks:

    Just ***incorporate*** the necessary details and __________ the rest.

    A. differentiate B. exclude
    C. dissect D. disjoin

13. Choose the alternative that best expresses the meaning of the idiom in italics:

    There was opposition to the new policy by ***the rank and file*** of the Government.

    A. the ordinary members
    B. the cabinet members
    C. the official machinery
    D. the majority

14. What is one word for **"a government run by a dictator"**?
    A. Democracy B. Autocracy
    C. Theocracy D. Oligarchy

15. Select the word which is nearest in meaning to the word **"DISMAL"**.
    A. Watery B. Deformed
    C. Impolite D. Bleak

16. Pick the word which would complete the following sentence correctly and meaningfully:

    Lots of people had come to attend his lecture because he is a very __________ scholar.

    A. imminent B. engaging
    C. eminent D. popular

17. Choose the word nearest in meaning to the italicised word in the following sentence:

    He spoke ***impromptu*** on the occasion.

    A. eloquently
    B. without preparation
    C. without enthusiasm
    D. with great force

18. Select the combination of numbers so that letters arranged accordingly will form a meaningful word:

    T P S L O I

    1 2 3 4 5 6

    A. 4 6 2 5 3 1
    B. 2 5 4 3 6 1
    C. 3 6 4 2 5 1
    D. 2 6 3 1 5 4

19. Which word is closest in meaning to the word **"INTIMIDATE"**?
    A. Bluff B. Frighten
    C. Harm D. Inform

20. Which of the choices expresses the following sentence in Indirect Speech:

He said to them, "Don't make a noise."

A. He asked them not to make a noise.

B. He told them not to make noise.

C. He told them that don't make a noise.

D. He told them do not make a noise.

21. Which part(s) of the following sentence has an error:

He could not plan his strategy (A)/ until he knew (B)/ whom his opponents could be. (C)

A. Only C B. No Error

C. Only B D. Both A and B

22. Which of the following means both **"small line"** and **"rush"**?

A. void B. blank

C. bustle D. dash

23. Select the word most appropriate for the blank space in this sentence:

I haven't seen you ________ a week.

A. since B. within

C. from D. for

24. What is the active voice of the following:

Have the box broken.

A. Break the box.

B. The box is broken.

C. He will break the box.

D. They broke the box.

25. The first sentence of a passage is given. Which of the four alternatives would be the most logical sequence of the sentences in the passage?

The mail is first collected from different letter boxes.

P: From there it is sent to the head post office.

Q: It is then sorted out at the sorting office.

R: The mail is again sorted out at the head post office by the concerned beat postman.

S: The sorted mail is sent to the zonal post office.

A. RPQS B. RSQP

C. QSPR D. QPRS

26. Ram leaves his office in a car and drives 15 km towards north and then 10 km towards west. He then turned to the south and covered 5 km. Further, he turned to the east and moved 8 km. Finally, he turned right and drove 10 km. How far and in which direction is he from his starting point?

A. 6 km South

B. 5 km East

C. 2 km West

D. 3 km North

27. Which of the following pairs has the same relationship as "Carpenter : Chair"?

A. King : Empire

B. Mason : Wall

C. Farmer : Agriculture

D. Teacher : Teaching

28. Sanjeev ranks seventh from the top and twenty-eighth from the bottom in a class. How many students are there in the class?

A. 36 B. 35

C. 37 D. 34

29. If 1st October is Sunday, then 16th October shall be:

A. Tuesday B. Wednesday

C. Monday D. Sunday

30. Five girls are sitting in a row. Rashi is not adjacent to Sulekha or Abha. Anuradha is not adjacent to Sulekha. Rashi is adjacent to Monika. Monika is at the middle of the row. Then, Anuradha is adjacent to whom out of the following?

A. Rashi B. Abha

C. Monika D. Sulekha

31. Pune is bigger than Jhansi. Sitapur is bigger than Chittor. Raigarh is not as big as Jhansi, but is bigger than Sitapur. Which is the smallest?

A. Sitaput B. Pune

C. Chittor D. Jhanshi

32. Two ladies and two men are playing cards and are seated at North, East, South and West of a table. No lady is facing East. Persons sitting opposite to each other are not of the same sex. One man is facing South. Which direction are the ladies facing?

A. South and East
B. North and West
C. East and West
D. North and East

33. Numbers from 1 to 100 are written on a page. The digit "3" occurs how many times on the page?

A. 20 B. 11
C. 21 D. 10

34. Rajan is the brother of Sachin and Manik is the father of Rajan. Jagat is the brother of Priya and Priya is the daughter of Sachin. Who is the uncle of Jagat?

A. Manik
B. Sachin
C. Rajan
D. None of the above

35. Which of the following does **NOT** belong with the others?

A. Tiger B. Elephant
C. Lion D. Leopard

36. "Every library has books." Which of the following conclusions logically follows from this statement?

A. Some libraries do not have readers.
B. Books are only in the library
C. Libraries are meant for books only
D. No library is without books

37. The number of boys in a class is three times the number of girls. Which of the following numbers cannot represent the total number of children in the class?

A. 44 B. 48
C. 42 D. 40

38. Ram is older than Shyam. Moti is older than Ram while Naresh is younger to Moti but older than Shyam. Who is the youngest?

A. Naresh B. Ram
C. Moti D. Shyam

39. Which one of the following is different from the others?

Mussoorie, Darjeeling, Jaipur, Shimla

A. Mussoorie B. Jaipur
C. Shimla D. Darjeeling

40. ACE : FHJ : : OQS : ?

A. TVX B. RTU
C. PRT D. UWY

41. A watch reads 4.30. If the minute hand points East, in which direction will the hour hand point?

A. South-east B. North
C. North-east D. North-west

42. Which is the next figure in the series?

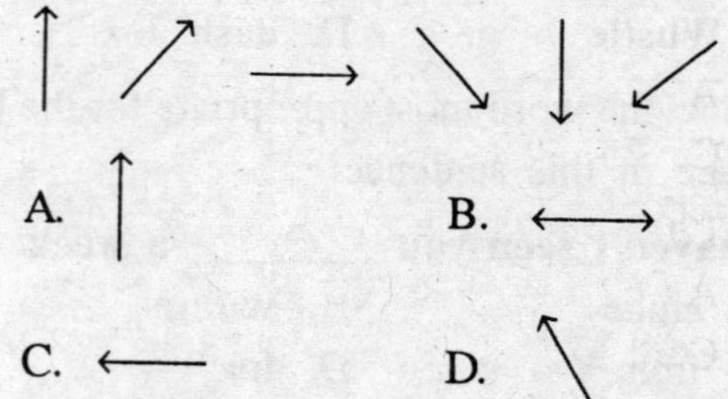

A. B.
C. D.

43. Which is the odd one out?

A. Tamil Nadu
B. Karnataka
C. Kerala
D. Puducherry

44. If 2 men can duild 2 walls in 2 days, how many days will 4 men take to build 4 walls?

A. 4 days B. 2 days
C. 16 days D. 8 days

45. If in a certain language MADRAS is coded as NBESBT, how is BOMBAY coded in that language?

A. CPNCBZ B. CQOCBZ
C. CPNCBX D. CPOCBZ

46. If X is the brother of the son of Y's son, how is X related to Y?

A. Brother B. Cousin
C. Grandson D. Son

47. Police is to Crime as Doctor is to .... ?

A. Medicine
B. Hospital
C. Disease
D. Injection

48. What is the next number in the series?
1, 4, 9, 16, 25, ...

A. 30 B. 50
C. 36 D. 45

49. If *pen* is *table, table* is *fan, fan* is *chair* and *chair* is *roof,* on which of the following will a person sit?

A. Fan B. Chair
C. Roof D. Table

50. Look at the series:

22, 21, 23, 22, 24, 23, ...

What number should come next?

A. 24 B. 26
C. 25 D. 22

51. 120% of 75 is:

A. 62.5 B. 90
C. 120 D. 80

52. The average salary of 20 workers in an office is ₹ 1300 per month. If the manager's salary is also added, then the average salary becomes ₹ 2000 per month. What is the manager's salary?

A. ₹ 16,000 per month
B. ₹ 12,000 per month
C. ₹ 24,000 per month
D. ₹ 20,000 per month

53. If $x = 2$, $y = 3$; find $x^y + y^x$

A. 12 B. 10
C. 25 D. 17

54. In what time will a sum of money double itself at 12.5% per annum simple interest

A. 6 yrs B. 8 yrs
C. 5 yrs D. 4 yrs

55. An almirah is sold at a profit of 16%. If it was sold for ₹ 100 more, then the seller's profit would have been 20%. What is the cost price of the almirah?

A. ₹ 1500 B. ₹ 2500
C. ₹ 1800 D. ₹ 2000

56. Find the value of
9 + 0.9 + 0.009 + 0.099

A. 9.9998 B. 9.008
C. 10.008 D. 9.908

57. 7 : 25 is equal to:

A. 175% B. 7.25%
C. 28% D. 35%

58. What is the value of 0.9 × 0.007?

A. 0.63 B. 0.0063
C. 0.063 D. 0.00063

59. A number is increased by 10% and then reduced by 10%. If the resultant number is 99, the original number was:

A. 98 B. 100
C. 95 D. 110

60. The average speed of a car which covers half the distance with a speed of 20 km/hr and the other half with a speed of 30 km/hr, will be:

A. 50 km/hr
B. 25 km/hr
C. 26 km/hr
D. 24 km/hr

61. A bag contains ₹ 90 in coins. If coins of 50p, 25p and 10p are in the ratio 2:3:5, how many 25p coins are there in the bag?

A. 110 B. 135
C. 120 D. 140

62. What is the value of $2^1 + 2^{-1}$?

A. 0 B. 2
C. 2.5 D. 4

63. $(2^8 \div 2^5)^2$ is equal to:

A. 64 B. 8/5
C. 32 D. 128

64. If the diameter of a circle is doubled, its area will become:

A. π^2 times B. Double
C. 2π times D. 4 times

65. The value of 0.5^2 will be:

A. Less than 0.5
B. Greater than 0.5
C. Equal to 0.5
D. None of the above

66. A train is moving with a speed of 92.4 km/hr. How many metres will it cover in 10 minutes?

A. 15.4 B. 1540
C. 15400 D. 154

67. The ratio between the length and breadth of a rectangular field is 5:4. If the breadth is 20 metres less than the length, the perimeter of the field is:

A. 280 m B. 260 m
C. 360 m D. 410 m

68. A cube painted red on all its faces is cut into 27 cubes of equal size. How many cubes would be there which are not painted on any face?

A. 3 B. 4
C. 1 D. 8

69. If '*a*' means plus, '*b*' means minus, '*c*' means multiplication and '*d*' means division, then 18 *a* 4 *c* 6 *b* 16 *d* 4 = ?

A. 20 B. 29
C. 38 D. 128

70. What number should be subtracted from 5/3 to get 5/6?

A. 5/6 B. 5/4
C. 5/3 D. 5/2

71. If $x = 1.5$, calculate $x^2 + 2x + \frac{3}{4}$

A. 6 B. 5¾
C. 4.5 D. 7½

72. If the selling price of 5 articles is same as the cost price of 6 articles, then what is the profit on each article?

A. 20% B. 1%
C. 12% D. 24%

73. The length of a rectangular field is twice its breadth. If the area of the field is 288 sq. m., the length of the field is :

A. 14 m B. 12 m
C. 24 m D. 16 m

74. By selling a suitcase for ₹ 570, a trader loses 5%. At what price must he sell it to gain 5%?

A. ₹ 580 B. ₹ 620
C. ₹ 630 D. ₹ 650

75. 18 binders bind 900 books in 10 days. How many binders will be required to bind 600 books in 12 days?

A. 16 B. 20
C. 10 D. 30

76. The largest island in the world is:

A. New Guinea B. Sumatra
C. Sri Lanka D. Greenland

77. Which planet rotates on its axis from east to west?

A. Jupiter B. Earth
C. Venus D. Mercury

78. Mahadev Govind Ranade founded the:

A. Theosophical Society
B. Arya Samaj
C. Prarthana Samaj
D. Brahmo Samaj

79. Prime Minister of which country was the Chief Guest for the India's Republic Day Parade in 2012?

A. Hong Kong
B. Thailand
C. Malaysia
D. South Korea

80. Where was the first cotton mill established in India?

A. Ahmedabad B. Surat
C. Bombay D. Coimbatore

81. Who was known as 'Punjab Kesari'?

A. Chandagi Ram
B. Maharaja Ranjit Singh
C. Bhagat Singh
D. Lala Lajpat Rai

82. The Rowlatt Act was passed in:
A. 1918 B. 1920
C. 1917 D. 1919

83. Kuchipudi dance belongs to which state?
A. Punjab B. Andhra Pradesh
C. Rajasthan D. Karnataka

84. Christopher Columbus discovered:
A. India B. Africa
C. West Indies D. East Indies

85. Where was Osama bin Laden killed in 2011?
A. Rawalpindi B. Kohat
C. Abbottabad D. Peshawar

86. Which is the International Date Line?
A. 180 Degree Longitude
B. 90 Degree E Longitude
C. Zero Degree Longitude
D. Equator

87. The American War of Independence took place in the years:
A. 1876 – 1879
B. 1775 – 1783
C. 1788 – 1789
D. 1878 – 1881

88. Fundamental Rights are enshrined in which part of our Constitution?
A. Part IV B. Part III
C. Part I D. Part VI

89. Which river is also called the 'Sorrow of Bihar'?
A. Alaknanda B. Teesta
C. Mahanadi D. Kosi

90. Who is the author of Harry Potter series of novels?
A. Jeff Kinney B. Rick Riordan
C. Roald Dahl D. J.K. Rowling

91. Which of the following is also called the 'City of Lakes'?
A. Udaipur B. Jaipur
C. Indore D. Mysore

92. McMahon Line is the demarcation between:
A. India – Myanmar
B. India – China
C. India – Pakistan
D. Pakistan – China

93. Who gave the slogan "Do or Die" during the Quit India Movement?
A. Vallabhbhai Patel
B. Mahatma Gandhi
C. Jawaharlal Nehru
D. Balgangadhar Tilak

94. The artist of the painting entitled "The Last Supper" was:
A. Rafael
B. Vincent Ben Gaug
C. Leonardo-da-vinci
D. Michael Angelo

95. Where the final match of cricket World Cup 2011 were held?
A. Eden Garden
B. Chinnaswami Stadium
C. Wankhede Stadium
D. Brabourne Stadium

96. In which reign the Jama Masjid of Delhi was constructed?
A. Akbar B. Shahjehan
C. Babur D. Jahangir

97. India, which date is being observed as Anti-Terrorism Day?
A. 31 January B. 26 November
C. 30 January D. 21 May

98. At present, who is the captain of the Australian Cricket Team?
A. Ricky Ponting
B. Andreu Stross
C. Michael Clark
D. Greem Smith

99. When was the Pakistan formed?
A. 14 August, 1947 B. 13 August, 1947
C. 15 August, 1947 D. 16 August, 1947

100. The maximum number of the member of the Rajya Sabha is:
A. 248 B. 250
C. 245 D. 249

ANSWERS

1	2	3	4	5	6	7	8	9	10
A	C	D	B	D	D	D	B	A	D
11	**12**	**13**	**14**	**15**	**16**	**17**	**18**	**19**	**20**
B	B	D	B	D	C	B	D	B	A
21	**22**	**23**	**24**	**25**	**26**	**27**	**28**	**29**	**30**
A	D	D	A	D	C	B	D	C	A
31	**32**	**33**	**34**	**35**	**36**	**37**	**38**	**39**	**40**
C	B	A	C	B	D	C	D	B	A
41	**42**	**43**	**44**	**45**	**46**	**47**	**48**	**49**	**50**
C	C	D	B	A	C	C	C	A	C
51	**52**	**53**	**54**	**55**	**56**	**57**	**58**	**59**	**60**
B	A	D	B	B	C	C	B	B	D
61	**62**	**63**	**64**	**65**	**66**	**67**	**68**	**69**	**70**
C	C	A	D	A	C	C	C	C	A
71	**72**	**73**	**74**	**75**	**76**	**77**	**78**	**79**	**80**
A	A	C	C	C	D	C	C	B	C
81	**82**	**83**	**84**	**85**	**86**	**87**	**88**	**89**	**90**
D	D	B	C	C	A	B	B	D	D
91	**92**	**93**	**94**	**95**	**96**	**97**	**98**	**99**	**100**
A	B	B	C	C	B	D	C	A	B

SOME SELECTED EXPLANATORY ANSWERS

26.

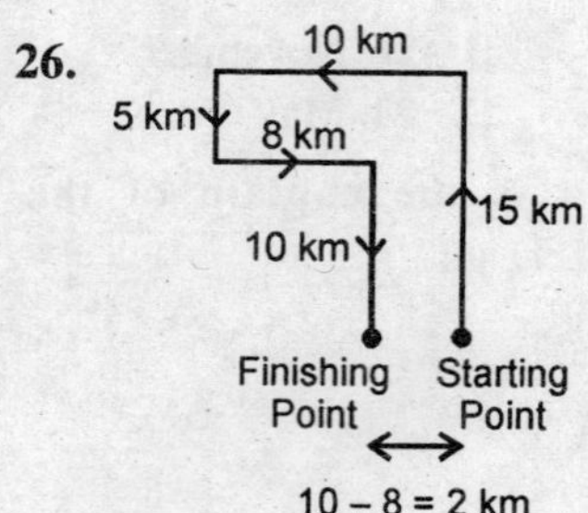

Ram is finally at 10 – 8 = 2 km west.

28. Number of students in the class

$= 7 + 28 - 1 = 34$

29. As 1st October is Sunday

then $1 + 2 \times 7 =$ 15th October will again Sunday.

Hence, 16th October will be Monday.

30. Probable sitting arrangement is like this

Sulekha Abha Monika Rashi Anuradha

Hence, Anuradha is adjacent to Rashi.

31. Pune > Jhansi > Raigarh > Sitapur > Chittor

↑ Biggest city ↑ Smallest city

32.

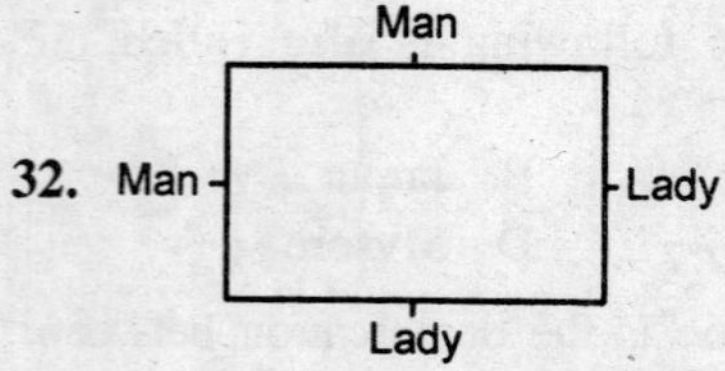

So, two ladies are facing North and West.

33. Number of 3 between:

1	to	10	→	1
11	to	20	→	1
21	to	30	→	2
31	to	40	→	10
41	to	50	→	1
51	to	60	→	1
61	to	70	→	1
71	to	80	→	1
81	to	90	→	1
91	to	100	→	1
		Total	→	20

34. Manik has two sons, Rajan and Sachin. And Sachin has one son and one daughter. They are Jagat and Priya. From this information we can say Jagat uncle name is Rajan.

35. Tiger, Lion and Leopard are non-vegetarian animal while elephant is a pure vegetarian animal.

37. Let number of girls in the class is x

then number of boys in the class = $3x$

total number of children in the class

$$= x + 3x = 4x$$

for $x \in N$, $4x \neq 42$.

38. Moti > Ram > Naresh > Shyam

↑ Oldest ↑ Youngest

39. Mussoorie, Darjeeling and Shimla are fomous hill stations in India, while Jaipur is the capital city of Rajasthan.

40. A C E : F H J :: O Q S : T V X (+2, +2; +1; +2, +2)

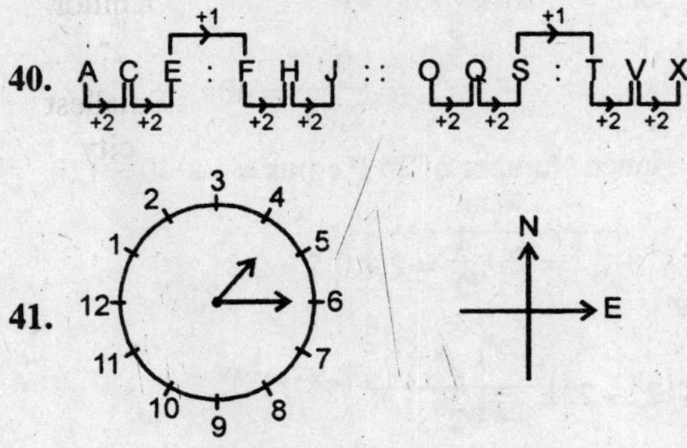

41. At 4 : 30

when minute hand points cast, hour hand. Points toward North-east.

42. Puducherry is one of the seven UT states.

44. Here 1 man can build 1 wall in 2 days.

$\therefore$ 4 men can build 4 wall in $\frac{2 \times 4}{4} = 2$ days

45.

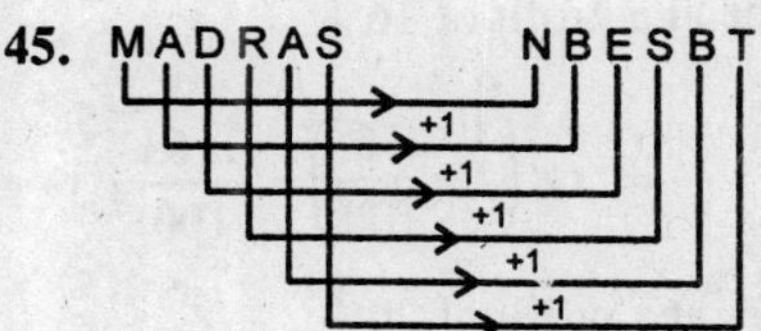

Similarly,

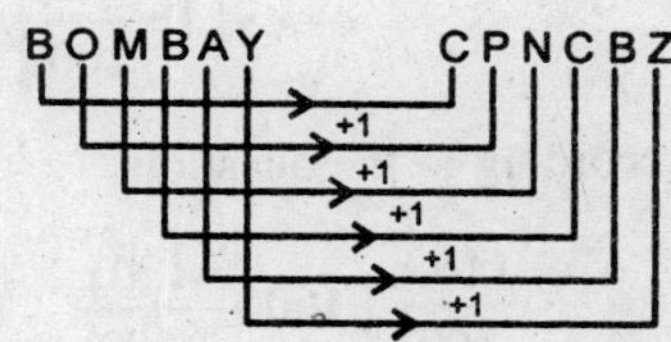

48. $(1)^2, (2)^2, (3)^2, (4)^2, (5)^2, (6)^2$ ......

$$(6)^2 = 36.$$

49. A person sit on chair and chair is called Roof so, person sit on roof.

50. 22, 21, 23, 22, 24, 23, 25, 24 ....

51. $75 \times \frac{120}{100} = 3 \times 30 = 90.$

52. Total salary of 20 workers

= 1300 × 20 = ₹ 26000 / month

Total salary of 20 workers and 1 manager

= 2000 × 21 = ₹ 42000 / month

Hence, salary of Manager = 42000 – 26000 = ₹ 16000 / month

53. $x^y + y^x = 2^3 + 3^2 = 8 + 9 = 17.$

54. From formula: $A = P + \frac{Prt}{100}$

According to the question, A = 2P

$$\therefore \quad 2P = P + \frac{Prt}{100}$$

$$P = \frac{Prt}{100} = \frac{12.5 \times t}{100}$$

$$\Rightarrow \quad t = \frac{100}{12.5} = 8 \text{ years.}$$

55. Let cost price of almirah = ₹ x

Selling price at a profit of 16%

$$= x \times \left(1 + \frac{16}{100}\right) = \frac{116x}{100}$$

Selling price at a profit of 20%

$$= x \times \left(1 + \frac{12}{100}\right) = \frac{120x}{100}$$

According to the question,

$$\frac{116x}{100} + 100 = \frac{120x}{100}$$

$$\text{or,} \quad \frac{(120 - 116)x}{100} = 100$$

$$\Rightarrow \quad \frac{120x}{100} - \frac{116x}{100} = 100$$

$$\Rightarrow \quad 4x = 100 \times 100$$

$$\Rightarrow \quad x = \frac{100 \times 100}{4}$$

= ₹ 2500

Hence, cost price = ₹ 2500

56. $9 + 0.9 + 0.009 + 0.099$

```
  9.000
  0.900
  0.009
+ 0.099
 10.008
```

57. $7 : 25 = \frac{7}{25} \times 100 = 28\%$.

58. $0.9 \times 0.007 = \frac{9}{10} \times \frac{7}{1000} = \frac{63}{10000} = 0.0063$.

59. Let original number is x.

$$10\% \text{ increament} = x \times \left(1 + \frac{10}{100}\right) = \frac{11x}{10}$$

$$\text{Again } 10\% \text{ reduction} = \frac{11x}{10} \times \frac{90}{100} = \frac{99x}{100}$$

According to the question,

$$\Rightarrow \quad x = \frac{99 \times 100}{99} = 100$$

$$\frac{99x}{100} = 99 \quad \therefore \ x = 100.$$

60. Time taken to cover half the distanced d is

$$t_1 = \frac{d}{20} \text{ hr.}$$

Time taken to cover another half distance d is

$$t_2 = \frac{d}{30} \text{ hr.}$$

$$\text{Total time taken } t_1 + t_2 = \left(\frac{d}{20} + \frac{d}{30}\right) \text{ hr}$$

$$\therefore \text{ Average speed} = \frac{2d}{\left(\frac{d}{20} + \frac{d}{30}\right)} = \frac{2 \times 20 \times 30}{50}$$

= 24 km/hr.

61. 50 P = ₹ 0.50, 25 P = ₹ 0.25 and 10 P = ₹ 0.10

According to the question,

$$0.5 \times 2x + 0.25 \times 3x + 0.10 \times 5x = 90$$

$$x + 0.75x + 0.5x = 90$$

$$2.25x = 90$$

$$x = \frac{90}{2.25} = 40$$

Hence Number of 25 P coins = 3 × 40 = 120.

62. $2^1 + 2^{-1} = 2 + \frac{1}{2} = 2 + 0.5 = 2.5$

63. $(2^8 \div 2^5)^2 = \left(\frac{2^8}{2^5}\right)^2 = (2^{8-5})^2$

$$= (2)^{3 \times 2} = (2)^6 = 64.$$

64. Area of circle $A = \pi r^2 = \frac{\pi d^2}{4}$

$$A \propto d^2$$

Now, when diameter is doubled, area will become 4 times.

65. $0.5^2 = 0.25,\ 0.25 < 0.5$

66. Speed in m/see $= 92.4 \times \frac{5}{18} = 25.66$ m/sec.

Now, 10 mints = 10 × 60 = 600 secs.

Distance travelled in 600 secs = 25.667 × 600

= 15400 m.

67. According to the question,

$$5x - 4x = 20$$

$$x = 20$$

∴ Length $5x = 100$, breadth $4x = 80$.

Perimeter P = 2(length + breadth)

= 2(100 + 80) = 360 m.

69. $18 + 4 \times 6 - 16 \div 4 = 18 + 24 - 4$

$= 18 + 20 = 38$

70. Required number $= \frac{5}{3} - \frac{5}{6} = \frac{5\times2-5}{6} = \frac{5}{6}$.

71. $x^2 + 2x + \frac{3}{4} = (1.5)^2 + 2\times1.5 + 0.75$

$= 2.25 + 3 + 0.75 = 6$

72. Let selling price of 5 articles = x = cost price of 6 articles

∴ Selling Price of 1 article $= \frac{x}{5}$

Cost price of 1 article $= \frac{x}{6}$

Profit = Selling price – Cost price

$$= \frac{x}{5} - \frac{x}{6} = \frac{x}{30}.$$

$$\text{Profit Percent} = \frac{\frac{x}{30}}{\frac{x}{6}} \times 100 = \frac{6}{30} \times 100 = 20\%.$$

73. Let breadth of the rectangular field = x m

then length = $2x$ m

Area of the field A = $x \times 2x$

$$288 = 2x^2$$

$$x^2 = 144$$

$$x = 12 \text{ m}$$

Length of the field $2x$ = 24 m.

74. Cost price $= 570 \times \frac{100}{(100-5)} = \frac{570\times100}{95}$

= ₹ 600

Selling price to gain a profit of 5%.

$$= 600 \times \left(\frac{100+5}{100}\right) = ₹\,630$$

75. Number of binders required

$$= \frac{900\times10}{18} \times \frac{12}{600} = 10.$$

Arithmetic/Numerical Ability

1. LCM AND HCF

LCM

Multiple : A number is said to be multiple of other when it is exactly divisible by the other.

Common multiple : A common multiple of two or more numbers is a number which is exactly divisible by each of them. For example, for 2 and 3, common multiples are 6, 12, 18, 24 and so on.

Explanation:

Consider the two numbers 2 and 3

Multiple of 2 are 2, 4, 6, 8, 10, 12, ...

Multiple of 3 are 3, 6, 9, 12, 15, ...

$\therefore$ Common multiples are 6, 12, 18, ...

Least Common Multiple (L.C.M.) : L.C.M. of two or more given numbers is the least number which is exactly divisible by each of them. For example,

6 is a common multiple of 2 and 3

12 is also common multiple of 2 and 3

18 is also common multiple of 2 and 3

But 6 is the least common multiple (L.C.M.) of 2 and 3.

Methods to find out L.C.M.

L.C.M. of two or more given numbers is determined by following two methods:

1. By prime factorization method
2. By division method

1. By prime factorization method : Resolve the given numbers into their prime factors and then find the product of the highest power of all the factors that occur in the given numbers. This product will be the L.C.M.

Example 1 : Find the L.C.M. of 40, 50, 60 and 80.

Sol : $40 = 2 \times 2 \times 2 \times 5 = 2^3 \times 5$

$50 = 2 \times 5 \times 5 = 2 \times 5^2$

$60 = 2 \times 2 \times 3 \times 5 = 2^2 \times 3 \times 5$

$80 = 2 \times 2 \times 2 \times 2 \times 5 = 2^4 \times 5$

Here, the prime factors that occur in the given numbers are 2, 3 and 5 and their highest powers are respectively 2^4, 5^2 and 3.

Hence, the required L.C.M. $= 2^4 \times 3 \times 5^2 = 1200$.

2. By division method : This is the quicker method to find the prime factors and hence L.C.M.

For determining L.C.M. of the numbers 40, 50, 60 and 80, following process of division is adopted:

2	40, 50, 60, 80
2	20, 25, 30, 40
2	10, 25, 15, 20
5	5, 25, 15, 10
	1, 5, 3, 2

Now required L.C.M. $= 2 \times 2 \times 2 \times 5 \times 5 \times 3 \times 2 = 1200$

L.C.M. of decimal : First of all, we find out the L.C.M. of numbers without decimal and then, we see the number in which decimal is given in the minimum digit from right to left. We put the decimal in our result which is equal to that number of digits.

Example : Find the L.C.M. of 0.6, 9.6 and 0.36.

Sol : The given numbers are equivalent to 0.60, 9.60 and 0.36.

Now, we find out the L.C.M. of 60, 960 and 36, which is equal to 2880.

Hence, the required L.C.M. = 2880.

L.C.M. of fraction : The L.C.M. of two or more fractions is the least fraction or integer which is exactly divisible by each of them.

If $\frac{a}{b}, \frac{c}{d}, \frac{e}{f}$ be the proper fractions, then their L.C.M. is given by

$$\frac{\text{L.C.M. of numerators } a, c, e}{\text{H.C.F. of denominators } b, d, f}$$

An example : Find the L.C.M. of $\frac{1}{2}, \frac{3}{5}, \frac{4}{7}$ and $\frac{5}{12}$

Sol : $$\text{L.C.M.} = \frac{\text{L.C.M. of } 1, 3, 4, 5}{\text{H.C.F. of } 2, 5, 7, 12}$$

$$= \frac{60}{1} = 60$$

HCF

Factor : One number is said to be a factor of other when it divides the other exactly. Hence, 5 and 7 are factors of 35.

Common factor : A common factor of two or more numbers is a number that divides each of them exactly. Hence, 5 is a common factor of 15, 25, 35 and 55.

Highest Common Factor (H.C.F.) : H.C.F. of two or more numbers is the largest number by which each given number is divisible without leaving any remainder.

An example : It is required to find the H.C.F. of 6 and 8.

Factors of 6 are 1, 2, 3, 6 and

Factors of 8 are 1, 2, 4, 8.

The common factors are 1, 2, but highest of these is 2. Hence, 2 is the H.C.F.

Note : *The terms Highest Common Divisor (H.C.D.) and Greatest Common Measure (G.C.M.) are often used in the sense of Highest Common Factor (H.C.F.)*

We can find H.C.F. by two methods:

1. By prime factorization method :

An example : Find the H.C.F. of 144, 336 and 2016.

Sol : $144 = 2 \times 2 \times 2 \times 2 \times 3 \times 3 = 2^4 \times 3^2$

$336 = 2 \times 2 \times 2 \times 2 \times 3 \times 7$

$= 2^4 \times 3 \times 7$

$2016 = 2 \times 2 \times 2 \times 2 \times 2 \times 7 \times 3 \times 3$

$= 2^5 \times 7 \times 3^2$

$\therefore$ H.C.F. of given numbers $= 2^4 \times 3 = 48$.

2. By division method : Divide the greater number by the smaller number, divide the divisor by the remainder, divide the remainder by the next remainder, and so on until no remainder is left. The last divisor is the required H.C.F.

An example : Find the H.C.F. of 48, 168 and 324.

Sol :

```
48 ) 168 ( 3
     144
     ---
      24 ) 48 ( 2
           48
           --
           ××
```

Thus, the H.C.F. of 48 and 168 is 24.

Now, we find out the H.C.F. of 24 and 324

```
24 ) 324 (13
     24
     --
     84
     72
     --
     12 ) 24 ( 2
          24
          --
          ××
```

$\therefore$ Required H.C.F. = 12.

H.C.F. of Decimals : First of all find the H.C.F. of the given numbers ignoring decimals and then put decimal at maximum digits from right to left.

An example : Find the H.C.F. of 0.0012, 1.6 and 2.8.

Sol : First we find the H.C.F. of 12, 16 and 28, which comes to 4.

So, H.C.F. of 0.0012, 1.6 and 2.8 will be 0.0004.

H.C.F. of Fractions : If $\frac{a}{b}, \frac{c}{d}, \frac{e}{f}, \ldots$ be the proper fraction, their H.C.F. is equal to

$$\frac{\text{H.C.F. of numerators}}{\text{L.C.M. of denominators}}$$

An example : Find the H.C.F. of $\frac{54}{9}, 3\frac{9}{17}$ and $\frac{36}{51}$

Sol : Here, $\frac{54}{9} = \frac{6}{1}$; $3\frac{9}{17} = \frac{60}{17}$ and $\frac{36}{51} = \frac{12}{17}$

Hence, the fractions are $\frac{6}{1}, \frac{60}{17}$ and $\frac{12}{17}$

$$\therefore \text{ H.C.F.} = \frac{\text{H.C.F. of } 6, 60, 12}{\text{L.C.M. of } 1, 17, 17} = \frac{6}{17}.$$

Relationship Between Two Numbers and Their L.C.M. and H.C.F.

Product of the H.C.F. and the L.C.M. of two numbers is equal to the product of the given numbers.

i.e., 1st number × 2nd number = H.C.F. × L.C.M.

MULTIPLE CHOICE QUESTIONS

1. The largest three-digit number, when divided by 6, 9 and 12 leaves 1 as remainder in each case, will be

A. 887 B. 987
C. 973 D. 730

2. Two numbers are in the ratio of 8 : 15. If their H.C.F. is 4, the numbers are

A. 32 and 60 B. 16 and 30
C. 80 and 150 D. 64 and 120

3. The largest number that will divide 226 and 272 leaving 1 and 2 as remainders respectively, is

A. 36 B. 45
C. 55 D. 59

4. Which of the following is the greatest common divisor of 1170 and 102?

A. 8 B. 4
C. 6 D. 3

5. A number, when 3 is added to it, becomes divisible by 36, 45 and 50. The smallest such number is

A. 987 B. 798
C. 986 D. 897

6. The least perfect square number which is completely divisible by 10, 20, 30 and 40 is

A. 4800 B. 3600
C. 4400 D. 2500

7. The product of two numbers is 2160 and their H.C.F. is 12. How many such pairs of numbers can be possibly formed?

A. 3 B. 1
C. 2 D. None

8. The greatest number that will divide 366, 513 and 324 leaving the same remainder in each case is

A. 21 B. 18
C. 27 D. 42

9. The sum of two numbers is 216 and their H.C.F. is 27. These numbers are

A. 60 and 90 B. 81 and 135
C. 64 and 128 D. 30 and 84

10. The L.C.M. of two numbers is 45 times their H.C.F. If the sum of the L.C.M. and the H.C.F. of these two numbers is 1150 and one of the numbers is 125, then the other number is

A. 256 B. 225
C. 250 D. 255

11. The H.C.F. and the L.C.M. of two numbers are 50 and 250 respectively. On dividing one of these numbers by 2, 50 is obtained as quotient. The numbers are

A. 100, 125 B. 80, 100
C. 125, 100 D. 200, 250

12. The largest three-digit number, which when successively divided by 6, 9 and 12, leaves 3 as remainder in each case, is

A. 575 B. 795
C. 975 D. 525

13. The greatest number that will divide 33, 64 and 80 leaving 3, 4 and 5 as remainders respectively, is

A. 10 B. 20
C. 15 D. 22

14. The H.C.F. of three numbers is 12. If the three numbers are in the ratio of 1 : 2 : 3, then the numbers are

A. 14, 28, 42 B. 12, 24, 36
C. 15, 30, 45 D. 24, 48, 72

15. The greatest four-digit number completely divisible by 2, 3, 4 and 5 is

A. 9960 B. 9690
C. 8990 D. 9980

16. Three bells ring respectively at an interval of 15 seconds, 20 seconds and 24 seconds. If they ring continuously for 12 minutes then how many times, during this period, will they ring together?

A. 2 times B. 6 times
C. 5 times D. 3 times

17. The smallest number, on being successively divided by 5, 6, 8, 9 and 12 leaves 1 as remainder in each case and is completely divisible by 13, will be

A. 4603 B. 6305
C. 4503 D. 3601

18. If in the process of finding H.C.F. of two numbers by continued division method, 49 is the last divisor and quotients obtained (from the beginning) are 17, 3 and 2 respectively, then the numbers are

A. 432 and 4929 B. 343 and 5829
C. 388 and 5880 D. 472 and 5930

19. A, B and C start running together in a particular direction from a particular point on a 12 kms long circular path. If the speeds of A, B and C are 3 kms/h, 7 kms/h and 13 kms/h respectively, then after how many hours will they meet together again?

A. 8 B. 6
C. 12 D. 10

20. Which of the following has most numbers of divisors?

A. 182 B. 176
C. 101 D. 99

ANSWERS

1	2	3	4	5	6	7	8	9	10
C	A	B	C	D	B	C	A	B	B
11	**12**	**13**	**14**	**15**	**16**	**17**	**18**	**19**	**20**
A	C	C	B	A	B	D	B	C	B

SOME SELECTED EXPLANATORY ANSWERS

1. L.C.M. of 6, 9 and 12

3	6, 9, 12
2	2, 3, 4
	1, 3, 2

$\therefore$ LCM = 3 × 2 × 3 × 2 = 36.

$\because$ Largest 3-digit number = 999

36) 999 (27
72
279
252
× 27

$\therefore$ Largest 3-digit number which is exactly divisible by 6, 9 and 12

= 999 − 27 = 972

$\therefore$ The required number = 972 + 1 = 973.

2. Let the numbers be $8x$ and $15x$

$$8x = 2 \times 2 \times 2 \times x$$
$$15x = 3 \times 5 \times x$$

$\therefore$ LCM of $8x$ and $15x = 2 \times 2 \times 2 \times x \times 3 \times 5 = 120x$

Now, 1st number × 2nd number = HCF × LCM

$\Rightarrow 8x \times 15x = 4 \times 120x$

$\Rightarrow 120x^2 = 4 \times 120x$

$\Rightarrow x = 4$

$\therefore$ Numbers are 8 × 4 = 32 and 15 × 4 = 60.

3. 226 − 1 = 225 and 272 − 2 = 270

Now, HCF of 225 and 270

225) 270 (1
225
45) 225 (5
225
×

$\therefore$ The required number is 45.

4. $1170 = 2 \times 5 \times 3 \times 3 \times 13$

$102 = 2 \times 3 \times 17$

$\therefore$ Greatest common divisor $= 2 \times 3 = 6.$

5. It is clear from the given conditions of the problem that the smallest number will be 3 less than the LCM of 36, 45 and 50.

$\therefore$ LCM of 36, 45 and 50

3	36, 45, 50
2	12, 15, 50
3	6, 15, 25
5	2, 5, 25
	2, 1, 5

$\therefore$ LCM $= 3 \times 2 \times 3 \times 5 \times 2 \times 5 = 900$

$\therefore$ Required number $= 900 - 3 = 897.$

6. LCM of 10, 20, 30 and 40

2	10, 20, 30, 40
5	5, 10, 15, 20
2	1, 2, 3, 4
	1, 1, 3, 2

$\therefore$ LCM $= 2 \times 2 \times 5 \times 3 \times 2$

But the number is a perfect square number

$\therefore$ Required number $= 2 \times 2 \times 5 \times 5 \times 3 \times 3 \times 2 \times 2 = 3600.$

7. Product of two numbers = their HCF × their LCM

$2160 = 12 \times \text{LCM}$

$\therefore \quad \text{LCM} = \frac{2160}{12} = 180$

Therefore such pairs of numbers in which product of numbers is 2160 and HCF is 12 will be only 2. *i.e.*, 12×180 and 36×60.

8. Difference between 366 and 513

$= 513 - 366 = 147$

and difference between 513 and 324

$= 513 - 324 = 189$

$\therefore$ HCF of 147 and 189

```
147 ) 189 ( 1
      147
      × 42 ) 147 ( 3
             126
             × 21 ) 42 ( 2
                    42
                     ×
```

$\therefore$ The required largest number is 21.

9. Let the numbers be x and y.

$\therefore x + y = 216 = 27 \times 8$

Since HCF of these two numbers is 27, hence, common factor of these two numbers is 27. Therefore these numbers will be of the form of $27 \times 1, 27 \times 2, 27 \times 3$, ... etc.

According to the condition of the problem sum of these numbers is 216.

$\therefore$ The numbers will be $27 \times 3 = 81$

and $27 \times 5 = 135.$

10. LCM of the two numbers $= 45 \times \text{HCF}$

and $\text{LCM} + \text{HCF} = 1150$

$\Rightarrow \quad 45 \times \text{HCF} + \text{HCF} = 1150$

$\Rightarrow \quad \text{HCF}(45 + 1) = 1150$

$\Rightarrow \quad \text{HCF} = \frac{1150}{46} = 25$

$\therefore \quad \text{LCM} = 45 \times 25 = 1125$

$\because$ 1st number × 2nd number = LCM × HCF

$\therefore$ 125 × 2nd number $= 1125 \times 25$

$\therefore \quad \text{2nd number} = \frac{1125 \times 25}{125} = 225.$

11. According to the condition of the problem, 50 is obtained on dividing one of the numbers by 2

$\therefore$ One of the numbers $= 50 \times 2 = 100$

Now, 1st number × 2nd number = LCM × HCF

$\therefore \quad 100 \times \text{2nd number} = 250 \times 50$

$\therefore \quad \text{2nd number} = \frac{250 \times 50}{100} = 125$

Hence, numbers are 100 and 125.

12. LCM of 6, 9 and 12 = 36 and largest 3-digit number = 999

$\therefore$ HCF of 36 and 999

```
36 ) 999 ( 27
     72
     279
     252
      27
```

$\therefore$ Largest three-digit number completely divisible by 6, 9 and 12

$= 999 - 27 = 972$

Since 3 is left as remainder in each case,

$\therefore$ Required largest number of 3-digit

$= 972 + 3 = 975.$

13. $33 - 3 = 30$, $64 - 4 = 60$ and $80 - 5 = 75$

Now, HCF of 30, 60 and 75:

$$30 = 2 \times \underline{3 \times 5}$$
$$60 = 2 \times 2 \times \underline{3 \times 5}$$
$$75 = \underline{3 \times 5} \times 5$$

$\because$ Common factor $= 3 \times 5 = 15$

$\therefore$ Required largest number = 15.

14. Let the numbers be x, $2x$ and $3x$ respectively. Here, HCF of the three numbers is 12, therefore 12 is the largest common factor of these three numbers. Thus, it is clear that $x = 12$

$\therefore$ These numbers are 12, 24 and 36 respectively.

15. LCM of 2, 3, 4 and 5 = 60

Largest 4-digit number = 9999

```
Now, 60 ) 9999 ( 166
          60
          399
          360
         × 399
           360
            39
```

$\therefore$ Largest 4-digit number completely divisible by 2, 3, 4 and 5

$= 9999 - 39 = 9960$

$\therefore$ Required number = 9960.

16. LCM of 15, 20 and 24

5	15, 20, 24
4	3, 4, 24
3	3, 1, 6
	1, 1, 2

LCM $= 5 \times 4 \times 3 \times 2 = 120$

$\because$ 12 minutes $= 12 \times 60 = 720$ seconds

$\therefore$ Number of times the bells will ring together during 12 minutes

$$= \frac{720}{120} = 6 \text{ times.}$$

17. LCM of 5, 6, 8, 9 and 12 = 360. Hence, the smallest number which when divided by 5, 6, 8, 9 and 12 leaves 1 as remainder in each case will be $360 + 1 = 361$. But 361 is not completely divisible by 13. Hence, on considering $360 \times 2 + 1$, $360 \times 3 + 1, \ldots, 360 \times n + 1$, we conclude that $360 \times 10 + 1 = 3601$ is the required number.

18. This question is based on finding HCF by continued division method. Now according to the condition of the problem,

Last divisor = 49

and Last quotient = 2

$\therefore$ dividend $= 49 \times 2 = 98$

Now, divisor = 98 and quotient = 3

and remainder = 49

$\therefore$ dividend $= 98 \times 3 + 49 = 343$

Now, divisor = 343

quotient = 17

and remainder = 98

$\therefore$ Dividend $= 343 \times 17 + 98 = 5829$

Therefore, these numbers are 343 and 5829.

19. A, B and C will take 4 hours, $\frac{12}{7}$ hours and $\frac{12}{13}$ hours respectively in completing one round on the circular path.

$\therefore$ LCM of $\frac{4}{1}$, $\frac{12}{7}$ and $\frac{12}{13}$

$$= \frac{\text{LCM of 4,12 and 12}}{\text{HCF of 1,7 and 13}}$$

$\because$ LCM of 4, 12 and 12= 12 and HCF of 1, 7 and 13 = 1

$\therefore$ Required LCM $= \frac{12}{1} = 12$

Hence, they will meet together again after 12 hrs.

20.

Numbers	***Their divisors***
182	→ 1, 2, 7, 13, 14, 26, 91 and 182
176	→ 1, 2, 4, 8, 16, 22, 44, 88 and 176
101	→ 1 and 101
99	→ 1, 3, 9, 11, 33 and 99

Therefore, 176 has the most number of divisors.

2. Ratio and Proportion

Some Important Facts:

1. If a and b are two quantities, then

(*a*) Duplicate ratio of $a : b = a^2 : b^2$

(*b*) Sub-duplicate ratio of $a : b = \sqrt{a} : \sqrt{b}$

(*c*) Triplicate ratio of $a : b = a^3 : b^3$

(*d*) Sub-triplicate ratio $a : b = \sqrt[3]{a} : \sqrt[3]{b}$

(*e*) Inverse or reciprocal ratio of $a : b = \frac{1}{a} : \frac{1}{b}$

2. If $a : b = c : d$, then

(*a*) Third proportional (c) to 'a' and 'b' $= \frac{b^2}{a}$

(*b*) Fourth proportional (d) $= \frac{bc}{a}$

(*c*) Mean proportional between a and $b = \sqrt{ab}$

(*d*) If $\frac{a}{b} = \frac{c}{d}$ then $\frac{a+b}{a-b} = \frac{c+d}{c-d}$

(Componendo and dividendo)

3. (*a*) Comparision of ratios $(a : b) > (c : d) \Leftrightarrow \frac{a}{b} > \frac{c}{d}$

(*b*) Compounded ratio of $(a : b)$, $(c : d)$, $(e : f) = \frac{ace}{bdf}$

4. If $A : B = x : y$ and $B : C = p : q$, then

(*a*) $A : C = \frac{x \times p}{y \times q}$

(*b*) $A : B : C = px : py : qy$

5. In what *ratio* the two kinds of tea must be mixed together one at ₹ x per kg and another at ₹ y per kg, so that the mixture may cost ₹ z per kg?

$$\text{Ratio} = \frac{z-y}{x-z}$$

6. A grey hound persues a hare as takes J_1 leaps for every J_2 leaps of the hare. If K_1 leaps of the hound are equal to K_2 leaps of the hare, then the Ratio of speeds of the hound and hare is $\frac{J_2 \times K_1}{J_1 \times K_2}$

7. The incomes of two persons are in the ratio of $a : b$ and their expenditure are in the ratio of $x : y$. If the saving of each person is ₹ s, then income of each is ₹ $\frac{as(y-x)}{ay-bx}$ and ₹ $\frac{bs(y-x)}{ay-bx}$ respectively.

8. In a mixture of z litre, the ratio of milk and water is $x : y$. If another p litres of water is added to the mixture, the ratio of milk and water in the resulting mixture $= \frac{xz}{yz + p(x+y)}$

9. There are four members a, b, c and d, then formula for

(*a*) What should be added to each of these numbers so that the remaining numbers may be proportional $= \frac{ad-bc}{(b+c)-(a+d)}$.

(*b*) What should be subtracted from each of these numbers so that the remaining numbers may be proportional

$$= \frac{ad-bc}{(a+d)-(b+c)}.$$

10. In a mixture the ratio of milk and water is $a : b$. If in this mixture another K litre of water is added, then the ratio of milk and water in the resulting mixture becomes $a : m$. Then the quantity of milk in the original mixture $= \frac{ak}{m-b}$ and quantity of water $= \frac{bk}{m-b}$.

SOLVED EXAMPLES

Example 1: The ratio between the three angles of a quadrilateral is 6 : 7 : 8 respectively. The value of the fourth angle of the quadrilateral is 108°. What is the difference between the largest and the smallest angles of the quadrilateral?

Solution: $6x + 7x + 8x = 360° - 108°$

$\Rightarrow \quad 21x = 252°$

$\Rightarrow \quad x = 12°$

$\therefore$ Required difference $= 108° - 6 \times 12°$

$= 108° - 72° = 36°.$

Example 2: Three-fifth of a number is equal to 70% of another number. What is the ratio between the first number and the second number respectively?

Solution: Let the numbers are x and y respectively.

$$\therefore \quad x \times \frac{3}{5} = y \times \frac{70}{100}$$

$$\Rightarrow \quad x \times \frac{3}{5} = y \times \frac{7}{10}$$

$$\Rightarrow \quad \frac{x}{y} = \frac{7}{10} \times \frac{5}{3} = 7 : 6.$$

Example 3: The respective ratio between the speeds of a car, a train and a bus is 5 : 9 : 4. The average speed of the car, the bus and the train is 72 km/hr together. What is the average speed of the car and the train together?

Solution: Let the speed of car, train and bus be $5x$, $9x$ and $4x$ km/hr respectively.

$\because \quad 5x + 9x + 4x = 72 \times 3$

$\therefore \quad x = 12$

$\therefore$ Average speed of car and train

$$= \frac{5x + 9x}{2} = \frac{14 \times 12}{2} = 84 \text{ km/hr}.$$

Example 4: The ratio between the present ages of Meena and Priya is 3 : 4 respectively. Ten years ago the ratio between their ages was 4 : 7 respectively. What will be Meena's age after 5 years?

Solution: Let the present age of Meena be $3x$ years

$\therefore$ The present age of Priya $= 4x$ years

$$\frac{3x - 10}{4x - 10} = \frac{4}{7}$$

$$21x - 70 = 16x - 40$$

$$x = \frac{70 - 40}{5} = 6$$

$\therefore$ Meena's age after 5 years $= 3 \times 6 + 5$

$= 23$ years.

MULTIPLE CHOICE QUESTIONS

1. An amount of rupees 4500 is to be distributed among Shrinath, Ramnath and Raghunath in the ratio of 3 : 7 : 5 respectively. If ₹ 500 is added to each of the share, the new ratio will become ......?

A. 7 : 10 : 13

B. 9 : 16 : 13

C. 2 : 4 : 3

D. None of these

2. The total number of students studying in a school is 10396. The ratio of the total number of girls to the total number of boys studying in the school is 52 : 61 respectively. What is the total number of girls studying in the school?

A. 4874 B. 4784

C. 5216 D. 5612

3. In a box the numbers of one rupee, half rupee and quarter rupee are in the ratio 3 : 4 : 5 and the total value of the coins is ₹ 100. Find the number of each kind of coins respectively:

A. 48, 64, 80

B. 48, 60, 70

C. 55, 78, 90

D. 44, 68, 80

4. The ratio of the ages of two persons is 4 : 7 and the age of one of them is more than the other by 30 years. What is the sum of their ages in years?

A. 100 B. 110

C. 120 D. 130

5. The ratio of the amounts of A and B is 4 : 3 and the sum of their amount is ₹ 700. What amount in rupees should A give B to make the ratio 1 : 1?

A. 100 B. 200
C. 150 D. 50

6. The ratio of the volumes of water and glycerine in 240 c.c. glycerine mixed with water is 1 : 3. What additional volume of water should be mixed with it so that the ratio of the volumes of water and glycerine becomes 2 : 3?

A. 70 c.c. B. 80 c.c.
C. 60 c.c. D. 50 c.c.

7. If 15% of A is the same as 20% of B, then A : B is :

A. 9 : 11 B. 4 : 3
C. 3 : 4 D. 6 : 7

8. The fourth proportional to 1, 3 and the third proportional to 1 and 3 is :

A. 9 B. 81
C. 3 D. 27

9. The ratio of third proportional to 12 and 30 and the mean proportional to 9 and 25 is :

A. 5 : 1 B. 2 : 1
C. 9 : 14 D. 7 : 15

10. If $a + b : b + c : c + a = 6 : 7 : 8$ and $a + b + c = 14$ then the value of c is :

A. 14 B. 7
C. 8 D. 6

11. ₹ 120 are divided among P, Q, R such that P's share is ₹ 20 more than Q's and ₹ 20 less than R's share. What is Q's share?

A. ₹ 20 B. ₹ 15
C. ₹ 25 D. ₹ 10

12. If four numbers are in the ratio 5 : 7 : 11 : 13 be such that the sum of their cubes is 3996, find the average of four numbers.

A. 13 B. 11
C. 12 D. 9

13. If 2A = 3B = 4C then A : B : C is :

A. 2 : 3 : 4 B. 4 : 3 : 2
C. 6 : 4 : 3 D. 3 : 4 : 6

14. If $\frac{1}{5} : \frac{1}{x} = \frac{1}{x} : \frac{1}{1.25}$, then the value of x is :

A. 1.25 B. 1.5
C. 2.5 D. 2.25

15. A fraction bears the same ratio to $\frac{1}{27}$ as $\frac{3}{7}$ does to $\frac{5}{9}$. The fraction is :

A. $\frac{7}{45}$ B. $\frac{1}{35}$
C. $\frac{45}{7}$ D. $\frac{5}{21}$

16. The fourth proportional to 0.2, 0.12 and 0.3 is:

A. 0.13 B. 0.15
C. 0.18 D. 0.8

17. A bag contains 25 paise, 10 paise and 5 paise coins in the ratio 1 : 2 : 3. If their total value is ₹ 30, the number of 5 paise coins is :

A. 50 B. 100
C. 150 D. 200

18. In a class, the number of boys is more than the number of girls by 12% of the total strength. The ratio of boys to girls is :

A. 11 : 14 B. 14 : 11
C. 25 : 28 D. 28 : 25

19. A right cylinder and a right circular cone have the same radius and the same volume. The ratio of the height of the cylinder to that of the cone is :

A. 3 : 5 B. 2 : 5
C. 3 : 1 D. 1 : 3

20. The speeds of three cars are in the ratio 3 : 4 : 5. The ratio between times taken by them to travel the same distance is :

A. 3 : 4 : 5
B. 5 : 4 : 3
C. 12 : 15 : 20
D. 20 : 15 : 12

ANSWERS

1	2	3	4	5	6	7	8	9	10
D	B	A	B	D	C	B	D	A	D
11	**12**	**13**	**14**	**15**	**16**	**17**	**18**	**19**	**20**
A	D	C	C	B	C	C	B	D	D

SOME SELECTED EXPLANATORY ANSWERS

2. From question,

The total number of students in the school = 10396

and ratio of number of girls : boys = 52 : 61

∴ The total number of girls in that school

$$= \frac{10396 \times 52}{(52+61)} = \frac{10396 \times 52}{113}$$

$= 92 \times 52 = 4784.$

3. $3x + 4x \times \frac{1}{2} + 5x \times \frac{1}{4} = 100$

$12x + 8x + 5x = 400$

$x = 16$

Number of 1 rupee = 48

Number of 1/2 rupee = 64

Number of quarter rupee = $5 \times 16 = 80$.

4. $\because$ $7x - 4x = 30,$

$x = 10$

∴ Sum of their ages = $(4 + 7) \times 10$

$= 11 \times 10 = 110$ years.

5. $\because$ $4x + 3x = 700$

$\Rightarrow$ $x = 100$

400 (A) 300 (B)

$\because$ $\frac{400 - x}{300 + x} = \frac{1}{1}$

$\Rightarrow$ $400 - x = 300 + x$

$\therefore$ $x = 50.$

6. Quantity of water in 240 cc glycerine and water

$= \frac{1}{4} \times 240$ cc = 60 cc

Quantity of glycerine = (240 – 60) cc

= 180 cc

$\because$ $\frac{60 + x}{180} = \frac{2}{3}$

$\Rightarrow$ $x = 60$ cc.

8. First we find the third proportional to 1 and 3. Let the third proportional to 1 and 3 is

$\Rightarrow$ $1 : 3 :: 3 : x$

$\Rightarrow$ $x = 3 \times 3$

$\Rightarrow$ $x = 9$

The fourth proportional to 1, 3 and the third proportional to 1 and 3

= The fourth proportional to 1, 3 and 9. Let the fourth proportional to 1, 3 and 9 is y, then $1 : 3 :: 9 : y$

$\Rightarrow$ $1 \times y = 3 \times 9$

$\Rightarrow$ $y = 27$

∴ Required answer is 27.

9. Let the third proportional to 12 and 30 be y, then $12 : 30 :: 30 : y$

$\Rightarrow$ $12y = 30 \times 30$

$y = \frac{30 \times 30}{12} = 75$

Mean proportional to 9 and 25

$= \sqrt{9 \times 25} = 3 \times 5 = 15$

∴ The required ratio is 75 : 15 = 5 : 1.

10. Given

$$\left.\begin{array}{l} a + b = 6x \\ b + c = 7x \text{ and } c + a = 8x \end{array}\right\} \quad ...(1)$$

and $a + b + c = 14$ ...(2)

adding equations in (1) we get

$2(a + b + c) = 21x$

using (2) we get

$$2 \times 14 = 21x$$

$$\Rightarrow \quad x = \frac{2\times14}{21}$$

$$= \frac{2\times2}{3} = \frac{4}{3}$$

$$a + b = 6x = 6\times\frac{4}{3} = 8.$$

Using $a + b + c = 14$ and $a + b = 8$

We get $c = 6$.

11. Given P's share = Q's share + ₹ 20

P's share = R's share − ₹ 20

let Q's share be y.

then P's share = $y + 20$

$y + 20$ = R's share − ₹ 20

$\Rightarrow$ R's share = $y + 40$

P's share + Q's share + R's share = 120

$$y + 20 + y + y + 40 = 120$$

$$3y + 60 = 120$$

$$3y = 120 - 60 = 60$$

$$y = 20$$

$\therefore$ Q's share = y = ₹ 20.

12. Let the four numbers be $5x$, $7x$, $11x$ and $13x$.

Given $(5x)^3 + (7x)^3 + (11x)^3 + (13x)^3 = 3996$.

$$125x^3 + 343x^3 + 1331x^3 + 2197x^3 = 3996$$

$$\Rightarrow \quad 3996x^3 = 3996$$

$$\Rightarrow \quad x^3 = 1 \quad \Rightarrow \quad x = 1$$

$\therefore$ The four numbers are 5, 7, 11 and 13.

Average of these four numbers

$$= \frac{5+7+11+13}{4} = \frac{36}{4} = 9.$$

13. Let $2A = 3B = 4C = x$.

Then, $A = \frac{x}{2}$, $B = \frac{x}{3}$ and $C = \frac{x}{4}$.

$$\therefore A : B : C = \frac{x}{2} : \frac{x}{3} : \frac{x}{4} = 6 : 4 : 3.$$

Hence, A : B : C = 6 : 4 : 3.

14. $$\frac{1}{x}\times\frac{1}{x} = \frac{1}{5}\times\frac{1}{1.25}$$

or, $$\frac{1}{x^2} = \frac{4}{25}$$

or, $$x^2 = \frac{25}{4}$$

$$\therefore \quad x = \frac{5}{2} = 2.5.$$

15. $x : \frac{1}{27} = \frac{3}{7} : \frac{5}{9} \Rightarrow \frac{5}{9}x = \frac{1}{27}\times\frac{3}{7}$.

$$\therefore \frac{5}{9}x = \frac{1}{63} \text{ or } x = \left(\frac{1}{63}\times\frac{9}{5}\right) = \frac{1}{35}.$$

16. Let $0.2 : 0.12 :: 0.3 : x$.

Then, $0.2x = 0.12 \times 0.3$ or

$$x = \frac{0.12\times0.3}{0.2} = 0.18.$$

17. Ratio of their values $= \frac{1}{4} : \frac{2}{10} : \frac{3}{20}$

$$= 5 : 4 : 3.$$

$\therefore$ Value of 5-paise coins = ₹ $\left(30\times\frac{3}{12}\right)$

= ₹ 7.50.

$$\therefore \text{Number of 5-paise coins} = \frac{750}{5} = 150.$$

19. Let the heights of the cylinder and cone be h and H respectively. Then, $\pi r^2 h = \frac{1}{3}\pi r^2 H$ or

$$\frac{h}{H} = \frac{1}{3}.$$

So, their heights are in the ratio 1 : 3.

20. Ratio of time taken $= \frac{1}{3} : \frac{1}{4} : \frac{1}{5} = 20 : 15 : 12.$

---

3. Age and Average

IMPORTANT FACTS

1. The present age of the father is x times the age of his son. T years hence, the father's age become y times the age of his son. Then the present ages of the father and his son are:

   Present age of the son $= \frac{(y-1)T}{x-y}$ years and

   age of the father $= \frac{(y-1)T \times x}{x-y}$ years.

2. T years ago, the father's age was x times that of his son and at present the father's age is y times the age of his son. Then their present ages are:

   Son's age $= \frac{T(x-1)}{x-y}$ years;

   Father's age $= \frac{T(x-1)}{x-y} \times y$ years.

3. Average Speed $= \frac{\text{Total travelled distance}}{\text{Total taken time}}$

4. If equal distances are travelled at the rate X and Y, then Average Speed $= \frac{2XY}{X+y}$

5. When a person leaves a group and another person joins the group in the place of person left, then

   I. In the case of increasing of average age, Age of the newcomer = Age of person left + no. of persons in the group X increase in average age.

   II. In the case of decreasing of average age, Age of the newcomer = Age of person left – no. of persons in the group X decrease in average age.

6. When a person joins a group without replacing any previous person from that group, then

   I. In the case of increasing of average age, Age of the newcomer = Previous of the age + no. of all persons (including newcomer) × increaser in average age.

   II. In the case of decreasing of average age, Age of the newcomer = Previous average age – no. of all persons (including new comer) × decrease in average age.

7. When a person leaves the group but nobody joins this group, then

   I. In the case of increasing of average age, Age of man left = Previous Average of the age – no. of present persons × decrease in the average age.

   II. In the case of decreasing of average age, Age of man left = Previous Average age + no. of present persons × increase in average age.

8. Average related to Natural Numbers

   I. Average of consecutive natural numbers till n $= \frac{(n+1)}{2}$

   II. Average of squares of numbers till n $= \frac{(n+1)(2n+1)}{6}$

   III. Average of cubes of consecutive natural numbers till $n = \frac{n(n+1)^2}{4}$

9. Average related to Even Numbers

   I. Average of n = consecutive even numbers $= n + 1$

II. Average of consecutive even number till $n = (n/2+1)$

III. Average of squares of n consecutive even numbers $= \frac{2(n+1)(2n+1)}{3}$

IV. Average of squares of consecutive even numbers till $n = \frac{(n+1)(2n+1)}{3}$

10. Average related to Odd Numbers

I. Average of n consecutive odd numbers $= n$

II. Average of consecutive odd numbers till $n = \frac{n(n+1)}{3}$

III. Average of squares of consecutive odd numbers till $n = \frac{n(n+1)}{3}$

SOLVED EXAMPLES

Example 1: Ankur's present age is 12 years more than Raman's age 5 years ago. Presently Raman is 24 years older than Raju's present age who is 12 years younger than Amit. If Amit's present age is 42 years, what is Ankur's age 3 years ago?

Solution: Amit's present age = 42 years

Raju's present age = 42 – 12 = 30 years

Raman's present age = 30 + 24 = 54 years

Ankur's present age = 54 – 5 + 12 = 61 years

$\therefore$ Ankur's age 3 years ago = 58 years.

Example 2: Present ages of Leela and Shivani are in the ratio of 4 : 5 respectively. Three years hence this ratio becomes 5 : 6. What is the difference between their present ages?

Solution: Let Leela's and Shivani's present ages be $4x$ and $5x$ years respectively.

After 3 years,

$$\frac{4x+3}{5x+3} = \frac{5}{6}$$

$\Rightarrow$ $25x + 15 = 24x + 18$

$\Rightarrow$ $25x - 24x = 18 - 15 = 3$

$\therefore$ $x = 3$ = Required difference.

Example 3: Radha's present age is three years less than twice her age 12 ages ago. Also the respective ratio between Raj's present age Radha's present age is 4 : 9. What will be Raj's age after 5 years?

Solution: Let the present age of Radha be x years. As per question,

$\because$ $x = (x - 12) \times 2 - 3$

$\Rightarrow$ $x = 2x - 27$

$\therefore$ $x = 27$

$\because$ Present age of Raj

$$= \frac{4}{9} \times 27 = 12 \text{ years}$$

$\therefore$ Raj's age after 5 years = 12 + 5 = 17 years.

Example 4: If $12a + 12b = 45$, what is the average of a and b?

Solution: $\because$ $12a + 12b = 45$

$\Rightarrow$ $12(a + b) = 45$

$\therefore$ $\frac{a+b}{2} = \frac{45}{12 \times 2} = 1.875.$

Example 5: The sum of five numbers is 555. The average of first two numbers is 75 and the third number is 115. What is the average of last two numbers?

Solution: Average of last two numbers

$$= \frac{555 - 2 \times 75 - 115}{2}$$

$$= \frac{555 - 150 - 115}{2} = \frac{290}{2} = 145.$$

Example 6: The average marks of nine students in a group is 63. Three of them scored 78, 69 and 48 marks. What are the average marks of remaining six students?

Solution: The average marks of remaining 6 students

$$= \frac{9 \times 63 - (78 + 69 + 48)}{6}$$

$$= \frac{567 - 195}{6} = 62.$$

MULTIPLE CHOICE QUESTIONS

1. The sum of 8 consecutive odd numbers is 656. Also average of four consecutive even number is 87. What is the sum of the smallest odd number and second largest even number?
A. 165
B. 175
C. 163
D. Cannot be determined

2. The ages of Meena, Tina and Seema are in the ratio of 6 : 4 : 7 respectively. If the sum of their ages is 34 years, what is Seema's age?
A. 12 years B. 10 years
C. 18 years D. None of these

3. The average of 4 positive integers is 52.5. The highest integer is 76 and the lowest integer is 34. The difference between the remaining two integers is 4. Which of the following integers is higher of the remaining two integers?
A. 52
B. 54
C. 48
D. Cannot be determined

4. The present age of Deepa is 3 times the present age of his son. Five years hence the ratio of their ages will be 34 : 13 respectively. What is the present age of Deepa?
A. 63 years B. 68 years
C. 58 years D. 60 years

5. The average of 5 consecutive even numbers A, B, C, D and E is 66. What is the product of B and E?
A. 4352 B. 4340
C. 4620 D. None of these

6. The present age of father is 34 years more than that of his son. Twelve years ago father's age was 18 times the age of his son. What is the present age of the son in years?
A. 16 B. 14
C. 12 D. 18

7. A father is older than his first son by 30 years, the first son is older than the second son by 10 years. If the sum of their ages by 95 years, find the age of father.
A. 65 years B. 55 years
C. 45 years D. 50 years

8. In 10 years, Alok will be twice as old as Babul was 10 years ago. If Alok is now 9 years older than Babul, the present age of Babul is :
A. 19 years B. 29 years
C. 39 years D. 49 years

9. The difference between the ages of two persons is 10 years. 15 years ago, the elder one was twice as old as the younger one. The present age of the elder person is :
A. 25 years B. 35 years
C. 45 years D. 55 years

10. Ratio of Anshu's age to Jolly's age is equal to 4 : 3. Anshu will be 26 years old after 6 years. How old is Jolly now?
A. 12 years B. 15 years
C. $19\frac{1}{2}$ years D. 21 years

11. The ratio between the ages of Asha and Bhushan at present is 2 : 3. Five years hence the ratio of their ages will be 3 : 4. What is the present age of Asha?
A. 10 years B. 15 years
C. 25 years D. data inadequate

12. Three years ago the average age of A and B was 18 years. With C joining them, the average becomes 22 years. How old is C now?
A. 24 years B. 27 years
C. 28 years D. 30 years

13. Ten years ago A was half of B in age. If the ratio of their present ages is 3 : 4, what will be the total of their present ages?
A. 8 years B. 20 years
C. 35 years D. 45 years

14. Out of three numbers, the first is twice the second and is half of the third. If the average of the three numbers is 56, the three numbers in order are :

A. 48, 96, 24 B. 48, 24, 96
C. 96, 24, 48 D. 96, 48, 24

15. The average of 50 numbers is 38. If two numbers, namely 45 and 55 are discarded, the average of the remaining numbers is :
A. 36.5 B. 37.0
C. 37.5 D. 37.52

16. The average temperature of the first three days is 27°C and that of the next three is 29°C. If the average of the whole week is 28.5°C, the temperature of the last day of the week is:
A. 10.5°C B. 21°C
C. 31.5°C D. 42°C

17. The average of an adult class is 40 years. 12 new students with an average age of 32 years join the class, thereby decreasing the average by 4 years. The original strength of the class was :
A. 10 B. 11
C. 12 D. 15

18. The average weight of 8 persons is increased by 2.5 kg when one of them whose weight is 56 kg is replaced by a new man. The weight of the new man is :
A. 66 kg B. 75 kg
C. 76 kg D. 86 kg

19. In a TV factory, an average of 60 TVs are produced per day for the first 25 days of the month. A few workers fell ill for the next five days, reducing the daily average for the month to 58 sets per day. The average production per day for the last 5 days is :
A. 45 B. 48
C. 52 D. 58

20. The average expenditure of a man for the first five months is ₹ 120 and for the next seven months it is ₹ 130. If he saves ₹ 290 in that years, his monthly average income is :
A. ₹ 140 B. ₹ 150
C. ₹ 160 D. ₹ 170

ANSWERS

1	2	3	4	5	6	7	8	9	10
C	D	A	A	D	B	B	C	B	B
11	**12**	**13**	**14**	**15**	**16**	**17**	**18**	**19**	**20**
A	A	C	B	C	C	C	C	B	B

SOME SELECTED EXPLANATORY ANSWERS

1. Let the smallest odd and smallest even numbers are x and y respectively. Then,

$\because x + (x + 2) + (x + 4) + (x + 6) + (x + 8) + (x + 10) + (x + 12) + (x + 14) = 656$

$\Rightarrow 8x + 56 = 656$

$\therefore x = \frac{656 - 56}{8} = 75$

$\because y + (y + 2) + (y + 4) + (y + 6) = 4 \times 87$

$\Rightarrow 4y + 12 = 348$

$y = \frac{348 - 12}{4} = 84$

$\therefore$ Reqd. sum of the smallest odd number and second largest even number

$= x + (y + 4) = 75 + (84 + 4) = 163.$

2. Seema's age $= \frac{7 \times 34}{(6 + 4 + 7)} = 14$ years.

3. Let the 4 positive integers, kept in descending order be a, b, c and d respectively. Then from question,

$\because a + b + c + d = 4 \times 52.5 = 210$

$\Rightarrow 76 + (b + c) + 34 = 210$

$\Rightarrow (b + c) = 100$ ...(*i*)

Again from question,

$b - c = 4$ ...(*ii*)

Solving (*i*) and (*ii*), we get

$b = 52$

and $c = 48$

Hence, higher integer $= b = 52$.

4. Let the present age of Deepa's son = x years.
Then from question,
Deepa's present age = $3x$ years

$\because \quad \frac{3x+5}{x+5} = \frac{34}{13}$

$\Rightarrow \quad 39x + 65 = 34x + 170$

$\Rightarrow \quad 5x = 105$

$\therefore \quad x = 21$

Deepa's present age = $3x = 3 \times 21 = 63$ years

5. From question,
A + B + C + D + E = 66 × 5 = 330
Let the 1st even number A be n, then

$\because n + (n + 2) + (n + 4) + (n + 6) + (n + 8) = 330$

$\Rightarrow \quad 5n + 20 = 330$

$\Rightarrow \quad 5n = 310$

$\therefore \quad n = 62$

Thus the required product
$= B \times E = (n + 2) \times (n + 8)$
$= 64 \times 70 = 4480.$

7. Age of 1st son = x
Father's age = $x + 30$
Age of 2nd son = $x - 10$

$\therefore x + (x + 30) + (x - 10) = 95$

$\Rightarrow \quad 3x + 20 = 95$

$\Rightarrow \quad 3x = 75$

$\therefore \quad x = 25$

$\therefore$ Father's age = (25 + 30) years = 55 years.

8. Let the present ages of Babul and Alok be x years and $(x + 9)$ years respectively.
Then, $(x + 9 + 10) = 2(x - 10)$ or $x = 39$.

9. Let the present age of the elder person be x years.
Then, the present age of the other person = $(x - 10)$ years
$(x - 15) = 2(x - 10 - 15)$ or $x = 35$
$\therefore$ The present age of the elder person is 35 years.

10. Let Anshu's age = $4x$ and Jolly's age = $3x$ years.
$\therefore 4x + 6 = 26 \quad \Rightarrow \quad x = 5$
$\therefore$ Jolly's age = $3x$ = 15 years.

11. Let the ages of Asha and Bhushan be $2x$ and $3x$ years.

$\frac{2x+5}{3x+5} = \frac{3}{4}$

$\Rightarrow \quad 4(2x + 5) = 3(3x + 5)$

$\Rightarrow \quad x = 5.$

$\therefore$ Asha's present age = $2x$ = 10 years.

12. Sum of ages of A and B, 3 years ago
= (18 × 2)
= 36 years.
Sum of ages of A, B and C = (22 × 3)
= 66 years.
Sum of ages of A and B = (36 + 6) years
= 42 years.
$\therefore$ C's age = (66 – 42) years = 24 years.

14. Let second number = x. Then, first one = $2x$ and third number = $4x$.

$\therefore \quad \frac{x+2x+4x}{3} = 56 \Rightarrow 7x = 168$ or $x = 24.$

So, the numbers are 48, 24, 96.

15. Total of 50 numbers = (50 × 38) = 1900.
Total of 48 numbers = [1900 – (45 + 55)]
= 1800.

$\therefore$ Required average = $\frac{1800}{48} = \frac{225}{6} = 37.5.$

16. $3 \times 27 + 3 \times 29 + x = 7 \times 28.5$

$\therefore \quad x = 31.5.$

17. Let original strength = x. Then,
$40x + 12 \times 32 = (x + 12) \times 36$
or $40x + 384 = 36x + 432$ or $4x = 48$
or $x = 12.$

18. Total increase = (8 × 2.5) kg = 20 kg.
Weight of new man = (56 + 20) kg = 76 kg.

19. Production during these 5 days
= (30 × 58 – 25 × 60) = 240.

$\therefore$ Average for 5 days = $\frac{240}{5} = 48.$

20. Total income = ₹ 120 × 5 + 130 × 7 + 290)
= ₹ 1800.

Average monthly income = ₹ $\left(\frac{1800}{12}\right)$
= ₹ 150.

4. PERCENTAGE

IMPORTANT FACTS

To solve quickly the problems related to percentage, remember following rules:

Rule 1:

(a) Of the given two numbers if the first is $x\%$ more than the second, then the second will be $\left(\frac{100 \times x}{100 + x}\right)\%$ less than the first.

(b) Of the given two numbers if the first is $x\%$ less than the second, then the second will be $\left(\frac{100 \times x}{100 - x}\right)\%$ more than the first.

(c) If two numbers are respectively $x\%$ and $y\%$ more than a third number, then the first number will be $\left(\frac{100 + x}{100 + y} \times 100\right)\%$ of the second.

(d) If two numbers are respectively $x\%$ and $y\%$ less than a third number, then the first number will be $\left(\frac{100 - x}{100 - y} \times 100\right)\%$ of the second.

Rule 2 :

(a) If a number or quantity is increased by $x\%$ then in order to restore its original value it must be decreased by $\left[\frac{100 \times x}{100 + x}\right]\%$.

(b) If a number or quantity is decreased by $x\%$ then in order to restore its original value it must be increased by $\left[\frac{100 \times x}{100 - x}\right]\%$.

Rule 3 :

(a) If a number is successively increased by $x\%$ and $y\%$ then a single equivalent increase in that number will be $\left(x + y + \frac{xy}{100}\right)\%$

(b) If two successive discounts of $x\%$ and $y\%$ are allowed on a particular amount, then a single discount that is equivalent to the two successive discounts will be $\left(x + y - \frac{xy}{100}\right)\%$

(c) If a number is successively increased by $x\%$, $y\%$ and $z\%$, then a single equivalent increase in that number will be

$$\left[(x + y + z) + \left(\frac{xy + yz + zx}{100}\right) + \frac{(xyz)}{10000}\right]\%$$

(d) If three successive discounts of $x\%$, $y\%$ and $z\%$ are allowed on an amount, then a single discount that is equivalent to the three successive discounts will be

$$\left[x + y + z - \frac{(xy + yz + zx)}{100} + \frac{xyz}{10000}\right]\%$$

Rule 4 :

(a) If a number is increased by $x\%$ and thereafter reduced by $x\%$, then the number will be reduced by $\left(\frac{x^2}{100}\right)$ per cent.

(b) If a number is reduced by $x\%$ and thereafter increased by $x\%$ then the number will be reduced by $\left(\frac{x^2}{100}\right)$ per cent.

(*c*) If due to an increase of $x\%$ in the selling price of certain commodity the sell/consumption of the commodity decreases by $y\%$, then gross receipts on account of sale of that commodity will be increased or decreased by $\left(x - y - \frac{xy}{100}\right)\%$, where $x > y$ and will be decreased by $\left(y - x + \frac{xy}{100}\right)\%$, where $y > x$.

SOLVED EXAMPLES

Example 1: If the numerator of a fraction is increased by 200% and the denominator is increased by 400%. The resultant fraction is $1\frac{1}{20}$. What was the original fraction?

Solution: Let original fraction = $\frac{x}{y}$; then

$$\frac{x + 2x}{y + 4y} = \frac{21}{20}$$

$$\frac{3x}{5y} = \frac{21}{20}$$

$$\frac{x}{y} = \frac{21 \times 5}{20 \times 3} = \frac{7}{4} = 1\frac{3}{4}.$$

Example 2: In a class of 65 students and 4 teachers, each student got sweets that are 20% of the total number of students and each teacher got sweets that are 40% of the total number of students. How many sweets were there?

Solution: The share of each student = $\frac{20}{100} \times 65$ = 13 sweets

The share of each teacher = $\frac{40}{100} \times 65$ = 26 sweets

Total number of sweets = $65 \times 13 + 4 \times 26$ = $845 + 104 = 949$.

Example 3: Bovina spent ₹ 44,668/- on her air tickets, ₹ 56,732/- on buying gifts for the family members and the remaining 22% of the total amount had as cash with her. What was the total amount?

Solution: Let total amount = ₹ x ; then

$$\frac{78}{100} \times x = 44668 + 56732$$

$$\Rightarrow x = \frac{101400 \times 100}{78} = ₹\ 1{,}30{,}00.$$

Example 4: Rubina decided to donate 16% of her monthly salary to an NGO. On the day of donation she changed her mind and donated ₹ 6,567/- which was 75% of what she had decided earlier. How much is Rubina's monthly salary?

Solution: Let her monthly salary be ₹ x ; then

$$\frac{16}{100} \times \frac{75}{100} \times x = 6567$$

$$\Rightarrow \frac{3}{25} x = 6567$$

$$\Rightarrow x = \frac{6567 \times 25}{3} = ₹\ 54725$$

Thus, her monthly salary = ₹ 54725.

MULTIPLE CHOICE QUESTIONS

1. Mr. Rajesh spent 20% of his monthly income on grocery and household expenses. Out of the remaining he spent 25% on children's education 20% on transport and 15% on entertainment. He is left with an amount of ₹ 14,400 after incurring above expenses. What was his monthly income?

   A. ₹ 45,000 B. ₹ 24,000
   C. ₹ 36,000 D. ₹ 32,000

2. Number of students in a school in June every year increases by 10% from the previous year. If the school had 2,400 students in June 2009, how many students did it have in June 2011?

A. 2,840 B. 2,880
C. 2,904 D. 2,920

3. On a test consisting of 150 questions, Reema answered 40% of the first 75 questions correctly. What per cent of the other 75 questions does she need to answer correctly for her grade on the entire exam to be 60%?

A. 80 B. 70
C. 40 D. 50

4. If the numerator of a fraction is increased by 200% and the denominator is increased by 300%. The resultant fraction is $\frac{9}{17}$. What was the original fraction?

A. $\frac{11}{17}$ B. $\frac{9}{11}$
C. $\frac{13}{17}$ D. None of these

5. One-sixth of a number is 53. What will 57% of that number be?

A. 181.26 B. 136.74
C. 197.16 D. 149.46

6. Mrs. Sudha Jain invests 14% of her monthly salary, *i.e.* ₹ 7,014 in Insurance Policies. Later she invests 21% of her monthly salary on Family Mediclaim Policies; also she invests another 6.5% of her salary on Mutual Funds. What is the total annual amount invested by Mrs. Sudha Jain?

A. ₹ 25,050
B. ₹ 50,100
C. ₹ 2,42,550
D. ₹ 2,49,498

7. A sum of ₹ 817 is divided among A, B and C such that 'A' receives 25% more than 'B' and 'B' receives 25% less than 'C'. What is the 'A's share in the amount?

A. ₹ 228 B. ₹ 247
C. ₹ 285 D. ₹ 304

8. Ms. Sujan invests 7% *i.e.* ₹ 2170 of her monthly salary in mutual funds. Later she invests 18% of her monthly salary in recurring deposits also, she invests 6% of her salary on NSC's. What is the total annual amount invested by Ms. Sujan?

A. ₹ 1,25,320
B. ₹ 1,13,520
C. ₹ 1,35,120
D. ₹ 1,15,320

9. What is the 30% of 40% of $\frac{2}{5}$th of 2500?

A. 500 B. 400
C. 360 D. 120

10. A sum of ₹ 731 is divided among A, B and C, such that 'A' receives 25% more than 'B' and 'B' receives 25% less than 'C'. What is C's share in the amount?

A. ₹ 172 B. ₹ 200
C. ₹ 262 D. None of these

11. Thirty five per cent of 740 is 34 more than a number. What is two-fifth of the number?

A. 45 B. 90
C. 180 D. 120

12. Ramu scored 456 marks in an exam and Shama got 54 per cent marks in the same exam which is 24 marks less than Ramu. If the minimum passing marks in the exam is 34 per cent, then how much more marks did Ramu score than the minimum passing marks?

A. 184 B. 196
C. 190 D. 180

13. Shreyas bought an article and sold for 125% of its cost price. What was the cost price of the article, if Shreyas sold it for ₹ 30,750?

A. ₹ 24,600 B. ₹ 25,640
C. ₹ 24,250 D. ₹ 23,200

14. When 20% of a number is added to another number the number increases by 50%. What is the respective ratio between the first and the second number?

A. 3 : 2
B. 2 : 3
C. 5 : 2
D. Cannot be determined

15. If a number is added to seven-ninth of thirty five per cent of 900, the value so obtained is 325. What is the number?

A. 60 B. 120
C. 90 D. None of these

16. The difference between 60% of a number and 20% of the same number is 316. What is 35% of that number?

A. 270.5 B. 285.5
C. 276.5 D. 275

17. In an examination it is required to get 36% of the aggregate marks to pass. A student gets 174 marks and is declared failed by 96 marks. What is the maximum aggregate marks a student can get?

A. 750
B. 650
C. 600
D. Cannot be determined

18. There is a rebate of 15%, if electric bills are paid in time. A man got a rebate of ₹ 54 by paying the bill in time. What was his electric bill in rupees?

A. 300 B. 350
C. 360 D. 380

19. A number is increased by 20% then again by 20%. By what per cent the original number is changed?

A. 40% B. 50%
C. 44% D. 36%

20. In an examination 62% of the examinees got plucked in Mathematics, 52% passed in English and 22% failed in both the subjects. If 108 is the number of examinees who passed in both the subjects then find out the total number of candidates.

A. 1200 B. 900
C. 800 D. 1000

ANSWERS

1	2	3	4	5	6	7	8	9	10
A	C	A	D	A	D	C	D	D	D
11	**12**	**13**	**14**	**15**	**16**	**17**	**18**	**19**	**20**
B	A	A	C	D	C	A	C	C	B

SOME SELECTED EXPLANATORY ANSWERS

1. Let Rajesh's monthly income be ₹ 100.

∴ Expenditure on grocery and household expenses = ₹ 20.

Expenditure on education etc. = $\frac{80 \times 60}{100}$

= ₹ 48

Saving = 100 − 20 − 48 = ₹ 32

Now,

When saving ₹ 32 then income = ₹ 100

When saving ₹ 14400 then income

$= ₹\ \frac{100}{32} \times 14400 = ₹\ 45000.$

2. Required number of students

$= 2400\left(1+\frac{10}{100}\right)^2 \quad \left[P = P_0\left(1+\frac{R}{100}\right)^T\right]$

$= 2400 \times \frac{11}{10} \times \frac{11}{10} = 2904.$

3. Required % $= \frac{150 \times \frac{60}{100} - 75 \times \frac{40}{100}}{75} \times 100\%$

$= \frac{90-30}{75} \times 100\% = 80\%.$

4. Let the fraction be $\frac{x}{y}$

$\therefore \quad \frac{x+2x}{y+3y} = \frac{9}{17}$

$\Rightarrow \quad \frac{3x}{4y} = \frac{9}{17}$

$\therefore \quad \frac{x}{y} = \frac{9}{17} \times \frac{4}{3} = \frac{12}{17}.$

5. Let the number be x

$\because \quad \frac{x}{6} = 53$

$\Rightarrow \quad x = 53 \times 6$

$\therefore \quad x \times \frac{57}{100} = \frac{53 \times 6 \times 57}{100} = 181.26.$

6. Let the monthly salary be ₹ x

$\because \quad x \times \frac{14}{100} = 7014$

$\Rightarrow \quad x = \frac{7014 \times 100}{14} =$ ₹ 50100

∴ Total amount of annual investment

$= \frac{(14+21+6.5)}{100} \times 50100 \times 12 =$ ₹ 249498.

8. Monthly salary of Ms. Sujan $= \frac{2170 \times 100}{7}$

= ₹ 31,000.

∴ Total money invested by her in a year

$= 31000 \times \frac{(7+18+6)}{100} \times 12$

= ₹ 9610 × 12

= ₹ 115320.

9. $2500 \times \frac{30}{100} \times \frac{40}{100} \times \frac{2}{5} = 120.$

10. Let the share of C be ₹ x

∴ Share of B $= \frac{75x}{100} =$ ₹ $0.75x$

and share of A $= 0.75x \times \frac{125}{100} =$ ₹ $0.9375x$

$\because 0.9375x + 0.75x + x = 731$

$\therefore \quad x = \frac{731}{2.6875} =$ ₹ 272.

11. Number $= 740 \times \frac{35}{100} - 34 = 225$

$\therefore \frac{2}{5}$ of the number $= 225 \times \frac{2}{5} = 90.$

12. Let the maximum marks of the eximination be x. Then, from question—

$\because \quad 54\%$ of $x = 456 - 24 = 432$

$x = \frac{432 \times 100}{54} = 800$

⇒ Minimum passing marks $= \frac{34}{100} \times 800$

$= 272$

∴ Required difference = 456 − 272 = 184.

13. C.P. of the article $= \frac{30750 \times 100}{125} =$ ₹ 24600.

14. Let the two numbers be x and y respectively. Then,

$\because \quad \frac{20x}{100} + y = y + \frac{50y}{100}$

$\Rightarrow \quad \frac{x}{5} + y = y + \frac{y}{2}$

$\Rightarrow \quad \frac{x}{5} = \frac{y}{2}$

$\Rightarrow \quad \frac{x}{y} = \frac{5}{2}$

$\therefore \quad x : y = 5 : 2.$

15. Let the number be x.

$\because \quad 900 \times \frac{35}{100} \times \frac{7}{9} + x = 325$

$\therefore \quad x = 325 - 245 = 80.$

16. Let the number be 'n', then from question,

$\because \quad (60\% - 20\%)$ of $n = 316$

$\Rightarrow \quad 40\%$ of $n = 316$

$\Rightarrow \quad 35\%$ of $n = \frac{316}{40} \times 35$

$= 276.5.$

17. Let the maximum marks of the exam. paper $= n$.

Then from question,

$$n \times \frac{36}{100} = 174 + 96$$

$$\Rightarrow \quad n = \frac{270 \times 100}{36}$$

$$\therefore \quad n = 750.$$

18. $15\% = ₹\ 54$

$$100\% = ₹\ \frac{54}{15} \times 100$$

$$= ₹\ 360.$$

19. Let the first number be 100.

After 20% increase, the number becomes = 120

After again 20% increase, the number becomes

$$= 120 \times \frac{120}{100} = 144$$

∴ Original number is changed by (144 – 100)% = 44%.

20. **Failed in Mathematics = 62%**

Failed in English = (100 – 52)% = 48%

Failed in both = 22%

Failed only in Maths = (62 – 22)% = 40%

Failed only in English = (48 – 22)% = 26%

∴ Total failed = (40 + 26 + 22)%

= 88%

∴ Passed in both = (100 – 88)% = 12%

12% = 108

$$100\% = \frac{108}{12} \times 100 = 900.$$

5. Profit and Loss

GENERAL FORMULAE

1. Gain % = $\left(\frac{\text{Gain}}{\text{C.P}} \times 100\right)$

2. Loss % = $\left(\frac{\text{Loss}}{\text{C.P}} \times 100\right)$

3. S.P = $\left(\frac{100 + \text{Gain \%}}{100}\right) \times$ C.P

4. S.P = $\left(\frac{100 - \text{Loss \%}}{100}\right) \times$ C.P

5. C.P = $\left(\frac{100}{100 + \text{Gain \%}}\right) \times$ S.P

6. C.P = $\left(\frac{100}{100 - \text{Loss \%}}\right) \times$ S.P

Formulae For Short Cut Solution

Type 1 :

Conditional Tricks

If cost price of X goods = Selling price of Y goods then,

I. Gain % = $\frac{X - Y}{Y} \times 100$ (In case of $X > Y$)

II. Loss % = $\frac{Y - X}{Y} \times 100$ (in case of $X < Y$)

Type 2 :

I. If X_1 and X_2 both are the rate of gain or both are the rate of loss, then, C.P. = $\left(\frac{100}{X_1 - X_2}\right) \times$ amount of difference between S.Ps.

II. If in X_1 and X_2 one is the rate of gain and another is the rate of loss, then C.P.= $\left(\frac{100}{X_1 + X_2}\right) \times$ amount of difference between S.Ps

Type 3 :

Miscellaneous Tricks

I. When a man buys two things on equal price and in those things one is sold on the profit of X % and another is sold on the loss of X %, then there is no loss or gain percent.

II. When a man sells two things at the same price each and in this process his loss on first thing is X % and gain on second thing is X % then in such type of questions, there is always a loss.

Loss % = X % of $X = \frac{X^2}{100} = \left(\frac{X}{10}\right)^2$

III. Dishonest dealer and less weight

$$\text{Gain} = \frac{\text{Error}}{\text{True value} - \text{Error}} \times 100$$

Where, error = 100 gm – used weight of goods

IV. If A sells a thing to B at a gain of R_1 %, B sells it to C at a gain of R_2 % and C sells it to D at a gain of R_3 %

Then, cost price of D = Cost Price of $A\,(1 + R_1/100)\,(1 + R_2/100)\,(1 + R_3/100)$

V. If A sells a thing, to B at a loss of R %, B sells it to C at a loss of R % and C sells it to D at a loss of R % then, Cost price of D = Cost price of $A\,(1 - R_1/100)\,(1 - R_2/100)\,(1 - R_3/100)$

SOLVED EXAMPLES

Example 1: Suman purchased an item of ₹ 72,000 and sold it at a loss of 27 percent. With that amount she purchased another item and sold it at a gain of 30 percent. What is her overall profit/loss?

Solution: First S.P. = $\frac{72000 \times 73}{100}$ = ₹ 52560

Second S.P. = $\frac{52560 \times 130}{100}$ = ₹ 68328

Loss = 72000 – 68328 = ₹ 3672.

Example 2: Mr. Babulal purchased 100 pieces of an article at the rate of ₹ 480 per piece. He then listed the price so as to gain a profit of 25%. While selling the articles he offered a discount of 5%. What is the percentage of profit earned in the deal?

Solution: Profit per cent = $\left(x + y + \frac{xy}{100}\right)\%$

Here, $x = 25\%$, $y = -5\%$

$= \left(25 - 5 - \frac{25 \times 5}{100}\right)\% = 18.75\%.$

Example 3: The profit earned after selling an article for ₹ 625 is the same as loss incurred after selling the article for ₹ 435. What is the cost price of the article?

Solution: C.P. of the article = $\frac{625 + 435}{2}$ = ₹ 530.

Example 4: A man sold an item for ₹ 6,750 at a loss of 25%. What will be the selling price of same item if he sells it at a profit of 15%?

Solution: C.P. of the item = $\frac{6750 \times 100}{75}$ = ₹ 9000

∴ Required S.P. of the item = $\frac{9000 \times 115}{100}$
= ₹ 10350.

Example 5: A man sold a wristwatch for ₹ 2,400 at a loss of twenty-five per cent. At what rate should he have sold the wristwatch to earn a profit of twenty five per cent?

Solution: C.P. of the wristwatch = $\frac{100 \times 2400}{100 - 25}$
= ₹ 3200

∴ Required S.P. of the wristwatch

= $\frac{125 \times 3200}{100}$ = ₹ 4000.

MULTIPLE CHOICE QUESTIONS

1. What profit/loss per cent did Raveena earn if she purchased an item of ₹ 5,600 and sold it at three-fourth of its cost price?
   A. Loss of 20 per cent
   B. Gain of 25 per cent
   C. Neither gain nor loss
   D. None of these

2. By what per cent must the cost price be raised in fixing the sale price in order that there may be a profit of 20% after allowing a commission of 10%?
   A. 30% B. $33\frac{1}{3}\%$
   C. 25% D. 40%

3. A sold a watch to B at a loss of 10% B sold it to C at a gain of 10%. If A had sold at the same price which C paid for it, what would have been his gain or loss per cent?
   A. 1% loss B. 10% gain
   C. 12% gain D. 11% loss

4. A shopkeeper purchased two cycles at ₹ 1600 and sold the first at 10% profit and second one at 20% profit. If he could sell the first cycle at a profit of 20% and the second one at a profit of 10% then he could get ₹ 5 more. What will be the cost price of each in rupees?
   A. 925, 675 B. 1000, 600
   C. 825, 775 D. 900, 700

5. A person makes a profit of 25%, by selling an article for ₹ 35.50. By how much should he increase his selling price so as to make a profit of 40%?

A. ₹ 4.60 B. ₹ 4.26
C. ₹ 4 D. ₹ 3.90

6. A man bought a pen and sold it at a loss of 20%. If he had bought it for 30% less and sold it for ₹ 60 more, he would have made a profit of 50%. Find the C.P. of the article.

A. ₹ 200 B. ₹ 140
C. ₹ 240 D. ₹ 210

7. The cost price of 15 article is equal to S.P. of 10 articles. The gain per cent is:

A. 50% B. 25%
C. $16\frac{2}{3}\%$ D. 100%

8. Raghav bought a radio with 20% discount on the labelled price. Had he bought it with 25% discount, he would have saved ₹ 500. At what price did he buy the radio?

A. ₹ 1000 B. ₹ 500
C. ₹ 5000 D. ₹ 10000

9. A man buys mangoes at ₹ 5 a dozen and an equal number at ₹ 4 a dozen. He sells them at ₹ 5.50 a dozen and makes a profit of ₹ 50. How many mangoes does he buy?

A. 30 dozens B. 40 dozens
C. 50 dozens D. 60 dozens

10. How many for a rupee must a shopkeeper sell to gain 25%, if he bought toys at 10 for a rupee?

A. 10 B. 9
C. 8 D. 6

11. Suppose the ratio of two investment be 3 : 2. What is the gain or loss on the two investments taken together if a man loses 20% on an investment but gains 25% on another investment.

A. 2.5% B. 0.2%
C. 2% D. 3%

12. A shopkeeper gives 12% additional discount after giving an initial discount of 20% on the labelled price of a T.V. If the sale price of the T.V. is ₹ 704. What is the labelled price of the T.V?

A. ₹ 844.80 B. ₹ 929.28
C. ₹ 1000 D. ₹ 900

13. By selling 12 oranges for a rupee, a man loses 10%. How many oranges for a rupee be sold to gain 20%?

A. 5 B. 4
C. 9 D. 12

14. A dishonest shopkeeper professes to sell pulses at his cost price but uses a false weight of 950 gm for each kilogram. His gain per cent is :

A. $5\frac{5}{19}\%$ B. 19%
C. $4\frac{5}{19}\%$ D. 95%

15. Sushil bought two boxes for ₹ 1300. He sold one box at a profit of 20% and the other box at a loss of 12%. If the selling price of both boxes is the same. Then the cost price of each box is :

A. ₹ 850, ₹ 650
B. ₹ 750, ₹ 750
C. ₹ 550, ₹ 750
D. ₹ 750, ₹ 650

16. A producer sells his articles to a wholesaler at 10% profit. The wholesaler sells it to a retailer at 20%. The retailer sells it to a customer at ₹ 41.25 making 25% profit. Then the cost of production is :

A. ₹ 52 B. ₹ 132
C. ₹ 110 D. ₹ 25

17. A bought two oxen for ₹ 1080. He sold one at a loss of 5% and the other at a gain of 7%. He neither gained nor lost in this transaction. C.P. of each is :

A. ₹ 630, ₹ 450
B. ₹ 680, ₹ 400
C. ₹ 600, ₹ 480
D. ₹ 540, ₹ 540

18. A businessman makes a profit of 20% in the first year. In the subsequent year, he had a loss of 25% on the capital which he had at the beginning of the second year. His overall gain or loss per cent in the capital is:

A. 120% B. 90%
C. 100% D. 10%

19. A co-operative society manufactures note books. It makes a profit of ₹ 9.00 when it sells 100 copies to a local shop. The local shop, in turn, makes a profit of ₹ 2 on selling 50 copies at 69 paisa per copy. How much did it cost the society to manufacture 100 note books?

A. ₹ 65 B. ₹ 55
C. ₹ 56 D. ₹ 32.50

20. A man marks his goods at a price that would give him 40% profit. He sells three-fourths of his goods at the marked price. For the remaining, he has to lower the marked price by 40%. His per cent profit on the entire transaction is:

A. 21% B. 84%
C. 52% D. 26%

ANSWERS

1	2	3	4	5	6	7	8	9	10
D	B	A	C	B	C	A	D	C	C
11	**12**	**13**	**14**	**15**	**16**	**17**	**18**	**19**	**20**
C	C	C	A	C	D	A	D	C	D

SOME SELECTED EXPLANATORY ANSWERS

1. S.P. of the item $= 5600 \times \frac{3}{4} = ₹\ 4200$

$\therefore$ Loss % $= \frac{5600 - 4200}{5600} \times 100 = 25.$

2. Let x% must the cost price be raised

$\therefore$ S.P. = (100 + x)

$\because \quad (100 + x)\frac{90}{100} = 120$

$\Rightarrow \quad 3x = 100$

$\therefore \quad x = 33\frac{1}{3}\%.$

3. Let A's C.P. = ₹ 100

A's S.P. $= 100 \times \frac{90}{100}$;

B's S.P. $= 100 \times \frac{90}{100} \times \frac{110}{100}$

C paid = B's S.P. $= 100 \times \frac{90}{100} \times \frac{110}{100}$

= 99

If A had sold at ₹ 99

Then, his loss = (100 – 99)% = 1%.

4. Let the C.P. of 1st cycle = ₹ x

and C.P. of 2nd cycle = ₹ (1600 – x)

Total S.P. in 1st case

$= x \times \frac{110}{100} + (1600 - x) \times \frac{120}{100}$

$= \frac{12 \times 1600 - x}{10}$

Total S.P. in 2nd case

$= x \times \frac{120}{100} + (1600 - x) \times \frac{110}{100}$

$= \frac{11 \times 1600 + x}{10}$

$\because \quad \frac{11 \times 1600 + x}{10} - \frac{12 \times 1600 - x}{10} = 5$

$\therefore \quad x = \frac{1650}{2} = 825$

C.P. of 1st cycle = 825

C.P. of 2nd cycle = 1600 – 825 = 775.

5. Let new S.P. be ₹ x

Then (100 + Gain%) : (1st S.P.)

= (100 + Gain%) : (2nd S.P.)

125 : 35.50 = 140 : x

$\Rightarrow \quad x = \frac{35.50 \times 140}{125} = ₹\ 39.76$

∴ Increased in S.P. = ₹ (39.76 − 35.50)

= ₹ 4.26.

6. Let original C.P. be ₹ x

$$\text{S.P.} = 80\% \text{ of } x = \frac{80x}{100} = \frac{4x}{5}$$

$$\text{New C.P.} = 70\% \text{ of } x = \frac{70x}{100} = \frac{7x}{10}$$

$$\text{New S.P.} = 150\% \text{ of } \frac{7x}{10} = \frac{21x}{20}$$

$$\therefore \quad \frac{21x}{20} - \frac{4x}{5} = 60$$

$$\Rightarrow \quad \frac{x}{4} = 60$$

$$x = 240$$

7. Let C.P. of each article be ₹ 1

Then C.P. of 10 article = ₹ 10

S.P. of 10 article = ₹ 15

$$\text{Gain \%} = \left(\frac{15-10}{10} \times 100\right)\% = \left(\frac{5}{10} \times 100\right)\%$$

= 50%.

8. Let the labelled price be x

$$\therefore \quad \text{S.P.} = 80\% \text{ of } x = \frac{4x}{5}$$

$$\text{New S.P.} = 75\% \text{ of } x = \frac{3x}{4}$$

$$\therefore \quad \frac{4x}{5} - \frac{3x}{4} = 500$$

$$\Rightarrow \quad x = ₹\ 10000.$$

9. C.P of 2 dozens of mangoes = ₹ (5 + 4)

= ₹ 9

S.P. of 2 dozens of mangoes = ₹ 11

2 dozens of mangoes are bought at a profit of ₹ 2.

If profit is ₹ 50, mangoes bought = $\frac{2}{2} \times 50$

= 50 dozens.

10. C.P of 10 toys = ₹ 1

Gain = 25%

$$\text{S.P of 10 toys} = \frac{125}{100} \times 1 = ₹\ \frac{5}{4}$$

Thus S.P of 10 toys is ₹ $\frac{5}{4}$

∴ For ₹ 1, Number of toys = $10 \times \frac{4}{5} = 8$

So he must sell 8 toys for a rupee.

11. Let the investments are $3x$ and $2x$

Then total investment = $5x$

Receipt = (80% of $3x$ + 125% of $2x$)

= ($2.4x + 2.5x$) = $4.9x$

$$\therefore \quad \text{loss} = \left(\frac{0.1x}{5x} \times 100\right)\% = 2\%.$$

12. Let the labelled price of the T.V be ₹ x

$$\text{Initial S.P} = 80\% \text{ of } x = \frac{80x}{100}$$

$$\text{New S.P} = 88\% \text{ of } \frac{80x}{100}$$

$$= \frac{88}{100} \times \frac{80x}{100} = \frac{704x}{1000}$$

From question,

$$\frac{704x}{1000} = 704$$

$$704x = 704 \times 1000$$

$$\Rightarrow \quad x = 1000$$

∴ The labelled price of the T.V = ₹ 1000.

14. Let C.P. of 1 gm pulses be ₹ 1

∴ C.P. of 950 gm pulses = ₹ 950

S.P. of 950 gm = C.P. of 1 kg

= C.P. of 1000 gm = ₹ 1000

∴ Gain = ₹ (1000 − 950) = ₹ 50

$$\therefore \quad \text{Gain \%} = \frac{50}{950} \times 100 = 5\frac{5}{19}\%.$$

17. From question,

∴ Loss on one = Gain on other

∴ 5% of the C.P. of one = 7% of the C.P. of the other

$$\Rightarrow \frac{\text{C.P. of 1st}}{\text{C.P. of 2nd}} = \frac{7\%}{5\%} = \frac{7}{5}$$

or, C.P. of 1st : C.P. of 2nd = 7 : 5

Divide ₹ 1080 in the ratio of 7 : 5

$$\therefore \text{ C.P. of the 1st} = \frac{7}{12} \times 1080 = ₹\ 630.$$

$$\text{and C.P. of the 2nd} = ₹\ \frac{5}{12} \times 1080 = ₹\ 450.$$

18. Let his capital at the beginning of first year be ₹ 100

Profit during first year = 20% of ₹ 100 = ₹ 20

∴ Capital at the beginning of the second year

= ₹ (100 + 20) = ₹ 120

Loss during second year = 25% of ₹ 120

$$= ₹\left(120 \times \frac{25}{100}\right) = ₹\ 30$$

∴ Capital at the end of second year

= ₹ (120 – 30) = ₹ 90

∴ Loss = ₹ (100 – 90) = ₹ 10

$$\text{Overall Loss \% on his capital} = \left(\frac{10}{100} \times 100\right)\%$$

= 10%.

19. The local shop sells 50 copies @ 69 paisa per copy

= ₹ (50 × 0.69) = ₹ 34.50

His profit = ₹ 2

∴ The local shop purchases 50 copies for

= S.P. – Profit = ₹ (34.50 – 2) = ₹ 32.50

∴ The local shop purchases 100 copies for

$$= ₹\left(\frac{32.50}{50} \times 100\right) = ₹\ 65$$

∴ Co-operative society sells 100 copies for ₹ 65

Profit = ₹ 9

∴ Co-operative society manufactures 100 copies for

= ₹ (65 – 9) = ₹ 56.

6. MIXTURE AND ALLIGATION

Alligation deals with calculation of values or properties of a mixture. Alligation is the rule that enables us—

(1) to find the proportion in which the two or more ingredients at the given prices must be mixed to yield a mixture at the given price. This is termed as "Alligation Alternate".

(2) to calculate the average or mean value of a mixture when the prices of two or more ingredients which are to be mixed together and proportion in which they are to be mixed are given. This is termed as "Alligation Medial".

1. Rule of Alligation:

$$\frac{\text{A of Cheap mixture}}{\text{A of Dearer mixture}} = \frac{\text{CP of Dearer} - \text{Mean Price}}{\text{Mean Price} - \text{CP of Cheaper}}$$

Here cost price of unit quantity of the mixture is called the *Mean Price.*

The above rule may be represented schematically as under:

CP of unit quantity of cheaper ingredient (c)

CP of unit quantity of dearer ingredient (d)

Mean Price (m)

$(d - m)$ $(m - c)$

(Cheaper quantity) : (Dearer quantity) $= (d - m) : (m - c)$

This relationship is very helpful in solving problems on mixture involving percentage values, rates, prices, speeds etc.

2. m gm of sugar solution has x % sugar in it. To increase the sugar content in the solution to y %,

quantity of sugar need to be added $= \dfrac{m(y-x)}{100-y}$

3. A vessel contains x litres of liquid A. y litres are withdrawn and replaced by liquid B. Next y litres of the mixture is withdrawn and again replaced by liquid B.
This operation is repeated n times.

$$\frac{\text{Quantity of liquid A left after } n\text{th operation}}{\text{Whole quantity of liquid A initially present}}$$

$$= \left(\frac{x-y}{x}\right)^n \text{ or } \left(1-\frac{y}{x}\right)^n$$

SOLVED EXAMPLES

Example 1: Find the quantities of two types of wheat, one @ ₹ 6 per kg and the other @ ₹ 4 per kg. to get 20 kgs. of wheat mixture worth ₹ 4.5 per kg.

Solution:

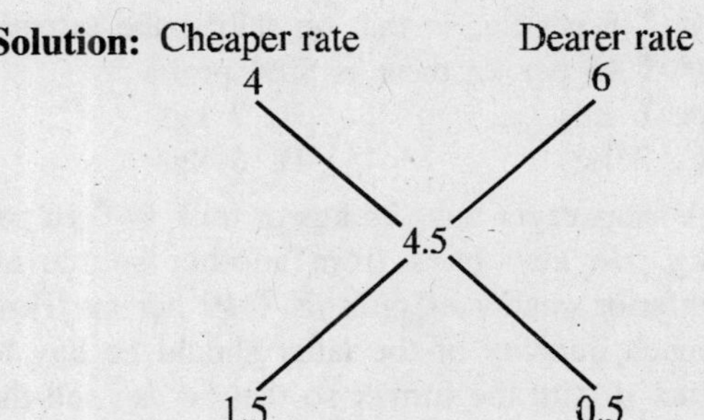

$$\frac{\text{Quantity of cheaper wheat}}{\text{Quantity of dearer wheat}} = \frac{1.5}{0.5} = \frac{3}{1}$$

Quantity of cheaper wheat

$$= \frac{3}{3+1} \times 20 = 15 \text{ kgs}$$

Quantity of dearer wheat

$= \frac{1}{3+1} \times 20 = 5$ kgs.

Example 2: In what proportion water be mixed with pure milk in order to make a profit of 20% by selling it at cost price?

Solution: Let cost price of pure milk be Re. 1 per litre.

The SP of mixture = ₹ 1 per litre

Profit = 20%

So, CP of 1 litre of mixture

$= ₹ \left(1 \times \frac{100}{120}\right) = ₹ \frac{5}{6}$

We assume that CP of 1 litre of water is zero. Using the rule of alligation on 1 litre,

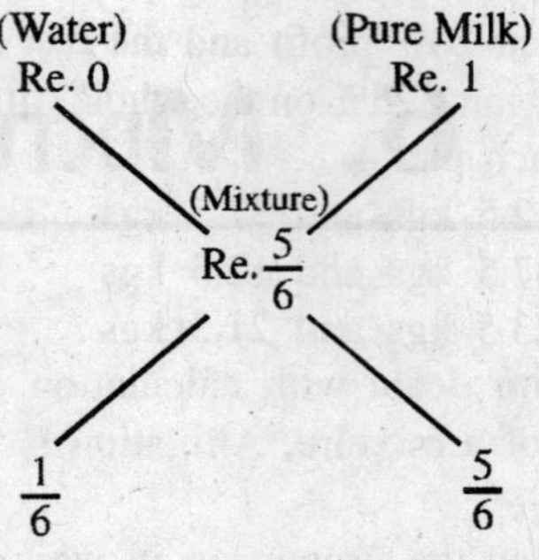

$$\frac{\text{Quantity of water}}{\text{Quantity of pure milk}} = \frac{\frac{1}{6}}{\frac{5}{6}} = \frac{1}{5}$$

or, Ratio of water to pure milk in the mixture = 1 : 5.

MULTIPLE CHOICE QUESTIONS

1. In what proportion must tea at ₹ 62 per kg be mixed with tea at ₹ 72 per kg in order to obtain the mixture worth ₹ 65 per kg?

A. 4 : 6 B. 7 : 3
C. 2 : 3 D. 4 : 7

2. Find the quantity of rice @ ₹ 10 per kg. which should be mixed with 25 kgs of rice @ ₹ 8 per kg, so that on selling the mixture @ ₹ 15 per kg there is 80% profit.

A. 6 kgs B. 7 kgs
C. 3 kgs D. 5 kgs

3. A shopkeeper buys 26 kgs of milk @ ₹ 16 per kg. He also buys from another source an inferior quality of milk @ ₹ 10 per kg. How much quantity of the latter should he buy to mix it with the former so that he can sell the mixture @ ₹ 14 per kg without making any loss?

A. 13 kgs B. 12 kgs
C. 14 kgs D. 16 kgs

4. Two vessels A and B contain milk and water in the ratio 7 : 5 and 17 : 7 respectively. In what ratio mixtures from two vessels should be mixed to get a new mixture containing milk and water in the ratio 5 : 3?

A. 1 : 2 B. 2 : 1
C. 2 : 3 D. 3 : 2

5. Two vessels A and B contain mixture of milk and water in the ratio 4 : 1 and 9 : 11 respectively. They are mixed in the ratio of 3 : 2. Find the ratio of milk : water in the resulting mixture.

A. 34 : 16 B. 33 : 17
C. 16 : 34 D. 17 : 33

6. A person has two solutions of sugar with 30% and 50% concentration respectively. In what proportion should he mix two solutions to get 45% concentration in the resulting mixture?

A. 1 : 3 B. 3 : 1
C. 2 : 3 D. 3 : 2

7. 6 litres of milk and water mixture has 75% milk in it. How much milk should be added to the mixture to make it 90% pure?

A. 8 litres B. 9 litres
C. 10 litres D. 12 litres

8. In what ratio must water be added to spirit to gain 25% by selling it at cost price?

A. 1 : 4 B. 4 : 1
C. 3 : 4 D. 4 : 3

9. A shopkeeper has 50 kgs of rice. He sells a part of it at 20% profit and the rest at 40% profit. If he gains 25% on the whole, find the quantity of each part.

A. 12.5 kgs and 37.5 kgs
B. 37.5 kgs and 12.5 kgs
C. 23.5 kgs and 21.5 kgs
D. 21.5 kgs and 23.5 kgs

10. A shopkeeper has 100 kgs of tea. He sells a part of it at 20% profit and the rest at 5% loss. If his overall profit is 10%, find the quantity for each part.

A. 20 kgs B. 25 kgs
C. 30 kgs D. 40 kgs

ANSWERS

1	2	3	4	5	6	7	8	9	10
B	D	A	B	B	A	B	A	A	D

SOME SELECTED EXPLANATORY ANSWERS

1. CP of 1 kg. Cheaper tea ₹ 62 CP of 1 kg. Dearer tea ₹ 72

Mean Price per kg
₹ 65

$d - m = 7$ $m - c = 3$

Using Alligation rule,

$$\frac{\text{Quantity of cheaper tea}}{\text{Quantity of dearer tea}} = \frac{d-m}{m-c} = \frac{7}{3}$$

Therefore, they must be mixed in the ratio of 7 : 3.

2. Cost price of the mixture $= 15 \times \frac{100}{180}$

$= ₹\ \frac{25}{3}$ per kg

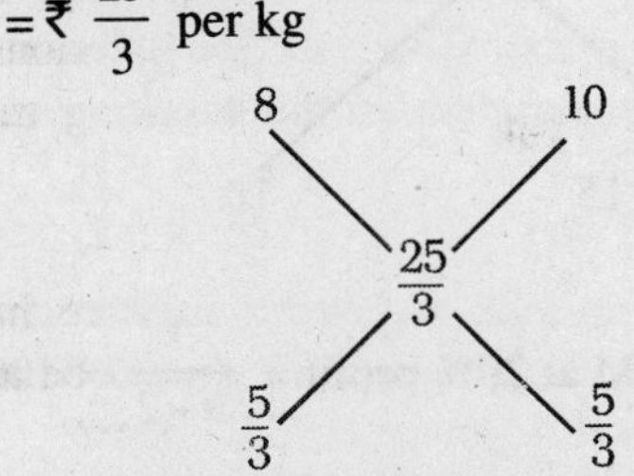

$$\frac{\text{Quantity of rice @ ₹ 8 per kg}}{\text{Quantity of rice @ ₹ 10 per kg}} = \frac{5/3}{1/3} = \frac{5}{1}$$

Quantity of rice @ ₹ 10 per kg $= 25 \times \frac{1}{5}$

= 5 kgs.

3.

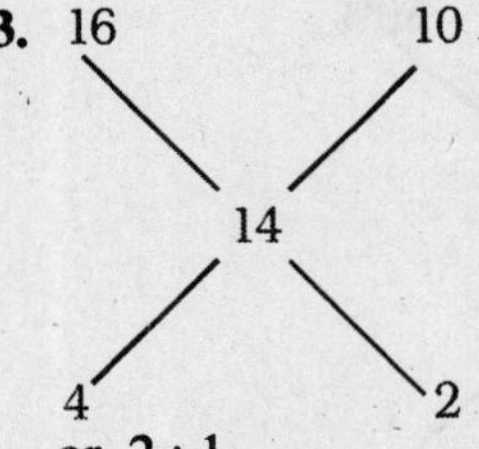

or 2 : 1

$$\frac{\text{Quantity of milk @ ₹ 10 per kg}}{\text{Quantity of milk @ ₹ 16 per kg}} = \frac{1}{2}$$

So, quantity of milk @ ₹ 10 per kg. $= \frac{26}{2}$

= 13 kgs.

4. First of all we write the fraction of milk present in three mixtures.

In A : $\frac{7}{12}$ In B : $\frac{17}{24}$

In combination of A and B : $\frac{5}{8}$

We now apply alligation rule on these fractions.

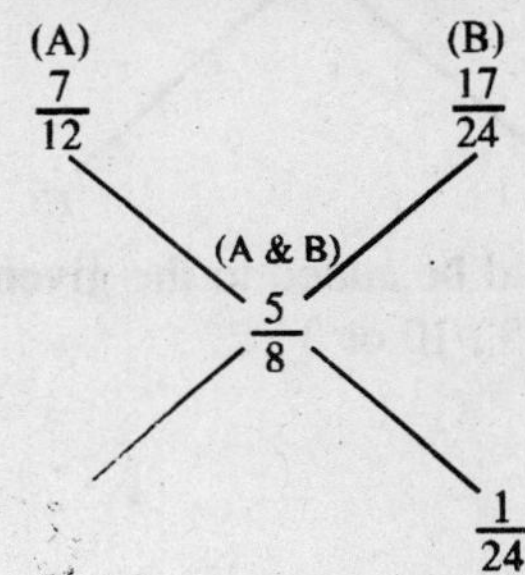

or, 2 : 1
So, Ratio of A : B = 2 : 1.

5. Fraction is *Milk* *Water*

A : $\frac{4}{5}$ $\frac{1}{5}$

B : $\frac{9}{20}$ $\frac{11}{20}$

(3A + 2B) = A and B : $\left(\frac{12}{5}+\frac{9}{10}\right)$ $\left(\frac{3}{5}+\frac{11}{10}\right)$

$\frac{33}{10}$ $\frac{17}{10}$

So, Ratio of milk : water in the resulting mixture = 33 : 17.

6. 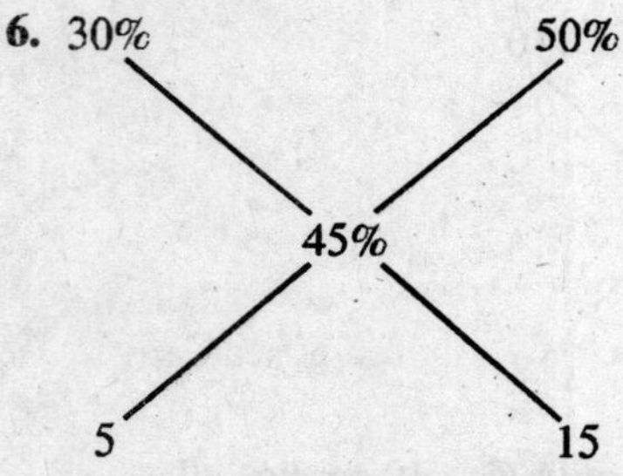

He should mix 30% and 50% in the ratio 5 : 15 or 1 : 3.

$\frac{30\% \text{ Solution}}{50\% \text{ Solution}} = \frac{1}{3}$

or 1 : 3

7. The given solution has 75% milk.
Milk to be added has 100% milk.

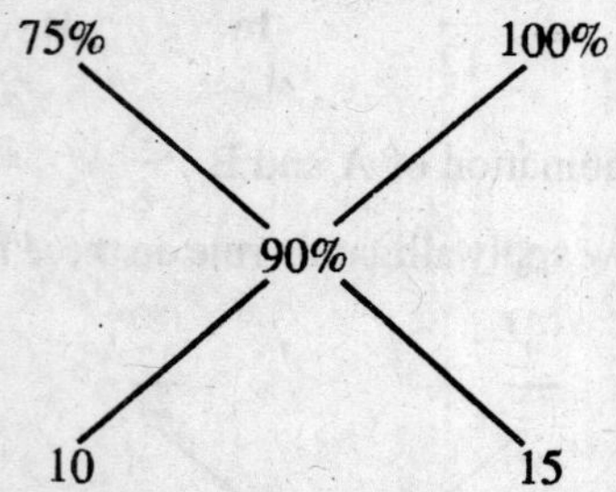

Milk should be added to the given mixture in the ratio 15 : 10 or 3 : 2.

∴ Quantity of milk to be added = $\frac{3}{2} \times 6$

= 9 litres.

8. Let cost price of spirit be Re. 1 per litre.
Then SP of mixture = Re. 1 per litre
Gain = 25%

So, CP of mixture $= 1 \times \frac{100}{125} = \text{Re. } \frac{4}{5}$

We assume that CP of water is zero.
Using alligation rule on cost price,
Water should be mixed to spirit in the ratio

$\frac{1}{5} : \frac{4}{5}$ or 1 : 4.

9. 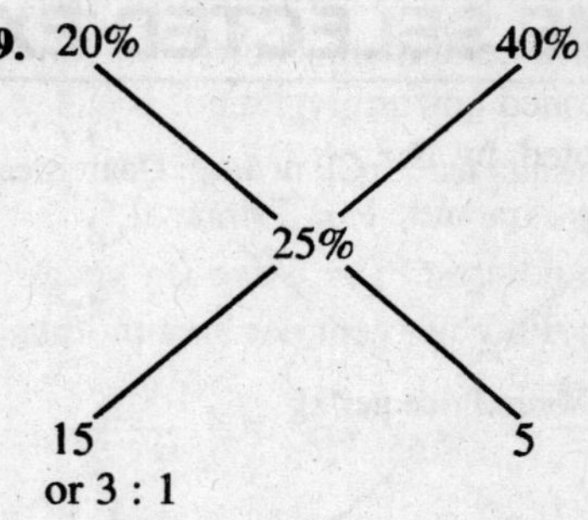

or 3 : 1

Quantity sold at 20% profit = $\frac{3}{3+1} \times 50$

= 37.5 kgs.

Quantity sold at 40% profit = (50 – 37.5)
= 12.5 kgs.

10. 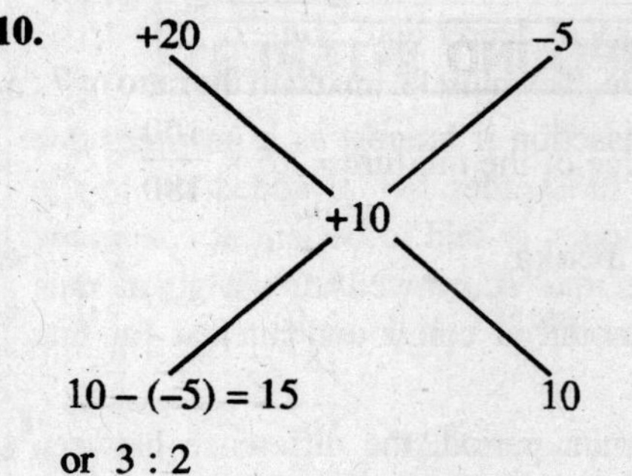

or 3 : 2

Quantity sold at 20% profit = $\frac{3}{3+2} \times 100$

= 60 kgs.

Quantity sold at 5% loss = (100 – 60)
= 40 kgs.

7. Simple and Compound Interests

SIMPLE INTEREST

Interest is the money paid for the use of money borrowed, *i.e.*, extra money paid for using other's money is called *interest.*

The sum borrowed is called the principal. The sum of interest and principal is called the *Amount.*

If the interest on a certain sum borrowed for a certain period is reckoned uniformly, then it is called simple interest, denoted by S.I.

Thus, if A = Amount, P = Principal,
I = Interest, T = Time (in year),
R = Rate per cent per annum, then

(*a*) $I = \frac{P \times R \times T}{100}$ (*b*) $P = \frac{100 \times I}{R \times T}$

(*c*) $T = \frac{100 \times I}{P \times R}$ (*d*) $R = \frac{100 \times I}{P \times T}$

(*e*) $P = \frac{100A}{100 + RT}$ (*f*) $A = P + I.$

COMPOUND INTEREST

In business transaction if interest as it becomes due is not paid to the lender but is added on to the principal, the money is said to be lent at *compound interest* and the total sum owed after a given time is called the amount at compound interest for that time.

After a certain period, the difference between the amount and the original principal is called the compound Interest (C.I.).

Some Important Formulae :

Let Principal = P
Time = n years
Rate = r% p.a.

then, the amount,

(*a*) when interest is compounded annually:

then, Amount = $P\left(1+\frac{r}{100}\right)^n$

(*b*) when interest is compounded half yearly:

then, Amount = $P\left(1+\frac{r/2}{100}\right)^{2n}$

(*c*) when interest is compounded quarterly :

then, Amount = $P\left(1+\frac{r/4}{100}\right)^{4n}$

(*d*) when time is fraction of a year, say $4\frac{1}{3}$ years,

then, Amount = $P\left(1+\frac{r}{100}\right)^4 \times \left(1+\frac{\frac{1}{3}r}{100}\right)$

(*e*) when rates are r_1%, r_2% and r_3% for Ist, IInd and IIIrd year respectively;
then, Amount =

$$P\left(1+\frac{r_1}{100}\right)\left(1+\frac{r_2}{100}\right)\left(1+\frac{r_3}{100}\right)$$

SOLVED EXAMPLES

Example 1: A man gets a simple interest of ₹ 1,000 on a certain principal at the rate of 5% p.a. in 4 years. What compound interest will the man get on twice the principal in two years at the same rate?

Solution: $\because$ Principal $= \frac{1000 \times 100}{4 \times 5} =$ ₹ 5000

$\therefore$ Required C.I. $= 1000\left[\left(1+\frac{5}{100}\right)^2 - 1\right]$

$= 1000\left[\frac{441-400}{400}\right]$

$= 1000 \times \frac{41}{400} =$ ₹ 1025.

Example 2: The simple interest accrued on an amount of ₹ 25,000 at the end of four years is ₹ 8,000. What would be the compound interest accrued on the same amount at the same rate in the same period?

Solution: Rate $= \frac{8000 \times 100}{25000 \times 4}\% = 8\%$

$\therefore$ C.I. $= 25000\left[\left(1+\frac{8}{100}\right)^4 - 1\right]$

$= 25000\left(\frac{27^4 - 25^4}{25^4}\right)$

$= 25000\left[\frac{531441-390625}{390625}\right]$

$=$ ₹ 9012.224

Example 3: The difference between the amount of compound interest and simple interest accrued on an amount of ₹ 26,000 at the end of 3 years is ₹ 2994.134. What is the rate of interest p.c.p.a.?

Solution: $\because$ $2994.134 = \frac{26000r^2}{(100)^2}\left(\frac{r}{100}+3\right)$

$= \frac{26r^2}{10}\left(\frac{r+300}{100}\right)$

$\Rightarrow$ $2994134 = 26r^3 + 7800r^2$

$\Rightarrow$ $115159 = r^3 + 300r^2$

$\therefore$ $r = 19$

Example 4: What would be the compound interest accrued on an amount of ₹ 45,400/- at the end of two years at the rate of 15% p.a.?

Solution: C.I. $= 45400\left[\left(1+\frac{15}{100}\right)^2 - 1\right]$

$= 45400\left[\frac{23}{20} \times \frac{23}{20} - 1\right]$

$= 45400 \times \frac{129}{400}$

$= \frac{29283}{2} =$ ₹ 14641.5

MULTIPLE CHOICE QUESTIONS

1. Anshul borrowed some money at the rate of 4% p.a. for the first three years, at the rate of 8% p.a. for the next two years and at the rate of 9% p.a. for the period beyond 5 years. If he pays a total simple interest of ₹ 19,550 at the end of 7 years, how much money did he borrow?

   A. ₹ 39,500   B. ₹ 42,500
   C. ₹ 41,900   D. ₹ 43,000

2. The simple interest accrued on an amount at the end of five years @ 12.5% p.a. ₹ 1,575. What is the amount?

   A. ₹ 2,050   B. ₹ 2,550
   C. ₹ 2,250   D. ₹ 2,520

3. Siyaram invested equal sum of money in two schemes. Under scheme X, the compound interest rate was 10% p.a. and under scheme Y, the compound interest rate was 12% p.a. The interest after two years on the sum invested in Scheme X was ₹ 63. How much is the interest earned under Scheme Y after two years?

   A. ₹ 79.0272
   B. ₹ 70.56
   C. ₹ 76.32
   D. Cannot be determined

4. What would be the compound interest accrued on an amount of ₹ 15,000 at the rate of 15% p.a. at the end of three years?

A. ₹ 7813.125 B. ₹ 7762.50
C. ₹ 7762.125 D. ₹ 11235.09375

5. If the difference between the simple interest and compound interest earned on an amount @ 15% p.a. at the end of 3 years is ₹ 595.35, what is the amount?
A. ₹ 8,400
B. ₹ 9,200
C. ₹ 6,800
D. Cannot be determined

6. What will be the simple interest earned on an amount of ₹ 988 @ 18% p.a., at the end of 5 years?
A. ₹ 711.36 B. ₹ 898.2
C. ₹ 799.25 D. None of these

7. The simple interest accrued on a sum of certain principal is ₹ 1,200 in four years at the rate of 8% p.a. What would be the simple interest accrued on thrice of that principal at the rate of 6% p.a. in 3 years?
A. ₹ 2,025 B. ₹ 3,025
C. ₹ 2,250 D. ₹ 2,150

8. What amount of compound interest can be obtained on an amount of ₹ 18,000 at the rate of 10% p.a. at the end of three years?
A. ₹ 5,628
B. ₹ 5,400
C. ₹ 5,940
D. None of these

9. Shrivastava invests ₹ 14500 for 6 years at the certain rate of simple interest. After 6 years his invested sum becomes ₹ 21460. Find out the rate of interest per annum:
A. 4% p.a. B. 10% p.a.
C. 6% p.a. D. 8% p.a.

10. A sum of ₹ 12,500 amounts to ₹ 15,500 in 4 years at the rate of simple interest. What is the rate of interest?
A. 3% B. 4%
C. 5% D. 6%

11. A sum fetched a total simple interest of ₹ 4016. 25 at the rate of 9% p.a. in 5 years. What is the sum?
A. ₹ 4462.50 B. ₹ 8032.50
C. ₹ 8900 D. ₹ 8925

12. ₹ 800 becomes ₹ 956 in 3 years at a certain rate of simple interest. If the rate of interest is increased by 4%, what amount will ₹ 800 become in 3 years?
A. ₹ 1020.80
B. ₹ 1025
C. ₹ 1052
D. Data inadequate

13. A certain amount earns simple interest of ₹ 1750 after 7 years. Had the interest been 2% more, how much more interest would it have earned?
A. ₹ 35
B. ₹ 245
C. ₹ 350
D. Cannot be determined

14. Neelam borrowed some money at the rate of 6% p.a. for the first three years, 9% p.a. for the next five years and 13% p.a. for the period beyond eight years. If the total interest paid by him at the end of eleven years is ₹ 8160, how much money did he borrow?
A. ₹ 8000 B. ₹ 10,000
C. ₹ 12000 D. Data inadequate

15. The simple interest on a sum of money will be ₹ 600 after 10 years. If the principal is trebled after 5 years, what will be the total interest at the end of the tenth year?
A. ₹ 600 B. ₹ 900
C. ₹ 1200 D. ₹ 1500

16. Simple interest on a certain sum at a certain annual rate of interest is $\frac{1}{9}$ of the sum. If the numbers representing rate percent and time in years be equal, then the rate of interest is :
A. $3\frac{1}{3}\%$ B. 5%
C. $6\frac{2}{3}\%$ D. 10%

17. A borrowed some money from B at 12% p.a. S.I. for 3 years. He then added some more money to the borrowed sum and lent it to C for the same period at 14% p.a. rate of interest. If A gains ₹ 93.90 in the whole transaction, how much money did he add from his side?

A. ₹ 35 B. ₹ 55
C. ₹ 80 D. ₹ 105

18. A sum of ₹ 725 is lent in the beginning of a year at a certain rate of interest. After 8 months, a sum of ₹ 362.50 more is lent but at the rate twice the former. At the end of the year, ₹ 33.50 is earned as interest from both the loans. What was the original rate of interest?

A. 3.6% B. 4.5%
C. 5% D. None of these

19. The difference between the simple interest received from two different sources on ₹ 1500 for 3 years is ₹ 13.50. The difference between their rates of interest is :

A. 0.1% B. 0.2%
C. 0.3% D. 0.4%

20. Priya invested an amount of ₹ 12,000 at the rate of 10% p.a. simple interest and another amount at the rate of 20% p.a. simple interest. The total interest earned at the end of one year on the total amount invested became 14% p.a. Find the total amount invested.

A. ₹ 20,000
B. ₹ 22,000
C. ₹ 24,000
D. ₹ 25,000

ANSWERS

1	2	3	4	5	6	7	8	9	10
B	D	C	A	A	D	A	D	D	D
11	**12**	**13**	**14**	**15**	**16**	**17**	**18**	**19**	**20**
D	C	D	A	C	A	D	D	C	A

SOME SELECTED EXPLANATORY ANSWERS

2. Required amount $= ₹\dfrac{1575 \times 100}{12.5 \times 5} = ₹\ 2520.$

3. Suppose Sriram invested ₹ P in each scheme.

$$\because \quad 63 = P\left[\left(1+\frac{10}{100}\right)^2 - 1\right]$$

$$\Rightarrow \quad 63 = P\left(\frac{121}{100} - 1\right) = \frac{21P}{100}$$

$$\therefore \quad P = \frac{63 \times 100}{21} = ₹\ 300$$

Compound interest of 2 years under scheme Y

$$= 300\left[\left(1+\frac{12}{100}\right)^2 - 1\right]$$

$$= \frac{300 \times 159}{625} = ₹\ 76.32.$$

5. $\because$ Required Difference $= \dfrac{P \times r^2}{(100)^2}\left(\dfrac{r}{100} + 3\right)$

$$\Rightarrow \quad 595.35 = \frac{P \times 15 \times 15}{100 \times 100}\left(\frac{15}{100} + 3\right)$$

$$= \frac{225P}{10000} \times \frac{315}{100}$$

$$\therefore \quad P = \frac{595.35 \times 1000000}{225 \times 315}$$

$$= ₹\ 8400$$

6. S.I. $= \dfrac{988 \times 18 \times 5}{100} = ₹\ 889.20$

7. Principal $= \dfrac{1200 \times 100}{4 \times 8} = ₹\ 3750$

$$\therefore \quad \text{S.I.} = \frac{3750 \times 3 \times 3 \times 6}{100} = ₹\ 2025$$

9. From question,

$$(21460 - 14500) = \frac{14500 \times r \times 6}{100}$$

$$\Rightarrow \quad \frac{6960}{145 \times 6} = r$$

$$\therefore \quad r = 8$$

Hence the rate of interest per annum = 8%.

10. S.I. = ₹ (15500 − 12500) = ₹ 3000.

$$\text{Rate} = \left(\frac{100 \times 3000}{12500 \times 4}\right)\% = 6\%.$$

11. $$\text{Principal} = ₹\left(\frac{100 \times 4016.25}{9 \times 5}\right)$$

$$= ₹\left(\frac{401625}{45}\right) = ₹\ 8925.$$

12. S.I. = ₹ (956 − 800) = ₹ 156.

$$\text{Rate} = \left(\frac{100 \times 156}{800 \times 3}\right)\% = 6\frac{1}{2}\%.$$

$$\text{New rate} = \left(6\frac{1}{2} + 4\right)\% = 10\frac{1}{2}\%.$$

$$\text{New S.I.} = ₹\left(800 \times \frac{21}{2} \times \frac{3}{100}\right) = ₹\ 252.$$

∴ New amount = ₹ (800 + 252) = ₹ 1052.

13. We need to know the S.I., principal and time to find the rate. Since the principal is not given, so data is inadequate.

14. Let the sum be ₹ x. Then,

$$\left(\frac{x \times 6 \times 3}{100}\right) + \left(\frac{x \times 9 \times 5}{100}\right) + \left(\frac{x \times 13 \times 3}{100}\right) = 8160$$

$$\Rightarrow \quad 18x + 45x + 39x = (8160 \times 100)$$

$$\Rightarrow \quad 102x = 816000 \quad \Rightarrow \quad x = 8000.$$

15. Let the sum be ₹ x. Now, S.I. = ₹ 600, T = 10 years.

$$\text{Rate} = \left(\frac{100 \times 600}{x \times 10}\right)\% = \left(\frac{6000}{x}\right)\%.$$

$$\text{S.I. for first 5 years} = ₹\left(\frac{x \times 5 \times 6000}{x \times 100}\right) = ₹\ 300.$$

$$\text{S.I. for last 5 years} = ₹\left(3x \times 5 \times \frac{6000}{x \times 100}\right) = ₹\ 900.$$

∴ Total interest = ₹ 1200.

16. Let sum = x. Then, S.I. = $\frac{x}{9}$.

Let rate = R% and time = R years.

$$\therefore \quad \left(\frac{x \times R \times R}{100}\right) = \frac{x}{9} \quad \Rightarrow R^2 = \frac{100}{9}$$

$$\Rightarrow \quad R = \frac{10}{3} = 3\frac{1}{3}.$$

Hence, rate = $3\frac{1}{3}\%$.

17. Let the money added be ₹ x Then,

$$\frac{(830 + x) \times 14 \times 3}{100} - \frac{830 \times 12 \times 3}{100} = 93.90$$

$$\Rightarrow \quad 830 \times 42 + 42x - 830 \times 36 = 9390$$

$$\Rightarrow \quad 42x + 830 \times (42 - 36) = 9390$$

$$\Rightarrow \quad 42x = 9390 - 4980 \Rightarrow x = \frac{4410}{42} = 105.$$

∴ Money added = ₹ 105.

18. Let the original rate be R%. Then, new rate = (2R)%.

$$\therefore \quad \left(\frac{725 \times R \times 1}{100}\right) + \left(\frac{36250 \times 2R \times 1}{100 \times 3}\right) = 33.50$$

$$\Rightarrow (2175 + 725)\, R = 33.50 \times 100 \times 3 = 10050$$

$$\Rightarrow R = \frac{10050}{2900} = 3.46.$$

∴ Original rate = 3.46%.

19. $$\left(\frac{1500 \times R_1 \times 3}{100}\right) - \left(\frac{1500 \times R_2 \times 3}{100}\right) = 13.50$$

$$\Rightarrow \quad 4500\,(R_1 - R_2) = 1350$$

$$\Rightarrow \quad R_1 - R_2 = \frac{1350}{4500} = 0.3\%.$$

8. Time and Work

IMPORTANT FACTS

1. If A can do a piece of work in n days, then work done by A in 1 day $= \frac{1}{n}$.
2. If work done by A in 1 day $= \frac{1}{n}$; then A can finish the whole work in n days.
3. If A is twice as good a workman as B then; Ratio of work done by A and B = 2 : 1
   Ratio of times taken by A and B to finish a work = 1 : 2.
4. If a pipe can fill a tank in x hours, then the part filled in 1 hour $= \frac{1}{x}$.
5. If a pipe can empty a tank in y hour, then the part of the tank emptied in 1 hour $= \frac{1}{y}$.
6. If two pipes can fill a tank in x and y hours respectively and both the pipes are opened simultaneously then, the part filled in 1 hour $= \frac{1}{x} + \frac{1}{y}$.
7. (*a*) A tap fills a cistern in x hours and the other can empty the cistern in y hours. If both the taps are opened simultaneously, then the net part of the tank filled in 1 hour $= \frac{1}{x} - \frac{1}{y}$; when $y > x$.

   (*b*) A tap can fill a tank in x hours and other can empty in y hours. If both the taps are opened simultaneously, then the net part of tank emptied in 1 hour $= \frac{1}{y} - \frac{1}{x}$; when $x > y$.

SOLVED EXAMPLES

Example 1: A and B together can complete a piece of work in 4 days. If A alone can complete the same piece of work in 5 days, in how many days will B alone complete it?

Solution: (A + B)'s 1 day's work $= \frac{1}{4}$

A's 1 day's work $= \frac{1}{5}$

$\therefore$ B's 1 day work $= \frac{1}{4} - \frac{1}{5} = \frac{5-4}{20} = \frac{1}{20}$

$\therefore$ B alone will complete the work 20 days.

Example 2: Four examiners can examine a certain number of answer papers in 10 days by working for 5 hours a day. For how many hours in a day would 2 examiners have to work in order to examine twice the number of answer papers in 20 days?

Solution:

No. of exam	Hrs. per day	No. of papers	Days
4 ↓	5 ↓	1 ↓	10 ↓
2	x	2	20

$$\left.\begin{array}{l} 2 : 4 \\ 1 : 2 \\ 20 : 10 \end{array}\right\} :: 5 : x$$

$$\therefore \quad x = \frac{4 \times 2 \times 10 \times 5}{2 \times 20} = 10 \text{ hrs./day}$$

Example 3: 6 women and 6 men together can complete a piece of work in 6 days. In how many days can 15 men alone complete the piece of work if 9 women alone can complete the work in 10 days?

Solution: $\because$ Work of 1 woman for 1 day

$$= \frac{1}{9 \times 10} = \frac{1}{90}$$

⇒ Work of 6 women for 6 days

$$= \frac{1}{90} \times 6 \times 6 = \frac{2}{5}$$

⇒ Work of 6 men for 6 days

$$= 1 - \frac{2}{5} = \frac{3}{5}$$

⇒ Work of 1 man for 1 day

$$= \frac{3}{5 \times 6 \times 6} = \frac{1}{60}$$

∴ Work of 15 men for 1 day

$$= \frac{1}{60} \times 15 = \frac{1}{4}.$$

Hence, 15 men will complete the work in 4 days.

Example 4: Six boys or four men can complete a piece of work in 24 days. In how many days will 3 boys and 10 men together complete the same piece of work?

Solution: 4 men = 6 boys

$$\therefore \quad 10 \text{ men} = \frac{6}{4} \times 10$$

$$= 15 \text{ boys}$$

$$\therefore \quad 10 \text{ men} + 3 \text{ boys} = 15 + 3$$

$$= 18 \text{ boys}$$

$$\therefore \text{ Required number of days} = \frac{6 \times 24}{18} = 8.$$

MULTIPLE CHOICE QUESTIONS

1. 24 men can complete a piece of work in 16 days. The same work can be completed by 8 women in 72 days, whereas 24 children take 32 days to complete it. If 10 men, 15 women and 24 children work together, in how many days can the work be completed?

A. 18 B. 8

C. 22 D. 12

2. 18 Men alone can complete a piece of work in 24 days. 54 Women alone can complete the same piece of work in 12 days and 16 children alone can complete the same piece of work in 54 days. In how many days can 3 men, 9 women and 6 children together complete the piece of work?

A. 18

B. 36

C. 27

D. Cannot be determined

3. If 80 persons can finish a work within 16 days by working 6 hours a day then how many hours per day should 64 persons work to complete that very job within 15 days?

A. 7 hrs B. 8 hrs

C. 6 hrs D. 5 hrs

4. A and B can do a piece of work in 12 days. B and C in 15 days and C and A in 20 days. In how many days A, B and C together can do the work?

A. 8 days B. 12 days

C. 10 days D. 14 days

5. 5 labourers can make 5 mats in 5 hours. How many mats will 10 labourers make in 10 hours?

A. 10 B. 20

C. 30 D. 35

6. A can do $\frac{1}{2}$ of a work in 9 days while B can do $\frac{1}{3}$ of the same work in 6 days. How long would it take for A and B together to complete the work?

A. 18 B. 6

C. 12 D. 9

7. A can do a piece of work in 40 days. He works on it for 5 days and then B completes it in 21 days. How long will A and B together take to complete the work?

A. 20 days B. 15 days

C. 30 days D. 10 days

8. A, B and C can complete a work separately in 24, 36 and 48 days respectively. They started together but C left after 4 days of start and A left 3 days before the completion of work. In how many days will the work be completed?

A. 15 days	B. 18 days
C. 10 days	D. 12 days

9. A and B can do a piece of work in 12 days. B and C together can do it in 15 days. If A is twice as good a work man as C, find in what time B alone can do it?

A. 12 days	B. 15 days
C. 20 days	D. 24 days

10. If 4 men or 6 boys can finish a piece of work in 20 days, in how many days can 6 men and 11 boys finish it?

A. 20 days	B. 12 days
C. 8 days	D. 6 days

11. 5 men and 2 boys together in 1 hour do 4 times work as 1 man and 1 boy do in an hour. Determine the ratio of the specified times of works of a man and a boy.

A. 4 : 1	B. 1 : 4
C. 3 : 4	D. 2 : 1

12. 75 boys finish a work in 24 days. How many men will complete twice the work in 20 days while 2 men do in a day same work as 3 boys do in a day?

A. 50	B. 24
C. 60	D. 120

13. If 3 men and 4 boys together earn ₹ 264 in 8 days and 2 men and 3 boys together earn ₹ 184 in the same time, then in how many days will 6 men and 7 boys together earn ₹ 315?

A. 5 days	B. 6 days
C. 9 days	D. 10 days

14. Pipes A and B can fill a tank in 36 and 48 hours respectively. Both pipes are opened together to fill the tank. After some time pipe B is closed and the tank is full in 24 hours. For how much time was the pipe B opend?

A. 20 hrs.	B. 16 hrs.
C. 48 hrs.	D. 36 hrs.

15. A tank is normally filled in 9 hours. But because of a leak in its bottom it takes 3 hours more to fill. How much time will it take the leak to empty the full tank?

A. 12 hrs.	B. 24 hrs.
C. 36 hrs.	D. 48 hrs.

16. Three pipes A, B and C are connected to a tank. A and B can fill it in 20 and 30 minutes respectively, while C can empty it in 15 minutes. If A, B and C are kept open successively for 1 minute each, how soon will the tank be filled?

A. 176 min	B. 167 min
C. 180 min	D. 170 min

17. Two pipes A and B can separately fill a cistern in $7\frac{1}{2}$ minutes and 5 minutes respectively and a waste pipe C can carry off 14 litres per minute. If all the pipes are opened when the cistern is full, it is emptied in 1 hour. How many litres does it hold?

A. 40 litres	B. 20 litres
C. 36 litres	D. 30 litres

18. Two workers A and B are engaged to do a work. A working alone takes 8 hours more to complete the job than if both worked together. If B worked alone, he would need $4\frac{1}{2}$ hours more to complete the job than they both working together. What time would they take to do the work together?

A. 4 hours	B. 5 hours
C. 6 hours	D. 7 hours

19. Savita can do a piece of work in 20 days. Tripti is 25% more efficient than Savita. The number of days taken by Tripti to do the same piece of work is :

A. 15	B. 16
C. 18	D. 25

20. A machine P can print one lakh books in 8 hours, machine Q can print the same number of books in 10 hours while machine R can print them in 12 hours. All the machines are started at 9 a.m. while machine P is closed at 11 a.m. and the remaining two machines complete the work. Approximately at what time will the work be finished?

A. 11:30 a.m. B. 12 noon
C. 12:30 p.m. D. 1 p.m.

ANSWERS

1	2	3	4	5	6	7	8	9	10
D	B	B	C	B	D	B	A	C	D
11	**12**	**13**	**14**	**15**	**16**	**17**	**18**	**19**	**20**
D	D	A	B	C	B	A	C	B	D

SOME SELECTED EXPLANATORY ANSWERS

1. In 16 days the work is completed by 24 men.

$\therefore$ In 1 day the work is completed by

$= 24 \times 16 = 384$ men.

Similarly in 1 day the work is completed by

$= 72 \times 8 = 576$ women

and in 1 day the work is completed by

$= 24 \times 32 = 768$ children

$\because$ 384 men = 768 children

$\therefore$ 10 men $= \frac{768 \times 10}{384} = 20$ children

and 576 women = 768 children

$\therefore$ 15 women $= \frac{768 \times 15}{576} = 20$ children

$\therefore$ (20 + 20 + 24) = 64 children

$\because$ 24 children complete the work in 32 days.

$\therefore$ 64 children complete the work in $= \frac{32 \times 24}{64}$

$= 12$ days.

2. Work done by 3 man + 9 women + 6 children in 1 day

$$= \frac{3 \times 1}{24 \times 18} + \frac{9 \times 1}{12 \times 54} + \frac{6 \times 1}{54 \times 16}$$

$$= \frac{1}{144} + \frac{1}{72} + \frac{1}{144} = \frac{1}{36}$$

$\because \frac{1}{36}$ work is done in 1 day.

$\therefore$ 1 work is done in $= \frac{1 \times 36}{1} = 36$ days.

3. 80 persons can do the job in 16 days by working = 6 hrs daily

1 person can do the job in 16 days by working

$= 6 \times 80$ hrs daily

1 person can do the job in 1 day by working

$= 6 \times 80 \times 16$ hrs daily

64 persons can do the job in 15 days by working

$$= \frac{6 \times 80 \times 16}{64 \times 15} \text{ hrs} = 8 \text{ hr.}$$

5. 5 labourers in 5 hrs. can make = 5 mats

1 labourer in 5 hrs. can make $= \frac{5}{5}$ mats

1 labourer in 1 hrs. can make $= \frac{5}{5 \times 5}$ mats

10 labourers in 10 hrs. can make

$$= \frac{5 \times 10 \times 10}{5 \times 5} = 20 \text{ mats.}$$

6. A's 9 day's work $= \frac{1}{2}$

$\therefore$ A's 1 day's work $= \frac{1}{2 \times 9} = \frac{1}{18}$

B's 6 day's work = $\frac{1}{3}$

∴ B's 1 day's work = $\frac{1}{3 \times 6} = \frac{1}{18}$

∴ (A + B)'s 1 day's work = $\frac{1}{18} + \frac{1}{18}$

$= \frac{2}{18} = \frac{1}{9}$

∴ A and B both together will complete the work in 9 days.

8. Let the work be completed in x days. Therefore, A worked for $x - 3$ days, B for x days and C for 4 days.

A's 1 day's work = $\frac{1}{24}$

B's 1 day's work = $\frac{1}{36}$

and, C's 1 day's work = $\frac{1}{48}$

$$\therefore (x-3) \times \frac{1}{24} + x \times \frac{1}{36} + 4 \times \frac{1}{48} = 1$$

$$\Rightarrow \frac{x-3}{24} + \frac{x}{36} + \frac{1}{12} = 1$$

$$\Rightarrow \frac{3x - 9 + 2x + 6}{72} = 1$$

$$\Rightarrow 5x - 3 = 72$$

$$\Rightarrow 5x = 75$$

$$\Rightarrow x = \frac{75}{5} = 15$$

Hence, the work was completed in 15 days.

11. Work of (5 men + 2 boys) = 4 (work of 1 man + 1 boy)

= Work of 4 men + 4 boys

⇒ Work of (5 men – 4 men)

= Work of (4 boys – 2 boys)

⇒ Work of 1 man = Work of 2 boys

∴ Required ratio = 2 : 1

12. Work of 3 boys = Work of 2 men

∴ Work of 1 boy = Work of $\frac{2}{3}$ man

∴ Work of 75 boys = Work of $\frac{2}{3} \times 75$

= 50 men

∵ 1 work is completed in 24 days by 50 men

∴ 1 work is completed in 1 day by 50 × 24 men

∴ 2 works are completed in 20 days by

$\frac{50 \times 24 \times 2}{20}$ = 120 men.

13. Let men be denoted by m and boys by b.

$3m + 4b$ earn in 8 days = ₹ 264

∴ $3m + 4b$ earn in 1 day = $\frac{264}{8}$ = ₹ 33 ...(*i*)

And, $2m + 3b$ earn in 8 days= ₹ 184

∴ $2m + 3b$ earn in 1 day = $\frac{184}{8}$ = ₹ 23 ...(*ii*)

By (*ii*) × 3 – (*i*) × 2, we have

$6m + 9b - 6m - 8b = 69 - 66$

⇒ $1b$ = ₹ 3

∴ $3m + 4b = 33$

$3m = 33 - 4 \times 3 = 21$

$1m = 7$

∴ Wages for 1 day of 6 men and 7 boys

= 6 × 7 + 7 × 3

= 42 + 21 = ₹ 63

∴ ₹ 63 are wages for 1 day

∴ ₹ 315 are wages for = $\frac{315}{63}$ = 5 days.

15. Without the leak, in 1 hour $\frac{1}{9}$ of the tank is filled.

∴ In extra 3 hrs, the pipe fills $\frac{3}{9} = \frac{1}{3}$ of the tank more.

In (9 + 3) = 12 hours, the leak empties this extra $\frac{1}{3}$ of the tank.

∴ The leak will empty the full tank in $12 \times \frac{3}{1}$ = 36 hrs.

16. $\left(\frac{1}{20}+\frac{1}{30}-\frac{1}{15}\right) = \frac{1}{60}$ of the tank is filled in first 3 minutes

$$\frac{1}{20}+\frac{1}{30} = \frac{5}{60}$$

$$1-\frac{5}{60} = \frac{55}{60}$$

This $\frac{55}{60}$ part of the tank will be filled in $3 \times 55 = 165$ minutes.

The last $\frac{5}{60}$ part will be filled in 2 minutes, successively by A and B.

Total time = 165 + 2 = 167 minutes.

17. Cistern filled by (A + B) in 1 minute

$$= \left(\frac{2}{15}+\frac{1}{5}\right) = \frac{1}{3}$$

Net emptying work done by (A + B + C) in 1 minute = $\frac{1}{60}$

Work done by C in 1 minute = $\left(\frac{1}{60}+\frac{1}{3}\right)=\frac{7}{20}$

$\therefore$ C alone can empty the cistern in $\left(\frac{20}{7}\right)$ minutes

Water thrown out by C in 1 minute = 14 litres

Water thrown out by C in $\left(\frac{20}{7}\right)$ minutes

$$= \left(14\times\frac{20}{7}\right) = 40 \text{ litres}$$

$\therefore$ Capacity of the cistern = 40 litres.

18. Let A and B together take x hours to complete the work. Then,

A alone takes $(x + 8)$ hrs and B alone takes $\left(x+\frac{9}{2}\right)$ hrs to complete the work. Then,

$$\frac{1}{(x+8)}+\frac{1}{\left(x+\frac{9}{2}\right)} = \frac{1}{x}$$

$$\Rightarrow \quad \frac{1}{(x+8)}+\frac{2}{(2x+9)} = \frac{1}{x}$$

$$\Rightarrow \quad x(4x + 25) = (x + 8)(2x + 9)$$

$$\Rightarrow \quad 2x^2 = 72$$

$$\Rightarrow \quad x^2 = 36$$

$$\Rightarrow \quad x = 6.$$

19. Ratio of times taken by Savita and Tripti

= 125 : 100

= 5 : 4.

Suppose Tripti takes x days to do the work.

$5 : 4 :: 20 : x \Rightarrow x = \left(\frac{4\times 20}{5}\right)$

$\Rightarrow x = 16$ days.

Hence, Tripti takes 16 days to complete the work.

9. Time and Distance

IMPORTANT FORMULAE

1. Speed = Distance ÷ Time
2. Distance = Time × Speed
3. Time = Distance ÷ Speed
4. x km/hr = $\left(x \times \frac{5}{18}\right)$ m/sec
5. x m/sec = $\left(x \times \frac{18}{5}\right)$ km/hr.
6. If the speed of a body is changed in the ratio $m : n$, then the ratio of the time taken changes in the ratio $n : m$.
7. When a man covers a certain distance with a speed of x km/h and another equal distance at the rate of y km/h, then for the whole journey, the average speed is given by

   Average speed = $\frac{2xy}{x+y}$ km/h.
8. The time taken by a train in passing a signal post or a telegraph pole or a man standing near a railway line = $\frac{\text{Length of the train}}{\text{Speed of the train}}$
9. The time taken by a train of length x passing a railway bridge or a platform or a tunnel or a train of length y at rest = $\frac{x+y}{\text{Speed}}$
10. (*a*) Time taken by faster train of length x and speed u to pass the slower train of length y and speed v in the same direction $= \frac{x+y}{u-v}$

    (*b*) Time taken by the trains in passing each other while moving in opposite direction $= \frac{x+y}{u+v}$
11. (*a*) Time taken by the train of length x and speed u to cross a man moving with speed v in same direction $= \frac{x}{u-v}$

    (*b*) Time taken by the train to cross a man moving in the opposite direction $= \frac{x}{u+v}$
12. If two trains start at the same time from two points A and B towards each other and after crossing, they take a and b hours in reaching B and A respectively. Then,

    A's speed : B's speed = $\left(\sqrt{b} : \sqrt{a}\right)$

SOLVED EXAMPLES

Example 1: Distance between two railway stations A and B is 1536 kms. A train covers a journey between A to B at the uniform speed of 60 km/hr and returns from B to A at the uniform speed of 40 km/hr. What is the average speed of the train during the whole journey?

Solution: Average speed of train = $\frac{2 \times 40 \times 60}{40+60}$

$= \frac{2 \times 40 \times 60}{100}$ = 48 km/hr.

Example 2: A car covers the first 39 km of its journey in 45 minutes and covers the remaining 25 km in 35 minutes. What is the average speed of the car?

Solution: Total time = $\frac{45}{60} + \frac{35}{60} = \frac{4}{3}$ hrs.

and total distance = 39 + 25 = 64 km

∴ Average speed = $\frac{64 \times 3}{4}$ = 48 km/hr.

Example 3: A train covered a distance of 1235 km in 19 hours. Also, the average speed of a car is four-fifth the average speed of the train. How much distance will the car cover in 22 hours?

Solution: Speed of the train $= \frac{1235}{19} = 65$ km/hr

$\therefore$ Speed of the car $= 65 \times \frac{4}{5} = 52$ km/hr

$\therefore$ Reqd. distance $= 52 \times 22 = 1144$ km.

Example 4: A 320 metre long train moving with an average speed of 120 km/hr crosses a platform in 24 seconds. A man crosses the same platform in 4 minutes. What is the speed of man in metre/second?

Solution: Let the length of the platform be x metre. Then,

$\because$Speed of the train = 120 km/hr $= 120 \times \frac{5}{18}$

$= \frac{100}{3}$ m/sec.

From question,

$\because$ $320\text{m} + x = \frac{100}{3} \times 24$

$\therefore$ $x = 800 - 320$

$= 480$ metre.

$\therefore$ Reqd. speed of man $= \frac{480 \text{ m}}{4 \times 60 \text{ sec}} = 2$ m/sec.

Example 5: A 260 metre long train crosses a platform thrice its length in 80 seconds. What is the speed of the train in km/hour?

Solution: Speed of the train

$= \frac{(260+780)}{80} \times \frac{18}{5}$ km/hr.

$= 46.8$ km/hr.

MULTIPLE CHOICE QUESTIONS

1. A boat while travelling upstream covers a distance of 18 km at the speed of 3 km/hr, whereas while travelling downstream it covers the same distance at a speed of 9 km/hr. What is the speed of the boat in still waters?

A. 3 km/hr B. 5 km/hr
C. 7 km/hr D. None of these

2. The speed of a car is 1.5 times the speed of a bus. If the car travels at the speed of 60 km/hr what will be the difference in the time taken by the bus and the time taken by the car to cover 720 km?

A. 5 hours B. 6 hours
C. 4 hours D. 8 hours

3. A car covers a distance of 540 km in 9 hours. Speed of a train is double the speed of the car. Two-third the speed of the train is equal to the speed of a bike. How much distance will the bike cover in 5 hours?

A. 450 km B. 360 km
C. 400 km D. 500 km

4. A train travels at a speed of 30 km per hour for 12 minutes and then for the next 8 minutes at a speed of 45 km per hour. What is the average speed for the journey?

A. 40 km/hr B. 36 km/hr
C. 43 km/hr D. 46 km/hr

5. The ratio of the speeds of two trains is 7 : 8. If the second train runs 400 km in 5 hrs., find the speed of the first train.

A. 60 km/hr B. 55 km/hr
C. 70 km/hr D. 75 km/hr

6. A train travels from Dehradun to Delhi at a speed of 40 km/hr and returns at 60 km/hr. Find the average speed for the entire journey—

A. 50 km/hr B. 45 km/hr
C. 48 km/hr D. 52 km/hr

7. A car runs at 60 km per hr. A man runs at one-third the speed of the car and reaches office from his house in 15 minutes. How far is his office from his house?

A. 20 km B. 10 km
C. 5 km D. 4 km

8. Two men A and B start walking simultaneously from P to Q, a distance of 21 kms, at the speeds of 3 km and 4 km an hour respectively. B reaches Q, returns immediately and meets A at R. Then the distance from P to R is :

A. 6 km B. 12 km
C. 18 km D. 24 km

9. A monkey climbing up a greased pole ascends 12 metres and slips down 5 metres in alternate minutes. If the pole is 63 metres high, how long will it take him to reach the top?

A. $12\frac{7}{16}$ B. $7\frac{12}{16}$
C. $16\frac{7}{12}$ D. $10\frac{7}{12}$

10. A carriage driving in a fog passed a man who was walking at the speed of 6 km/hr. in the same direction. He could see the carriage for 4 minutes and it was visible to him up to a distance of 200 metres. The speed of the carriage is :

A. 9 km/hr B. 4 km/hr
C. 6 km/hr D. 8 km/hr

11. A train met with an accident 3 hours after starting, which detains it for one hour, after which it proceeds at 75% of its original speed. It arrives at the destination 4 hours late. Had the accident taken place 150 km further along the railway line, the train would have arrived only $3\frac{1}{2}$ hours late. Find the length of the trip :

A. 1200 km B. 1000 km
C. 2100 km D. 1050 km

12. Two places A and B are 162 kms apart. A train leaves A for B and at the same time another train leaves B for A. The two trains meet at the end of 6 hours. If the train travelling from A to B travels 8 km per hr. faster than the other. Then the speed of the faster train is :

A. $9\frac{1}{2}$ km/h B. 27 km/hr
C. $17\frac{1}{2}$ km/hr D. 19 km/hr

13. A train takes 18 seconds to pass completely through a station 162 metres long and 15 seconds to pass completely through another station 120 metres long. The length of the train is :

A. 60 m B. 75 m
C. 90 m D. 100 m

14. A man covered a distance of 3990 km partly by air, partly by sea and remaining by land. The time spent in air, on sea and on land is in the ratio 1 : 16 : 2 and the ratio of average speeds is 20 : 1 : 3 respectively. If total average speed is 42 km per hr, Then the distance covered by sea is :

A. 1502 kms B. 2520 kms
C. 1520 kms D. 1500 kms

15. A man is walking at a speed of 10 km/hr. After every kilometre, he takes rest for 5 minutes. How much time will he take to cover a distance of 5 km?

A. 1 hr B. 50 min
C. 20 min D. 30 min

16. Walking $\frac{5}{6}$ of his usual speed, a man reaches the station 10 min late. His usual time to reach the station is :

A. 30 min B. 40 min
C. 50 min D. 60 min

17. A is four times as fast as B and B is six times as fast as C. A certain distance is covered by B in 28 minutes. Then the time taken by C to cover the same distance is :

A. 2 : 48 hrs B. 2 : 40 hrs
C. 2 : 28 hrs D. 3 hrs

18. It takes eight hours for a 600 km journey, if 120 km is done by train and the rest by car. It takes 20 minutes more, if 200 km is done by train and the rest by car. The ratio of the speed of the train to the speed of the car is :

A. 2 : 3 B. 6 : 9
C. 3 : 4 D. 4 : 3

19. A bus takes two hours less for a journey of 300 km if its speed is increased by 5 kmph from its normal speed. The normal speed is

A. 30 kmph B. 25 kmph
C. 35 kmph D. 50 kmph

20. A boy goes to school with a speed of 3 km/hr and returns to the village with a speed of 2 km/hr. If he takes 5 hours in all, the distance between the village and the school is :

A. 6 km B. 7 km
C. 8 km D. 9 km

ANSWERS

1	2	3	4	5	6	7	8	9	10
D	B	C	B	C	C	C	C	C	A
11	**12**	**13**	**14**	**15**	**16**	**17**	**18**	**19**	**20**
A	C	C	C	B	C	A	C	B	A

SOME SELECTED EXPLANATORY ANSWERS

1. Speed of boat in still water = $\frac{9+3}{2}$ = 6 km/hr.

2. Speed of bus = $60\times\frac{1}{1.5}$ = 40 km/hr.

Hence, required difference = $\frac{720}{40}-\frac{720}{60}$ = 18 – 12 = 6 hrs.

3. Speed of the car = $\frac{540}{9}$ = 60 km/hr.

∴ Speed of train = 60 × 2 = 120 km/hr.

and speed of bike = $120\times\frac{2}{3}$ = 80 km/hr.

∴ Reqd. distance = 80 × 5 = 400 km.

4. In 12 minutes, the train with 30 km per hour speed goes

$= 30\times\frac{5}{18}\times60\times12$ m $= \frac{5\times5\times20\times12}{1000}$ km

= 6 km.

In 8 minutes, the train with 45 km per hr. speed goes

$= 45\times\frac{5}{18}\times60\times\frac{8}{1000}$ km = 6 km

Average speed = $\frac{12 \text{ km}}{20 \text{ min}} = \frac{12}{20}\times60$ km/hr

= 36 km/hr.

5. $x:\frac{400}{5} = 7 : 8$

$\Rightarrow x\times\frac{5}{400} = \frac{7}{8}$ ∴ x = 70 km/hr.

6. Reqd. average speed = $\frac{2\times40\times60}{(40+60)}$

$= \frac{2\times2400}{100}$ = 48 km/hr.

8. Let A and B meet after time t hours.

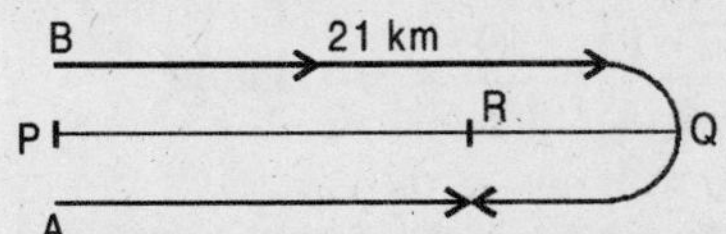

Distance covered by A in t hours = 3 t km.
Distance covered by B in t hours = 4 t km.
Total distance covered by A and B = $(3t + 4t)$ km = 7 t km.

From the diagram we can see that the total distance covered by A and B is equal to twice the distance between P and Q.

∴ $7t = 2 \times 21$

$t = \frac{2\times21}{7}$

t = 6 hours

Distance (PR) = 6 × 3 = 18 kms.

9. From question,
In 2 minutes the net ascending of the monkey is 12 – 5 = 7 metres. So, to cover 63 metres to above process is repeated $\frac{63}{7}$ = 9 times.

Since on 9th time, it will climb to the top.

Hence, Time taken to cover 56 metres = $\frac{56\times2}{7}$ = 16 minutes

Remaining distance = 63 – 56 = 7 metres

Time taken to ascend 7 metres = $\frac{7}{12}$ minutes

∴ Total time taken = $16+\frac{7}{12} = 16\frac{7}{12}$ minutes.

10. The distance covered by man in 4 minutes

$= \frac{6\times1000\times4}{60}$ = 400 metres

The distance coverd by carriage in 4 minutes $= 200 + 400 = 600$ metres

$\therefore$ Sepeed of carriage $= \frac{600}{4} \times \frac{60}{1000}$ km/hr.

$= 9$ km/hr.

12. Both trains meet after 6 hours.

$\therefore$ The relative speed of two trains $= \frac{162}{6}$

$= 27$ km/hr.

The speed of the slower train starting from B

$= \frac{27-8}{2} = \frac{19}{2} = 9\frac{1}{2}$ km/hr.

$\therefore$ The speed of the faster train $= 9\frac{1}{2} + 8$

$= 17\frac{1}{2}$ km/hr.

13. Let the length of the train $= x$ metres

Then, in 18 sec. the train travels $(x + 162)$ metres ...(*i*)

and in 15 sec. the train travels $(x + 120)$ metres

$\therefore$ In $(18 - 15) = 3$ sec. the train travels $(x + 162) - (x + 120) = 42$ m

$\therefore$ In 1 sec the train travels $= \frac{42}{3} = 14$ metes ...(*ii*)

$\therefore$ In 18 sec. the train travels $= 14 \times 18 = 252$ metres ...(*iii*)

From equations (*i*) and (*iii*)

$\therefore \quad x + 162 = 252$

$\Rightarrow \quad x = 252 - 162 = 90$

$\therefore$ Length of the train = 90 metres.

14. Total distance travelled = 3990 km

Ratio of time spent = 1 : 16 : 2

$\therefore$ Ratio of time $\times$ speeds $= 20 \times 1 : 16 \times 1 : 2 \times 3$

$= 20 : 16 : 6$

Sum of the ratios $= 20 + 16 + 6$

$= 42$

$\therefore$ Distance covered by sea $= \frac{3990}{42} \times 16$

$= 1520$ kms.

15. Total time = walking time + rest time

Walking time $= \frac{5}{10}$ hour $= \frac{1}{2}$ hour = 30 min

Rest time $= 4 \times 5$ min = 20 min

$\therefore$ Required time taken = 30 min + 20 min

= 50 min.

17. Let the speed of C be x kmph

$\therefore$ B's speed $= 6x$ kmph

and A's speed $= 4 \times 6x$ kmph $= 24x$ kmph

The distance covered by B in 28 minutes

$= 6x \times \frac{28}{60}$ km

$= \frac{28x}{10}$ km $= \frac{14x}{5}$ km

The time taken by C to cover the same distance

$= \frac{\frac{14x}{5}\text{ km}}{x\text{ kmph}} = \frac{14}{5}$ hrs

$= 2\frac{4}{5}$ hours = 2 hrs 48 minutes

19. Let s be the normal speed and t be the normal time taken by the bus

$\therefore \quad s \times t = 300$ ...(1)

new speed $= s + 5$

new time $= t - 2$

$\therefore \quad (s + 5)(t - 2) = 300$

$(s+5)\left(\frac{300}{s} - 2\right) = 300$ (from (1))

$(s + 5)(300 - 2s) = 300s$

$300s - 2s^2 + 1500 - 10s = 300s$

$\Rightarrow \quad 2s^2 + 10s - 1500 = 0$

$\Rightarrow \quad 2s^2 + 60s - 50s - 1500 = 0$

$\Rightarrow \quad 2s(s + 30) - 50(s + 30) = 0$

$\Rightarrow \quad (s + 30)(2s - 50) = 0$

$\therefore \quad s = 25$

$\therefore$ The normal speed of the bus is 25 kmph.

20. Let the required distance be x km. Then,

$\frac{x}{3} + \frac{x}{2} = 5$

$\Rightarrow \quad 2x + 3x = 30$

$\Rightarrow \quad x = 6.$

10. MENSURATION

Triangle

1. Perimeter = 3 × side (Equilateral triangle)

2. Area = $\frac{1}{2} \times \text{base} \times \text{height}$, or

   Area = $\sqrt{s(s-a)(s-b)(s-c)}$

   where *a, b, c,* are the lengths of the sides of triangle and $s = \frac{a+b+c}{2}$

Right Angled Triangle : It is one whose one of the angles is right angle, *i.e.*, 90°.

1. $(\text{Hypotenuse})^2 = (\text{Perpendicular})^2 + (\text{Base})^2$

2. Area = $\frac{1}{2} \times \text{Base} \times \text{Perpendicular}$

Equilateral Triangle : All three sides are equal in length and all three angles are equal to 60°.

1. Area = $\frac{\sqrt{3}}{4} \times (\text{Side})^2$

2. Area = $\frac{(\text{Height})^2}{\sqrt{3}}$

3. Height = $\frac{\sqrt{3}}{2} \times \text{side}$

4. Perimeter = 3 × side

Isosceles Triangle : Two sides are equal in lengths.

1. Area = $\frac{b}{4}\sqrt{4a^2 - b^2}$

   where a = lengths of equal sides
   b = length of unequal side

2. In an isosceles right triangle,

   (*a*) Hypotenuse = $\sqrt{2} \times \text{congruent side}$ (a)

   (*b*) Area = $\frac{1}{2} \times a^2$

   (*c*) Perimeter = $\sqrt{2} \times a(\sqrt{2}+1)$

Rectangle :

1. Area = length(l) × breadth(b)
2. Perimeter = $2(l + b)$
3. Diagonal = $\sqrt{l^2 + b^2}$

Square :

1. Area = $(\text{Side})^2$
2. Perimeter = 4 × side
3. Diagonal = $\text{side} \times \sqrt{2}$

Parallelogram: Area = Base × Height.

Trapezium : Area = $\frac{1}{2} \times \text{Height} \times$ (Sum of parallel sides). Here, height is the distance between the two parallel sides.

Rhombus :

1. Area = $\frac{1}{2} \times \text{Product of diagonals}$

2. Side = $\sqrt{\left(\frac{d_1}{2}\right)^2 + \left(\frac{d_2}{2}\right)^2}$, where d_1 and d_2 are diagonals

3. Perimeter = 4 × side

Quadrilateral : Area = $\frac{1}{2} \times \text{One diagonal} \times$ (Sum of perpendicular to it from the opposite vertices)

$$= \frac{1}{2} \times d \times (a+b)$$

Circle :

1. Diameter = 2 × Radius

2. Area = $\pi r^2 = \frac{\pi}{4} d^2$;

   where d = diameter = $\sqrt{\frac{4A}{\pi}}$

3. Circumference = $2\pi r = \pi d$

4. Radius = $\dfrac{\text{Circumference}}{2\pi} = \dfrac{\sqrt{\text{Area}}}{\pi}$

5. Length of an Arc = $\dfrac{\theta}{360°} \times 2\pi r$

6. Area of sector = $\dfrac{\theta}{360°} \times \pi r^2 = \dfrac{1}{2} \times \text{Arc} \times r$

Polygon :

1. Interior angle + Exterior angle = 180°
2. Each interior angle = $\left(\dfrac{2n-4}{n}\right) \times 90°$

   where n = number of sides
3. Sum of Exterior angles = 360°
4. Perimeter = Number of sides × Length of side.
5. For an equilateral triangle of side 'a'

   (*a*) radius of inscribed circle = $\dfrac{a}{2\sqrt{3}}$

   and side of the triangle = $2\sqrt{3}r$,

   (*b*) radius of circumcircle = $\dfrac{a}{\sqrt{3}}$
6. Area of regular polygon = $\dfrac{1}{2}$(No. of sides) (Radius of the inscribed circle)
7. Area of regular hexagon = $\dfrac{3\sqrt{3}}{2}(\text{side})^2$

   = 2.598 $(\text{side})^2$
8. Area of a regular octagon

   $= 2\left(\sqrt{2}+1\right)(\text{side})^2$ = 4.828 $(\text{side})^2$
9. Area of quadrilateral, A

   $= \sqrt{s(s-a)(s-b)(s-c)(s-d)}$

   where, $s = \dfrac{a+b+c+d}{2}$

VOLUME AND SURFACE AREA OF SOLIDS

Cuboid : A cuboid has six faces, each one a ractangle. It has 12 edges. For example, a rectangular brick.

Let Length = l, Breadth = b and Height = h, then,

1. Volume = (Length × Breadth × Height)
2. Whole Surface Area = $2(lb + bh + lh)$
3. Diagonal = $\sqrt{l^2+b^2+h^2}$
4. Area of 4 walls of a room = $2 \times h\ (l + b)$

Cube : In a cube, Length = Breadth = Height

1. Volume = $(l)^3$
2. Length = $\sqrt[3]{\text{Volume}}$
3. Whole Surface Area = $6\ l^2$
4. Diagonal = $l \times \sqrt{3}$
5. Lateral Surface Area = $4\ l^2$

Cylinder :

1. Volume = $\pi r^2 h$
2. Curved Surface Area = $2\pi rh$
3. Total Surface Area = $2\pi r(r + h)$

   where r = radius, h = height

Spherical Cell :

1. Volume = $\dfrac{4}{3}\pi\left(R^3 - r^3\right)$
2. Total Surface Area= $4\pi(R^2 - r^2)$

   where R = Outer radius

   r = Inner radius

Sphere :

1. Volume = $\dfrac{4}{3}\pi r^3$
2. Surface Area = $4\pi r^2$

Semi-sphere :

1. Volume = $\dfrac{2}{3}\pi r^3$
2. Curved surface area = $2\pi r^2$
3. Total surface area = $3\pi r^2$

Cone :

1. Slant height (l) = $\sqrt{r^2+h^2}$
2. Volume = $\dfrac{1}{3}\pi r^2 h$
3. Curved surface area = πrl
4. Total surface area = $\pi r\ (l + r)$
5. If the depth of the frustum of a cone be k and the radii of its ends are r_1 and r_2, then

   (*i*) Slant height of the frustum of a cone

   $= \sqrt{k^2 + (r_1 - r_2)^2}$

(*ii*) Curved surface of the frustum

$= \pi(r_1 + r_2)\ l.$

(*iii*) Volume $= \dfrac{\pi k}{3}\left(r_1^2 + r_1 r_2 + r_2^2\right)$

SOLVED EXAMPLES

Example 1: What is the longest rod that can be placed in a room which is 7 m long, 9 m broad and $\sqrt{39}$ m high?

Solution: Required length of rod

$= \sqrt{7^2 + 9^2 + (\sqrt{39})^2} = \sqrt{49+81+39}$

$= \sqrt{169} = 13$ m.

Example 2: The total area of a circle and a square is equal to 5450 sq. cm. The diameter of the circle is 70 cms. What is the sum of the circumference of the circle and the perimeter of the square?

Solution: Let side of the square = x cm

Also $\pi \times 35 \times 35 + x^2 = 5450$

$\Rightarrow \dfrac{22}{7} \times 35 \times 35 + x^2 = 5450$

$\Rightarrow x^2 = 5450 - 3850 = 1600$

$\therefore x = 40$ cm

$\therefore$ Required sum $= \pi \times d + 4x$

$= \left(\dfrac{22}{7} \times 70 + 4 \times 40\right) = 380$ cm.

Example 3: Perimeter of a circle is equal to the prmimeter of a square whose area is 484 cm^2. What is the radius of the circle?

Solution: Side of a square $= \sqrt{\text{Area}} = \sqrt{484} = 22$ cm.

Perimeter of square $= 4 \times$ side $= 4 \times 22 = 88$ cm.

$\therefore 2\pi r = 88$

$\Rightarrow 2 \times \dfrac{22}{7} \times r = 88$

$\Rightarrow r = \dfrac{88 \times 7}{2 \times 22} = 14$ cm.

Example 4: The perimeter of a square is equal to twice the perimeter of a rectangle of length 8 cm and breadth 7 cm. What is the circumference of a semicircle whose diameter is equal to the side of the square? (Rounded off to the two decimal place)

Solution: $\because$ Perimeter of the square

$= 2 \times$ Perimeter of rectangle

$= 2(8 + 7) \times 2 = 60$ cm

One side of the square = 15 cm

Radius of the semicircle (R) $= \dfrac{15}{2}$ cm

$\therefore$ Perimeter of the semicircle $= \pi R + 2R$

$= \dfrac{22}{7} \times \dfrac{15}{2} + 15 = 23.57 + 15$

$= 38.57$ cm

MULTIPLE CHOICE QUESTIONS

1. What is the area of a circle whose radius is equal to the side of a square whose perimeter is 112 metres?

   A. 176 sq m B. 2504 sq m
   C. 284 sq m D. None of these

2. The sum of the circumference of a circle and the perimeter of a rectangle is 132 cm. The area of the rectangle is 112 sq cm and breadth of the rectangle is 8 cms. What is the area of the circle?

   A. 616 sq cm
   B. 540 sq cm
   C. 396 sq cm
   D. Cannot be determined

3. The total area of a circle and a rectangle is equal to 1166 sq cm. The diameter of the circle is 28 cm. What is the sum of the circumference of the circle and the perimeter of the rectangle if the length of the rectangle is 25 cm?

   A. 186 cm
   B. 182 cm
   C. 184 cm
   D. Cannot be determined.

7. One side of the square $= \sqrt{196} = 14$ cm

$\therefore$ Radius of the circle = 28 cm

$\therefore$ Circumference of the circle $= 2 \times \frac{22}{7} \times 28$

$= 176$ cm

$\therefore$ Breadth of the rectangle = 176 cm

$\therefore$ Length of the rectangle $= \frac{712}{2} - 176$

$= 356 - 176$

$= 180$ cm.

8. Let r be the radius of the circular plot then from problem,

$\because$ The circumference of the circular plot = 484 m

$\Rightarrow \quad 2\pi r = 484$

$r = 484 \times \frac{7}{22} \times \frac{1}{2} = 77$ metres

$\therefore$ Area of the circular plot $= \pi r^2 = \frac{22}{7} \times (77)^2$

$= 18634 \text{ m}^2$.

10. Area of the whole paper ABCD $= 22 \times 14$

$= 308 \text{ cm}^2$

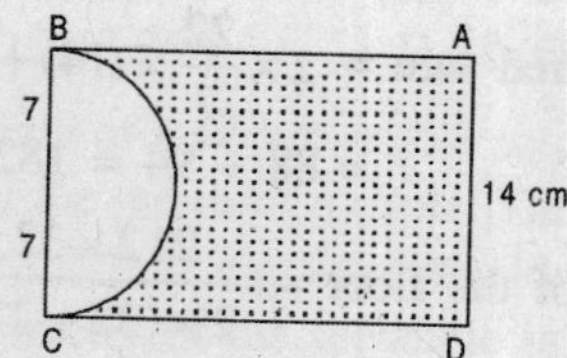

Radius of the semi-circle $= \frac{1}{2} \times 14 \text{ cm} = 7$ cm

$\therefore$ Area of the semi-circle $= \frac{1}{2}\pi r^2$

$= \frac{1}{2} \times \frac{22}{7} \times 7 \times 7$

$= 77 \text{ cm}^2$

$\therefore$ Area of the remaining part of the paper

$= 308 \text{ cm}^2 - 77 \text{ cm}^2 = 231 \text{ cm}^2$.

11. Circumference of flower bed = 880 dm

$\Rightarrow \quad 2\pi r = 880$ dm

$\Rightarrow \quad r = \frac{880}{2\pi}$ dm $= \frac{880 \times 7}{2 \times 22} = 140$ dm

Area of flower bed $= \pi r^2 = \frac{22}{7} \times (140)^2 \text{ dm}^2$

$\therefore$ Required number of plants

$= \frac{\frac{22}{7} \times 140 \times 140}{35} \text{ dm}^2$

$= \frac{22}{7} \times \frac{140 \times 140}{35} = 1760.$

13. Area of each quadrant $= \frac{\theta}{360} \times \pi r^2$

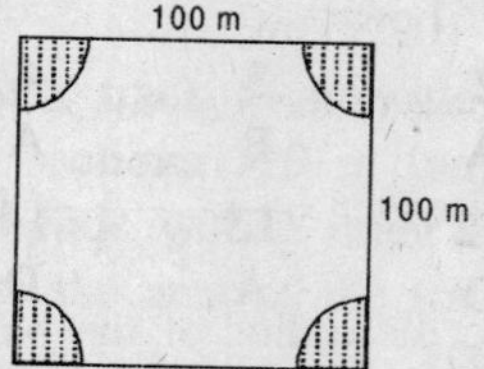

$= \frac{90}{360} \times \frac{22}{7} \times 14 \times 14 \text{ m}^2 = 154 \text{ m}^2$

$\therefore$ Area of 4 quadrants $= 154 \times 4 \text{ m}^2 = 616 \text{ m}^2$

Area of park $= (100)^2 = 10,000 \text{ m}^2$

Hence area of the remaining part of the park

$= 10,000 - 616 = 9,384 \text{ m}^2$.

14. Length of minute hand of clock $= r = 14$ cm

Central angle covered in 1 minute $= \frac{360}{60} = 6°$

$\therefore$ Area swept in one minute = Area of sector with central angle 6°

$= \frac{\theta}{360} \times \pi r^2 = \frac{6}{360} \times \frac{22}{7} \times 14 \times 14$

$= \frac{154}{15} = 10.26 \text{ cm}^2$.

15. Let R be the radius of outer circle and r the radius of inner circle.

Circumference of outer circle = 77 cm

$\therefore \quad 2\pi R = 77$

$\Rightarrow \quad R = \frac{77}{2\pi} = \frac{77 \times 7}{2 \times 22} = \frac{49}{4}$ cm

Circumference of inner circle = 55 cm

$\therefore\ 2\pi r = 55$

$\Rightarrow\ r = \frac{55}{2\pi} = \frac{55 \times 7}{2 \times 22} = \frac{35}{4}$ cm

$\therefore$ Area of ring $= \pi(R^2 - r^2)$

$= \frac{22}{7} \times \left(\frac{49}{4} + \frac{35}{4}\right)\left(\frac{49}{4} - \frac{35}{4}\right)$

$= 231$ cm^2

16. Volume of water that flows in one second

$= (18 \times 0.075 \times 0.045)$ m^3

Volume of water that flows in 30 minutes

$= 18 \times 0.075 \times 0.045 \times 30 \times 60$

$= 109.35$ m^3.

Area of the base of the reservoir $= 10.8 \times 3.75$ m^2

$\therefore$ Height of water $= \frac{109.35}{10.8 \times 3.75} = 2.7$ metres.

17. Let r cm be the radius of the base and h cm be the height. Then, $h = 18$ cm.

Now, circumference of the base = Length of the Sheet

$\Rightarrow$ Circumference = 44 cm

$\Rightarrow\ 2\pi r = 44$

$\Rightarrow\ 2 \times \frac{22}{7} \times r = 44$

$\Rightarrow\ r = 7$ cm

Volume of the cylinder $= \pi r^2 h$ cm^3

$= \frac{22}{7} \times (7)^2 \times 18$ cm^3

$= 2772$ cm^3

18. Slant height, $l = \sqrt{r^2 + h^2}$

$= \sqrt{7^2 + 24^2} = 25$ metres

Curved surface area of cone $= \pi r l$

$= \frac{22}{7} \times 7 \times 25$

$= 550$ m^2

$\therefore$ Area of the cloth required = 550 m^2

$\therefore$ Length of the cloth $= \frac{550}{5}$

$= 110$ metres.

11. PERMUTATION AND COMBINATION

IMPORTANT RESULTS

(*i*) Number of permutations of n distinct things taken r at a time, $0 \le r \le n$
$= n(n-1)(n-2)\ldots(n-r+1)$
$= n!/(n-r)! = {}^nP_r$.
This is equivalent to filling r places by r objects taking from n distinct objects.

(*ii*) The number of permutations of n distinct objects taken all at a time $= n!$

(*iii*) The number of combinations of n objects taken r at a time, $0 \le r \le n$. $= {}^nC_r$

$$= \frac{n!}{(n-r)!.r!}.$$

(*iv*) The number of permutations of n dissimilar things taken r at a time when each thing can be repeated any number of times $= n^r$.

(*v*) The number of combinations of n distinct objects taken r at a time when any object may be repeated any number of times
$=$ coefficient of x^r in $(1 + x + x^2 + \ldots + x^r)^n$
$=$ coefficient of x^r in $(1-x)^n = {}^{n+r-1}C_r$.

(*vi*) Number of combinations of n distinct things taken r at a time when p particular things always occur $= {}^{(n-p)}C_{(r-p)}$.

(*vii*) The number of permutations of n distinct things taken r at a time when p particular things always occur $= {}^{(n-p)}C_{(r-p)}.r!$.

(*viii*) Number of combinations of n distinct things taken r at a time when p particular things never occur $= {}^{(n-p)}C_r$.

(*ix*) Number of permutations (arrangements) of n distinct things taken r at a time when p particular things never occur $= {}^{(n-p)}C_r.r!$.

(*x*) Number of permutations of n things, taken all at a time when p_1 are alike of one kind, p_2 are alike of second kind, ..., p_r of them are alike of the r-th kind $p_1 + p_2 + \ldots + p_r \le n$,
and remaining things are all different $= n!/\{p_1!p_2! \ldots p_r!\}$.

(*xi*) If $3n$ things are to be divided into three equal groups, then the number of ways

$$= \frac{(3n)!}{n!.n!.n!.3!}.$$

(*xii*) If $3n$ things are to be divided equally between 3 persons (*i.e.,* division of $3n$ things into 3 equal groups with permutation of groups) then the number of ways $= \dfrac{(3n)!}{(n!)^3}$.

(*xiii*) Greatest value of ${}^nC_r$
${}^nC_r$ is greatest when $r = n/2$ if n is even
$r = (n-1)/2$ or $(n+1)/2$ if n is odd.

(*xiv*) ${}^nC_r = {}^nC_{n-r}$.

(*xv*) ${}^nC_r + {}^nC_{r+1} = {}^{n+1}C_{r+1}$.

(*xvi*) ${}^nC_r = {}^nC_s \Rightarrow r = s$ or $r + s = n$.

(*xvii*) The number of circular permutations of n different things taken all at a time $= (n-1)!$

(*xviii*) The number of arrangements of n persons on a round table $= (n-1)!$.

(*xix*) The number of arrangements of n flowers to make a garland $= \dfrac{1}{2}(n-1)!$.

SOLVED EXAMPLES

Example 1: In how many different ways can the letters of the word 'PRIDE' be arranged ?

Solution: Required number of arrangements

$= {}^5P_5 = 5! = 120$

Example 2: In how many different ways can the letters of the word 'PRAISE' be arranged ?

Solution: Required number of ways

$= {}^6P_6 = 6! = 720$

Example 3: On a shelf there are 4 books on Economics, 3 books on Management and 4 books on Statistics. In how many different ways can the books be arranged so that the books on Economics are kept together ?

Solution: Required number of different ways

$= {}^8P_8 \times {}^4P_4 = \lfloor 8 \times \lfloor 4$

$= 40320 \times 24 = 967680$

Example 4: In how many different ways can the letters of the word 'PRETTY' be arranged?

Solution: Required ways = $\frac{\lfloor 6}{\lfloor 2} = 360$

Example 5: In how many different ways can the letters of the word 'PEANUT' be arranged ?

Solution: Required ways = ${}^6P_6 = \lfloor 6$

$= 6 \times 5 \times 4 \times 3 \times 2 \times 1 = 720.$

MULTIPLE CHOICE QUESTIONS

1. How many seven digit numbers can be made from the number 3428651, using each digit only once ?

A. 49 B. 180
C. 5040 D. 2520

2. How many words can be formed from the letters of the word 'DIRECTOR' so that the vowels are always together?

A. 2106
B. 1206
C. 360
D. 2160

3. In how many ways a committee of 5 members can be selected from 6 men and 5 ladies, consisting of 3 men and 2 ladies?

A. 120 B. 220
C. 200 D. 320

4. In how many ways can the letters of the word 'APPLE' be arranged?

A. 720 B. 120
C. 60 D. 180

5. How many words can be formed by using all the letters of the word. 'ALLAHABAD'?

A. 3780 B. 1890
C. 7560 D. 2520

6. How many words can be formed from the letters of the word 'SIGNATURE' so that the vowels always come together?

A. 720 B. 1440
C. 2880 D. 17280

7. In how many different ways can the letters of the word 'BANKING' be arranged so that the vowels always come together?

A. 120 B. 240
C. 360 D. 720

8. In how many ways can a group of 5 men and 2 women be made out of a total of 7 men and 3 women?

A. 63 B. 90
C. 126 D. 45

9. In a group of 6 boys and 4 girls, four children are to be selected. In how many different ways can they be selected such that at least one boy should be there?

A. 159 B. 194
C. 205 D. 209

10. A box contains 2 white balls, 3 black balls and 4 red balls. In how many ways can 3 balls be drawn from the box, if at least one black ball is to be included in the draw?

A. 32 B. 48
C. 64 D. 96

11. In how many ways can a team of 3 boys and 3 girls be selected from 5 boys and 4 girls?
A. 14 B. 40
C. 18 D. 140

12. The number of ways of selecting 9 balls from 6 red, 5 white and 5 blue if each selection consists of 3 balls of each colour is :
A. 1200 B. 20000
C. 2200 D. 2000

13. In how many ways can we select 4 red balls and 3 blue balls from 8 red balls and 9 blue balls?
A. 8550 B. 5850
C. 5880 D. 8580

14. Find the number of diagonals of a decagon
A. 45 B. 35
C. 55 D. 25

15. In how many ways can a student choose a programme of 5 courses if 9 courses are available and 2 specific courses are compulsary for every student?
A. 53 B. 14
C. 35 D. 28

16. Seven different lecturers are to deliver lectures in seven periods of a class on a particular day. A, B and C are three of the lecturers. The number of ways in which a routine for the day can be made such that A delivers his lecuture before B, and B before C, is
A. 420 B. 120
C. 210 D. 840

17. The number of words that can be made by rearranging the letters of the word APURBA so that vowels and consonants alternate is
A. 18 B. 35
C. 36 D. 24

18. The number of ways in which the letters of the word ARTICLE can be rearranged so that the even places are always occupied by consonants is
A. 576 B. ${}^4C_3 \times (4!)$
C. 2(4!) D. 288

19. The number of ways in which a couple can sit around a table with 6 guests if the couple take consecutive seats is
A. 1440 B. 720
C. 5040 D. 2880

20. The number of ways in which 20 different pearls of two colours can be set alternately on a necklace, there being 10 pearls of each colour, is
A. $9! \times 10!$ B. $5(9!)^2$
C. $(9!)^2$ D. $(18!)^2$

ANSWERS

1	2	3	4	5	6	7	8	9	10
C	D	C	C	C	D	D	A	D	C
11	**12**	**13**	**14**	**15**	**16**	**17**	**18**	**19**	**20**
B	D	C	B	C	D	C	A	A	B

SOME SELECTED EXPLANATORY ANSWERS

1. Required number of ways = ${}^7P_7 = \underline{|7} = 5040$

2. In the given word, we treat the vowels IEO as one letter.
Thus, we have DRCTR (IEO).
This group has 6 letters of which R occurs 2 times and others are different.
Number of ways arranging these letters $= \frac{6!}{2!} = 360.$

Now 3 vowels can be arranged among themselves in 3! = 6 ways.

∴ Required number of ways = (360 × 6) = 2160.

3. (3 men out of 6) and (2 ladies out of 5) are to be chosen.

∴ Required number of ways = $({}^6C_3 \times {}^5C_2)$

$$= \left(\frac{6\times5\times4}{3\times2\times1}\times\frac{5\times4}{2\times1}\right) = 200.$$

4. The word 'APPLE' contains 5 letters, 1A, 2P, 1L and 1E.

∴ Required number of ways

$$= \frac{5!}{(1!)(2!)(1!)(1!)} = 60.$$

5. The word 'ALLAHABAD' contains 9 letters, namely 4A, 2L, 1H, 1B and 1D.

∴ Required number of words

$$= \frac{9!}{(4!)(2!)(1!)(1!)(1!)} = 7560.$$

6. The word 'SIGNATURE' contains 9 different letters.

When the vowels IAUE are taken together, they can be supposed to form an entity, treated as one letter.

Then, the letters to be arranged are SGNTR (IAUE).

These 6 letters can be arranged in $^6P_6 = 6! = 720$ ways.

The vowels in the group (IAUE) can be arranged amongst themselves in $^4P_4 = 4! = 24$ ways.

∴ Required number of words = (720 × 24) = 17280.

7. In the word 'BANKING', we treat the two vowels AI as one letter. Thus, we have BNKNG (AI).

This has 6 letters of which N occurs 2 times and the rest are different.

Number of ways of arranging these letters

$$= \frac{6!}{(2!)(1!)(1!)(1!)(1!)} = 360.$$

Now, 2 vowels AI can be arranged in 2! = 2 ways.

∴ Required number of ways = (360 × 2) = 720.

8. Required number of ways = $({}^7C_5 \times {}^3C_2)$

$$= ({}^7C_2 \times {}^3C_1) = \left(\frac{7\times6}{2\times1}\times3\right) = 63.$$

9. We may have (1 boy and 3 girls) or (2 boys and 2 girls) or (3 boys and 1 girl) or (4 boys).

∴ Required number of ways

$$= ({}^6C_1\times{}^4C_3) + ({}^6C_2\times{}^4C_2) + ({}^6C_3\times{}^4C_1) + ({}^6C_4)$$

$$= ({}^6C_1\times{}^4C_1) + ({}^6C_2\times{}^4C_2) + ({}^6C_3\times{}^4C_1) + ({}^6C_2)$$

$$= (6\times4)+\left(\frac{6\times5}{2\times1}\times\frac{4\times3}{2\times1}\right)+\left(\frac{6\times5\times4}{3\times2\times1}\times4\right)+\left(\frac{6\times5}{2\times1}\right)$$

= (24 + 90 + 80 + 15) = 209.

10. We may have (1 black and 2 non-black) or (2 black and 1 non-black) or (3 black)

∴ Required number of ways

$$= ({}^3C_1 \times {}^6C_2) + ({}^3C_2 \times {}^6C_1) + ({}^3C_3)$$

$$= \left(3\times\frac{6\times5}{2\times1}\right)+\left(\frac{3\times2}{2\times1}\times6\right)+1 = (45+18+1)$$

= 64.

13. 4 red balls from 8 red balls can be selected in $^8C_4$ ways

3 blue balls from 9 balls can be selected in $^9C_3$ ways

∴ Total number of selection = $^8C_4 \times {}^9C_3$

$$= \frac{8\times7\times6\times5}{1\times2\times3\times4}\times\frac{9\times8\times7}{1\times2\times3}$$

= 70 × 84 = 5880.

14. A decagon has 10 vertices

Join any two vertices in $^{10}C_2$ lines 10 lines will be sides.

∴ Number of diagonals = $^{10}C_2 - 10$

$$= \frac{10\times9}{1\times2} - 10$$

= 45 − 10 = 35

16. As the order of A, B and C is not to change they are to be treated identical in arrangement.

So, the required Number of ways = $\frac{7!}{3!}$.

$$= \frac{7\times6\times5\times4\times3\times2\times1}{3\times2\times1} = 840.$$

18. The number of ways to fill the three even places by 4 consonants = $^4P_3$.
After filling the even places, remaining places can be filled in $^4P_4$ ways.
So, the required number of words = $^4P_3 \times {}^4P_4$
$= 4! \times 4! = 24 \times 24 = 576$.

19. A couple and 6 guests can be arranged in $(7 - 1)!$ ways. But the two people forming the couple can be arranged among themselves in $2!$ ways.

$\therefore$ The required number of ways $= 6! \times 2!$
$= 720 \times 2 = 1440$.

20. Ten pearls of one colour can be arranged in 1/2 $(10 - 1)!$ ways. The number of arrangements of 10 pearls of the other colour in 10 places between the pearls of the first colour = $10!$.

$\therefore$ The required number of ways $= \frac{1}{2} \times 9! \times 10!$
$= 5 \times 9! \times 9! = 5(9!)^2$.

12. PROBABILITY

1. **Random Experiment:** If the result of an experiment is not certain and is any one of the several possible outcomes, the experiment is called a trial or a random experiment.
2. **Sample Space:** The set of all possible outcome of an experiment is called the sample space provided no two or more of these outcomes can occur simultaneously and exactly one of these outcomes must occur whenever the experiment is conducted.
3. **Events:** The outcomes of an experiment, *i.e.*, sample points of the sample space are usually known as simple events and any subset of the sample space 'S' is called an event.

   Thus throwing of a dice is an experiment, $S = \{1, 2, 3, 4, 5, 6\}$ is the sample space, $\{1\}$, ... $\{6\}$ are simple events and $\{1, 2\}$, etc., are events. The empty set ϕ is also an event as $\phi \subset S$ and it is called an impossible event. The sample space S is also a subset of S and so it is also an event. S represents the sure event, *i.e.*, certainty.
4. **Equally Likely Events:** A set of events is said to be equally likely if taking into consideration all the relevant factors there is no reason to expect one of them in preference to others.

   For example, when a fair coin is tossed, the occurrence of a tail or a head are equally likely.
5. **Exhaustive Events:** A set of events is said to be exhaustive if the performance of the experiment always results in the occurrence of atleast one of them.

   For example, if we throw a dice, then the events $A_1 = \{1, 2\}$, $A_2 = \{2, 3, 3\}$ are not exhaustive as we can get 5 as outcome of the experiment which is not the member of any of the events A_1 and A_2. If we consider the events $E_1 = \{1, 2, 3\}$ and $E_2 = \{2, 4, 5, 6\}$, then the set E_1, E_2, is exhaustive.
6. **Mutually Exclusive Events:** A set of events is said to be mutually exclusive if they have no point in common, *i.e.*, happening of one of them eliminates the happening of any of the remaining events. Thus E_1, E_2, E_3, ... are mutually exclusive iff $E_i \cap E_j = \phi$ for $i \neq E_1$ and E_2 are mutually exclusive.
7. **Complement of An Events:** The complement of an event A, denoted by $\overline{A}$, A' or A^c, is the set of all sample points of the space other than the sample points in A.

   e.g., In the experiment of throwing a fair dice, $S = \{1, 2, 3, 4, 5, 6\}$. If $A = \{1, 3, 5, 6\}$, then $\overline{A} = \{2, 4\}$

   Note that $A \cap \overline{A} = S$.
8. **Classical Definition of Probability:** If there are n exhaustive mutually exclusive and equally likely outcomes of an experiment and m of them are favourable to an event A, the probability of the happening of A is defined as the ratio m/n.

   Thus, denoting the probability of the happening of an event A by p, we have $p = m/n$.

   Clearly p is a positive number not greater than unity, so that $0 \leq p \leq 1$.

   Since the number of cases in which the event A will not happen is $n - m$, the probability q that the event will not happen is given by

   $$q = \frac{(n-m)}{n} = 1 - \frac{m}{n} = 1 - p. \therefore p + q = 1$$

If probability of happening of an event A is 1, then A is certain event and if probability of happening of an event A is 0, then A is impossible event.

9. Odds in Favour and Odds against an Event: As a result of an experiment if a of the outcomes are favourable to an event E and b of the outcomes are against it, then we say that odds are a to b in favour of E or odds are b to a against E.

Thus, odds in favour of an event E

$$= \frac{\text{number of favourable cases}}{\text{number of unfavourable cases}}.$$

Similarly, odds against an event E

$$= \frac{\text{number of unfavourable cases}}{\text{number of favourable cases}}.$$

If odds in favour of an event are $a : b$ then the probability of the occurrence of that event is $\frac{a}{a+b}$ and the probability of the non-occurrence of that event is $\frac{b}{(a+b)}$.

Addition Theorem:

(*a*) If 'A' and 'B' are any two events in a sample space S, then $P(A \cup B) = P(A) + P(B) - P(A \cap B)$.

(*b*) If 'A' and 'B' are mutually exclusive then $P(A \cap B) = 0$ so that $P(A \cup B) = P(A) + P(B)$.

(*c*) If A is any event in S, then $P(A') = 1 - P(A)$.

Total Probability Theorem:

The probability that one of several mutually exclusive events $A_1, A_2, ..., A_n$ will happen, is the sum of the probabilities of the separate events. In symbol,

$$P(A_1 + A_2 + ... + A_n) = P(A_1) + P(A_2) + ... + P(A_n).$$

Conditional Probability:

The probability of B under the assumption that A has occurred is called the conditional probability of B under the condition that the event A has taken place and is denoted by P(B/A). P(B/A) is read as "probability at the event B given A^B."

Conditional Probability Theorem:

If A and B are any two events in the sample space S, the conditional probability of B relative to A is given by $P(B/A) = \frac{P(B \cap A)}{P(A)} = \frac{n(B \cap A)}{n(A)}, A \neq \phi.$

Some Important Remarks about Coins, Dice and Playing Cards:

(*a*) **Coins:** A coin has a head side and a tail side. If an experiment consist of more than a coin, coins are considered to be distinct if not otherwise stated.

(*b*) **Dice:** A die (cubical) has six faces marked 1, 2, 3, 4, 5, 6. We may have tetrahedral (having four faces 1, 2, 3, 4) or pentagonal (having five faces 1, 2, 3, 4, 5) die. As in the case of dice, if we have more than one die, all dice are considered to be distinct if not otherwise stated.

(*c*) **Playing Cards:** A pack of playing cards usually contain 52 cards.

There are 4 suits (spade, heart, diamond and club) each having 13 cards. There are two colours — red (heart and diamond) and black (spade and club) each having 26 cards.

In thirteen cards of each suit, there are 3 face cards namely king, queen and jack, so there are in all 12 face cards (4 kings, 4 queens and 4 jacks).

Also there are 16 honours cards, 4 of each suit namely ace, king, queen and jack.

SOLVED EXAMPLES

Example 1: A bag contains 7 Red balls, 4 Green balls and 5 Yellow balls. What is the probability that 3 balls drawn at random are either Green or Yellow?

Solution: Total ways $= {}^{16}C_3 = \frac{\lfloor 16}{\lfloor 13 \lfloor 3} = 560$

Favourable ways = $^4C_3 \times {^5C_3} = \frac{\lfloor 4}{\lfloor 3 \lfloor 1} \times \frac{\lfloor 5}{\lfloor 3 \lfloor 2}$

$= 4 \times 10 = 40.$

$\therefore$ Reqd. Probability $= \frac{40}{560} = \frac{1}{14}.$

Example 2: A basket contains three Red and four Green balls. If four balls are drawn at random from the basket, what is the probability that two are Red and two are Green?

Solution: Reqd. Probability $= \frac{^3C_2 \times {^4C_2}}{^7C_4} = \frac{3 \times 6}{35}$

$= \frac{18}{35}.$

Example 3: A box contains 8 Red, 16 Blue, 4 Yellow and 12 Black bolls. Two balls are picked up randomly. What is the chance that both are Red?

Solution: Total results $= {^{40}C_2} = \frac{40 \times 39}{2} = 780$

and favourable results $= {^8C_2} = \frac{\lfloor 8}{\lfloor 2 \lfloor 6} = \frac{8 \times 7}{2}$

$= 28.$

$\therefore$ Required probability $= \frac{28}{780} = \frac{7}{195}.$

Example 4: A bag contains 8 Red, 16 Blue, 12 Black and 4 Yellow marbles. One marbles is picked up randomly. What is the probability that it is not Blue?

Solution: Total results $= {^{40}C_1} = 40$

Favourable results when it is Blue $= {^{16}C_1} = 16.$

$\therefore$ Favourable results when it is not Blue

$= 40 - 16 = 24$

$\therefore$ Reqd. probability $= \frac{24}{40} = 0.6.$

MULTIPLE CHOICE QUESTIONS

Directions (Qs. 1 to 3) : *Study the information carefully to answer the questions that follow.*

A bucket contains 8 Red, 3 Blue and 5 Green marbles.

1. If 4 marbles are drawn at random, what is the probability that 2 are Red and 2 are Blue?

A. $\frac{11}{16}$ B. $\frac{3}{16}$

C. $\frac{11}{72}$ D. $\frac{3}{65}$

2. If 2 marbles are drawn at random, what is the probability that both are Green?

A. $\frac{1}{8}$ B. $\frac{5}{16}$

C. $\frac{2}{7}$ D. None of these

3. If 3 marbles are drawn at random, what is the probability that none is Red?

A. $\frac{3}{8}$ B. $\frac{1}{16}$

C. $\frac{1}{10}$ D. None of these

Directions (Qs. 4 to 5) : *Study the information and answer the questions that follow.*

A basket contains 3 Red balls, 5 Blue balls and 2 Green balls.

4. If three balls are drawn at random, what is the probability that none is Blue?

A. $\frac{1}{6}$ B. $\frac{1}{12}$

C. $\frac{1}{5}$ D. $\frac{3}{10}$

5. If four balls are drawn at random, what is the probability that at least one is Green?

A. $\frac{2}{3}$ B. $\frac{1}{2}$

C. $\frac{1}{3}$ D. $\frac{2}{5}$

6. If two balls are drawn at random, what is the probability that both are Red?

A. $\frac{1}{5}$ B. $\frac{3}{10}$

C. $\frac{3}{5}$ D. $\frac{1}{15}$

7. A dice is thrown once. Find the probability of getting a number greater than 3.

A. $\frac{2}{3}$ B. $\frac{1}{3}$

C. $\frac{1}{2}$ D. $\frac{3}{2}$

8. A bag contains 5 Red balls, 8 White balls, 4 Green balls and 7 Black balls. If one ball is drawn at random, find the probability that it is Black.

A. $\frac{7}{24}$ B. $\frac{5}{24}$

C. $\frac{5}{6}$ D. $\frac{1}{4}$

9. Find the probability that a number selected from the numbers 1 to 25 is not a prime number when each of the given number is equally to be selected.

A. $\frac{9}{25}$ B. $\frac{16}{25}$

C. $\frac{21}{25}$ D. $\frac{14}{25}$

10. A bag contains 3 Red balls and 5 Black balls. A ball is drawn at random from the bag. What is the probability that the ball drawn is not Red?

A. $\frac{3}{8}$ B. $\frac{5}{8}$

C. $\frac{1}{8}$ D. $\frac{7}{8}$

11. A die is thrown once. Find the probability of getting an odd number.

A. $\frac{1}{2}$ B. $\frac{3}{2}$

C. $\frac{2}{3}$ D. $\frac{1}{3}$

12. A letter is chosen at random from the word REED the probability of choosing an E is–

A. $\frac{3}{4}$ B. $\frac{1}{2}$

C. $\frac{1}{4}$ D. $\frac{2}{3}$

13. A card is drawn at random from a well-shuffled deck of playing cards. Find the probability that the card drawn is a card of spade or an ace.

A. $\frac{11}{13}$ B. $\frac{1}{26}$

C. $\frac{4}{13}$ D. $\frac{9}{13}$

14. If a letter is chosen at random from the word TRIANGLE.
What is the probability that it a vowel?

A. $\frac{3}{8}$ B. $\frac{5}{8}$

C. $\frac{1}{4}$ D. $\frac{3}{4}$

15. What is the chance that a leap year, selected at random, will contain 53 Sundays?

A. $\frac{52}{365}$ B. $\frac{52}{366}$

C. $\frac{2}{7}$ D. $\frac{5}{7}$

16. In a book of 300 pages, if a page is opened at random; find the probability that the sum of the digits in its number is 10.

A. $\frac{8}{15}$ B. $\frac{9}{15}$

C. $\frac{7}{75}$ D. $\frac{14}{15}$

17. A die is thrown once. Find the probability of getting an even number.

A. $\frac{1}{3}$ B. $\frac{1}{2}$

C. $\frac{1}{4}$ D. $\frac{1}{6}$

18. Two friends were born in the year 2000. What is the probability that they have the same birthday?

A. $\frac{1}{500}$ B. $\frac{1}{730}$

C. $\frac{1}{365}$ D. $\frac{1}{366}$

19. A number is chosen at random from among the first 30 natural numbers. The probability of the number chosen being prime is :

A. $\frac{1}{3}$ B. $\frac{3}{10}$

C. $\frac{1}{30}$ D. $\frac{11}{30}$

20. The probability that a number selected at random from the set of numbers {1, 2, 3, 4, ..., 100} is a cube is :

A. $\frac{1}{25}$ B. $\frac{2}{25}$

C. $\frac{3}{25}$ D. $\frac{4}{25}$

ANSWERS

1	2	3	4	5	6	7	8	9	10
D	D	D	B	C	D	C	A	B	B
11	**12**	**13**	**14**	**15**	**16**	**17**	**18**	**19**	**20**
A	B	C	A	C	C	B	D	A	A

SOME SELECTED EXPLANATORY ANSWERS

1. Total number of ways = ${}^{16}C_4 = \frac{\lfloor 16}{\lfloor 12 \lfloor 4}$

$= 1820$

And favourable number of ways = ${}^{8}C_2 \times {}^{3}C_2$

$= \frac{\lfloor 8}{\lfloor 6 \lfloor 2} \times \frac{\lfloor 3}{\lfloor 1 \lfloor 2} = 84$

$\therefore$ Reqd. probability $= \frac{84}{1820} = \frac{3}{65}$.

2. Total number of ways = ${}^{16}C_2 = \frac{\lfloor 16}{\lfloor 14 \lfloor 2} = 120$

And favourable number of ways = ${}^{5}C_2$

$= \frac{\lfloor 5}{\lfloor 3 \lfloor 2} = 10$

$\therefore$ Reqd. probability $= \frac{10}{120} = \frac{1}{12}$.

3. Total number of ways = ${}^{16}C_3 = \frac{\lfloor 16}{\lfloor 13 \lfloor 3} = 560$

Total number of ways when all the marbles are Red

$= {}^{8}C_3 = \frac{\lfloor 8}{\lfloor 5 \lfloor 3} = 56$

$\therefore$ Probability when all the three are Red

$= \frac{56}{560} = \frac{1}{10}$

$\therefore$ And probability when none is Red $= 1 - \frac{1}{10}$

$= \frac{9}{10}$.

4. Probability that none is blue

$= \frac{{}^{5}C_3}{{}^{10}C_3} = \frac{10}{120} = \frac{1}{12}$

5. Probability that none is green

$= \frac{{}^{8}C_4}{{}^{10}C_4} = \frac{70}{210} = \frac{1}{3}$

$\therefore$ Probability that at least one is green

$= 1 - \frac{1}{3} = \frac{2}{3}$

6. Probability that both are red

$= \frac{{}^{3}C_2}{{}^{10}C_2} = \frac{3}{45} = \frac{1}{15}$

7. Sample space S = {1, 2, 3, 4, 5, 6} ; $n(S) = 6$

Let A = "getting a number grater than 3" then

$$A = \{4, 5, 6\} ; n(A) = 3$$

$$P(A) = \frac{n(A)}{n(S)} = \frac{3}{6} = \frac{1}{2}.$$

9. We are given numbers from 1 to 25.
$n(S) = 25$.
Prime numbers from 1 to 25 are 2, 3, 5, 7, 11, 13, 17, 19, 23.
These are 9 prime numbers.
Let E denote the event 'Number drawn is not prime'.

$\therefore \quad n(E) = 25 - 9 = 16$

$$p(E) = \frac{n(E)}{n(S)} = \frac{16}{25}.$$

10. Total number of balls in the bag = 3 + 5 = 8
Let E denote the event 'ball drawn is red'.

$\therefore \quad n(E) = 3$ and $n(S) = 8$.

(*i*) $\quad p(E) = \frac{n(E)}{n(S)} = \frac{3}{8}$

(*ii*) $\quad p(\text{not red}) = p(\bar{E})$

$$= 1 - p(E) = 1 - \frac{3}{8} = \frac{5}{8}.$$

11. Sample $S = \{1, 2, 3, 4, 5, 6\}$; $n(S) = 6$
Let F denote the event 'getting an odd number'.

$$F = \{1, 3, 5\} ; n(S) = 3$$

$$\therefore \quad P(F) = \frac{n(F)}{n(S)} = \frac{3}{6} = \frac{1}{2}.$$

12. The sample space is $\{R, E_1, E_2, D\}$
There are 2 ways to choose the letter E from the four letters

$$\therefore \quad P(E) = \frac{2}{4} = \frac{1}{2}.$$

13. There are 52 cards in a deck of 52 playing cards.
There are 13 spades and 4 aces in 52 playing cards. Out of 13 spades there is one ace.
∴ Favourable no ways for the card drawn to be spade or an ace = 13 spades + 3 aces = 16.

$$\therefore P(\text{a card of spade or an ace}) = \frac{16}{52} = \frac{4}{13}.$$

14. Since there are 3 vowels out of a total of 8 letters, the probability of choosing a vowel is 3/8.

15. A Leap year has 366 days. In a leap year, here are 52 complete weeks (52 Sundays) and 2 days over these two days can be as follows. Sunday and Monday, Monday and Tuesday, Tuesday and Wednesday, Wednesday and Thursday, Thursday and Friday, Friday and Saturday, Saturday and Sunday.
Out of these 7 possibilities, only two (Saturday and Sunday; Sunday and Monday) are favourable for having 53 Sundays)

$$\text{Required chance} = \frac{2}{7}.$$

17. A die is thrown once. Its sample space is

$$S = \{1, 2, 3, 4, 5, 6\}, n(S) = 6$$

Let E : an even number, then $E = \{2, 4, 6\}$
Number of favourable cases = $n(E) = 3$

$$\therefore \quad P(E) = \frac{n(E)}{n(S)} = \frac{3}{6} = \frac{1}{2}.$$

18. Year 2000 is a leap year. There are 366 days in the year 2000. Total number of cases in which two friends can be born on the same day are 366.
Out of 366 days, number of favourable ways in which two friends have the same birthday = 1

$$\therefore \text{Required probability} = \frac{1}{366}.$$

19. The prime numbers from first 30 natural numbers are 2, 3, 5, 7, 11, 13, 17, 19, 23, 29.
We find that there are 10 prime numbers from 1 to 30.
∴ Probability that the number chosen being prime is $= \frac{10}{30} = \frac{1}{3}$.

20. From the natural numbers 1 to 100 the four number 1, 8, 27 and 64 are cubes

$$\therefore \text{Required Probability} = \frac{4}{100} = \frac{1}{25}.$$

GENERAL INTELLIGENCE & REASONING

1. LETTER SERIES

In letter series, the letters follow a definite order. The given series of letters can be in natural order or in reverse order or combination of both. The letters may be skipped or repeated or consecutive. The given series may be single or may even comprise of two different series merged at alternate positions. While attempting questions on letter series one should note the pattern of alphabet series.

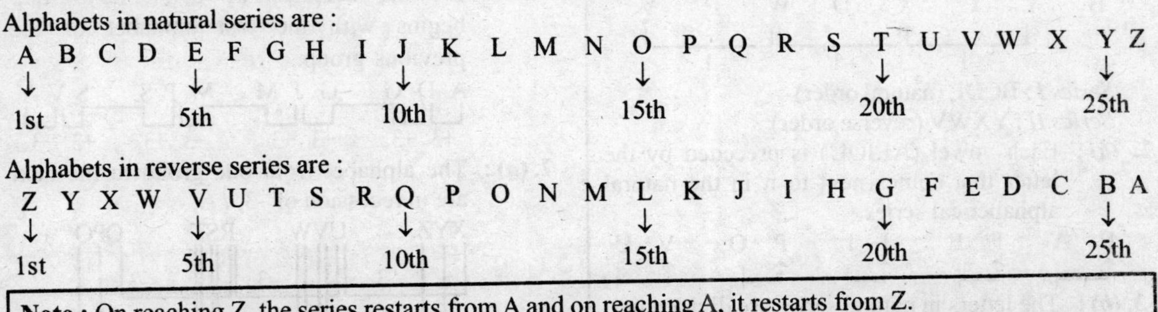

Note : On reaching Z, the series restarts from A and on reaching A, it restarts from Z.

EXERCISE

Directions : *In each of the following series determine the order of the letters. Then from the given options select the one which will complete the given series.*

1. B Y C X D W E ?
(*a*) S (*b*) T
(*c*) U (*d*) V

2. B A F E J I P O ? U
(*a*) V (*b*) T
(*c*) S (*d*) Q

3. B A D C ? H G J I
(*a*) EF (*b*) FE
(*c*) FG (*d*) DF

4. ADG, XVT, BEH, WUS, ?
(*a*) VTR (*b*) CFI
(*c*) DFJ (*d*) STU

5. GMSY, IOUA, KQWC, ?
(*a*) MSYE (*b*) NSYE
(*c*) MTYE (*d*) MSYF

6. ADG, GJM, ?, SVY
(*a*) MPS (*b*) MQR
(*c*) MQS (*d*) SPM

7. XYZ, UVW, ?, OPQ
(*a*) RST (*b*) STU
(*c*) QRS (*d*) TUV

8. JOBS, KMEO, LKHK, ?, NGNC
(*a*) MJLH (*b*) LIKG
(*c*) MIKG (*d*) MNGM

9. AZ, GT, MN, ?, YB
(*a*) KF (*b*) TS
(*c*) RX (*d*) SH

10. BMY, DNW, FOU, ?
(*a*) HPT (*b*) HPS
(*c*) HQS (*d*) GPS

11. AZ, CX, EV, ?
(*a*) HU (*b*) GS
(*c*) GT (*d*) HT

12. DMP, FLN, HKL, JJJ, ?
(*a*) MIH (*b*) III
(*c*) LIH (*d*) MII

13. ECA, JHF, OMK, ?, YWU
(*a*) TRP (*b*) LNP
(*c*) QPN (*d*) RPT

14. ABP, CDQ, EFR, ?
(*a*) GHS (*b*) HGS
(*c*) GHR (*d*) GHT

15. BEH, KNQ, TWZ, ?
(*a*) IJL (*b*) BDF
(*c*) CFI (*d*) ADG

EXPLANATORY ANSWERS

1. (*d*) : There are two alternate series.

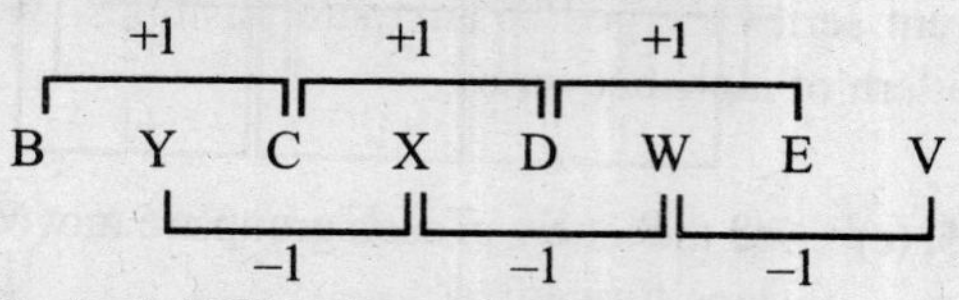

Series I : BCDE (natural order)
Series II : YXWV (reverse order)

2. (*a*) : Each vowel (AEIOU) is preceded by the letter that comes next to it in the natural alphabetical series.

3. (*b*) : The letters in natural series are divided into sections of two letters each. The letters in each section are written backward.
BA DC FE HG JI

4. (*b*) : There are two alternate series.

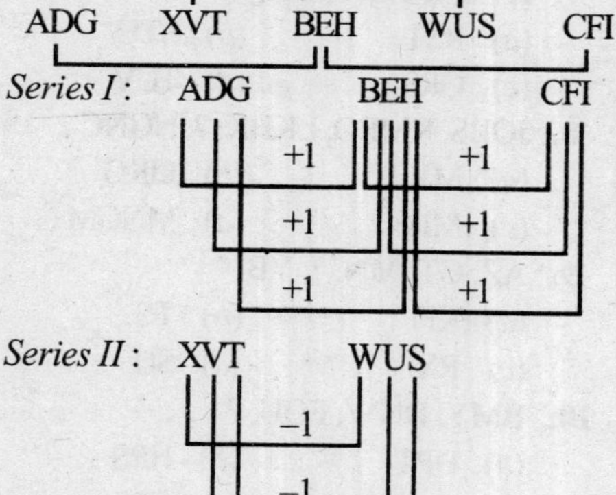

5. (*a*) : The series is formed by moving each letter two steps forward from one group to the next.

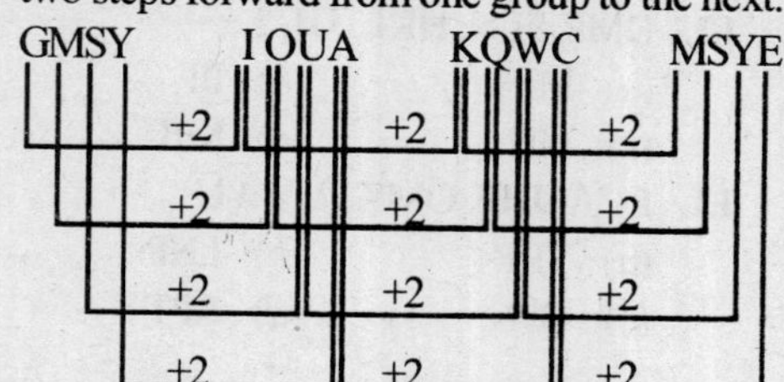

(The series restarts from A on reaching Z)

6. (*a*) : In each group of three letters the alphabet is in the succession of +3. The next group begins with the last alphabet of the previous group.

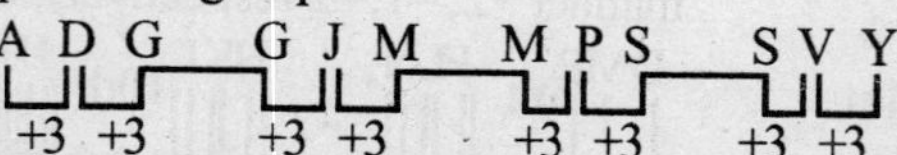

7. (*a*) : The alphabet from one group to the next are in recession of –3, *i.e.*,

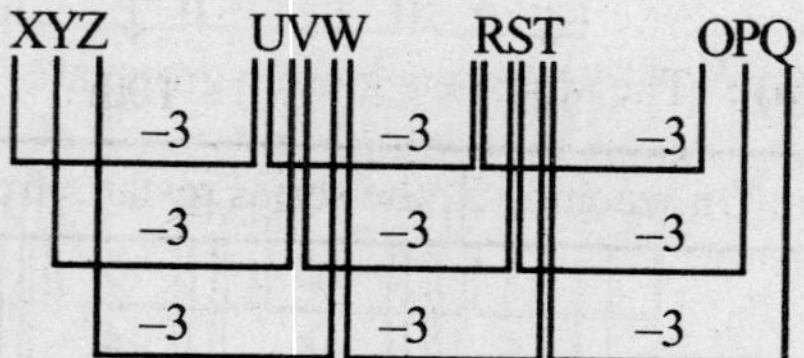

8. (*c*) : The alphabets in each group follow the pattern +1, –2, +3 and –4 respectively from one group to the next group.

9. (*d*) : The letters in one group correspond to the letters in the next group in the manner +6, –6 respectively, *i.e.*,

AZ GT MN SH YB
+6 +6 +6 +6
–6 –6 –6 –6

10. (*b*) : The letters in one group correspond to the letters in the next group in the manner +2, +1, -2 respectively, *i.e.*,

BMY DNW FOU HPS
+2 +2 +2
+1 +1 +1
–2 –2 –2

11. (*c*) : The letters in each group correspond to the letters in the next group in the manner +2, –2 respectively, *i.e.,*

AZ CX EV GT

+2 +2 +2

–2 –2 –2

12. (*c*) : The alphabets in each group correspond to the alphabets in the next group in the manner +2, –1, –2 respectively, *i.e.,*

13. (*a*) : The alphabets in each group are moved five steps forward, *i.e.,*

ECA JHF OMK TRP YWU

+5 +5 +5 +5

+5 +5 +5 +5

+5 +5 +5 +5

14. (*a*) : The letters in one group correspond to the letters in the next group in the manner +2, +2, +1 respectively, *i.e.,*

ABP CDQ EFR GHS

+2 +2 +2

+2 +2 +2

+1 +1 +1

15. (*c*) : All the letters in each group are moved nine steps forward.

BEH KNQ TWZ CFI

+9 +9 +9

+9 +9 +9

+9 +9 +9

5. WRONG NUMBER SERIES

In this type of series, the given series may be complete but what needs to be identified is the number in the given completed series which is disturbing the sequential pattern of that series and does not fit in with the relationship shared between the other numbers.

EXERCISE

Directions : *In the given series find the number which is wrong.*

1. 5, 25, 120, 625, 3125, 15625
(*a*) 15625 (*b*) 625
(*c*) 120 (*d*) 5

2. 4, 8, 11, 22, 18, 36, 24, 50
(*a*) 8 (*b*) 22
(*c*) 36 (*d*) 24

3. 2, 4, 12, 24, 72, 142, 432
(*a*) 432 (*b*) 12
(*c*) 142 (*d*) 72

4. 2, 3, 4, 4, 6, 8, 9, 12, 16
(*a*) 3 (*b*) 9
(*c*) 6 (*d*) 12

5. 97, 91, 86, 83, 79, 77, 76, 76
(*a*) 86 (*b*) 76
(*c*) 91 (*d*) 83

6. 7, 11, 11, 9, 15, 7, 19, 5, 23, 1
(*a*) 5 (*b*) 7
(*c*) 1 (*d*) 9

7. 3, 7, 12, 28, 48, 118, 192, 448
(*a*) 12 (*b*) 118
(*c*) 28 (*d*) 7

8. 10, 100, 1100, 11000, 111000, 1210000
(*a*) 1210000 (*b*) 11000
(*c*) 100 (*d*) 111000

9. 24576, 6144, 1536, 386, 96, 24
(*a*) 386 (*b*) 6144
(*c*) 96 (*d*) 1536

10. 11, 13, 15, 17, 19, 23, 29, 31, 37
(*a*) 13 (*b*) 23
(*c*) 15 (*d*) 31

11. 36, 43, 49, 54, 60, 61, 63, 64
(*a*) 60 (*b*) 63
(*c*) 54 (*d*) 43

12. 3, 10, 41, 206, 1236, 8660
(*a*) 10 (*b*) 41
(*c*) 206 (*d*) 1236

13. 17, 25, 37, 50, 65, 82, 101
(*a*) 25 (*b*) 17
(*c*) 101 (*d*) 65

14. 12, 20, 38, 42, 56, 72
(*a*) 20 (*b*) 38
(*c*) 56 (*d*) 72

15. 5, 6, 11, 22, 42, 88, 176
(*a*) 5 (*b*) 42
(*c*) 176 (*d*) 11

EXPLANATORY ANSWERS

1. (*c*) : The numbers in the series are multiplied by 5 to get the next number.
∴ 125 should be in place of 120.

2. (*d*) : Two numbers form a pair. The first number increases by 7 for the next pair and the second number is the double of first number.

4 8 (×2) 11 22 (×2) 18 36 (×2) 25 50 (×2)
4 → 11 → 18 → 25 (+7, +7, +7)

∴ 25 should be in place of 24.

3. (c) : There are two alternate series and in each series, the numbers are multiplied by 6 to get the next number.

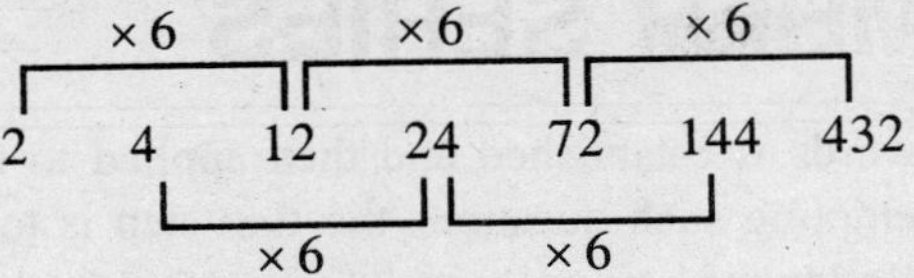

∴ 144 should be in place of 142.

4. (b) : There are three alternate series and in each series, the numbers are multiplied by 2 to get the next number.

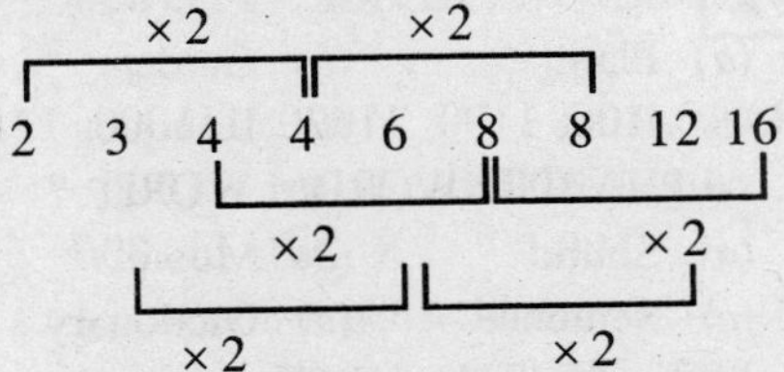

Series I : 2, 4, 8 *Series II* : 3, 6, 12
Series III : 4, 8, 16

∴ 8 should be in place of 9.

5. (d) : The difference between the consecutive numbers in the series decreases by 1 at each step.

97 91 86 82 79 77 76 76

−6 −5 −4 −3 −2 −1 −0

∴ 82 should be in place of 83.

6. (c) : There are two alternate series :

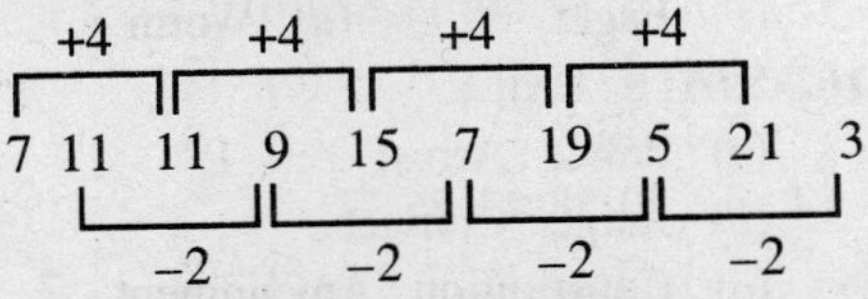

Series I : 7, 11, 15, 19, 23 (addition of 4)
Series II : 11, 9, 7, 5, 3 (subtraction of 2)

∴ 3 should be in place of 1.

7. (b) : There are two alternate series and in each series, the numbers are multiplied by 4 to get the next number.

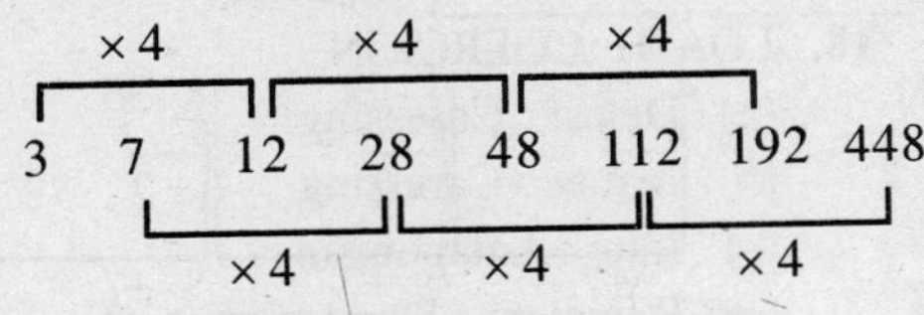

∴ 112 should be in place of 118.

8. (d) : The numbers in this series are multiplied by 10 and 11 alternately is, *i.e.*, × 10, × 11.

10 100 1100 11000 121000 1210000

× 10 × 11 × 10 × 11 × 10

∴ 121000 should be in place of 111000.

9. (a) : The numbers in this series are divided by 4 to get the next number.

24576 6144 1536 384 96 24

÷ 4 ÷ 4 ÷ 4 ÷ 4 ÷ 4

∴ 384 should be in place of 386.

10. (c) : The series comprises of prime numbers in increasing order. Only 15 is an exception.

11. (a) : The difference between two consecutive numbers is decreasing by 1 at each step.

36 43 49 54 58 61 63 64

+7 +6 +5 +4 +3 +2 +1

∴ 58 should be in place of 60.

12. (d) : The sequence followed in this series is :
$3 \times 3 + 1 = 10$, $10 \times 4 + 1 = 41$
$41 \times 5 + 1 = 206$, $206 \times 6 + 1 = 1237$; and
$1237 \times 7 + 1 = 8660$

∴ 1237 should be in place of 1236.

13. (a) : The numbers in the series are 1 plus the squares of numbers in natural order starting from 4.

17 26 37 50 65 82 101
↓ ↓ ↓ ↓ ↓ ↓ ↓
4^2+1 5^2+1 6^2+1 7^2+1 8^2+1 9^2+1 10^2+1

∴ 26 should be in place of 25.

14. (b) : The sequence followed in this series is :
$3 \times 4 = 12$, $4 \times 5 = 20$, $5 \times 6 = 30$,
$6 \times 7 = 42$, $7 \times 8 = 56$, $8 \times 9 = 72$

∴ 30 should be in place of 38.

15. (b) : The numbers in the series are the sum of all the numbers preceding them.

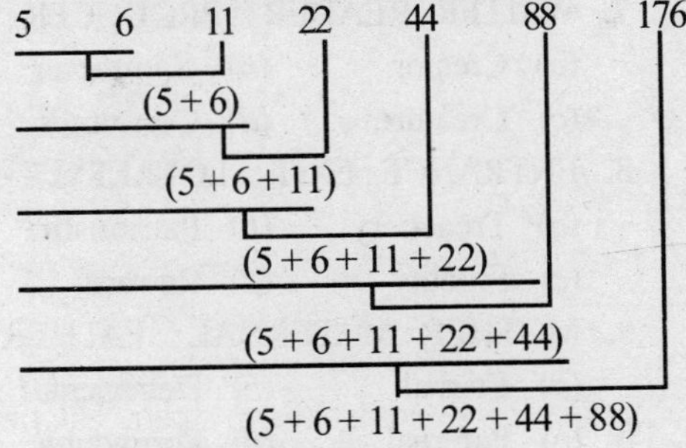

∴ 44 should be in place of 42.

6. WORD ANALOGY

In Analogy Tests, the relationship between two given words is established and then applied to the other words. The type of relationship may vary, so while attempting such questions the first step is to identify the type of relationship, which can be any one of the following.

EXERCISE

Directions : *In the questions given below one term is missing. Based on the relationship of the two given words find the missing term from the given options.*

1. HUNGER : FOOD : : THIRST : ?
(*a*) Water (*b*) Drink
(*c*) Tea (*d*) Coffee

2. HUNTER : GUN : : WRITER : ?
(*a*) Book (*b*) Pen
(*c*) Poem (*d*) Page

3. WOOL : SHEEP : : SILK : ?
(*a*) Saree (*b*) String
(*c*) Silkworm (*d*) Moth

4. FOOD : STOMACH : : FUEL : ?
(*a*) Engine (*b*) Automobile
(*c*) Rail (*d*) Aeroplane

5. WATER : SAND : : OCEAN : ?
(*a*) Island (*b*) River
(*c*) Desert (*d*) Waves

6. ADULT : BABY : : FLOWER : ?
(*a*) Seed (*b*) Bud
(*c*) Fruit (*d*) Butterfly

7. WRITER : READER : : PRODUCER : ?
(*a*) Creator (*b*) Contractor
(*c*) Creature (*d*) Consumer

8. ENTRANCE : EXIT : : LOYALTY : ?
(*a*) Treachery (*b*) Patriotism
(*c*) Fidelity (*d*) Reward

9. MOTHER : MATERNAL : : FATHER : ?
(*a*) Eternal (*b*) Detrimental
(*c*) Paternal (*d*) Formidable

10. PEARL : NECKLACE : : FLOWER : ?
(*a*) Plant (*b*) Garden
(*c*) Petal (*d*) Bouquet

11. ALPHABET : WORD : : WORD : ?
(*a*) Sound (*b*) Music
(*c*) Sentence (*d*) Dictionary

12. LIFE : DEATH : : HOPE : ?
(*a*) Cry (*b*) Pain
(*c*) Despair (*d*) Sad

13. GOOD : BAD : : VIRTUE : ?
(*a*) Blame (*b*) Sin
(*c*) Despair (*d*) Vice

14. BIRD : FLY : : SNAKE : ?
(*a*) Timid (*b*) Clatter
(*c*) Crawl (*d*) Hole

15. CAT : MOUSE : : BIRD : ?
(*a*) Cage (*b*) Trap
(*c*) Eagle (*d*) Worm

16. STATE : EXILE
(*a*) Police : Arrest
(*b*) Judge : Convict
(*c*) Constitution : Amendment
(*d*) Church : Excommunicate

17. CAPRICIOUSNESS : RELIABILITY
(*a*) Extemporaneous : Predictability
(*b*) Unreliable : Inhuman
(*c*) Tenacious : Practicality
(*d*) Arbitrary : Whimsical

18. LOATH : COERCION
(*a*) Detest : Caressing
(*b*) Irritate : Caressing
(*c*) Irate : Antagonism
(*d*) Reluctant : Persuasion

19. SCALES : FISH
(*a*) Lady : Dress (*b*) Tree : Leaves
(*c*) Bird : Feather (*d*) Skin : Man

20. TREE : SAPLING
(*a*) Hut : Mansion
(*b*) Giant : Dwarf
(*c*) Horse : Foal
(*d*) Ant : Elephant

21. CHALK : BLACKBOARD
(*a*) Door : Handle
(*b*) Table : Chair
(*c*) Ink : Paper
(*d*) Type : Paint

22. PRIMEVAL : MEDIEVAL
(*a*) Dinosaur : Dragon
(*b*) Gorilla : Soldier
(*c*) Evolution : Revelation
(*d*) Thorn : Rose

23. TRILOGY : NOVEL
(*a*) Rice : Husk
(*b*) Milk : Cream
(*c*) Fabric : Weaving
(*d*) Serial : Episode

24. PEDANT : ERUDITION
(*a*) Prude : Modesty
(*b*) Blunt : Politician
(*c*) Diplomats : Tactless
(*d*) Enemy : Friendly

25. FURY : IRE
(*a*) Convulsion : Spasm
(*b*) Amusement : Happiness
(*c*) Joke : Laugh
(*d*) Dispassion : Emotion

EXPLANATORY ANSWERS

1. (*a*) : Hunger is satiated by food, thirst by water.

2. (*b*) : Weapon of a hunter is a gun, weapon of a writer is a pen.

3. (*c*) : Wool is obtained from sheep, silk is obtained from silkworm.

4. (*a*) : Food is consumed in stomach, fuel is consumed in engine.

5. (*c*) : The related words are near opposites.

6. (*b*) : The youngone of an adult is a baby and that of a flower is a bud.

7. (*d*) : A writer aims to please the readers by his writings, a producer aims to please the consumers by his products.

8. (*a*) : The related words are opposites.

9. (*c*) : Relations on the mother's side are maternal and on the father's side paternal.

10. (*d*) : Many pearls make a necklace, many flowers make a bouquet.

11. (*c*) : More than one alphabet make a word, more than one word make a sentence.

12. (*c*) : The related words are opposites.

13. (*d*) : The related words are opposites.

14. (*c*) : Birds fly, snakes crawl.

15. (*d*) : Cat chases the mouse, bird chases the worm.

16. (*d*) : Punishment of leaving the State is exile, punishment of leaving the Church is excommunication.

17. (*c*) : The related words are antonyms.

18. (*d*) : Loathing is the result of constant coersion, reluctance is the result of constant persuasion.

19. (*d*) : Covering of the fish is scales, covering of man is skin.

20. (*c*) : Young tree is a sapling, young horse is a foal.

21. (*c*) : Chalk is used to write on blackboard, ink is used to write on paper.

22. (*a*) : The related words represent almost the same time period and answer option represents almost the same sized creatures.

23. (*d*) : Trilogy is section of a novel, episode is a section of a serial.

24. (*a*) : The related words are synonyms.

25. (*b*) : Fury causes ire, amusement causes happiness.

7. NUMBER ANALOGY

In number analogy also, the relationship between the given numbers is detected and then applied to the second part to find the missing numbers. This relationship between the numbers can be based on any of the following patterns : *(i)* numbers can be odd/even/prime numbers; *(ii)* numbers can be multiples of one number; *(iii)* numbers can be squares/cubes of different numbers; *(iv)* some numbers can be added to/ subtracted from/multiplied to/divided into the first number to get the second number; *(v)* the second number can be the sum/product/difference of the digits of first number; and *(vi)* combinations of any mathematical calculations given above can apply to the relationship between the two given numbers.

EXERCISE

Directions : *In the following questions, select the number from the given options which follows the same relationship as shared between the first two numbers.*

1. 1 : 11 : : 2 : ?
(*a*) 20 (*b*) 22
(*c*) 24 (*d*) 44

2. $\frac{1}{7} : \frac{1}{14} :: \frac{1}{9} : ?$
(*a*) $\frac{1}{88}$ (*b*) $\frac{1}{80}$
(*c*) $\frac{1}{81}$ (*d*) $\frac{1}{18}$

3. 0.16 : 0.0016 : : 1.02 : ?
(*a*) 10.20 (*b*) 0.102
(*c*) 0.0102 (*d*) 1.020

4. 663 : 884 : : 221 : ?
(*a*) 332 (*b*) 554
(*c*) 773 (*d*) 442

5. 16 : 0.16 : : ?
(*a*) 2 : 0.02 (*b*) 7 : 0.007
(*c*) 1.3 : 0.13 (*d*) 0.01 : 0.001

6. $3 : \frac{1}{3} :: ?$
(*a*) 6 : 12 (*b*) 5 : 2/15
(*c*) 8 : 1/8 (*d*) 9 : 27

7. 65 : 13 : : 180 : ?
(*a*) 93 (*b*) 36
(*c*) 133 (*d*) 102

8. 125 : 27 : : 343 : ?
(*a*) 729 (*b*) 64
(*c*) 216 (*d*) 512

9. 357 : 73 : : ?
(*a*) 429 : 94
(*b*) 201 : 21
(*c*) 138 : 38
(*d*) 93 : 39

10. 731 : 902 : : 655 : ?
(*a*) 646 (*b*) 800
(*c*) 793 (*d*) 556

11. 162 : 9 : : 310 : ?
(*a*) 33 (*b*) 27
(*c*) 16 (*d*) 4

12. 13 : 17 : : 15 : ?
(*a*) 19 (*b*) 11
(*c*) 21 (*d*) 16

13. 225 : 15 : : 256 : ?
(*a*) 26 (*b*) 16
(*c*) 20 (*d*) 28

14. 46 : 48 : : 54 : ?
(*a*) 59 (*b*) 40
(*c*) 67 (*d*) 62

15. 33 : 36 : : 21 : ?
(*a*) 9 (*b*) 18
(*c*) 25 (*d*) 32

EXPLANATORY ANSWERS

1. *(b)* : The first number is repeated to obtain the second number.

2. *(d)* : The first fraction is multiplied by half to obtain the second fraction.

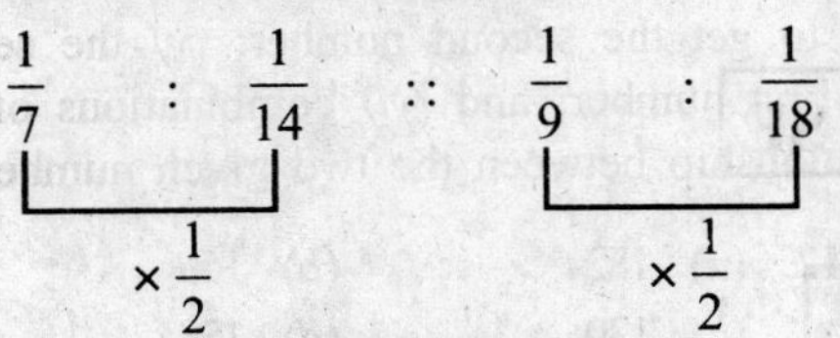

3. *(c)* : The decimals are divided by 100.

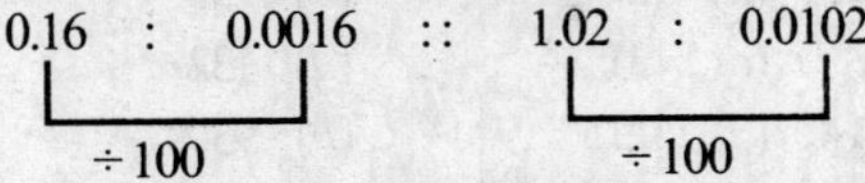

4. *(d)* : The digits at tens and hundreds place is same but the digit at the units place is half the other identical digits.

66<u>3</u> : 88<u>4</u> :: 22<u>1</u> : 44<u>2</u>

5. *(a)* : Of the two related numbers, the second number is the result of first number divided by 100.

16 : 0.16 :: 2 : 0.02
(÷ 100) (÷ 100)

6. *(c)* : Of the two related numbers, the second number is the part fraction of the first number, *i.e.* 3 is related to one-third $\left(\frac{1}{3}\right)$.

Similarly, 8 will be related to one-eighth $\left(\frac{1}{8}\right)$.

7. *(b)* : The first number is divided by 5 to get the second number.

8. *(a)* : The numbers are cubes of different odd numbers.

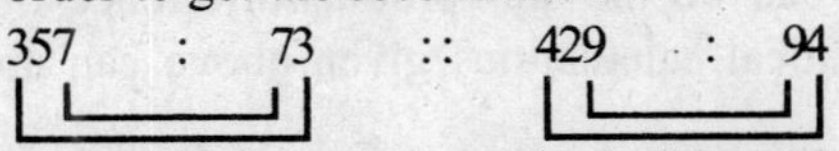

9. *(a)* : The central digit of the first number is left out and the corner digits written in reverse order to get the second number.

357 : 73 :: 429 : 94

10. *(a)* : The sum of the digits of both the numbers is same.

$731 : 902 \rightarrow 7+3+1 = 9+0+2$ *i.e.* $11 = 11$

$655 : 646 \rightarrow 6+5+5 = 6+4+6$ *i.e.* $16 = 16$

11. *(d)* : The sum of the digits of the first number is the second number.

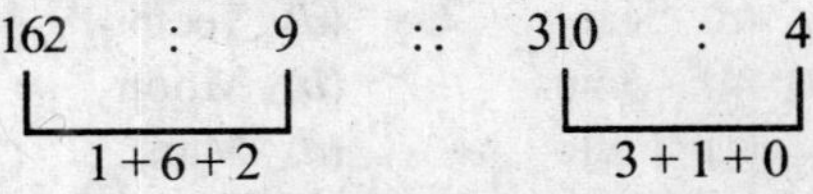

12. *(a)* : First number plus 4 gives the second number.

13 : 17 :: 15 : 19
(+4) (+4)

13. *(b)* : The root of first number is the second number.

14. *(b)* : The product of the digits of first number is multiplied by 2 to get the second number.

46 : 48 :: 54 : 40
$(4 \times 6)\,2$ $(5 \times 4)\,2$

15. *(a)* : The square of the sum of the digits of the first number is the second number.

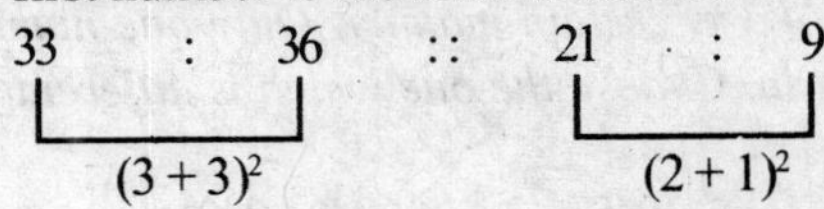

8. ODD ONE OUT

In this type of classification, four words are given out of which three are almost same in matter or meaning and only one word is different from the common three. One has to find out the word which is different from the rest.

EXERCISE

Directions : *In each of the following questions, three words are alike in some manner. Spot the odd one out.*

1. (*a*) Green (*b*) Red (*c*) Colour (*d*) Orange

2. (*a*) Stable (*b*) Hole (*c*) Canoe (*d*) Sty

3. (*a*) Nose (*b*) Eyes (*c*) Skin (*d*) Teeth

4. (*a*) Venus (*b*) Moon (*c*) Pluto (*d*) Mars

5. (*a*) Happy (*b*) Gloomy (*c*) Lively (*d*) Cheerful

Directions : *Three of the following four in each question are alike in a certain way and so form a group. Select the group of letters that does not belong to that group.*

6. (*a*) ACE (*b*) LOR (*c*) GIK (*d*) VXZ

7. (*a*) TSR (*b*) LKJ (*c*) PQO (*d*) HGF

8. (*a*) EF LM (*b*) KJ SR (*c*) XW HG (*d*) ED YX

9. (*a*) JOPK (*b*) BOPC (*c*) QOPR (*d*) TOPS

10. (*a*) DfH (*b*) MoQ (*c*) UwY (*d*) lnO

Directions : *In each of the following questions, there are four options. Three numbers, in these options, are alike in certain manner. Only one number does not fit in. Choose the one which is different from the rest.*

11. (*a*) 1948 (*b*) 2401 (*c*) 966 (*d*) 1449

12. (*a*) 182 (*b*) 169 (*c*) 130 (*d*) 158

13. (*a*) 129 (*b*) 130 (*c*) 131 (*d*) 132

14. (*a*) 3215 (*b*) 9309 (*c*) 4721 (*d*) 2850

15. (*a*) 1776 (*b*) 2364 (*c*) 1976 (*d*) 3776

Directions : *In the following questions select the pair which is different from the other three.*

16. (*a*) Chair - Furniture
(*b*) Shirt - Garment
(*c*) Necklace - Jewellery
(*d*) Bogie - Engine

17. (*a*) Crayon - Paper
(*b*) Pencil - Lead
(*c*) Pen - Ink
(*d*) Brush - Paint

18. (*a*) War - Peace
(*b*) Real - Natural
(*c*) Premiere - First
(*d*) Wrath - Anger

19. (*a*) Finger - Thimble
(*b*) Head - Cap
(*c*) Waist - Tiara
(*d*) Foot - Shoe

20. (*a*) Day - Night
(*b*) Clever - Foolish
(*c*) Clear - Blurred
(*d*) Arrive - Come

Directions : *In the following questions, which of the following pair of letters is different from the other three?*

21. (*a*) FGH - HIJ (*b*) PQR - RST (*c*) MNO - OPQ (*d*) CDE - DEF

22. (*a*) JuM - jUm (*b*) iLo - Ilo (*c*) PSa - psA (*d*) ZeX - zEx

23. (*a*) NQT - JMP (*b*) CFI - RUX (*c*) ADG - FGH (*d*) SVY - ORU

24. (*a*) DXD - XDX (*b*) KUK - UKU (*c*) FHF - EHE (*d*) RSR - SRS

25. (*a*) AYT - BZU (*b*) FNG - EMF (*c*) RWO - QVN (*d*) HJD - GIC

EXPLANATORY ANSWERS

1. (*c*) : All others are types of colour.

2. (*c*) : Canoe is a boat. Others are resting places of birds/animals.

3. (*d*) : All others are sense organs.

4. (*b*) : All others are planets.

5. (*b*) : All others are expressions of joy.

6. (*b*) : The sequence in each group is +2. Only option (*b*) has sequence in +3, *i.e.*,

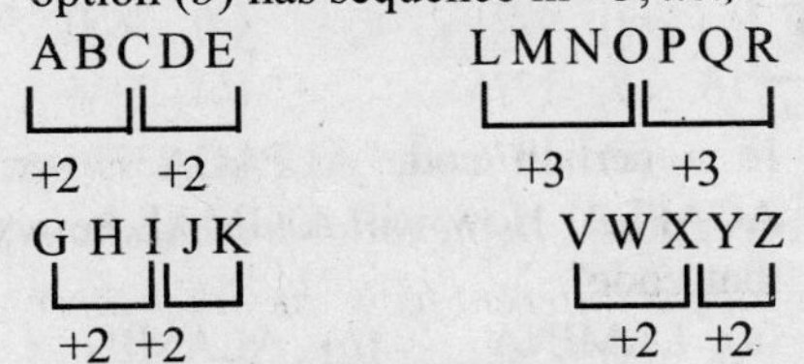

7. (*c*) : The sequence of alphabet in each group is in reverse order. Only option (*c*) has sequence in disturbed order.

8. (*a*) : Two consecutive alphabet in each group are in reverse sequence (–1), *i.e.*,

KJ SR; XW HG; ED YX
–1 –1 –1 –1 –1 –1

Only in option (*a*) the sequence is in natural order (+1), *i.e.*,

9. (*d*) : In each group, letters 'OP' are common. The two corner alphabet are in natural order (+1); *i.e.*,

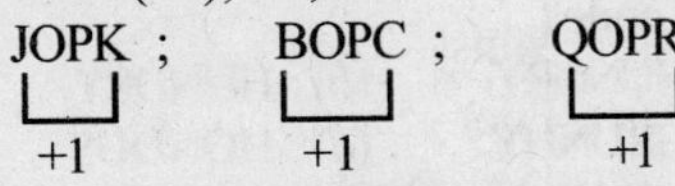

Only in option (*d*) they are in reverse order (–1); *i.e.*,

TOPS
–1

10. (*d*) : In other groups, only the alphabet in the centre is of lower case. In this option letter 'L' on the left is also in lower case.

11. (*a*) : Other numbers are divisible by 7.

12. (*d*) : Other numbers are multiples of 13.

13. (*c*) : 131 is a prime number.

14. (*b*) : In other numbers, no digit is repeated.

15. (*b*) : In other numbers, the last two digits are same.

16. (*d*) : Bogie is a part of train which is a type of conveyance. Chair, Shirt and Necklace are types of furniture, garment and jewellery respectively.

17. (*a*) : The medium used for writing with pencil is lead, with pen it is ink and with brush, it is paint. With crayon it should be wax.

18. (*a*) : The pair of words are opposite. Other pairs are synonyms.

19. (*c*) : Tiara is worn on the head.

20. (*d*) : Other words are opposite to each other.

21. (*d*) : In all other groups, the letters are in natural series and the last letter of first part is the first letter of the second part.

22. (*b*) : In all other groups, only the vowel is in lower case in the first part and in second part the case is reversed.

23. (*c*) : In all other groups, the letters jump two letters in between them.

24. (*c*) : In all other groups, the single letter in first part is repeated in the second and vice versa.

25. (*a*) : In all other groups, the letters in the first part are one step forward than the corresponding letters in the second part.

9. CODING AND DECODING

Coding is a secretive language which is used to change the representation of the actual term/word/value. This coded language can be framed by *(i)* moving the letters one or more steps forward or backward; *(ii)* substituting numbers for letters and vice–versa; *(iii)* writing the letters of the given word in reverse order in part or in whole; and *(iv)* replacing the letters in their natural series by the same positioned letters in their reverse series.

There is variety in ways of coding. Coding language is not only for words and numbers but also for hiding a group of words, statements or even sentences. This form of coding pattern may appear to be confusing but after solving only a few questions it is very easy to understand. Questions based on this coding pattern require no moving of steps or straining efforts of calculations, but only quick tallying or comparing ability. The codes can be letters or numbers.

EXERCISE

Directions : *In the following questions select the right option which indicates the correct code for the word or letter given in the question.*

1. If MUSK is coded as 146816, then ZERO will be coded as :
(*a*) 113811 (*b*) 122912
(*c*) 15915 (*d*) 2651815

2. If BAD is coded as 7, HIS as 9, LOW will be coded as :
(*a*) 50 (*b*) 8
(*c*) 23 (*d*) 5

3. In a certain code LIBERATE is written as 56403170, TRIBAL will be written in the same code as :
(*a*) 734615 (*b*) 736415
(*c*) 136475 (*d*) 034615

4. In certain military code, SYSTEM is written as SYSMET, and NEARER as AENRER, what will be the code for FRACTION?
(*a*) CRAFNOIT (*b*) FRCAITNO
(*c*) CARFNOIT (*d*) FRACNOIT

5. If CRUDE is written as BSTED, then MOIST will be coded as :
(*a*) NNJRU (*b*) LNHRS
(*c*) NPJTU (*d*) LPHTS

6. In a certain code ALPACA is written as ACAPLA. How will ANIMAL be written in that code?
(*a*) LAMINA (*b*) ALAMIN
(*c*) LAMNIA (*d*) AAMLIN

7. In a certain code FINGER is written as DGLECP. What will be the code for KIDNEY?
(*a*) IGBLCW (*b*) IGCLBW
(*c*) IBCGLE (*d*) IGBKCV

8. In a certain code QUESTION is written as NXBVQLLQ. How will REPLY be coded?
(*a*) YHMOV (*b*) OBMVI
(*c*) VHSOB (*d*) OHMOV

9. If in a certain code SKEW is coded as PNCY, then what will JXQV will stand for?
(*a*) MUTS (*b*) MUST
(*c*) MTSU (*d*) STUM

10. In a certain code LONDON is written as MPOEPO. What will IVOHSZ mean in the same code?
(*a*) HUNGRY (*b*) HUNDRY
(*c*) GRUNHY (*d*) HONDUS

11. In a certain code language 8514 is a code for HEAD, 3945 for RIDE and 057 for BEG. What will be the code for GRADE?
(*a*) 71345 (*b*) 73415
(*c*) 74135 (*d*) 73145

12. If MOTHERLAND is coded as 9501623748, how will DREAM be coded?
(*a*) 82697 (*b*) 86297
(*c*) 82769 (*d*) 82679

13. If OATH is coded in a certain language as TEYL, then how will WORD be coded?
(*a*) BWRH (*b*) HRWB
(*c*) BSWH (*d*) CSXI

14. If FINANCE is coded as GKQESIL, then how will BANK be coded in the same manner?
(*a*) CBOL (*b*) CDRP
(*c*) CCQO (*d*) CCPN

15. PLANNING is coded in a certain language as UFFHSCSA. How will AUTHORITY be coded in the same language?
(*a*) FOYBTLNND
(*b*) FYOTBNNLT
(*c*) FBOYTLNTN
(*d*) FBOYTNLTN

EXPLANATORY ANSWERS

1. (*b*) : The coded number signifies the position of the alphabet in its reverse order of the alphabetical series (ZYXW...)

M U S K → MUSK
↓ ↓ ↓ ↓
14th 6th 8th 16th → 146816

Similarly,

Z E R O → ZERO
↓ ↓ ↓ ↓
1st 22nd 9th 12th → 122912

2. (*d*) : The coded number is the sum of number digits signifying the position of the alphabet in the natural order.

B A D
↓ ↓ ↓
2nd 1st 4th *i.e.,* 2 + 1 + 4 = 7

Similarly,

H I S
↓ ↓ ↓
8th 9th 19th *i.e.,* 8 + 9 + 19 = 36
further, 3 + 6 = 9

Also,

L O W
↓ ↓ ↓
12th 15th 23rd *i.e.,* 12 + 15 + 23 = 50
further, 5 + 0 = 0

3. (*b*) : The letters of the word TRIBAL are picked from LIBERATE. So will be the coded numbers.

L I B E R A T E → given word
5 6 4 0 3 1 7 0 → codes

Similarly,

T R I B A L → word to be coded
7 3 6 4 1 5 → answer codes

4. (*c*) : The word is divided into two equal parts and the letters of each part are written in reverse order.

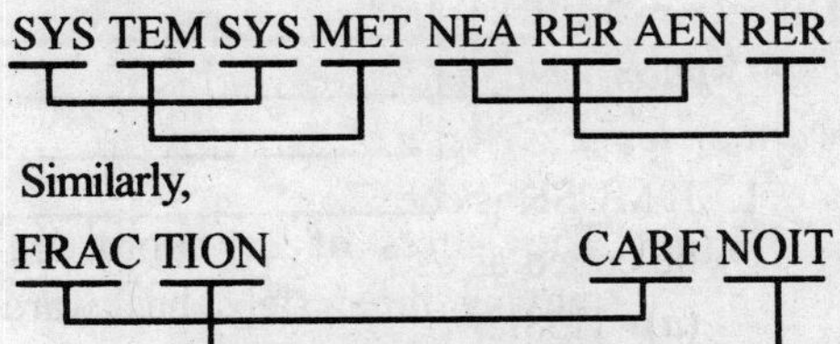

Similarly,

FRAC TION CARF NOIT

5. (*d*) : The code is formed by moving the letters one step backwards and one step forward alternately.

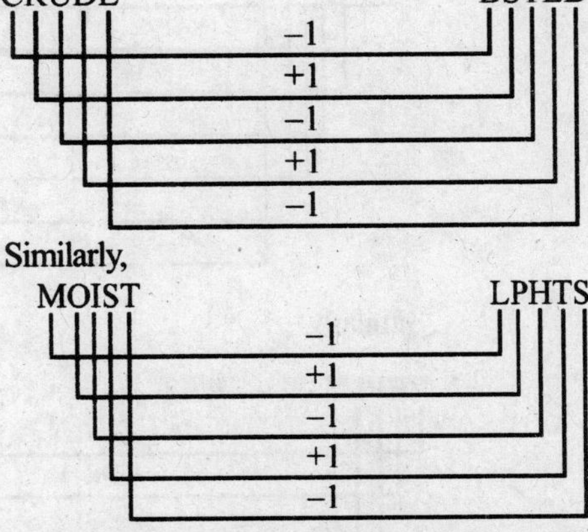

6. (*a*) : The letters of the word are written backwards.

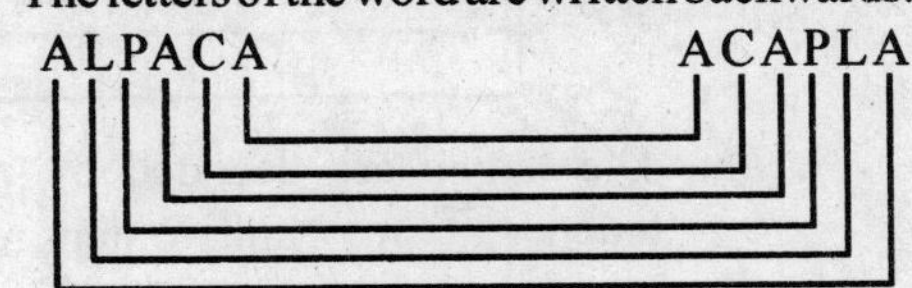

Similarly,

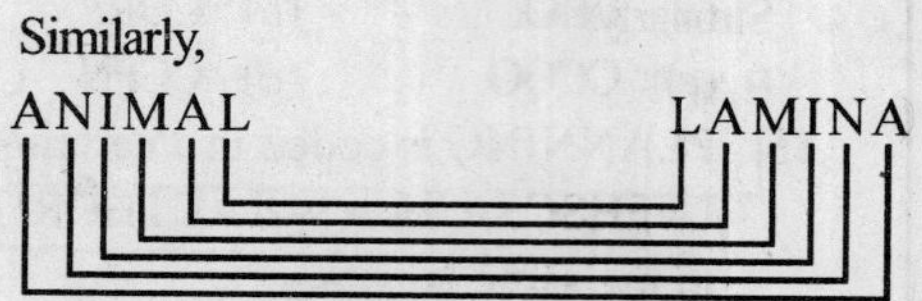

7. *(a)* : The word is coded by moving the letters two steps backwards.

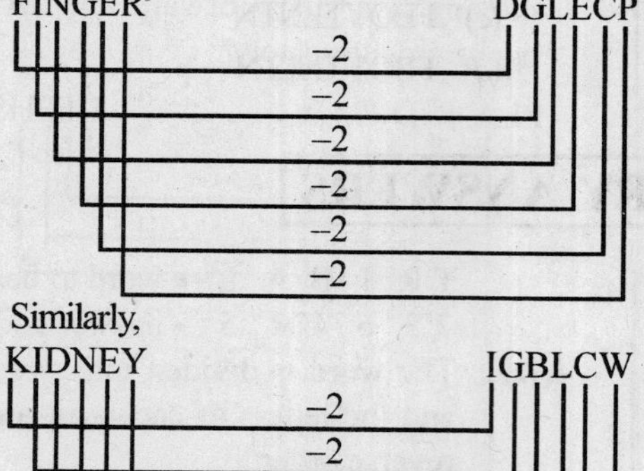

8. *(d)* : The letters of the word are coded by moving three steps backward and three steps forward alternately.

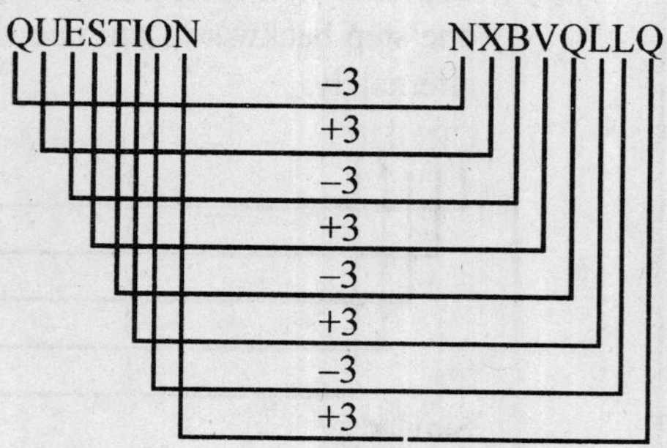

Similarly,

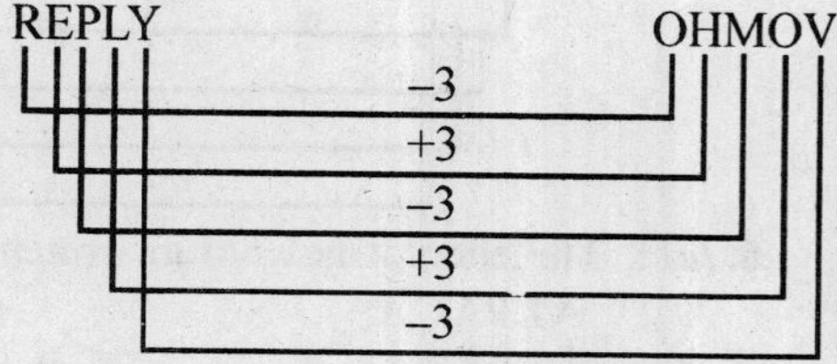

9. *(b)* : The letters are decoded by moving the letters +3, –3, +2 and –2 steps respectively.

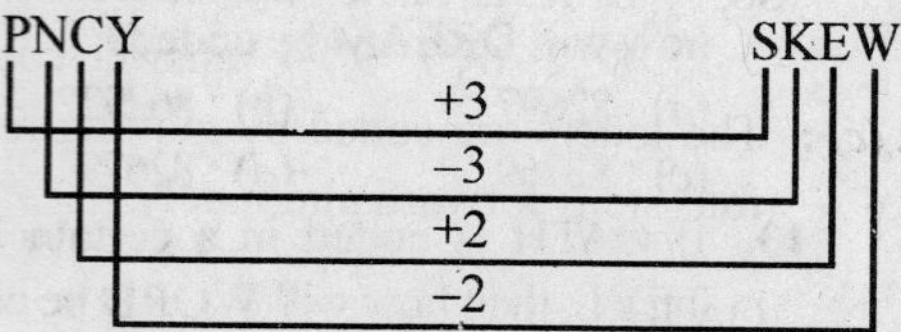

Similarly,

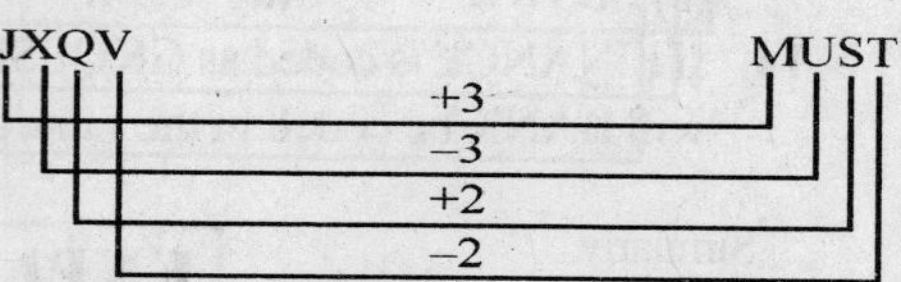

10. *(a)* : The letters of the coded word are moved one step backward.

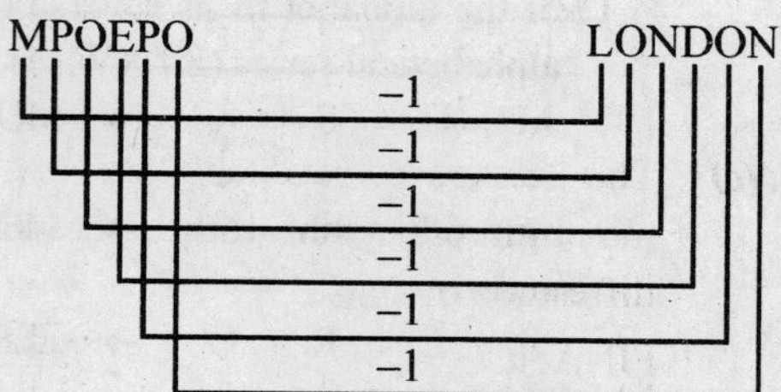

Similarly,

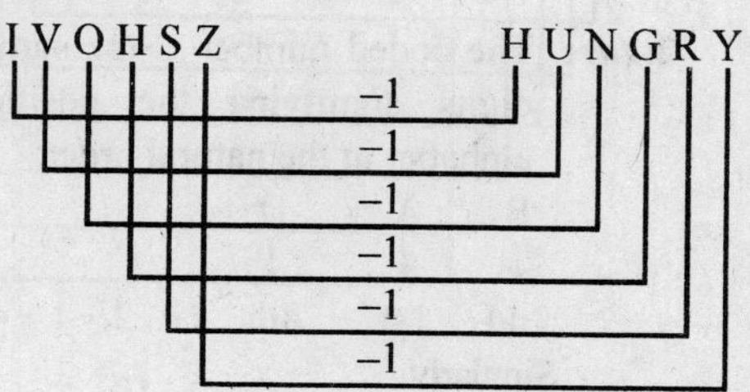

11. *(d)* : The word GRADE is framed by letters in the given words. So, in order to find the code for GRADE select the respective number codes.

H E A D R I D E B E G → letters

8 5 1 4 3 9 4 5 0 5 7 → codes

So,

G R A D E → letters

7 3 1 4 5 → answer codes

12. *(d)* : The letters of the word are coded by numbers. So to find the code for DREAM select the respective numbers.

M O T H E R L A N D → letters

9 5 0 1 6 2 3 7 4 8 → codes

So, D R E A M → letters
8 2 6 7 9 → answer codes

13. *(c)*: The letters are coded by moving five and four steps forward alternately.

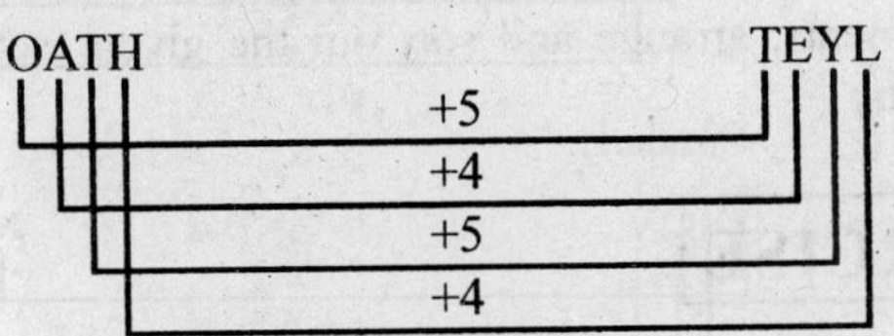

Similarly,

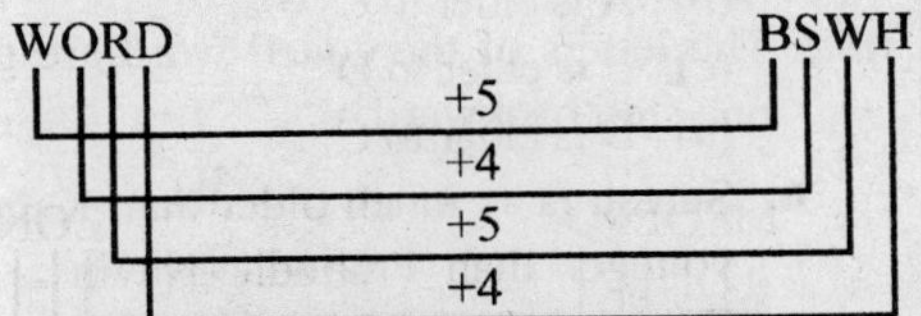

14. *(c)*: The letters of the word are coded by moving one step ahead and increasing the difference by one.

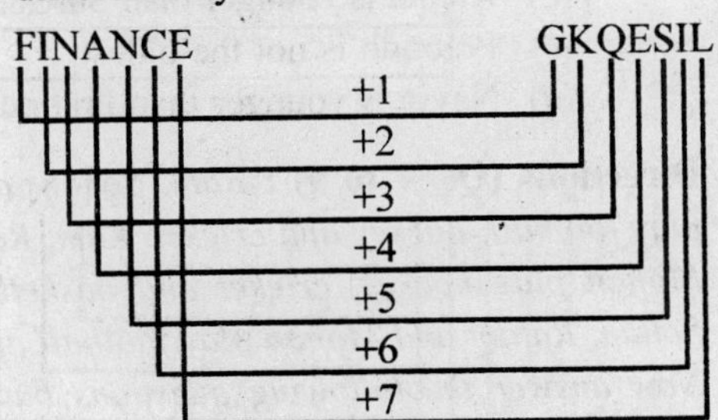

Similarly,

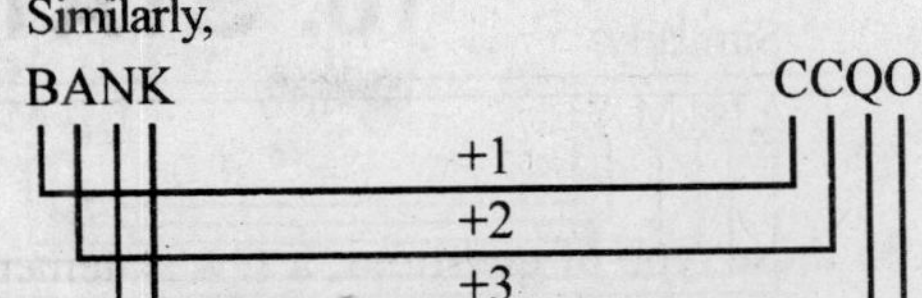

15. *(a)*: The letters of the word are coded by moving five steps forward and six steps backward alternately.

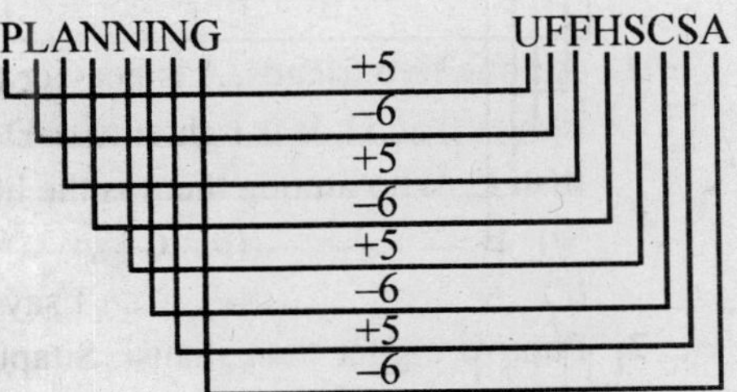

Similarly,

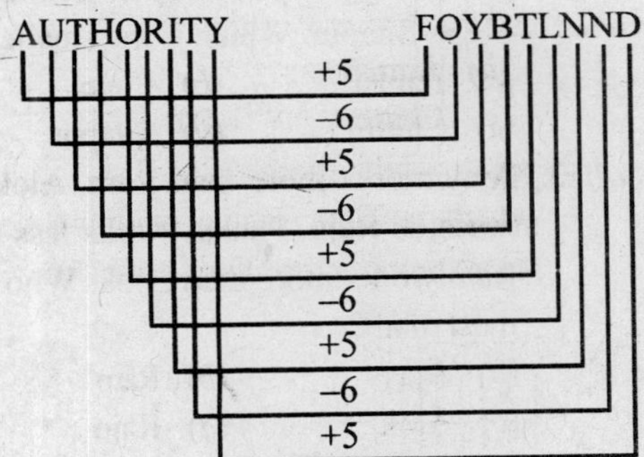

10. STATEMENT ANALYSIS

In these type of questions, a few statements are given. Certain facts are broken up and mentioned in these statements. What is required is to analyse the statements, arrange and sort out the given facts and then answer the questions related to the given statements.

EXERCISE

1. Among five friends, A is heavier than B; C is lighter than D; B is lighter than D but heavier than E. Who among them is the heaviest?

(*a*) B (*b*) C
(*c*) A (*d*) Can't say

2. Pune is bigger than Jhansi, Sitapur is bigger than Chittor. Raigarh is not as big as Jhansi, but is bigger than Sitapur. Chittor is not as big as Sitapur. Which is the smallest?

(*a*) Jhansi (*b*) Pune
(*c*) Chittor (*d*) Sitapur

3. Ajay works more than Ram. Alok works as much as Raju. Pankaj works less than Alok. Ram works more than Alok. Who works the most of all?

(*a*) Ajay (*b*) Ram
(*c*) Alok (*d*) Raju

4. Among five friends P, Q, R, S and T, who is the youngest? To arrive at the answer which of the following information given in the statements (A) and (B) is sufficient?

(A) R is younger than P and T.
(B) S is younger than Q.

(*a*) Only A alone is sufficient
(*b*) Either A or B is sufficient
(*c*) Both A and B together are needed
(*d*) Both A and B together are not sufficient

5. A is elder to B while C and D are elder to E who lies between A and B. If C be elder to B, which one of the following statements is necessarily true?

(*a*) E is elder to B
(*b*) A is elder to C
(*c*) C is elder to D
(*d*) D is elder to C

6. Suresh is as much older than Kamal as he is younger than Prabodh. Navin is as old as Kamal. Which of the following statements is wrong?

(*a*) Suresh is older than Navin
(*b*) Kamal is younger than Suresh
(*c*) Prabodh is not the oldest
(*d*) Navin is younger than Prabodh

Directions (Qs. 7 to 9) : *Ram, Sohan and Mohan play football, hockey and cricket. Ram, Ramesh and Mohan play hockey, cricket and basketball. Ram, Sohan, Rahim and Mohan play football and cricket. Now answer the following questions based on the above statements :*

7. Which game is played by all the boys?

(*a*) Football (*b*) Hockey
(*c*) Cricket (*d*) Basketball

8. Which two boys play all the games?

(*a*) Ram, Sohan (*b*) Ram, Ramesh
(*c*) Sohan, Mohan (*d*) Ram, Mohan

9. Who does not play football?

(*a*) Ramesh (*b*) Sohan
(*c*) Rahim (*d*) Mohan

Directions (Qs. 10 to 12) : *Read the following directions and answer the questions given below :*

There are five persons in a group. Out of these two are men. Only three persons know swimming, of which one is a man. There is a couple, of which the husband knows swimming. A is the younger sister of D and B is the husband of E. C is a swimming champion.

10. Who is the other man in the group?
(*a*) C (*b*) B
(*c*) A (*d*) D

11. The two women who know how to swim are:
(*a*) A and C (*b*) C and D
(*c*) D and E (*d*) A and E

12. The two persons who do not know how to swim are :
(*a*) B and D (*b*) D and E
(*c*) A and E (*d*) A and D

Directions (Qs. 13 to 15) : *Read the following statements and answer the questions given below :*

Rajat, Sushil and Nagesh play football, hockey and cricket. Rajat, Ramu and Nagesh play hockey, cricket and basketball. Rajat, Sushil, Mayank and Nagesh play football and cricket.

13. Which game is played by all the boys?
(*a*) Hockey (*b*) Basketball
(*c*) Football (*d*) Cricket

14. Who does not play football?
(*a*) Rajat (*b*) Nagesh
(*c*) Sushil (*d*) Ramu

15. Which of the following two boys play all the games?
(*a*) Nagesh, Rajat (*b*) Mayank, Ramu
(*c*) Ramu, Nagesh (*d*) Sushil, Mayank

EXPLANATORY ANSWERS

1. (*d*) : The five friends in descending order of weight are : A/D, B/C, E or A/D, B, C/E. Either A or D is the heaviest.

2. (*c*) : The order of cities in descending order of size is : Pune, Jhansi, Raigarh, Sitapur, Chittor.

3. (*a*) : On the basis of doing work, the descending order will be : Ajay, Ram, Alok/Raju, Pankaj.

4. (*d*) : Statements are not inter-related.

5. (*a*) : The order in descending seniority will be : A/C/D, E, B.

6. (*c*) : On the basis of age the descending order will be : Prabodh, Suresh, Kamal/Navin.

Chart for Answers 7 to 9

Boy	*Games Played*
Ram	Football, Hocky, Cricket, Basketball
Sohan	Football, Hockey, Cricket
Mohan	Football, Hockey, Cricket, Basketball
Ramesh	Hockey, Cricket, Basketball
Rahim	Football, Cricket.

7. (*c*) **8. (*d*)** **9. (*a*)**

For Answers 10 to 12 the information chart will be :

A. Woman ((younger sister of D); knows swimming.

B. Man (husband of E); knows swimming

C. Woman; Svimming champion

D. Man (brother of A)

E. Woman (wife of B)

From the couple B & E, B (husband) knows swimming. C is a swimming champion. Three persons know how to swim of which only B is a man. So, the two women who know how to swim are C and A (the younger sister of D). There are two men in the group of five. One is B and the other will be D.

10. (*d*) **11. (*a*)** **12. (*b*)**

Chart for Answers 13 to 15

Boy	*Games Played*
Rajat	— Football, Hockey, Cricket, Basketball
Sushil	— Football, Hockey, Cricket, Basketball
Nagesh	— Football, Hockey, Cricket, Basketball
Ramu	— Hockey, Cricket, Basketball
Mayank	— Football, Cricket

13. (*d*) **14. (*d*)** **15. (*a*)**

12. DIRECTION SENSE

In these type of tests, the directions in questions needs to be perceived. Such questions are based on the direction chart.

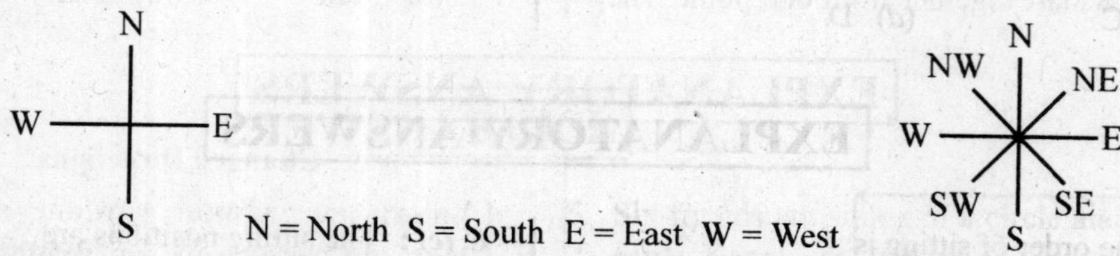

The sense of the different directions are guided by the left and right turns or angular turns.

EXERCISE

Directions : *In the following questions, select the right answer from the given options to depict the correct direction/distance.*

1. Kittu walks towards East and then towards South. After walking some distance he turns towards West and then turns to his left. In which direction is he walking now?
(*a*) North (*b*) South
(*c*) East (*d*) West

2. A person is driving towards West. What sequence of directions should he follow so that he is driving towards South?
(*a*) left, right, right
(*b*) right, right, left
(*c*) left, left, left
(*d*) right, right, right

3. Richa drives 8 km to the South, turns left and drives 5 km. Again, she turns left and drives 8 km. How far is she from her starting point?
(*a*) 3 km (*b*) 5 km
(*c*) 8 km (*d*) 13 km

4. Dingi runs 40 km towards North then turns right and runs 50 km. He turns right and runs 30 km, and once again turns right and runs 50 km. How far is he from his starting point?
(*a*) 90 km (*b*) 50 km
(*c*) 10 km (*d*) 5 km

5. If North is called North-West, North-West is called West, West is called South-West and so on. What will South-East be called?
(*a*) East (*b*) West
(*c*) North-East (*d*) South-East

6. A man travels 100 km towards South. From there he turns right and travels 100 km and again turns right to travel 50 km. Which direction is he in from his starting point?
(*a*) North (*b*) North-East
(*c*) East (*d*) South-West

7. A train runs 120 km in West direction, 30 km in South direction and then 80 km in east direction before reaching the station. In which direction is the station from the train's starting point?
(*a*) South-West (*b*) North-West
(*c*) South-East (*d*) South

8. Facing the West direction, Priya jogs for 20 m, turns left and goes further 40 m. She turns left again and jogs for 20 m. Then she turns right to go 20 m to reach the park. How far is the park from her starting point and in which direction?
(*a*) 20 m South (*b*) 40 m West
(*c*) 60 m South (*d*) 100 m East

9. If all the directions are rotated, *i.e.,* if North is changed to West and East to North and so on, then what will come in place of North-West?

(*a*) South-West (*b*) North-East

(*c*) East-North (*d*) East-West

10. A and B start together from one point. They walk 10 km towards North. A turns left and covers 5 km whereas B turns right and covers 3 km. A turns left again and covers 15 km whereas B turns right and covers his 15 km. How far is A from B?

(*a*) 18 km (*b*) 10 km

(*c*) 5 km (*d*) 8 km

EXPLANATORY ANSWERS

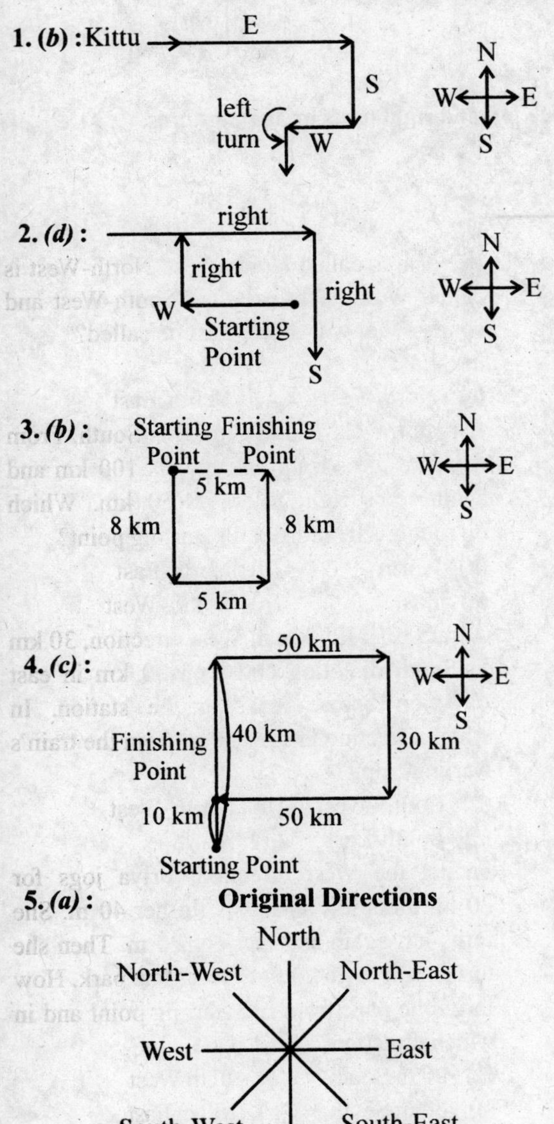

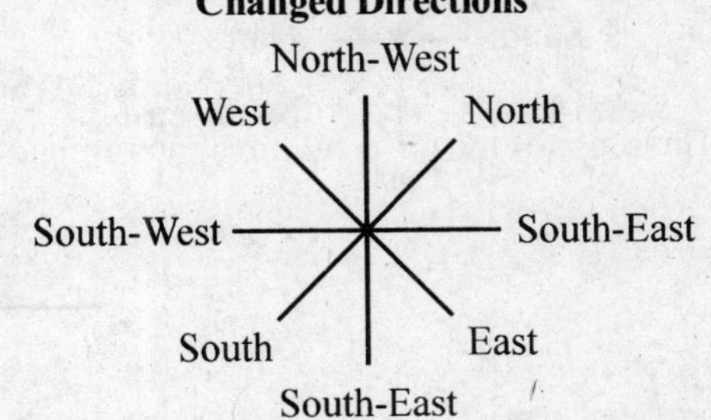

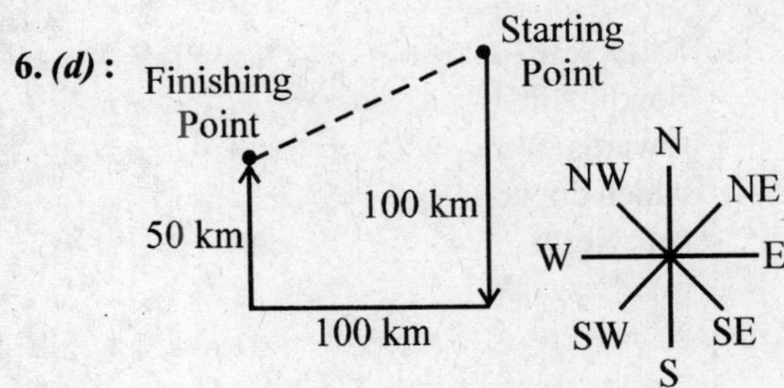

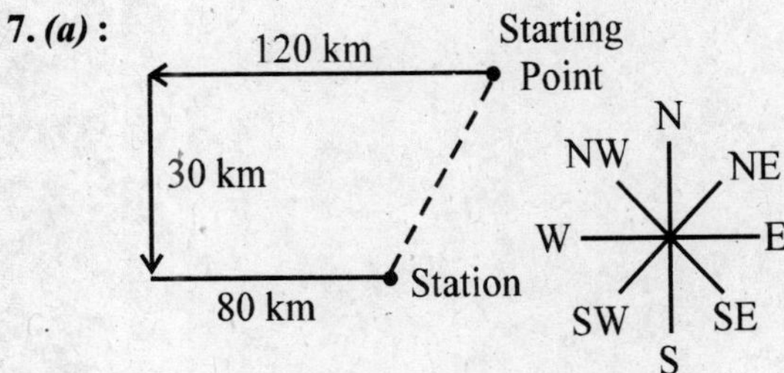

8. (*c*) : $(40 + 20) = 60$ metres South

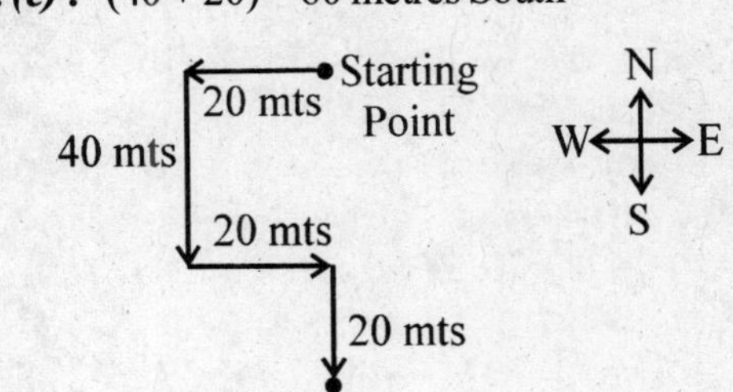

9. ***(a)*** **: Original Directions**

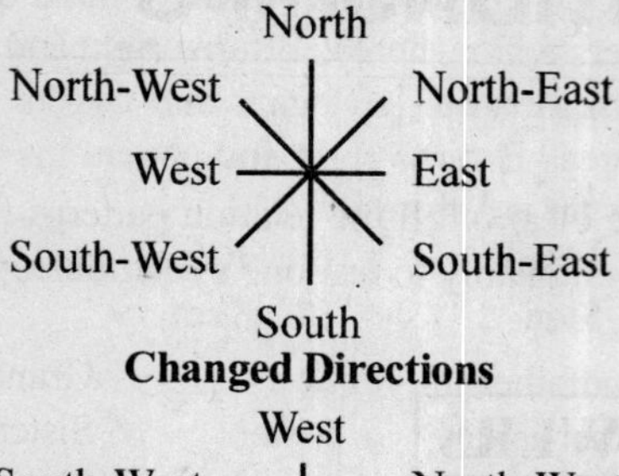

Changed Directions

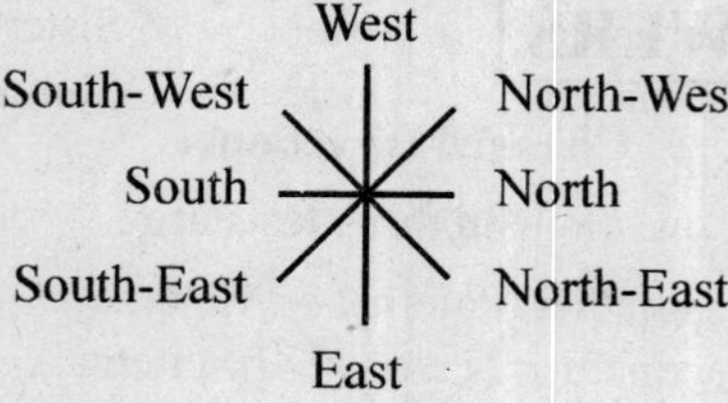

10. ***(d)*** **:**

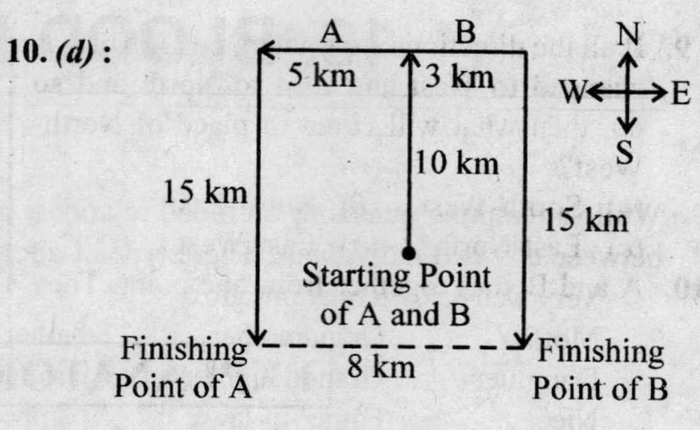

13. BLOOD RELATIONSHIPS

While attempting questions on blood relations, one should be clear of all the relation patterns that can exist between any two individuals. These type of questions are given mainly to test one's relationship ability.

Very well-known relations are :

Mother	Grandmother	Father	Grandfather	Son	Grandson
Daughter	Granddaughter	Brother	Brother-in-law	Sister	Sister-in-law
Niece	Father-in-law	Nephew	Mother-in-law	Uncle	Son-in-law
Aunt	Daughter-in-law	Husband	Cousin	Wife	

The patterns of some relationships which help in solving questions in these tests are :

Father's *or* Mother's Father	—	Grandfather (Paternal *or* Maternal)
Father's *or* Mother's Mother	—	Grandmother (Paternal *or* Maternal)
Father's *or* Mother's Son	—	Brother
Father's *or* Mother's Daughter	—	Sister
Father's Brother	—	Paternal Uncle
Father's Sister	—	Paternal Aunt
Mother's Brother	—	Maternal Uncle
Mother's Sister	—	Maternal Aunt
Uncle *or* Aunt's Son *or* Daughter	—	Cousin
Son's Wife	—	Daughter-in-law
Daughter's Husband	—	Son-in-law
Husband's *or* Wife's Brother	—	Brother-in-law
Husband's *or* Wife's Sister	—	Sister-in-law
Brother's Wife	—	Sister-in-law
Sister's Husband	—	Brother-in-law
Brother's Son	—	Nephew
Brother's Daughter	—	Niece

EXERCISE

Directions : *In each of the following questions keenly study the relationship mentioned between the persons, and then from the given options select the right relationship as the answer.*

1. A lady said, "The person standing there is my grandfather's only son's daughter". How is the lady related to the standing person?

(*a*) Sister (*b*) Mother
(*c*) Aunt (*d*) Cousin

2. Ajay is the brother of Vijay. Mili is the sister of Ajay. Sanjay is the brother of Rahul and Mehul is the daughter of Vijay. Who is Sanjay's Uncle?

(*a*) Rahul (*b*) Ajay
(*c*) Mehul (*d*) Data inadequate

3. A man introduced the boy coming with him as "He is son of the father of my wife's daughter". What relation did the boy bear to the man?

(*a*) Son-in-law (*b*) Son
(*c*) Brother (*d*) Father

4. If Amit's father is Billoo's father's only son and Billoo has neither a brother nor a daughter, what is the relationship between Amit and Billoo?

(*a*) Uncle — Nephew
(*b*) Father — Daughter
(*c*) Father — Son
(*d*) Cousins

5. Pointing to a woman in the photograph a man said, "She is the daughter of my grand-mother's only son." How is the woman related to the man?

(*a*) Mother (*b*) Daughter
(*c*) Sister-in-law (*d*) Sister

6. Pointing to a photograph, a woman said, "She is the only daughter of my mother's father." How is the woman related to the person in the photograph?

(*a*) Mother
(*b*) Grandmother
(*c*) Daughter
(*d*) Cannot be determined

7. Ram is the brother of Shyam and Mahesh is the father of Ram. Jagat is the brother of Priya and Priya is daughter of Shyam. Who is the uncle of Jagat ?

(*a*) Shyam (*b*) Mahesh
(*c*) Ram (*d*) Data insufficient

8. Introducing a man, a woman said, "His wife is the only daughter of my father". How is the man related to the woman?

(*a*) Husband (*b*) Father
(*c*) Father-in-law (*d*) Brother

9. If Maya is the only daughter of Richa's grandmother's brother, how is Maya's daughter related to Richa?

(*a*) Niece (*b*) Cousin
(*c*) Aunt (*d*) Mother

10. Pointing to a woman, a man said, "Her husband's mother is the wife of my father's only son". How is the man related to the woman?

(*a*) Son (*b*) Brother-in-law
(*c*) Uncle (*d*) Father-in-law

EXPLANATORY ANSWERS

1. (*a*) : Grandfather

Father
(only son)

Daughter ⟶ Lady
(standing person) (sister)

Lady's grandfather's son is lady's father and father's daughter will only be lady's sister.

2. (*d*) : 1. Mili ⟶ Ajay ⟶ Vijay ↓ Mehul
(sister) (brother) (daughter)

2. Sanjay ⟶ Rahul
(brother)

There are two sets of relationship. Information given is incomplete and no relation can be established between the two sets.

3. (*b*) : The relationship chart based on problem is :

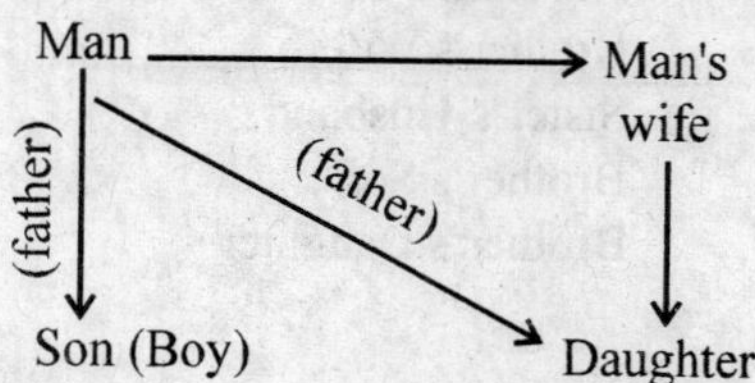

'Father of the man's wife's daughter' is the man himself and the boy in question is the man's son.

4. (*c*) : The relationship chart based on problem is :

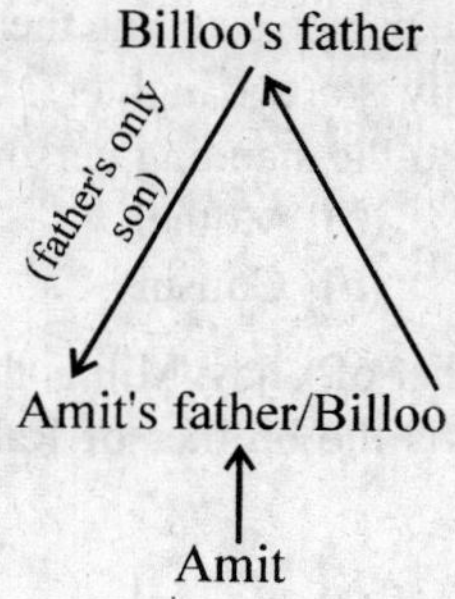

Amit's father is Billoo's father's only son means Billoo is the only son in question also, he is the father of Amit. It must be noted that Billoo has no brother which means he is single and also, when he has no daughter, Amit is his only son.

5. (*d*) :

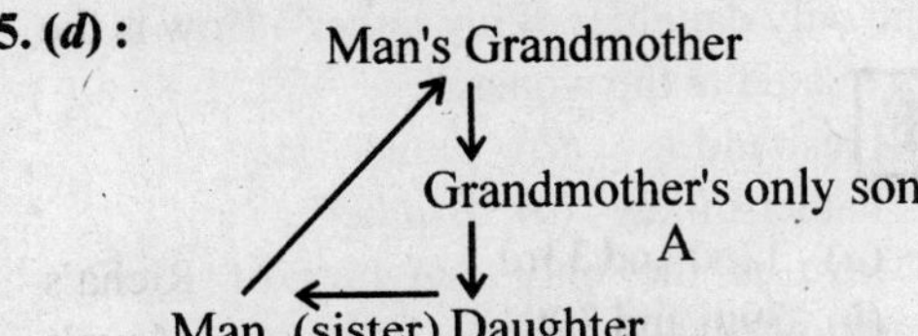

'My grandmother's only son' is the father of the man, and 'daughter of my grand-mother's only son' is the sister of the man.

6. (*c*) : Woman's mother's father

↕

Person in photograph (woman's mother/only daughter)

↑ (daughter)

Woman

'Only daughter of my mother's father' is the person in the photograph and she is also the mother of the woman. So, the woman is the daughter of the person in the photo-graph.

7. (*c*) :

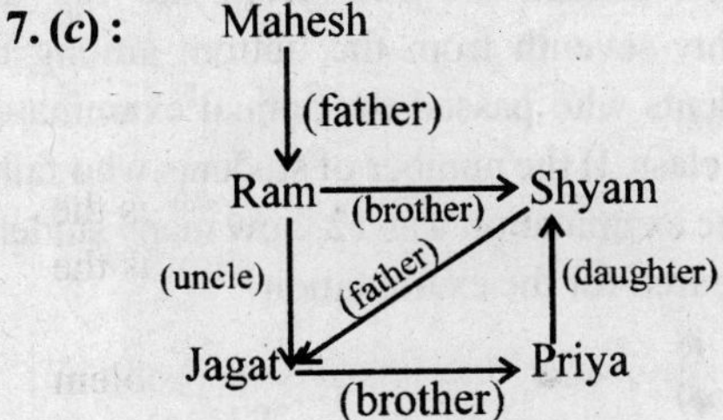

Jagat is brother of Priya and Priya is daughter of Shyam. So Shyam is also the father of Jagat. Ram is the brother of Shyam. So, Jagat's father's brother Ram is the uncle of Jagat.

8. (*a*) :

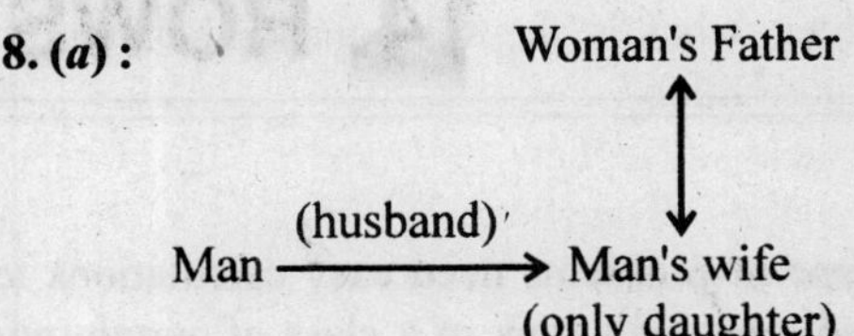

'Only daughter of my father' is the woman herself and the man is her husband.

9. (*b*) :

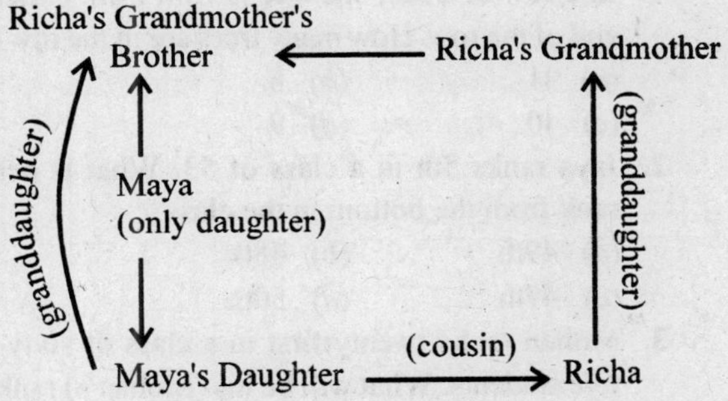

Both Maya's Daughter and Richa are granddaughters of a brother and a sister respectively. So Maya's daughter is the cousin of Richa.

10. (*d*) :

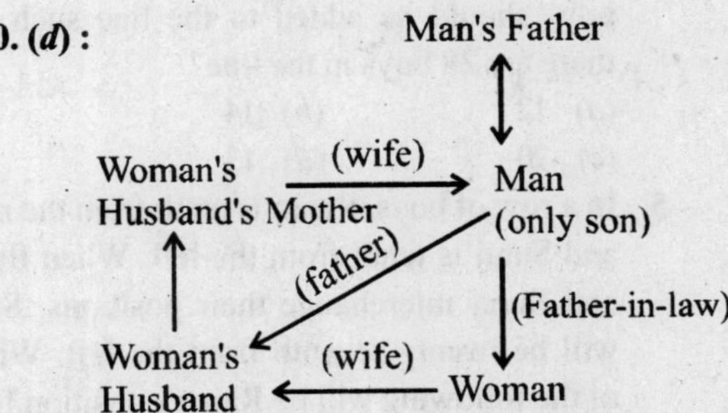

'My father's only son' is the man himself. 'Her husband's mother' is the wife of the man and so the man is the father of the woman's husband. As the woman is the wife of man's son, the man is the father-in-law of the woman.

14. ROWS AND RANKS

These type of problems need easy calculations to find out the number of objects in a row, lane or queue or to find a person's rank in a class of certain number of students; or to find the total number of students.

EXERCISE

1. In a row of trees, one tree is fifth from either end of the row. How many trees are in the row?

(*a*) 11 (*b*) 8
(*c*) 10 (*d*) 9

2. Jaya ranks 5th in a class of 53. What is her rank from the bottom in the class?

(*a*) 49th (*b*) 48th
(*c*) 47th (*d*) 50th

3. Mohan ranks twenty-first in a class of sixty-five students. What will be his (Mohan's) rank if the lowest candidate is assigned rank 1?

(*a*) 44th (*b*) 45th
(*c*) 46th (*d*) Data inadequate

4. If Rahul finds that he is 12th from the right in a line of boys and 4th from the left, how many boys should be added to the line such that there are 28 boys in the line?

(*a*) 12 (*b*) 14
(*c*) 20 (*d*) 13

5. In a row of boys, Rajan is tenth from the right and Suraj is tenth from the left. When Rajan and Suraj interchange their positions, Suraj will be twenty-seventh from the left. Which of the following will be Rajan's position from the right?

(*a*) Tenth
(*b*) Twenty-sixth
(*c*) Twenty-ninth
(*d*) None of these

6. Mahesh and Suresh are ranked 11th and 12th respectively from the top in a class of 41 students. What will be their respective ranks from the bottom?

(*a*) 32nd and 33rd
(*b*) 29th and 30th
(*c*) 30th and 31st
(*d*) 31st and 30th

7. Uma ranked 8th from the top and 37th from bottom in a class. How many students are there in the class?

(*a*) 47 (*b*) 46
(*c*) 45 (*d*) None of these

8. In a queue, Sadiq is 14th from the front and Joseph is 17th from the end, while Jane is in between Sadiq and Joseph. If Sadiq be ahead of Joseph and there be 48 persons in the queue, how many persons are there between Sadiq and Jane?

(*a*) 5 (*b*) 6
(*c*) 7 (*d*) 8

9. Rohan ranked eleventh from the top and twenty-seventh from the bottom among the students who passed the annual examination in a class. If the number of students who failed in the examination was 12, how many students appeared for the examination?

(*a*) 48
(*b*) 49
(*c*) 50
(*d*) Cannot be determined

10. Some boys are sitting in a row. P is sitting fourteenth from the left and Q is seventh from the right. If there are four boys between P and Q, how many boys are there in the row?

(*a*) 19 (*b*) 21
(*c*) 25 (*d*) 23

EXPLANATORY ANSWERS

1. (*d*):

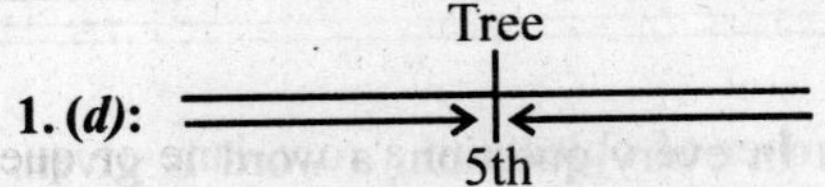

Total number of trees in the row are :
$(5+5)-1=9$.

2. (*a*) :

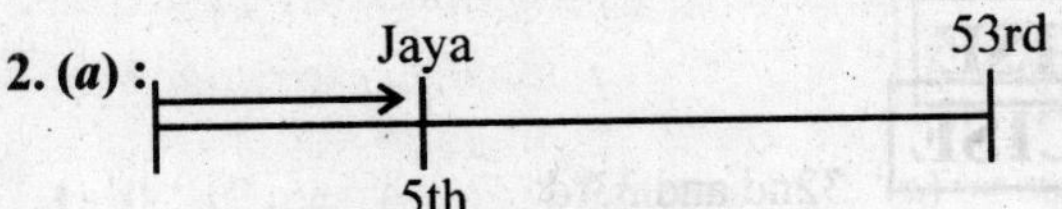

Jaya's rank from the bottom is :
$(53-5)+1=49$th.

3. (*b*) :

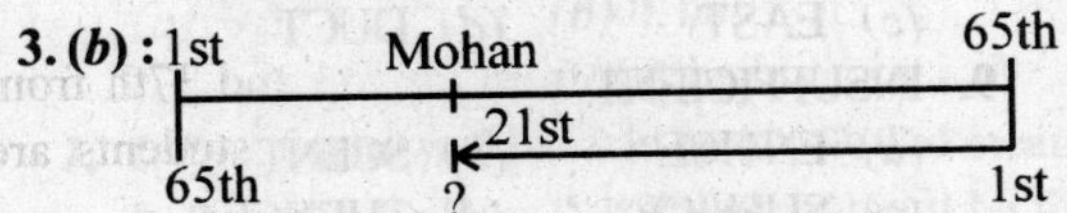

Note : Mohan's rank from the last or the question asked means the same.

Mohan's rank is $(65-21)+1=45$th.

4. (*d*) :

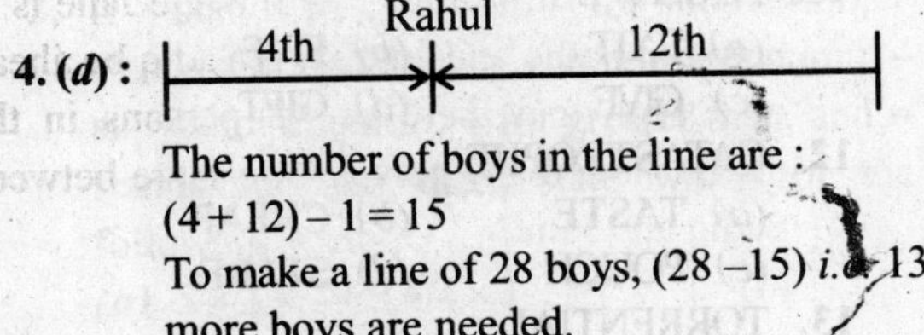

The number of boys in the line are :
$(4+12)-1=15$

To make a line of 28 boys, $(28-15)$ *i.e.* 13 more boys are needed.

5. (*d*) :

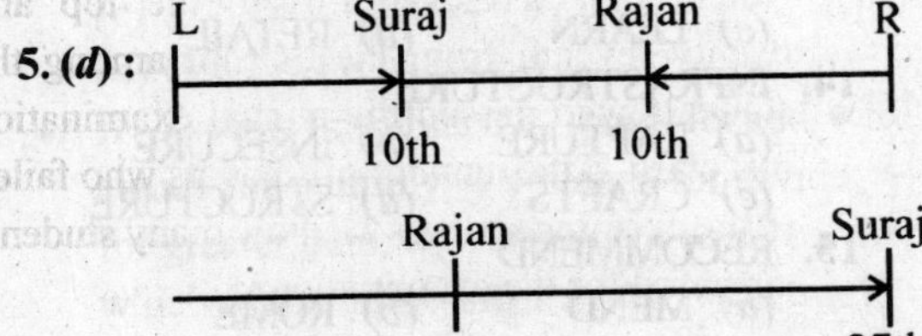

As the position of boys is equal from both ends, Rajan will also be 27th from the right after changing positions.

6. (*d*) :

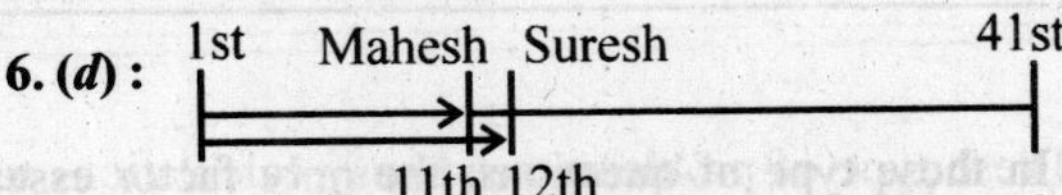

Mahesh's position from bottom is :
$(41-11)+1=31$st

Suresh's position from bottom is :
$(41-12)+1=30$th.

7. (*d*) :

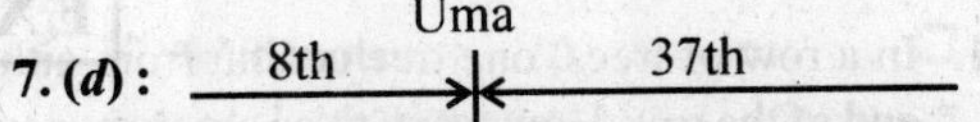

Total number of students in the class are :
$(8+37)-1=44$.

8. (*d*) :

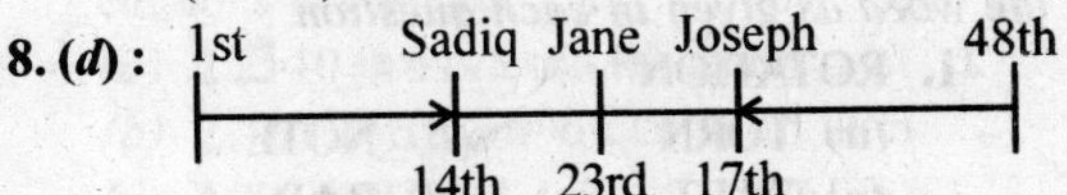

Sadiq's position from front : 14th

Joseph's position from last :
17th or $48-17+1=32$nd from front.

Middle postion between Sadiq & Joseph

$$=\frac{(32-14)}{2}+14=23\text{ rd.}$$

Hence, Jane position is 23rd from front

Person between Sadiq & Jane
$=23-14-1=8$.

9. (*b*) :

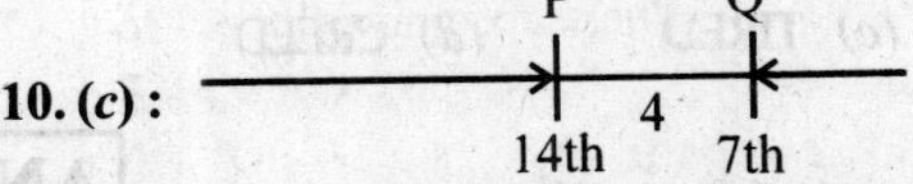

Number of students who passed the examination $(11+27)-1=37$

Those who failed $=12$

Total number of students who appeared in the examination $=37+12=49$.

10. (*c*) :

P Q

14th 4 7th

The number of boys in the row are :
$(14+4+7)=25$.

EXPLANATORY ANSWERS

1. (c) : $15 \div 5 + 10 - 5 \times 3$

$3 + 10 - 15 = -2$

2. (d) : $20 + 40 \div 4 - 5 \times 6$

$20 + 10 - 30 = 0$

3. (c) : *(a)* $5 + 3 - 7 > 8 \div 4 + 1$

$1 > 3$

(b) $3 + 4 \times 2 = 9 \div 3 - 3$

$11 = 0$

(c) $5 \times 2 \div 2 < 10 - 4 + 8$

$5 < 14$

(d) $3 + 2 - 4 > 16 \times 2 \div 4$

$1 > 8$

4. (b) : *(a)* $4 + 6 \times 2 = 3 - 12 + 12$

$16 = 3$

(b) $10 \div 5 \times 5 = 9 - 3 + 4$

$10 = 10$

(c) $15 \times 2 - 5 = 12 \div 4 + 3$

$25 = 6$

(d) $13 \div 13 + 1 > 20 - 5 \times 2$

$2 > 10$

5. (d) : What is given is $a > b < c$

The equations are :

(a) $b = c \neq a$ which is wrong

(b) $b \neq a < c$ which is wrong

(c) $a < b > c$ which is wrong

(d) $b < a > c$ which is correct

Therefore, *(d)* is the answer.

6. (c) : The solved equations will be :

(a) $2 - 10 \times 4 \div 5 = 5 + 12 \div 6$

$2 - 8 = 5 + 2$

$-6 = 7$ which is wrong

(b) $27 \div 9 + 6 \neq 3 \times 6 - 9$

$3 + 6 \neq 18 - 9$

$9 \neq 9$ which is wrong

(c) $4 \div 2 \times 0 = 7 \div 1 \times 0$

$2 \times 0 = 7 \times 0$

$0 = 0$ which is correct

(d) $5 + 6 \div 3 - 2 = 8 \div 4 \times 3$

$5 = 6$ which is wrong

7. (d) : $25 \div 5 + 3 \times 6 - 8$

$5 + 18 - 8 = 15$

8. (c) : After interchanging the signs the equations are :

(a) $7 + 5 \times 3 = 22$ which is wrong

(b) $4 \times 9 + 1 = 37$ which is wrong

(c) $6 + 5 \times 8 = 46$ which is correct

(d) $2 \times 11 + 4 = 26$ which is wrong

9. (c) : $7 + 4 - 10 + 2 \times 5$

$7 + 4 - 10 + 10 = 11$

10. (c) : $12 \times 4 \div 24 - 10 + 1$

$2 - 10 + 1 = -7$

17. MISSING NUMBERS

Playing with numbers and mathematical skills are needed to attempt these type of tests. The candidates have to work out the right combination of arithmetical symbols to arrive at the answer options which will take the place of the interrogation sign in the given questions.

EXERCISE

Directions: *In each question given below which one number can be placed at the sign of interrogation?*

1.

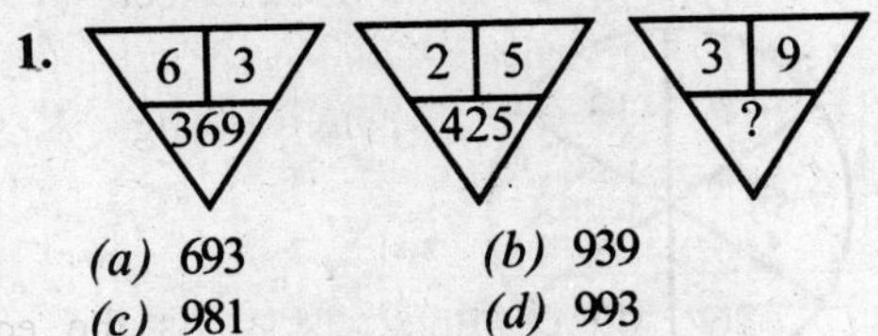

(*a*) 693 (*b*) 939
(*c*) 981 (*d*) 993

2.

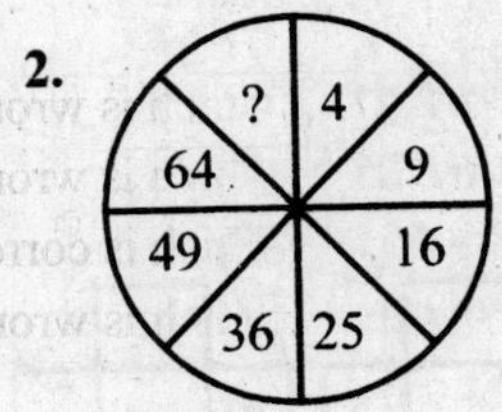

(*a*) 68 (*b*) 100
(*c*) 72 (*d*) 81

3.

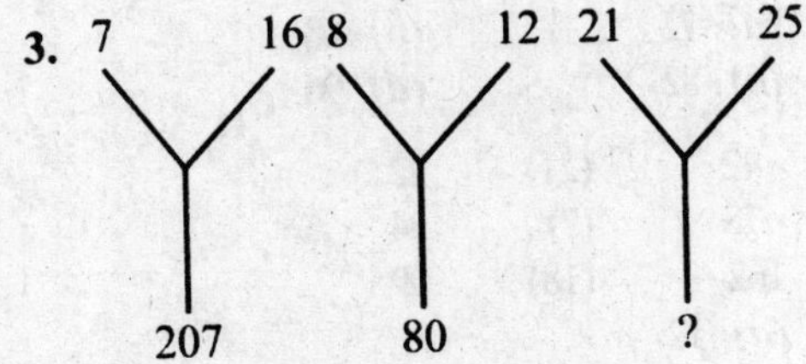

(*a*) 425 (*b*) 184
(*c*) 241 (*d*) 210

4.

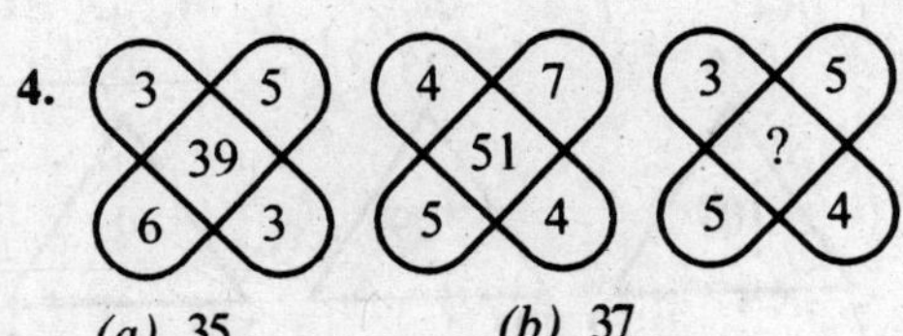

(*a*) 35 (*b*) 37
(*c*) 45 (*d*) 48

5.

7	5
6	

5	21
13	

24	4
?	

(*a*) 4 (*b*) 8
(*c*) 20 (*d*) 14

6.

14	9	4
12	7	2
10	5	0
16	11	?

(*a*) 9 (*b*) 6
(*c*) 3 (*d*) 7

7.

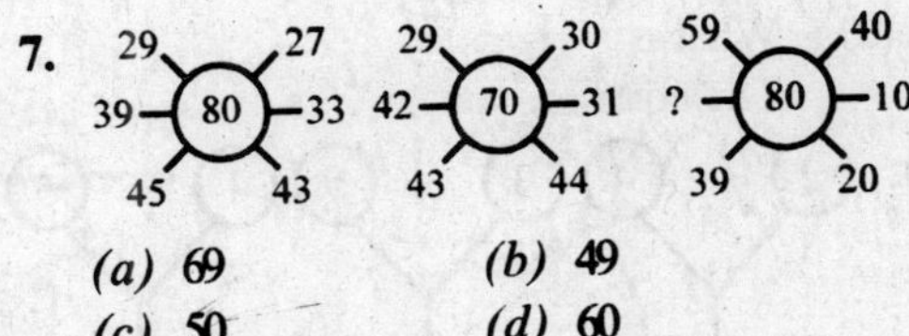

(*a*) 69 (*b*) 49
(*c*) 50 (*d*) 60

8.

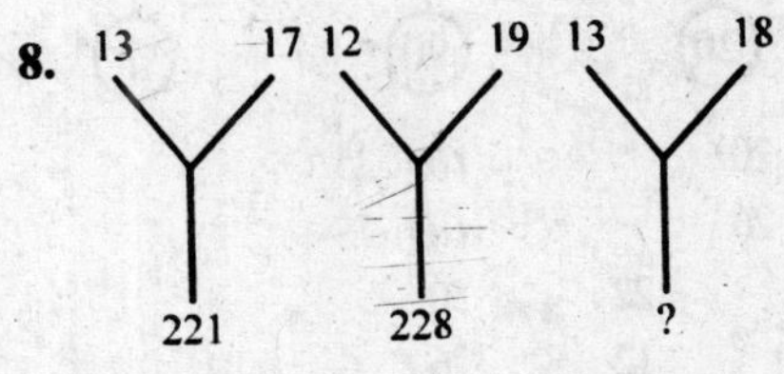

(*a*) 31 (*b*) 229
(*c*) 234 (*d*) 312

9.

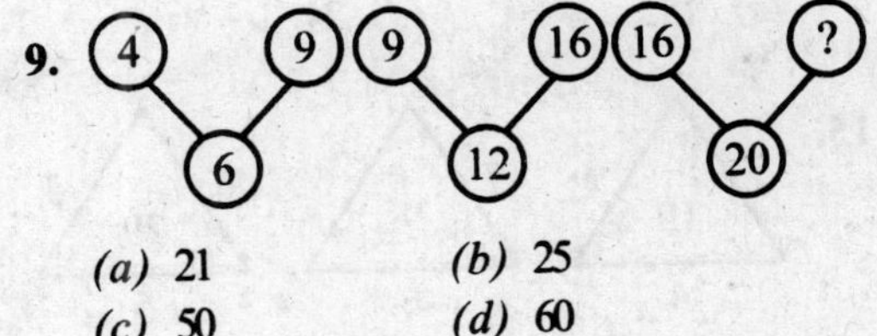

(*a*) 21 (*b*) 25
(*c*) 50 (*d*) 60

10. 51 (11) 61
64 (30) 32
35 (?) 43
(a) 25 *(b)* 27
(c) 32 *(d)* 37

11.

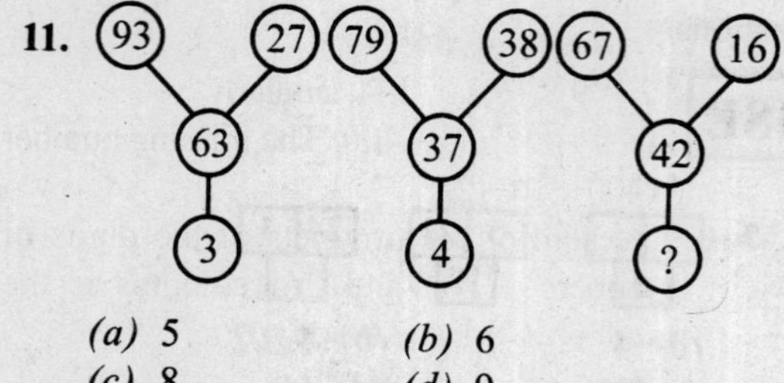

(a) 5 *(b)* 6
(c) 8 *(d)* 9

12.

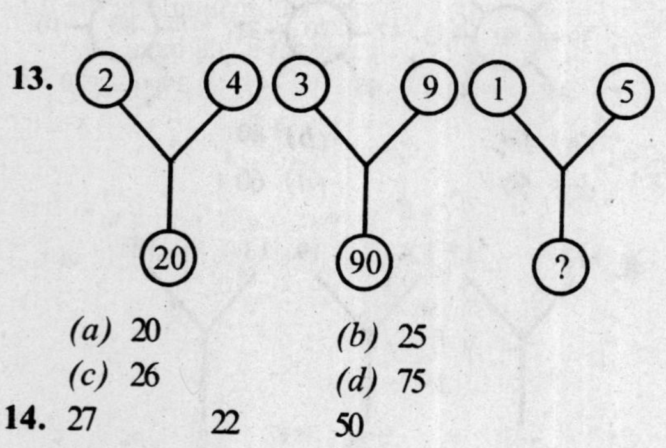

(a) 8 *(b)* 14
(c) 10 *(d)* 6

13.

(a) 20 *(b)* 25
(c) 26 *(d)* 75

14. 27 22 50
13 12 26
9 2 ?
(a) 12 *(b)* 39
(c) 18 *(d)* 24

15.

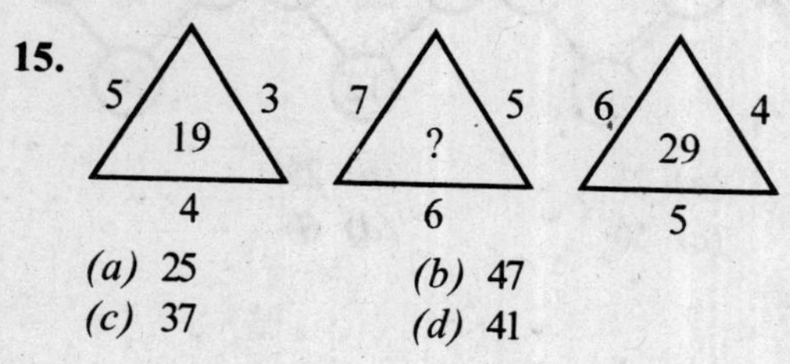

(a) 25 *(b)* 47
(c) 37 *(d)* 41

16.

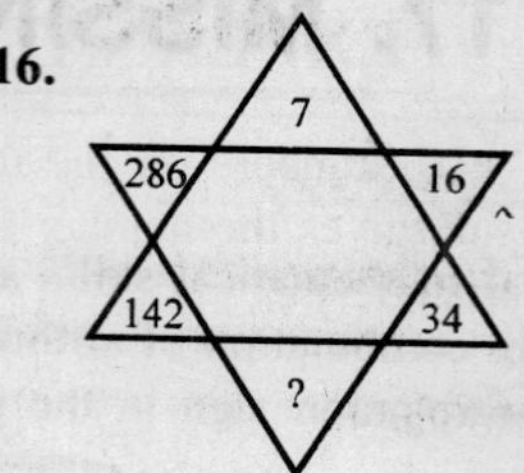

(a) 70
(b) 68
(c) 56
(d) 92

17.

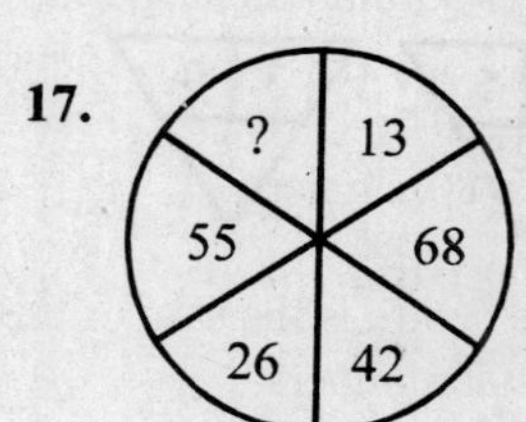

(a) 41 *(b)* 37
(c) 29 *(d)* 25

18.

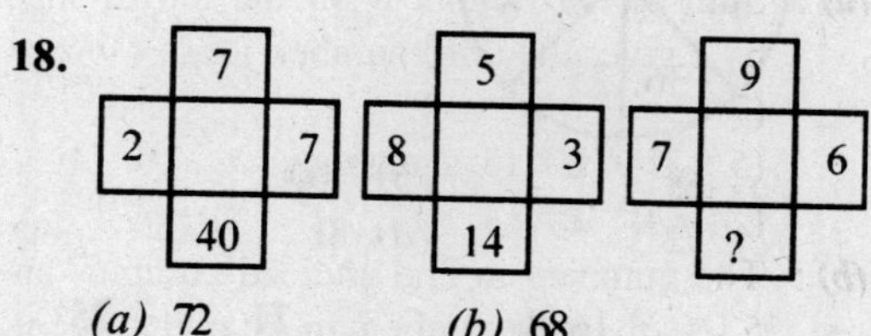

(a) 72 *(b)* 68
(c) 82 *(d)* 96

19. 42 (21) 22
78 (?) 84
162 (18) 99
(a) 12
(b) 13
(c) 60
(d) 72

20.

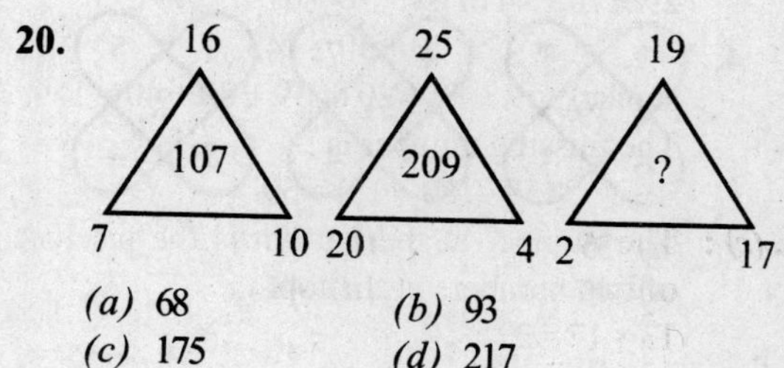

(a) 68 *(b)* 93
(c) 175 *(d)* 217

EXPLANATORY ANSWERS

1. (c) : The squares of two numbers on the top placed side by side gives the number inside the bottom triangle, *i.e.*,
6^2 and $3^2 = 369$
2^2 and $5^2 = 425$, similarly
3^2 and $9^2 = 981$.

2. (d) : Starting from number 4 the numbers are the squares of numbers in natural order *i.e.*, $2^2 = 4, 3^2 = 9, 4^2 = 16 \ldots\ldots 9^2 = 81$.

3. (b) : The number at the bottom is the difference of the squares of two numbers at the top, *i.e.*,
$16^2 - 7^2 = 256 - 49 = 207$
$12^2 - 8^2 = 144 - 64 = 80$, similarly
$25^2 - 21^2 = 625 - 441 = 184$.

4. (b) : The number in the centre is the sum of the products of diagonal numbers, *i.e.*,
$(3 \times 3) + (5 \times 6) = 39$
$(4 \times 4) + (7 \times 5) = 51$, similarly
$(3 \times 4) + (5 \times 5) = 37$.

5. (d) : Sum of two numbers on the top divided by 2 gives the third number, *i.e.*,
$(7 + 5) \div 2 = 6$
$(5 + 21) \div 2 = 13$, similarly
$(24 + 4) \div 2 = 14$.

6. (b) : The numbers in 2nd and 3rd columns are 5 less than the nunbers in 1st and 2nd columns respectively, *i.e.*,
$14 - 5 = 9$ and $9 - 5 = 4$
$12 - 5 = 7$ and $7 - 5 = 2, \ldots$ similarly
$16 - 5 = 11$ and $11 - 5 = 6$.

7. (a) : The sum of 3 numbers in each line in one figure is same, *i.e.*,
$29 + 80 + 43$ or $39 + 80 + 33$
or $45 + 80 + 27 = 152$
$29 + 70 + 44$ or $42 + 70 + 31$
or $43 + 70 + 30 = 143$,
similarly $59 + 80 + 20$ or $39 + 80 + 40 = 159$.
The missing number is :
$159 - (80 + 10) = 69$.

8. (c) : The number at the bottom is the product of two numbers at the top, *i.e.*,
$13 \times 17 = 221$
$12 \times 19 = 228$, similarly
$13 \times 18 = 234$.

9. (b) : Square of number at the bottom is equal to the product of two numbers at the top, *i.e.*,
$6^2 = 4 \times 9$, *i.e.*, 36
$12^2 = 9 \times 16$, *i.e.*, 144, similarly
$20^2 = 16 \times ?$, *i.e.*, 400. The missing number is $400 \div 16 = 25$.

10. (b) : The sum of the products of the digits of numbers in 1st and 3rd columns is the number in the 2nd column, *i.e.*,
$(5 \times 1) + (6 \times 1) = 11$
$(6 \times 4) + (3 \times 2) = 30$, similarly
$(3 \times 5) + (4 \times 3) = 27$.

11. (d) : The sum of numbers on right and centre subtracted from the number on the left gives the number at the bottom, *i.e.*,
$93 - (27 + 63) = 3$
$79 - (38 + 37) = 4$, similarly
$67 - (16 + 42) = 9$.

12. (c) : The number inside each triangle is the difference of the numbers at its base *i.e.*
$10 - 4 = 6$, $18 - 4 = 14$ and $18 - 10 = 8$
$14 - 8 = 6$, $22 - 8 = 14$ and $22 - 14 = 8$, similarly
$11 - 5 = 6$, $15 - 5 = 10$ and $15 - 11 = 4$.

13. (c) : The sum of squares of two numbers at the top gives the third number below, *i.e.*,
$2^2 + 4^2 = 20$
$3^2 + 9^2 = 90$, similarly
$1^2 + 5^2 = 26$.

14. (a) : The sum of numbers in 1st and 2nd column plus 1 is the number in the 3rd column, *i.e.*,
$27 + 22 + 1 = 50$
$13 + 12 + 1 = 26$, similarly
$9 + 2 + 1 = 12$.

15. (d) : The product of numbers on either side of the triangle plus the number at the base is the number inside the triangle, *i.e.*,
$(5 \times 3) + 4 = 19$
$(6 \times 4) + 5 = 29$, similarly
$(7 \times 5) + 6 = 41$.

16. *(a)* : Clockwise starting from number 7, the next number is obtained by doubling the number and adding 2, *i.e.,*

$(7 \times 2) + 2 = 16$

$(16 \times 2) + 2 = 34\ldots$, similarly

$(34 \times 2) + 2 = 70$

$(70 \times 2) + 2 = 142$

$(142 \times 2) + 2 = 286$.

17. *(c)* : The difference between the numbers in opposite sectors is 13, *i.e.,*

$26 - 13 = 13$

$68 - 55 = 13$, similarly

The missing number is $42 - 13 = 29$

($42 + 13 = 55$ is not given as option).

18. *(b)* : The number at the bottom is obtained by subtracting the sum of two numbers in the centre grid line from the square of the number at the top, *i.e.,*

$7^2 - (2 + 7) = 40$

$5^2 - (8 + 3) = 14$, similarly

$9^2 - (7 + 6) = 68$.

19. *(b)* : The number inside the brackets is obtained by multiplying the number on the left by 2 and then dividing the product by the sum of digits of number on the right, *i.e.,*

$(42 \times 2) \div (2 + 2) = 21$

$(162 \times 2) \div (9 + 9) = 18$, similarly

$(78 \times 2) \div (8 + 4) = 13$.

20. *(a)* : Subtracting the sum of squares of two numbers at the base from the square of number at the apex gives the number inside the triangle, *i.e.,*

$16^2 - (7^2 + 10^2) = 107$

$25^2 - (20^2 + 4^2) = 209$, similarly

$19^2 - (2^2 + 17^2) = 68$.

18. ALPHABET PROBLEMS

Alphabet problems are fun to attempt. They are based on alphabetical series in natural as well as reverse order.

Natural Order

A B C D E F G H I J K L M N O P Q R S T U V W X Y Z

Reverse Order

Z Y X W V U T S R Q P O N M L K J I H G F E D C B A

Note : The series starts from A on reaching Z and from Z on reaching A. Of these A E I O U are vowels and the rest are consonants.

EXERCISE

1. Which letter should be ninth letter to the left of ninth letter from the right if the first half of the alphabet is reversed?

(a) I *(b)* D
(c) F *(d)* E

2. Starting from the fifth letter from the left, if twelve letters are written in reverse order, then which letter will be the seventh to the left of the fourteenth letter from the right?

(a) N *(b)* H
(c) L *(d)* O

3. What letter will come in the centre of sixth letter from the right and thirteenth letter from the left?

(a) Q *(b)* R
(c) P *(d)* S

4. If in the word "DISTURBANCE", the first letter is interchanged with the last letter, the second letter is interchanged with the tenth letter and so on, which letter would come after the letter "T" in the newly formed word?

(a) I *(b)* U
(c) N *(d)* S

5. If it is possible to make a meaningful word with the third, the fifth, the seventh and the tenth letters of the word PROJECTION. If no such word can be made, give 'O' as the answer. If more than one such word can be made, give 'M' as the answer.

(a) T *(b)* N
(c) O *(d)* M

6. A meaningful word is made if we take the first, fourth, fifth, seventh, tenth, eleventh and the twelfth letters of the word "FELICITATIONS". Which of the following will be the fifth letter of that word from the right end of that word?

(a) T *(b)* C
(c) N *(d)* I

7. On rearranging the jumbled spelling of the word SKARTINS, a language is obtained. What is the fifth letter from the right of the rearranged word?

(a) N *(b)* K
(c) R *(d)* S

8. If the 1st, 3rd, 5th, 7th, 10th and 13th letters of the word "ENTERTAINMENT" are used to make a meaningful word, then what two letters will come in the centre?

(a) A M *(b)* T T
(c) RE *(d)* N A

9. On rearranging the jumbled spelling of the word GRUBY a sport is obtained. What is the letter in the centre?

(a) R *(b)* B
(c) G *(d)* U

EXPLANATORY ANSWERS

1. *(a)* :

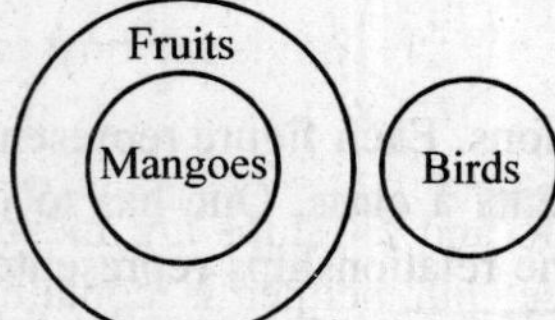

All mangoes are fruits, but neither fruits, nor mangoes can be birds.

2. *(a)* :

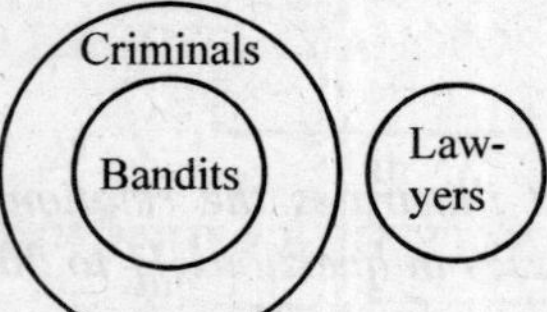

All bandits are criminal, but neither criminals nor bandits can be lawyers.

3. *(b)* :

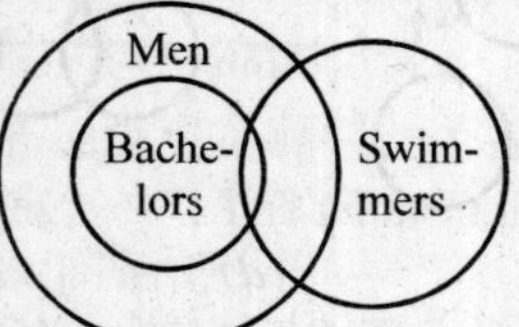

All bachelors are men and some men and bachelors can be swimmers.

4. *(c)* :

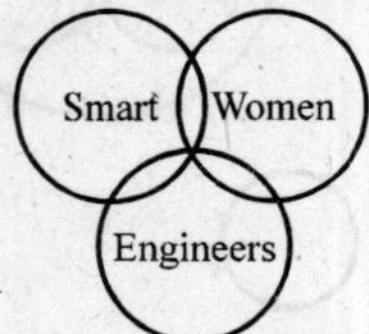

Some women can be smart and some women can be engineers and vice–versa. Some engineers can be women and some engineers can be smart and vice–versa.

5. *(d)* :

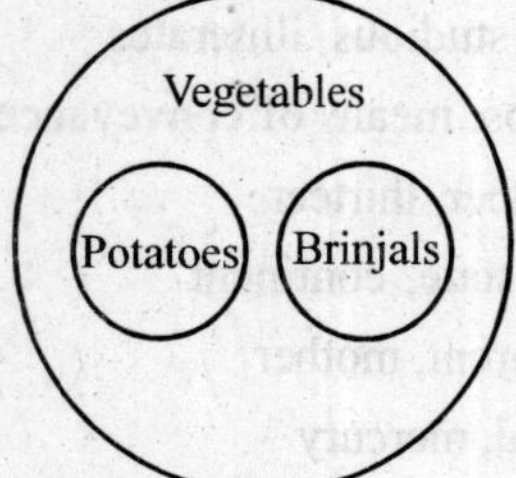

Potatoes and brinjals are vegetables but they have nothing in common. Some vegetables are potatoes and some are brinjals.

6. *(b)* :

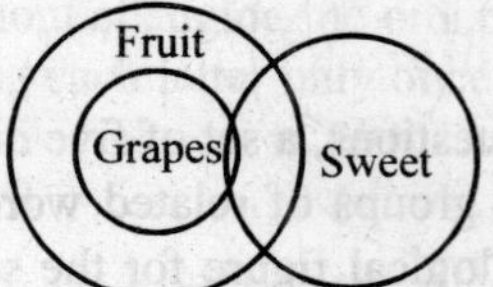

Some grapes are sweet and all grapes are fruit. But not all that is sweet is fruit.

7. *(d)* :

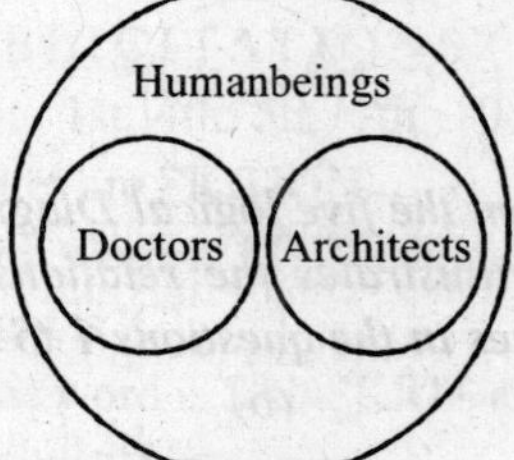

Doctors and architects are two separate classes, but all doctors and architects are humans and some humans are either doctors or architects.

8. *(e)* :

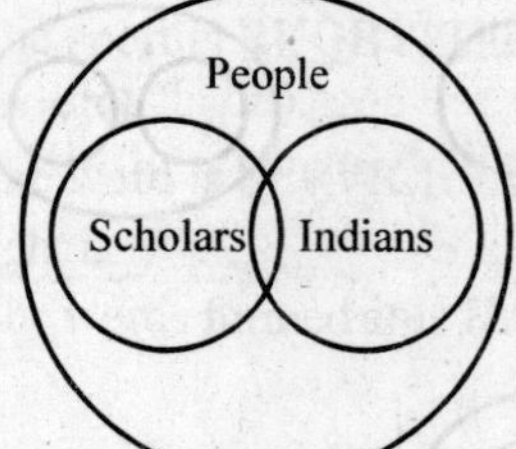

Some Indians can be scholars and some scholars can be Indians. All scholars and Indians are people.

9. *(c)* :

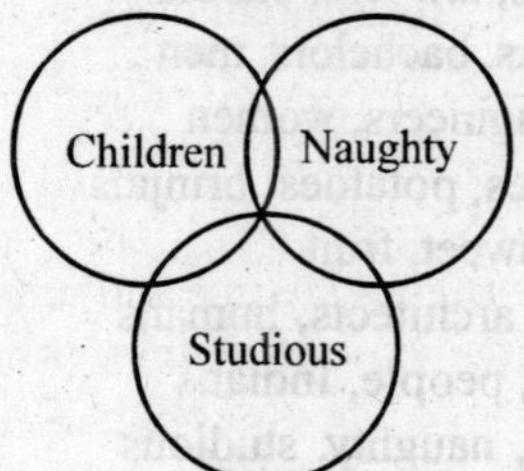

Some children can be naughty and some can be studious, some studious can be children and some naughty. Some naughty can be studious and some children.

10. *(d)* :

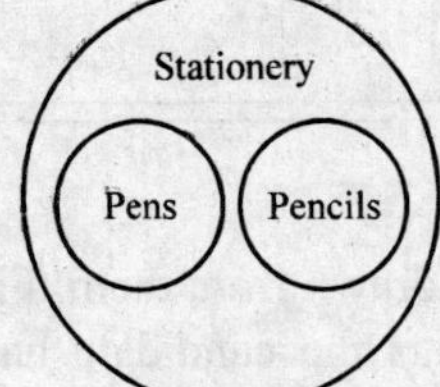

Pens and pencils both are items of stationery and some stationery is pens and pencils, but pens and pencils are two separate classes.

11. *(b)* :

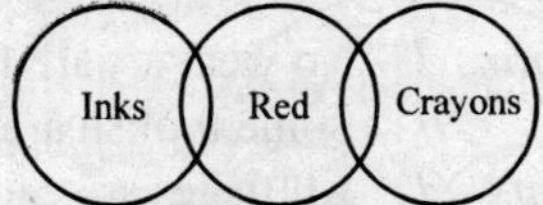

Some ink and some crayons can be red and some red units can be inks and crayons, but ink and crayon have nothing in common.

12. *(c)* :

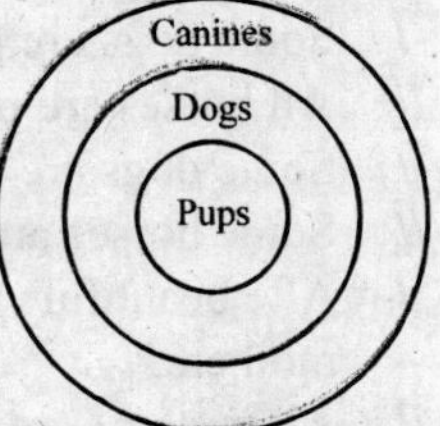

All pups are dogs and all dogs are canines. Some canines are dogs, of which some are pups.

13. *(a)* :

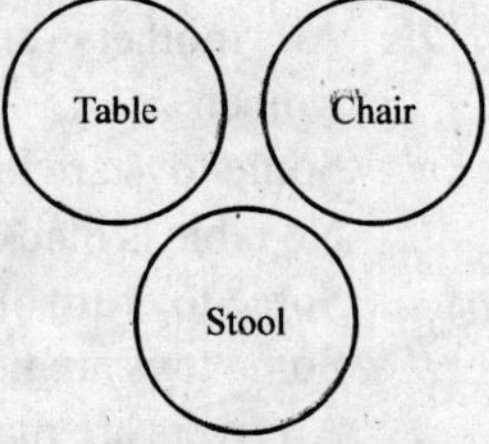

All three are different classes.

14. *(e)* :

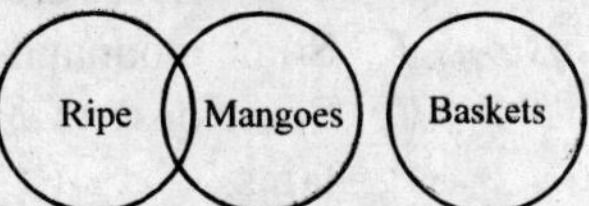

Some mangoes are ripe and some ripe units are mangoes, but neither ripe units nor mangoes can be baskets.

15. *(e)* :

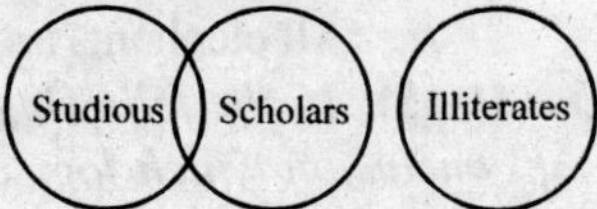

Some studious can be scholars and some scholars can be studious, but neither studious nor scholars can be illiterates.

16. *(d)* :

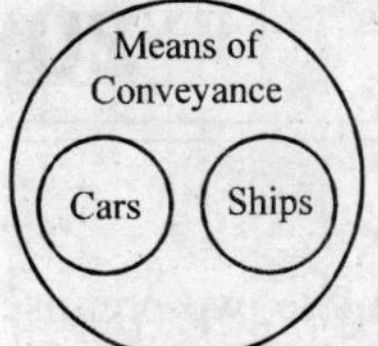

All cars and all ships are means of conveyance, but neither is contained in the other. Some means of conveyance are cars and some ships.

17. *(b)* :

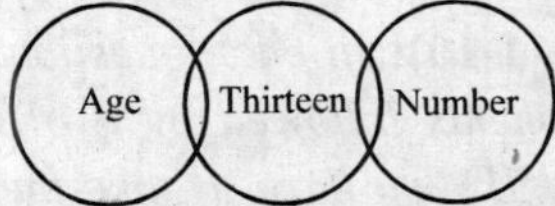

Some are aged thirteen and some numbers are thirteen. Some thirteen units are numbers and some ages. Age and number have nothing in common.

18. *(c)* :

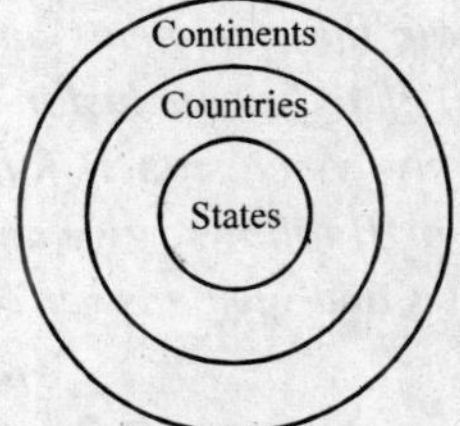

All continents contain countries within it and each country contains states within it.

19. *(d)* :

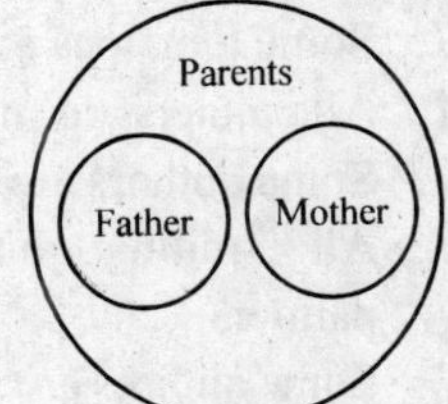

All fathers and mothers are parents, but they are two separate classes. Some of the parents are fathers and some are mothers.

20. *(d)* :

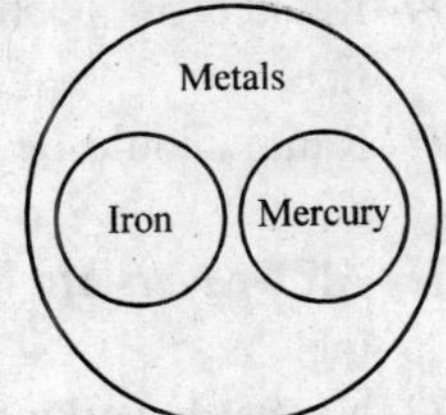

Iron and mercury are metals, but they have nothing in common. Some metals are iron and some mercury.

20. SYLLOGISM

In this reasoning pattern, the two premises are followed by two conclusions drawn from them. Five options *(a)*, *(b)*, *(c)*, *(d)* and *(e)* are given as answers. Based on the two statements the candidate has to select the right option as answer.

EXERCISE

Directions (Qs. 1-10): *In each question below are given two statements followed by two conclusions numbered I and II. You have to take the two given statements to be true even if they seem to be at variance from commonly known facts and then decide which of the given conclusions logically follows from the two given statements, disregarding commonly known facts. Read both the statements and—*

Give answer (a) if only conclusion I follows; give answer (b) if only conclusion II follows; give answer (c) if either I or II follows; give answer (d) if neither I nor II follows and give answer (e) if both I and II follows.

1. *Statements* *I*: All tomatoes are red.
II: All grapes are tomatoes.
Conclusions *I*: All grapes are red.
II: Some tomatoes are grapes.

2. *Statements* *I*: All painters are smilling.
II: Some authors are painters.
Conclusions *I*: All smiling authors are painters.
II: Some authors are smiling.

3. *Statements* *I*: All peons in this office are efficient.
II: Ramu is not efficient.
Conclusions *I*: Ramu is not peon in this office.
II: Ramu should be more efficient.

4. *Statements* *I*: All weavers are hard working.
II: No hard working men are foolish.
Conclusions *I*: No weavers are foolish.
II: Some foolish are weavers.

5. *Statements* *I*: All fishes are cars.
II: All cars are vegetables.
Conclusions *I*: Some vegetables are cars.
II: Some vegetables are fishes.

6. *Statements* *I*: Some dogs are pups.
II: All horses are pups.
Conclusions *I*: Some dogs are horses.
II: Some horses are dogs.

7. *Statements* *I*: All beautiful women are mothers.
II: All mothers are understanding.
Conclusions *I*: All beautiful women are understanding.
II: All mothers are beautiful women.

8. *Statements* *I*: Some toys are tables.
II: No table is black.
Conclusions *I*: Some toys are black.
II: Some toys are not black.

9. *Statements* *I*: All rivers are mountains.
II: Some rivers are deserts.
Conclusions *I*: Some mountains are deserts.
II: Some deserts are not mountains.

10. *Statements* *I*: All men are horses.
II: All horses are elephants.
Conclusions *I*: All men are elephants.
II: All elephants are men.

Directions (Qs. 11-15): *In the following questions, select the set of conclusion which logically follows from the given statements.*

11. *Statements* *I*: All foxes are plates.
II: All plates are trees.
Conclusions *I*: All foxes are trees.
II: All trees are foxes.
III: Some trees are foxes.
IV: Some trees are plates.
(*a*) All conclusions are correct.
(*b*) Only conclusions I, III, and IV follow.
(*c*) Only conclusions II, III, and IV follow.
(*d*) Only conclusions I and IV follow.
(*e*) None of the above.

12. *Statements* *I*: Some cubes are squares.
II: All squares are circles.
Conclusions *I*: All cubes are circles.
II: Some circles are cubes.
III: Some circles are squares.
IV: All squares are cubes.
(*a*) Only conclusion I follows.
(*b*) Only conclusion I, II and III follow.
(*c*) All conclusions are correct.
(*d*) Only conclusions II and III follow.
(*e*) None of the above.

13. *Statements* *I*: All cups are goats.
II: All goats are tins.
Conclusions *I*: All goats are cups.
II: All tins are goats.
III: No cups are tins.
IV: No tins are cups.
(*a*) Only conclusions III and IV follow.
(*b*) Only conclusios I and II follow.
(*c*) Only conclusions I, II and III follow.
(*d*) All conclusions are correct.
(*e*) None of the above.

14. *Statements* *I*: All bombs are bags.
II: Some bags are jets.
Conclusions *I*: All bombs are jets.
II: All jets are bombs.
III: Some jets are bombs.
IV: Some bombs are jets.
(*a*) Only conclusion III follows.
(*b*) Only conclusions I and II follow.
(*c*) All conclusions are correct.
(*d*) Only conclusions III and IV follow.
(*e*) None of these.

15. *Statements* *I*: Some thorns are jackets.
II: Some jackets are boats.
Conclusions *I*: No thorns are boats.
II: All jackets are boats.
III: Some boats are thorns.
IV: No jackets are thorns.
(*a*) Either conclusion I or IV follows.
(*b*) Either conclusion I or II follows.
(*c*) Either conclusion I or III follows.
(*d*) No conclusion is correct.
(*e*) All conclusions are correct.

EXPLANATORY ANSWERS

1. *(e)*: When all tomatoes are red and all grapes are tomatoes, then all grapes are also red. When all grapes are tomatoes, then some tomatoes must be grapes. Therefore, both conclusions I and II are correct.

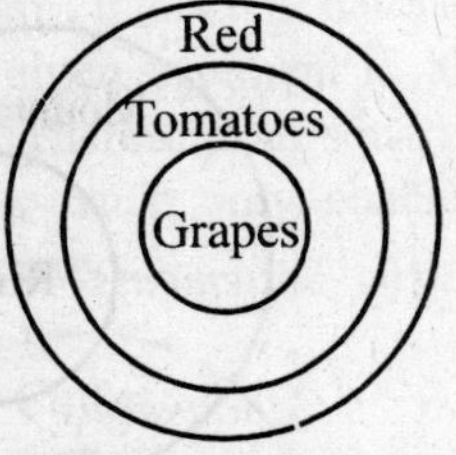

2. *(b)*: When all painters are smiling and some authors are painters, then some authors are smiling. Therefore, only conclusion II is correct.

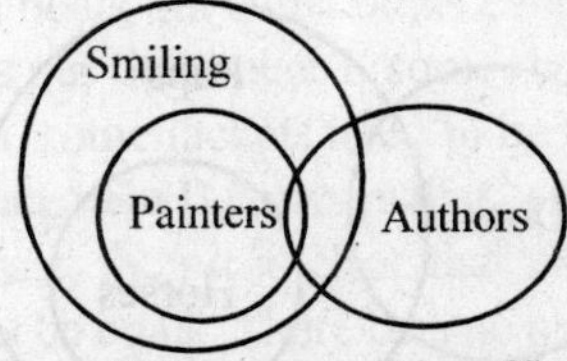

3. *(a)*: When all the peons of the office are efficient, then Ramu cannot be a peon in this office. Therefore, only conclusion I is correct.

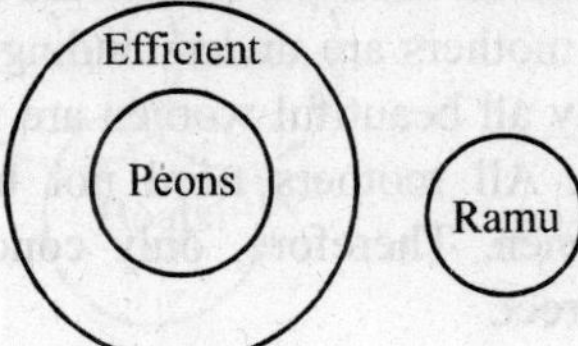

21. VENN DIAGRAMS

In these type of questions, diagrammatic representation presents a logical illustration of particular class or statements based on which the questions are asked. A clear view of the diagram makes the concepts clear for attempting such questions.

EXERCISE

1. What is the number which is common to only two geometrical figures?

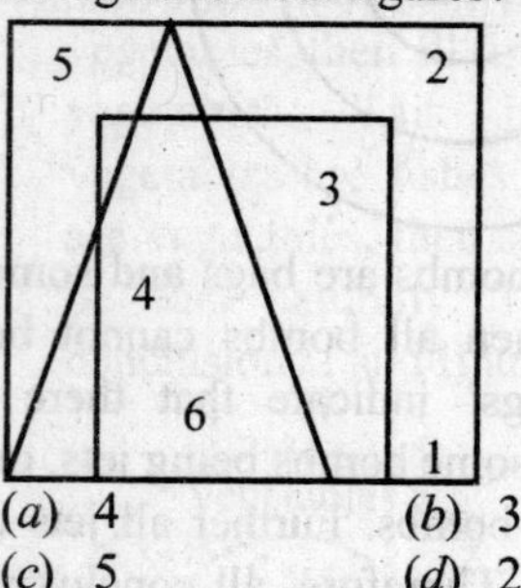

(*a*) 4 (*b*) 3
(*c*) 5 (*d*) 2

Directions (Qs. 2 and 3) : *In the following diagram, rectangle represents Hindi Announcers, circle represents English Announcers, square represents French Announcers, and triangle represents German Announcers.*

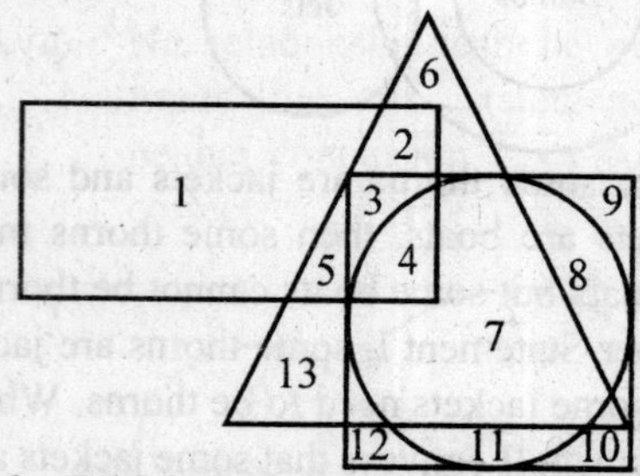

2. Which area represents those announcers who can present programmes in Hindi, French and German only?

(*a*) 1 (*b*) 2
(*c*) 3 (*d*) 4

3 Which area represents those announcers who can present programmes in French and English only?

(*a*) 7 (*b*) 9
(*c*) 11 (*d*) 13

Directions (Qs. 4 and 5) : *Study the diagram to answer these questions.*

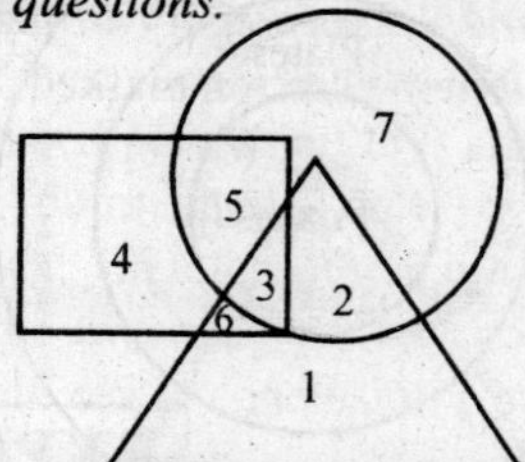

4. Which number is in all the geometrical figures?

(*a*) 5 (*b*) 6
(*c*) 2 (*d*) 3

5. Number 6 is in :

(*a*) Rectangle and triangle
(*b*) Circle and traingle
(*c*) Rectangle and circle
(*d*) Rectangle only

Directions (Qs. 6 to 9) : *In the following diagram*

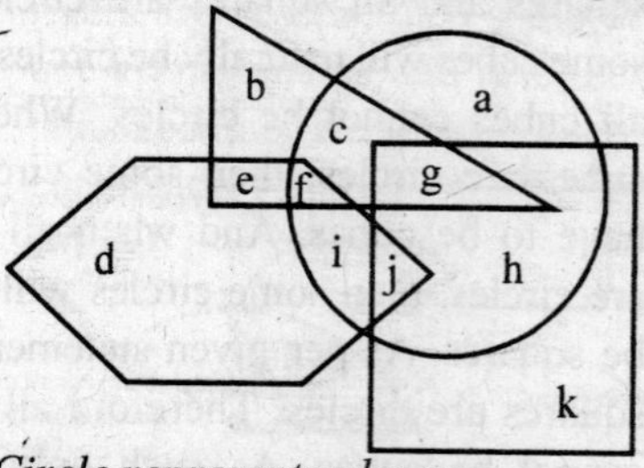

The Circle represents players
The Triangle represents outdoor games
The Hexagon represents indoor games and
The Square represents national level players
Study the diagram and answer the questions given below :

6. The letter in the section representing the players who play indoor games at national level is :

(*a*) f (*b*) i
(*c*) j (*d*) g

7. The letter representing the section of outdoor as well as indoor game players who do not play at the national level is :

(*a*) c (*b*) f

(*c*) e (*d*) i

8. The section representing national level players who do not play either outdoor or indoor games but still come under the category of players is :

(*a*) k (*b*) g

(*c*) c (*d*) h

9. Persons who play outdoor games but do not come under the category of players are represented in the section marked :

(*a*) b (*b*) c

(*c*) a (*d*) d

Direction (Qs. 10) : *Study the diagram given below.*

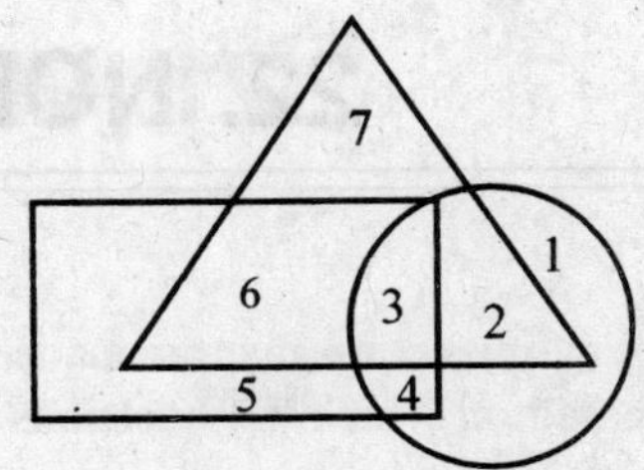

A college provides three different activities, students union represented by triangle, literary society represented by rectangle and social service league represented by circle.

10. Those who take part in both literary society and social service league but not in students union are represented by :

(*a*) 3 & 4 (*b*) 5 & 6

(*c*) 5 & 1 (*d*) 4

EXPLANATORY ANSWERS

1. *(b)* :

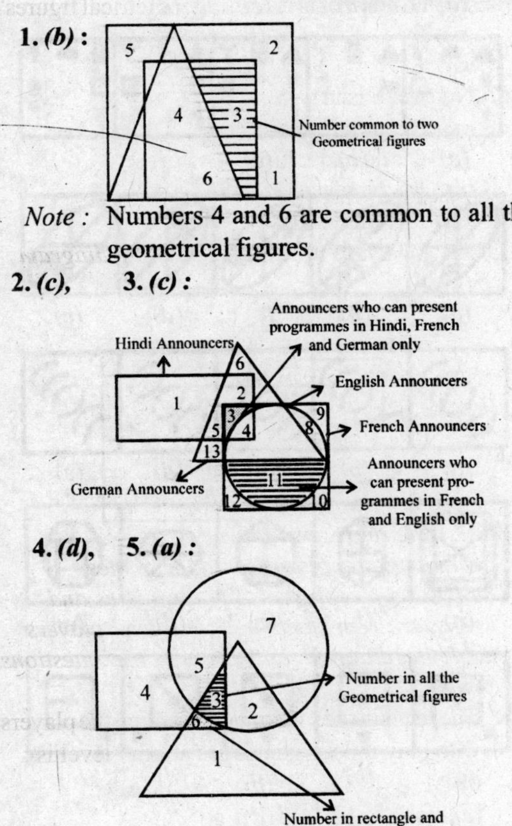

Note : Numbers 4 and 6 are common to all three geometrical figures.

2. *(c)*, **3.** *(c)* :

4. *(d)*, **5.** *(a)* :

6. *(c)*, **7.** *(b)*, **8.** *(d)*, **9.** *(a)* :

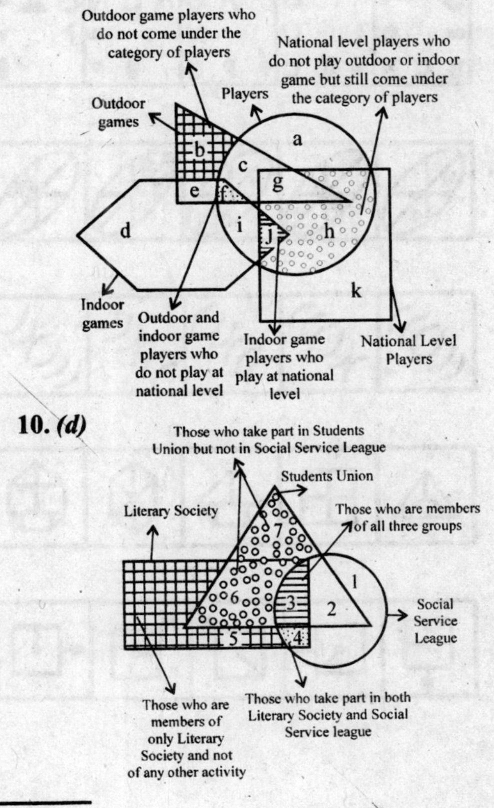

10. *(d)*

22. NON-VERBAL SERIES

EXERCISE

Directions (Q. 1–10) : *In each of the following questions which one of the five answer figures given below should come after the problem figures if the sequence are continued?*

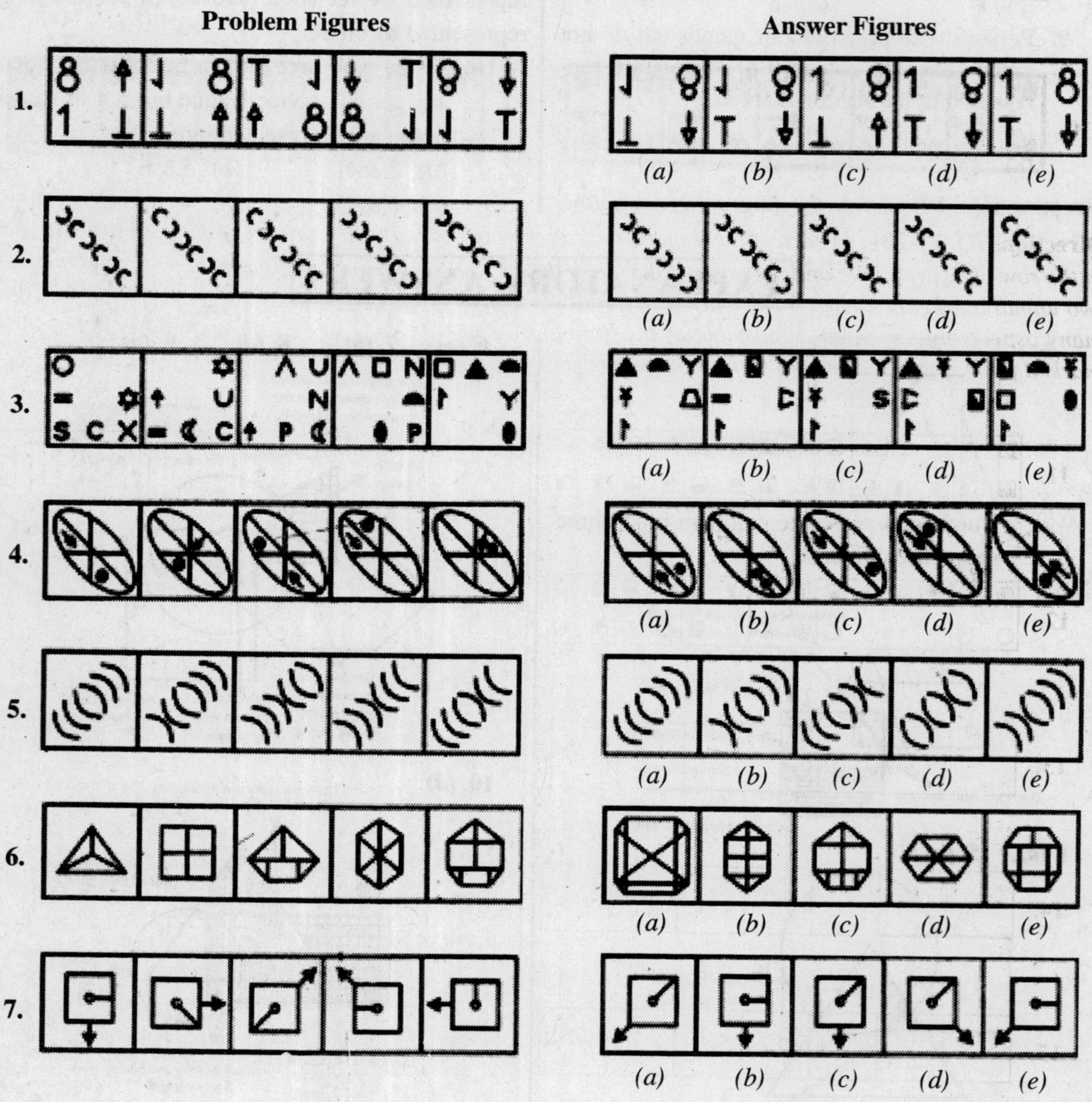

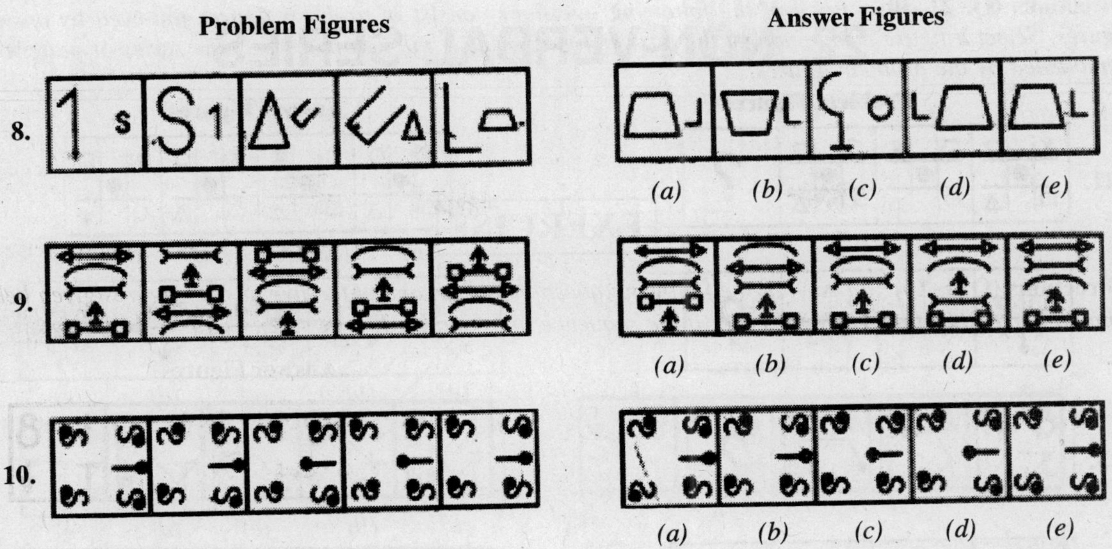

Directions (Q. 11-20) : *In each of these questions, a series begins with an unmarked figure on the extreme left in the row of figures. One and only one of the five lettered figures in the series does not fit into the series. The two unmarked figures, one on the extreme left and the other on the extreme right fit into the series. Take as many aspects into account as possible of the figures in the series and find out the one and only of the five marked figures which does not fit into the series. The letter of that figure is the answer.*

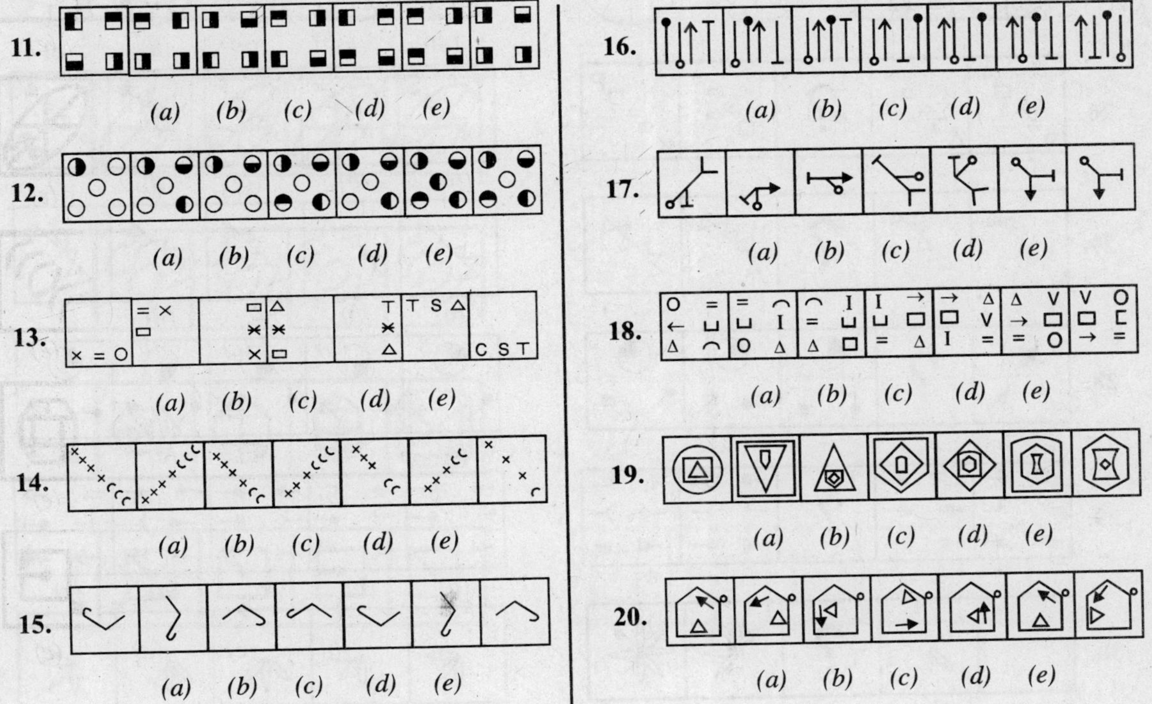

Directions (Q. 21–30) : *Each of the following questions consist of problem figures followed by answer figures. Select a figure from amongst the answer figures which will continue the same series or pattern as established by the problem figures.*

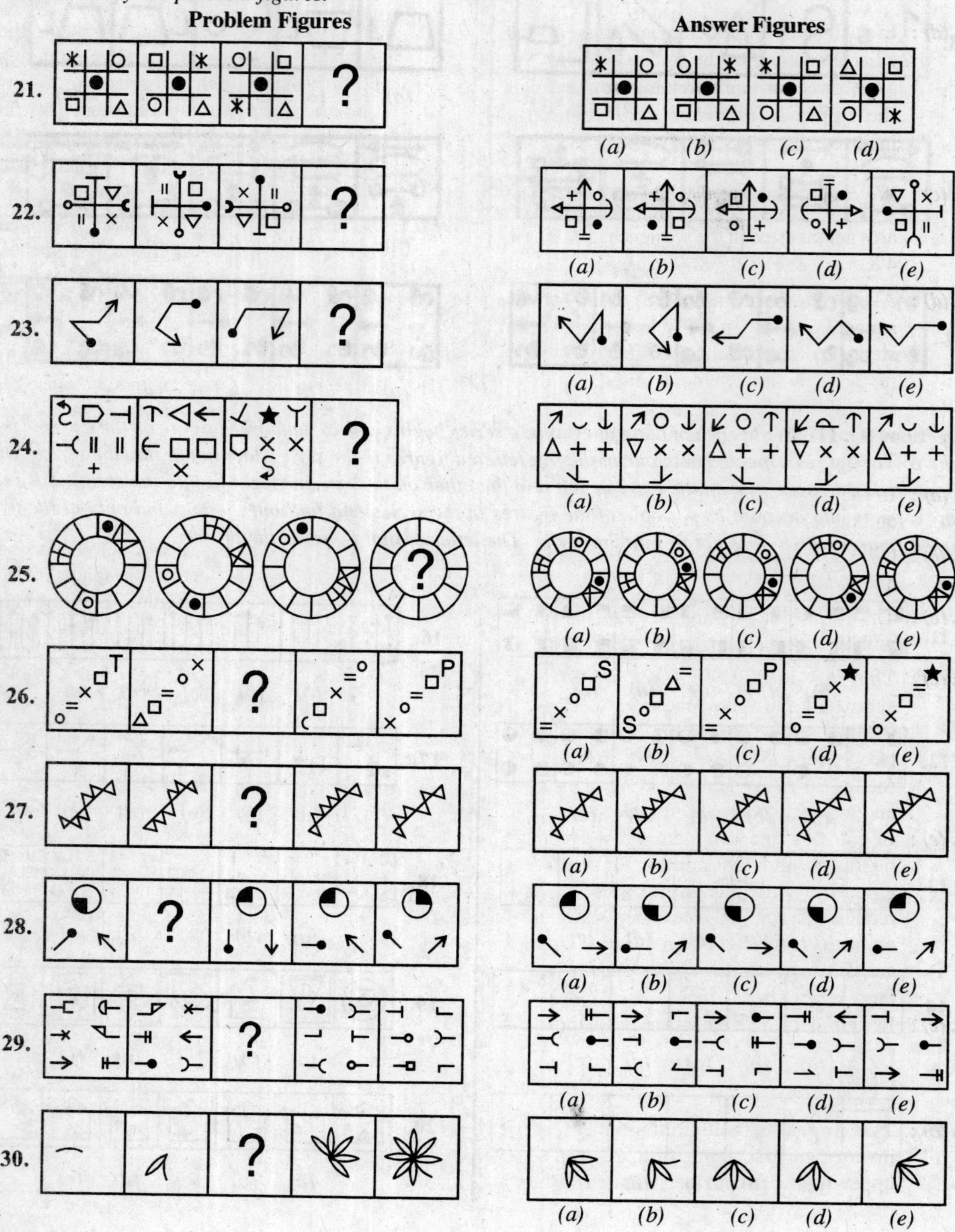

EXPLANATORY ANSWERS

1. (d) : In each step, all the elements move to the adjacent corner (of the square boundary) in a CW direction and the element that reaches the upper-left corner gets vertically inverted.

2. (c) : We can label the arcs as shown. The arcs get inverted in the sequence (1 & 2), (3, 4 & 5), (6 & 1), (2, 3 & 4), (5 & 6), ...

3. (d) : All the elements move half-a-side of the square boundary in ACW direction in each step. Also, first, third and fifth elements are replaced by new elements in one step and second, fourth and sixth elements are replaced by new elements in the next step. The two steps are repeated alternately.

4. (a) : In each step, the dot moves one space CW and the arrow moves two spaces CW.

5. (c) : One arc and four arcs get inverted alternately.

6. (e) : The number of parts increases by one along with the number of sides in the figure.

7. (c) : The pin rotates 45°CW and 90°CW alternately and moves one space (each space is equal to half-a-side of the square) and two spaces CW alternately. The arrow rotates 90°ACW and 45°ACW alternately and moves two spaces and one space.

8. (e) : In one step, the two elements interchange positions and the smaller element gets enlarged while the larger element gets reduced in size. In the next step, the smaller element is replaced by a new small element and the larger element is replaced by a new large element.

9. (c) : In each step, the elements move in the order

.

10. (b) : The upper-left element gets laterally inverted in first, third, fifth. .... steps; the upper-right element gets rotated through 180° is first, fourth, seventh,.... steps; the lower-left element gets laterally inverted in second, fourth, sixth, ... steps; the lower-right element gets rotated through 180° in third, sixth,... steps and the pin at the middle-right position gets laterally inverted in every second step.

11. (a) : The shade in the top left square is moved one step clockwise till figure B and then reversed, the process is repeated. The shade in the top right square is moved one step anticlockwise till figure D and then reversed. The shade in the bottom left square is moved one step clockwise in alternate figures and the shade in bottom right square is moved one step clockwise after two figures. In figure 'A' the rule is isolated by the shade in the bottom left square.

12. (e) : In alternate figures a new circle is shaded clockwise. The pattern of the shade is also moved clockwise. In figure 'E' right half of the circle in the centre should have been shaded.

13. (a) : The three elements are placed either horizontally or vertically. In option 'A' neither of the placements can be applied.

14. (c) : The placement of elements is same in alternate figures. The number and type of elements is same in two subsequent figures. In this manner, figure 'C' should have four crosses and two C shapes.

15. (c) : The element is moved one step anticlockwise and the arc at one end is turned outside and inside alternately. In figure 'C' the element should be on the right side with the arc turned outside on the top side.

16. (e) : The left most element, line segment with the dot is moved one step towards right till figure C where it reaches the extreme right position. This process is repeated from figure D where the element on the extreme

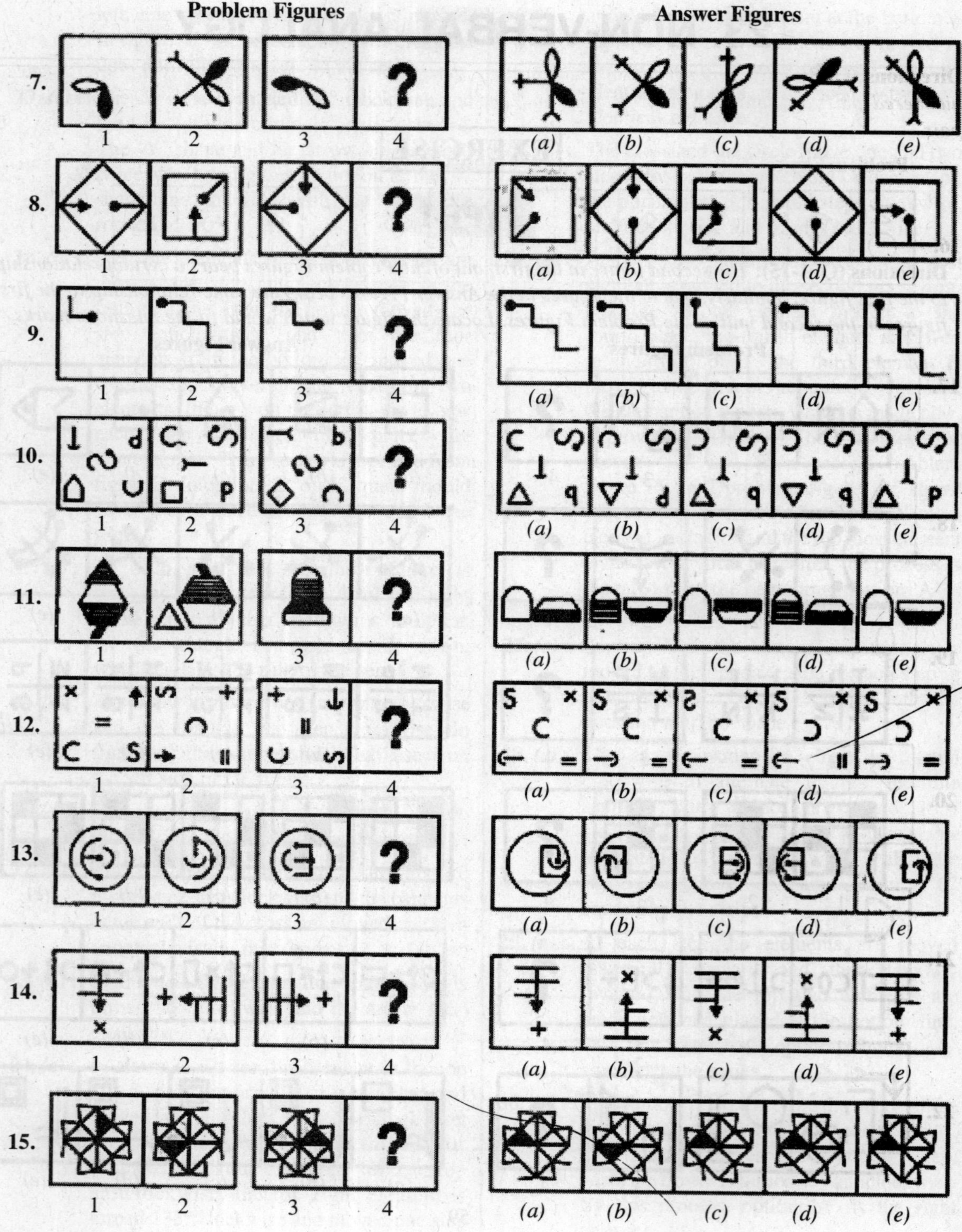
Problem Figures
Answer Figures
7.
8.
9.
10.
11.
12.
13.
14.
15.
1
2
3
4
?
(a)
(b)
(c)
(d)
(e)

TYPE-II

Directions (Q. 16–30): *In each of the following questions, a related pair of figures is followed by five numbered pairs of figures. Select the pair that has a relationship* **similar** *to that in the unnumbered pair.*

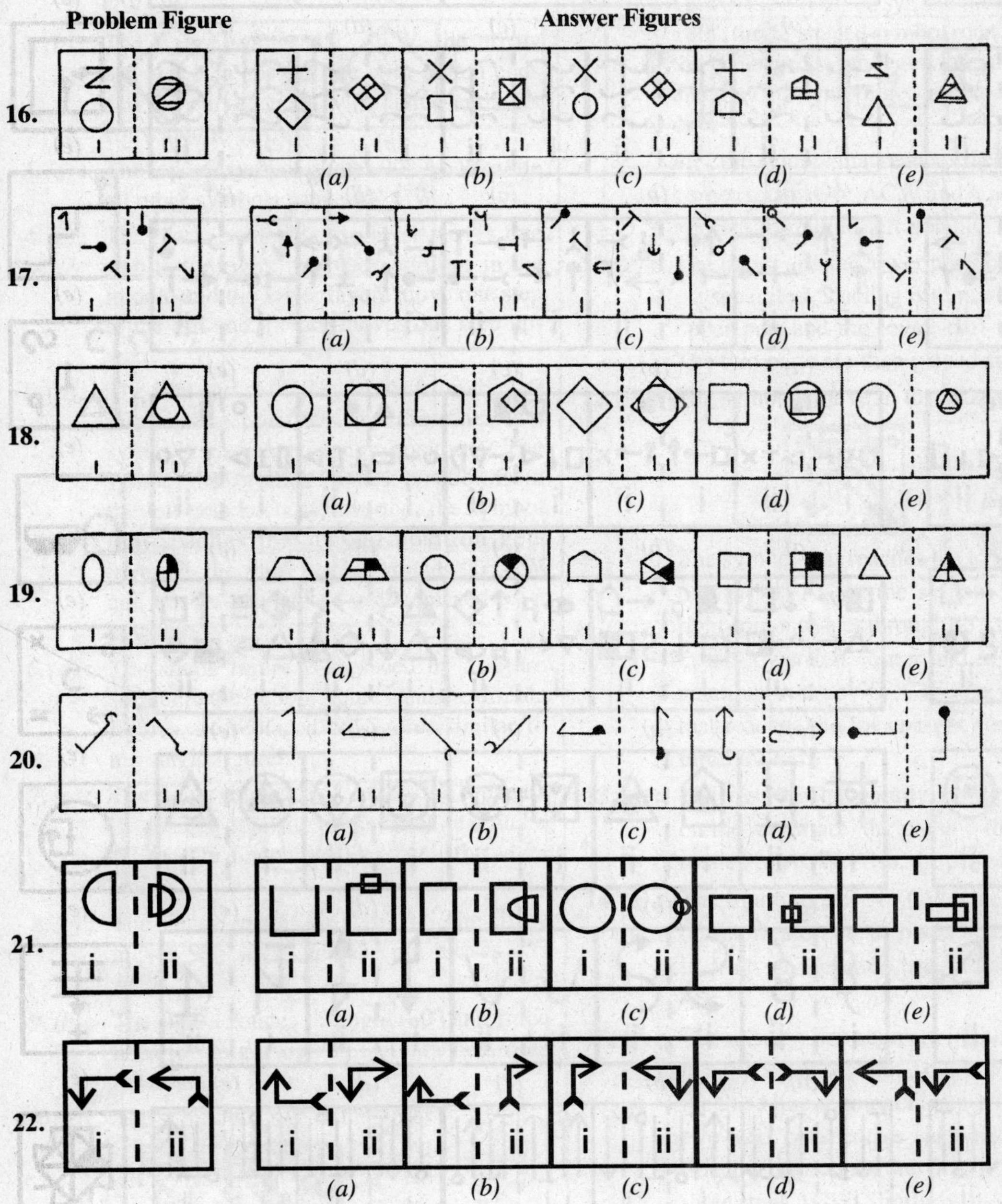

13.

(a) (b) (c) (d) (e)

14.

(a) (b) (c) (d) (e)

15.

(a) (b) (c) (d) (e)

16.

(a) (b) (c) (d) (e)

17.

(a) (b) (c) (d) (e)

18.

(a) (b) (c) (d) (e)

19.

(a) (b) (c) (d) (e)

20.

(a) (b) (c) (d) (e)

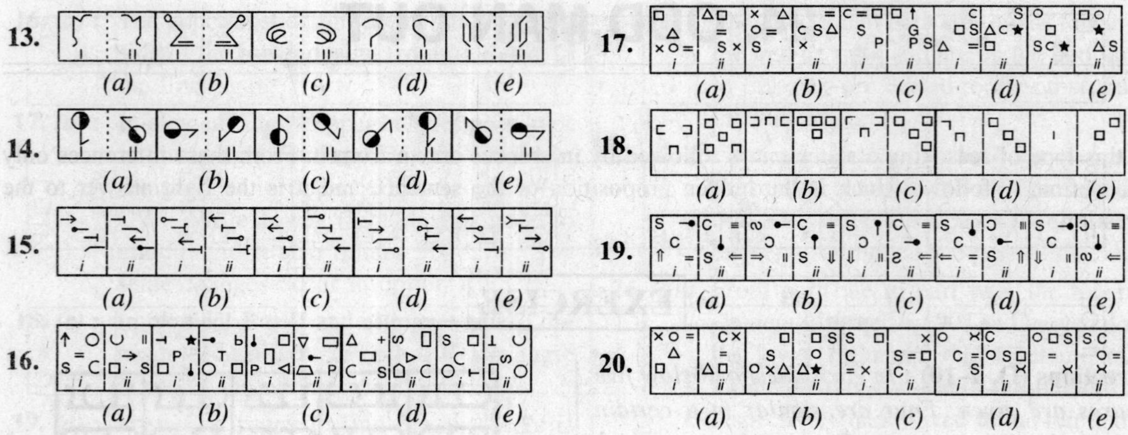

Directions (Q. 21–30) : *In each of the following questions, a related pair of figures (unnumbered) is followed by five numbered pairs of figures. Out of these five, four have relationship similar to that in the unnumbered pair. Only one pair of figures does not have similar relationship. Select that pair of figures which does not have a similar relationship to that in the unnumbered pair. Number of that pair is your answer.*

21.

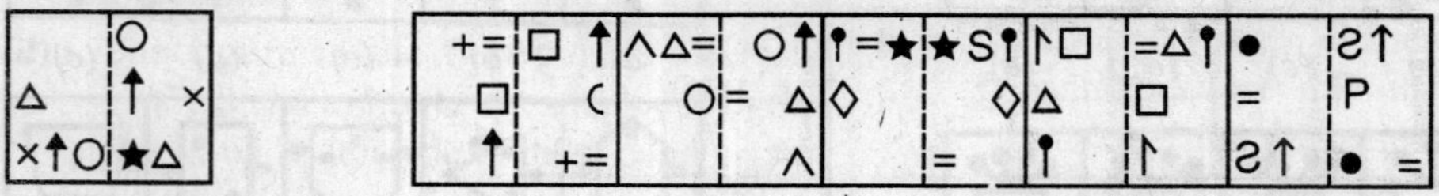

(a) (b) (c) (d) (e)

22.

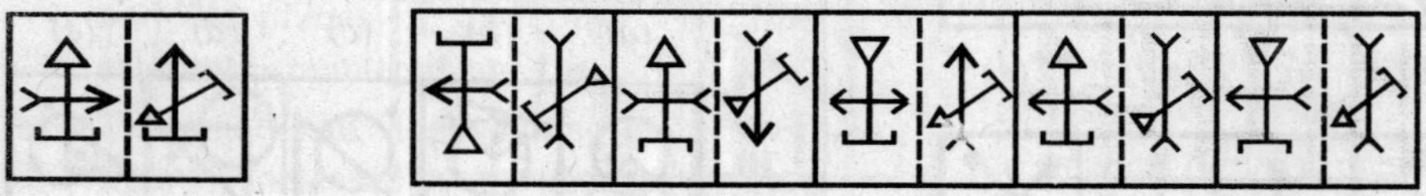

(a) (b) (c) (d) (e)

23.

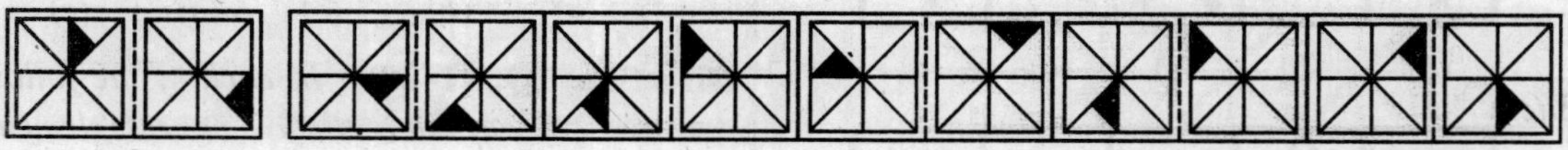

(a) (b) (c) (d) (e)

24.

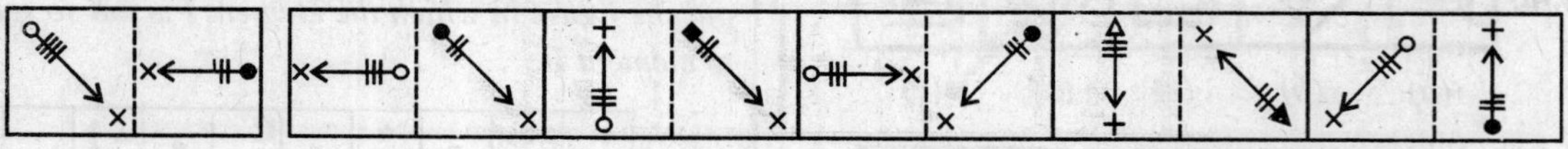

(a) (b) (c) (d) (e)

25.

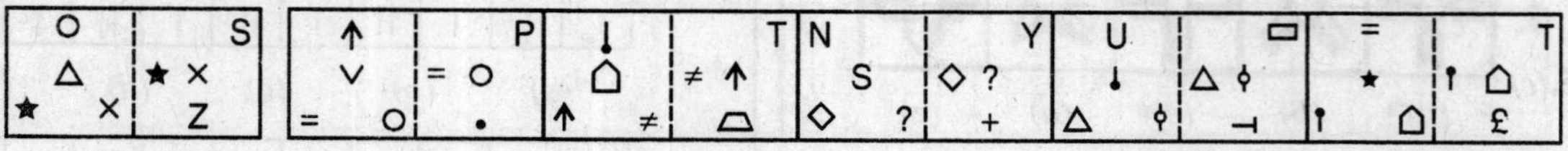

(a) (b) (c) (d) (e)

26.

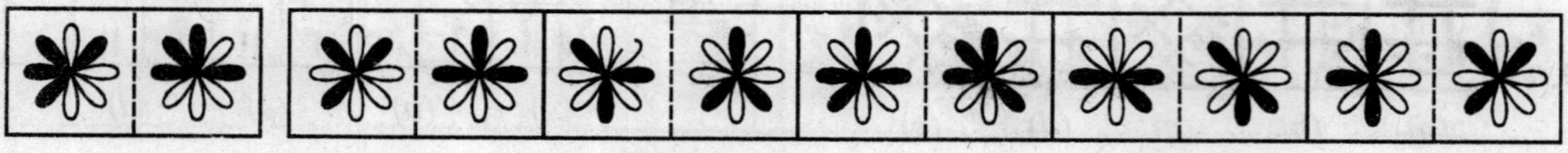

(a) (b) (c) (d) (e)

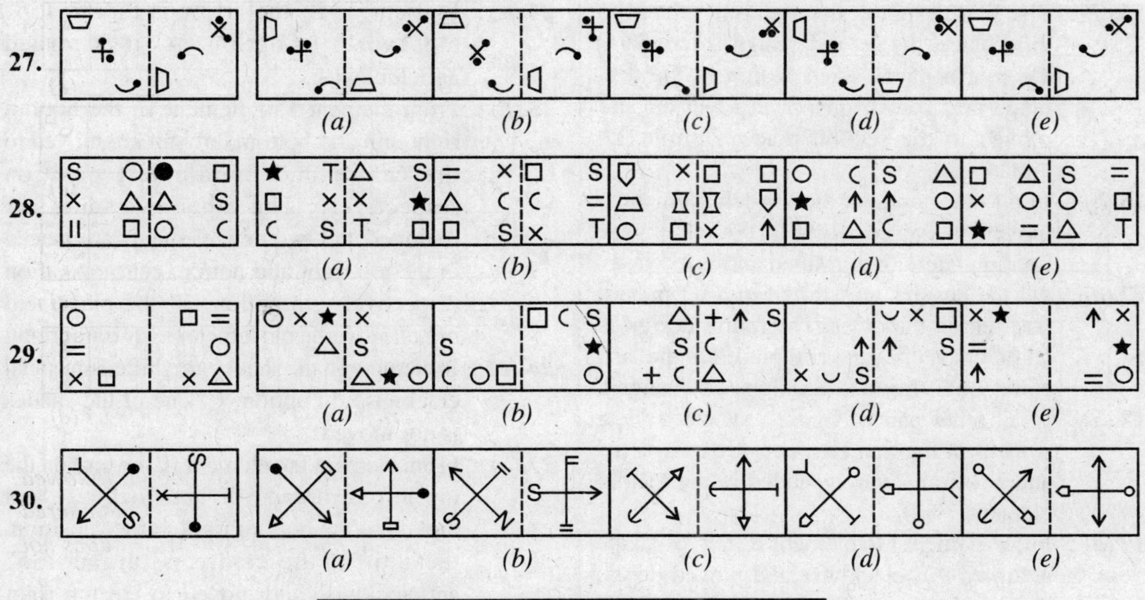

EXPLANATORY ANSWERS

1. *(d)* : In all other figures, the arrow and the + sign lie towards the black end of the main figure.

2.*(a)* : The pins, equal in number of sides in the main figure are attached to the midpoint of a side of the main figure in case of figures (B), (C), (D) and (E). In figure (A), these pins are attached to a vertex of the main figure.

3.*(c)* : In all other figures, the dot appears in the angle formed between the arrow and the pin.

4.*(a)* : All other figures can be rotated into each other. (In each figure except figure (A), the middle element is obtained by rotating the outer element through 90° CW and the inner element is obtained by rotating the middle element through 90° CW).

5.*(c)* : All other figures have at least one line of symmetry.

6.*(c)* : All other figures can be rotated into each other.

7.*(e)* : In each one of the other four figures, four arcs are curved towards the left and four other arcs are curved towards the right.

8.*(c)* : All other figures can be rotated into each other.

9.*(d)* : In all other figures, the number of dots outside the main figure is one more than the number of dots inside the main figure.

10.*(a)* : In all other figures, one of the dots lies outside the triangle as well as the circle.

11.*(e)* : Except in figure (B), in all other figures, from element I to II two new designs are added in one side of the main design.

12.*(c)* : In each figure from element I to II the main design rotates through 135° clockwise or anticlockwise. Except in figure (C), in all other figures, the smaller line segment moves to other side from element I to II.

13.*(a)* : In all other figures the element II can be obtained by the lateral inversion of the element I. In figure (A), the lower design has not been inverted.

14.*(b)* : In figure (B), the small segment is on the same side as that of the half shaded circle in both the elements.

15.(*d*) : The first design is inverted and moved to third place, the second design is moved to the fourth place, third design to the first place and fourth design is inverted and moved to the second place. Option (D) violates this.

16.(*b*) : In all other options the top-left element is moved to the centre with 90° clockwise rotation. Here, it is rotated anticlockwise.

17.(*d*) : All the designs are shifted in a set pattern one behind the other. The fourth design in all others is changed and placed in the last. Here, the fifth and last designs are changed.

18.(*a*) : In all other pair of figures, all incomplete squares in the first elements are completed and an extra square is added in the second element.

19.(*a*) : From element I to element II, the 'S' shape is turned 90° clockwise and moved down, the double arrow shape '⇒' is turned 90° clockwise and moved to the right, the two parallel lines one turned by 90°; one parallel line is added and all three lines are moved up, the line with a dot is turned 90° clockwise and moved to the centre and the 'C' shape in the centre is turned by 180°. and moved to top left position. Here, the double arrow is turned anticlockwise.

20.(*c*) : Starting from one unit, all units are moved in a set pattern, the places of last two units moved are interchanged and the last unit is then made new. Here, no changes are made in the last two units.

21.(*d*) : From element I to element II clockwise the first unit is moved 2 steps forward, the second unit 1 step forward, the third unit 2½ steps forward and the fourth unit 3 steps forward. In option 'D' the third unit violates the rule.

22.(*e*) : From element I to element II, the horizontal bar is turned 135° anticlockwise and the unit at the lower end is turned by 180°. The vertical bar is turned 90° anticlockwise and the unit at the lower end is turned by 180°. In option 'E' one more unit at the top is turned by 180°.

23.(*e*) : In element II, the shade is moved two sections clockwise and shifted from the centre to the base. In option 'E' it is not so.

24.(*a*) : In element II, the arrow is turned 135° clockwise. In option 'A' it is turned anticlockwise.

25.(*b*) : From element I to element II, the bottom right unit and bottom left unit are moved to the centre and middle left position respectively. The other two units are removed and two new elements are placed in the top right and bottom centre position respectively. In option 'B' the placement of bottom right and left elements is not right.

26.(*c*) : In element II, the shades are shifted one petal clockwise. In option 'C' one of the shades is not moved.

27.(*b*) : From element I to element II, the unit on the top left is turned 90° anticlockwise and moved to the bottom right corner position, the unit in the centre is turned 135° anticlockwise and moved to the top right position, and the unit in the bottom right is turned by 180° and moved to the centre. In option 'B', the middle unit is turned 135° clockwise.

28.(*a*) : From element I to element II, a new unit is placed in the top left position, the top left unit is moved to the middle right position, the middle right unit is moved to the left position, the middle left unit is replaced by a new unit and placed in bottom right position, the bottom right unit is moved to the top right position, and the top right unit is moved diagonally to replace the bottom left unit. In option 'A', the middle left unit is not changed when moved to the bottom right position.

29.(*e*) : From element I to element II starting anticlockwise, the first and second units are moved 1½ steps clockwise respectively, the third unit ½ step anticlockwise, the fourth unit 2 steps clockwise, and a new unit is placed ahead of the first unit. Option 'E' violates the rules.

30.(*e*) : In element II, the cross is turned 135° clockwise and then the positions of left and top units on the cross are interchanged. In option 'E' it is not so.

ENGLISH LANGUAGE

1. Comprehension Passages

In the English language paper, questions on comprehension test are very important for the examinees appearing in the competitive examinations.

Comprehension means the act of comprehending or the capacity of the mind to understand. In the examination papers, questions on comprehension test are included to judge the ability of the examinees to understand the given passage.

Therefore, they should understand how to solve these questions. Practice of solving these questions will greatly help them in the examination.

Directions: *Read the following passages carefully and answer the questions given after each passage. Out of the four alternatives, choose the correct answer according to the context of the passage.*

PASSAGE-1

This is the age of the Machine, Machines are everywhere, in the fields, in the factory, at home, in the street, in the city, in the country, every where. To fly, it is not necessary to have wings; there are machines. The swim under the sea, it is not necessary to have gills; there are machines. To kill our fellowmen in over-whelming numbers, there are machines. Petrol machines alone provide ten times more power than all human beings in the world. In the busiest countries, each individual has six hundred human slaves in his machines.

What are the consequences of this abnormal power? Before the War, it looked as though it might be possible, for the first time in history to provide food and clothing and shelter for the teeming population of the world—every man, woman and child. This would have been the greatest triumphs of science. And yet, if you remember, we saw the world crammed, full of food and people hungry. Today, the larders are bare and millions, starving. That's the war, you would say. When the machines of peace once more begin to ....

1. According to the passage, which of the following is not necessary to fly?

A. Wings B. Arms

C. Feet D. Machines

2. Petrol machinery is used to provide:

A. ten times more power than human beings in the world

B. less power than human beings in the world

C. as much power as human beings in the world

D. none of the above is correct

3. What could be one of the greatest triumphs of science?

A. to provide food, clothing and shelter to everyone

B. none would get food, clothing and shelter

C. only rich people would get food, clothing and shelter

D. people would get only clothing

4. This is the age of the:

A. machine B. animal husbandry

C. agriculture D. wars

5. The machine age produces:

A. goods

B. food

C. goods but avoids the consequences

D. none of the above

Answers

1	2	3	4	5
A	A	A	A	C

PASSAGE-2

What are the good parts of our civilization? First and foremost there are order and safety. If today I have a quarrel with another man, I do not get beaten merely because I am physically weaker and he can knock me down. I go to law and the law will decide as fairly as it can between the two of us. Thus in disputes between man and man. Right has taken the place of might. Moreover, the law protects me from robbery and violence. Nobody may come and break into my house, steal my books or run off with my children. Of course, there are burglars, but they are very rare and the law punishes them whenever, it catches them.

It is difficult for us to realize how much this safety means. Without safety those higher activities of mankind which make up civilization could not go on. The inventor could not invent, the scientist find out or the artist make beautiful things. Hence, order and safety, although they are not themselves civilization, are things without which civilization could be impossible. They are as necessary to our civilization as the air we breathe is to us; and we have-grown so used to them that we do not notice them any more than we notice the air.

1. The first and foremost good parts of civilization are:
   A. order and insecurity
   B. only insecurity
   C. order and safety
   D. insecurity and lawlessness.

2. In disputes between man and man:
   A. right has taken the place of might
   B. might has taken the place of right
   C. might is right
   D. none of the above

3. According to the passage, the burglars are:
   A. many B. rare
   C. found nowhere D. not punished

4. An artist can create beautiful things only if:
   A. there is disorder
   B. there is no safety
   C. there is safety
   D. there is neither safety nor order

5. According to the writer, man does not notice order and safety as:
   A. he does not notice the air he breathes
   B. he does not notice the food he eats
   C. he does not notice the shelter he needs
   D. none of the above is correct

Answers

1	2	3	4	5
C	A	B	C	A

PASSAGE-3

The purpose of education is to make the student an expert in his subject. This must be clearly understood, and mere muddling through lessons and lectures and books and passing examination are relegated to secondary importance as means to the end—which is excellence in the field choosen.

But there are so many fields, and no man can become an expert in all the fields. It is necessary to decide which fields are the important ones that a man should know well.

It is clear that one's own work is the most important. This has been realised and modern civilization has accordingly provided vocational education. It is now possible to acquire high professional skill in the various fields, medicine, engineering production, commerce and so on—but with good and bad mixed together, and no standard for guidance.

1. The purpose of education is to make the student:
   A. an expert in all fields
   B. an expert in his subject
   C. only capable of earning
   D. confident only

2. What, according to the writer, is the end?
   A. excellence in the field choosen
   B. passing the examination
   C. earning more and more money
   D. cramming lectures and books

3. According to the passage, can a man become an expert in all fields?
   A. Yes B. Partially yes
   C. Sometimes D. No

4. According to the writer, which of the following is the most important work?
   A. someone else's work
   B. one's own work
   C. nobody's work
   D. everyone's work

5. The modern civilization has provided
   A. vocational education
   B. art of conversation
   C. adult education
   D. higher education

Answers

1	2	3	4	5
B	A	D	B	A

PASSAGE-4

English education, which was introduced in India in the earlier part of the nineteenth century, established her cultural contact with the West. Prior to this, India had for centuries remained in a state of isolation, although in very early times she had sent out cultural missions to the other Asiatic countries. India really began to borrow from the West and assimilate new ideas on an extensive scale only after the British had taken up the direction of her educational policy.

It is true that Western education at first exerted an unsettling: influence on young men and led to errors in life and conduct. They hated everything Indian, aped western manners and modes of life, and forgot their glorious past. There were scholars who ignored modern Indian languages, avoided classical Indian literature, and made a fetish of speaking and writing English.

1. When was English education introduced in India?
   A. in the twentieth century
   B. in the later part of the nineteenth century
   C. in the earlier part of the nineteenth century
   D. in the eighteenth century
2. When did India begin to borrow from the West?
   A. after the British had taken up the direction of her educational policy
   B. before the British had taken up the direction of her educational policy
   C. in the twentieth century
   D. none of the above is correct
3. What did India send out to other Asiatic countries?
   A. economic mission B. military forces
   C. cultural missions D. none of these
4. Western education exerted an unsettling influence on:
   A. old men B. young men
   C. old women D. children
5. Young men forgot their:
   A. glorious past B. present
   C. future D. originality

Answers

1	2	3	4	5
C	A	C	B	A

PASSAGE-5

Each nation has its own peculiar character which distinguishes it from others. But the peoples of the world have more points in which they are all like each other than points in which they are different. One type of person that is common in every country is the one who always tries to do as little as he possibly can and to get as much in return as he can. His opposite, the man who is in the habit of doing more than is strictly necessary and is ready to accept what is offered in return, is rare everywhere.

Both these types are usually unconscious of their character. The man who avoids effort is always talking about his 'rights'; he appears to think that society owes him a pleasant easy life. The man who is always doing more than his sheer talks of 'duties' feels that the individual is in debt to society, and not society to the individual. As a result of their view, neither of these men thinks that he behaves at all strangely.

1. What type of person is common in every nation?
   A. A person who wants to do little and get more
   B. A person who wants to do more and get little
   C. Each person is different
   D. There is no such type of person that is common in every country
2. A person doing more and getting little:
   A. is rare everywhere
   B. is found in our country
   C. is common in all countries
   D. is found nowhere

2. Cloze Test

A cloze test is a procedure in which an examinee is asked to supply words that have been removed from a passage as a test of his ability to comprehend text. Practise it regularly to score well.

TEST 1

Today most Indian businessmen are very worried. To begin with, they are not used to competition. In the past, they sold whatever ..... (1) ..... produced at whatever prices thay chose. But ..... (2) ..... increasing competition, customers began to ..... (3) ..... and choose. Imports suddenly became ..... (4) ..... available and that too at cheaper ..... (5) .....

1. A. it B. he C. they D. we
2. A. with B. by C. after D. from
3. A. buy B. take C. pick D. want
4. A. hardly B. easily C. frequently D. conveniently
5. A. costs B. returns C. dividend D. prices

TEST 2

As a rule of thumb, a manned mission costs from fifty to a hundred times more than a comparable unamanned mission. Thus, for scientific exploration alone, ... (1) ..... missions, employing machine intelligence, are ..... (2) ..... However, there may well be ..... (3) ..... other than scientific for exploring ..... (4) ..... social, economic, political, cultural or ..... (5) .....

1. A. manned B. unmanned C. space D. lunar
2. A. liked B. wanted C. used D. preferred
3. A. reasons B. causes C. clues D. objects
4. A. moon B. sun C. space D. mission
5. A. casual B. historic C. historical D. histrionic

TEST 3

The principal advantage in having a clear-cut objective of business is that it does not derail; the enterprise does not stray ..... (1) ..... the direct route that it has set for ..... (2) ..... Enterprises with well-defined objectives can conveniently undertake ..... (3) ..... and follow long-range development policies. Recognition of objectives ..... (4) ..... the temptation to compromise long-range ..... (5) ..... for short-term gains and improves coordination in work and consistency in policy.

1. A. from B. on C. along D. towards
2. A. others B. industry C. itself D. government
3. A. production B. research C. audit D. appraisal
4. A. invites B. defers C. shifts D. removes
5. A. objectives B. losses C. interests D. profits

TEST 4

Let children learn to judge their own work. A child ..... (1) ..... to talk does not learn ..... (2) ..... being corrected all the time ..... (3) ..... corrected too much, he will ..... (4) ..... talking. He notices a thousand times a day the difference between the ..... (5) ..... he uses and the language those around him use.

1. A. endeavouring B. learning
   C. experimenting D. experiencing
2. A. in B. on
   C. by D. to
3. A. unless B. being
   C. until D. if
4. A. stop B. halt
   C. avoid D. shun
5. A. speech B. language
   C. talk D. skill

TEST 5

His talk used to be full of wit and humours. He liked reading. He was a ..... **(1)** ..... reader and would pore over books ..... **(2)** ..... a wide range of interest as ..... **(3)** ..... he got them. He had ..... **(4)** ..... a standing order to two bookshops ..... **(5)** ..... city.

1. A. voracious B. fervent
   C. anxious D. enthusiastic
2. A. covering B. barring
   C. including D. containing
3. A. firmly B. quickly
   C. soon D. urgently
4. A. offered B. proclaimed
   C. intimated D. given
5. A. at B. in
   C. within D. inside

TEST 6

An old scholar ..... **(1)** ..... that Truth was in the country. He ..... **(2)** ..... to find her, as he had devoted his life to studying her in all her ..... **(3)** ..... . He came upon the cottage in the ..... **(4)** ..... where Truth lived. He ..... **(5)** ..... on the door. Truth ..... **(6)** ..... what he wanted. The scholar ..... **(7)** ..... who she was. He added that he had ..... **(8)** ..... a thousand times ..... **(9)** ..... she really was ..... **(10)** .....

1. A. hard B. herd
   C. heard D. hired
2. A. decide B. decides
   C. decided D. decision
3. A. firms B. forms
   C. farms D. ferns
4. A. maintain B. fountain
   C. mountain D. plantain
5. A. locked B. shocked
   C. knocked D. pocked
6. A. told B. said
   C. asked D. advised
7. A. explored B. exhorted
   C. explained D. exported
8. A. wandered B. wondered
   C. wondrous D. wounded
9. A. which B. what
   C. whom D. whose
10. A. like B. lake
    C. lick D. lack

TEST 7

Each species has its special place or habitat. An ..... **(1)** ..... bird-watcher can look at ..... **(2)** ..... forest, meadow, lake, swamp or field and ..... **(3)** ..... almost exactly what birds he ..... **(4)** ..... find there ..... **(5)** ..... birds are found all over the world; others ..... **(6)** ..... themselves to certain areas. Still ..... **(7)** ..... migrate from one country to another in ..... **(8)** ..... in search of warmth and ..... **(9)** ..... and then return in spring, ... **(10)** ..... the season is more favourable.

1. A. expert B. experienced
   C. advanced D. active
2. A. the B. some
   C. a D. certain
3. A. predict B. suggest
   C. prophesy D. calculate
4. A. should B. must
   C. might D. will
5. A. more B. some
   C. most D. all
6. A. keep B. entrust
   C. confine D. involve
7. A. some B. others
   C. few D. all
8. A. winter B. summer
   C. spring D. autumn
9. A. seeds B. crops
   C. fruit D. food
10. A. while B. until
    C. after D. when

TEST 8

In the large shops ..... **(1)** ..... for Diwali are begun ..... **(2)** ..... or six weeks before ..... **(3)** ..... actual day. Shop owners ..... **(4)** ..... Diwali because lots of ..... **(5)**

..... are given, which means ..... **(6)** ..... goods are bought than ..... **(7)** ..... any other time of ..... **(8)** ..... year. The main shops ..... **(9)** ..... decorated many weeks before ..... **(10)** ..... to tempt people to buy things.

1. A. preparations B. shopping C. purchases D. preparing
2. A. two B. five C. few D. couple
3. A. a B. an C. the D. which
4. A. hate B. anticipate C. recommend D. like
5. A. purchases B. prizes C. presents D. presentation
6. A. many B. more C. few D. less
7. A. at B. in C. on D. for
8. A. any B. a C. the D. this
9. A. were B. are C. have been D. will be
10. A. occasion B. festival C. festivities D. Diwali

TEST 9

Many parents greet their children's teenage years with needless dread. While teens ..... **(1)** ..... assault us with heavy-metal music ..... **(2)** ..... outlandish clothes and spend all ..... **(3)** ..... time with friends, such behaviour ..... **(4)** ..... adds up to full-scale revolt. Teenage ..... **(5)** ..... according to psychologist Laurence Steinberg, has been ..... **(6)** ..... exaggerated. Sociologist Sanford Dornbusch agrees. "The ..... **(7)** ..... that teenagers inevitably rebel is a ..... **(8)** ..... that has the potential for great family ..... **(9)**," say Dornbusch. He believes the notion can ..... **(10)** ..... communication during this critical time for parents to influence youngsters.

1. A. should B. may C. must D. can
2. A. put B. show C. dress D. flaunt
3. A. our B. their C. his D. her
4. A. infrequently B. sporadically C. scarcely D. always
5. A. revolution B. mania C. subversion D. rebellion
6. A. greatly B. hardly C. never D. always
7. A. surmise B. idea C. complaint D. accusation
8. A. story B. reality C. fact D. myth
9. A. ruin B. harm C. defeat D. downfall
10. A. damage B. destroy C. injure D. suffocate

TEST 10

Well, it was done and the debt was paid. But I began to feel ..... **(1)** ..... sorry for myself that I could not ..... **(2)** ..... it. I made up my mind never to steal ..... **(3)** ..... I also made up my mind to tell ..... **(4)** ..... to my father. But I did not have the ..... **(5)** ..... to speak to him. It was not that ..... **(6)** ..... was afraid that my father would beat me. I ..... **(7)** ..... not remember any time when he beat ..... **(8)** ..... of us. I was afraid that my confession ..... **(9)** ..... cause him great pain. But I ..... **(10)** ..... felt that I had to take this risk. I would never be happy again unless I told everything to my father.

1. A. so B. as C. very D. too
2. A. accept B. like C. bear D. understand
3. A. also B. again C. still D. ever
4. A. anything B. something C. nothing D. everything
5. A. bravery B. courage C. fortitude D. gallantry
6. A. I B. he C. she D. me
7. A. would B. should C. do D. did
8. A. all B. some C. any D. none
9. A. shall B. can C. will D. would
10. A. soon B. again C. once D. since

TEST 11

It is difficult to find a person who would put in a good word for the kind of bureaucracy we have in India. Incidentally, things may now be seen as coming to a head. ..... **(1)** ..... the attainment of Independence, India ..... **(2)** from time to time several ..... **(3)** ..... power Committees or Commissions to ..... **(4)** ..... administration. In spite of all this, the impression ..... **(5)** ..... that the Indian variety of bureaucracy has been slow and slothful. Fact is that the ..... **(6)** ..... of bureaucracy happens to be ..... **(7)** ..... the same all over the world. Even in the U.S.A. Presidents have ..... **(8)** ..... a great deal of concern ..... **(9)** ..... the manner in which bureaucracy has been functioning at various levels. In spite of all this, not much change can be ..... **(10)** ..... in the near future. One may feel like hanging one's head the despair unless one believes in some super-human power that looks after our universe.

1. A. From B. With C. Till D. Since
2. A. arranged B. appointed C. framed D. selected
3. A. great B. super C. high D. multiple
4. A. perform B. reform C. revive D. transform
5. A. insists B. subsists C. consists D. persists
6. A. structure B. function C. growth D. behaviour
7. A. practically B. structurally C. precisely D. strictly
8. A. asserted B. declared C. voiced D. waged
9. A. on B. at C. with D. from
10. A. accepted B. expected C. affected D. admitted

ANSWERS

Test 1

1	2	3	4	5
C	A	C	B	D

Test 2

1	2	3	4	5
B	D	A	C	C

Test 3

1	2	3	4	5
A	C	A	D	A

Test 4

1	2	3	4	5
B	C	D	C	B

Test 5

1	2	3	4	5
A	A	C	D	B

Test 6

1	2	3	4	5
C	C	B	C	C
6	7	8	9	10
C	B	B	B	A

Test 7

1	2	3	4	5
A	C	D	B	B
6	7	8	9	10
C	A	A	D	D

Test 8

1	2	3	4	5
A	B	C	D	C
6	7	8	9	10
B	A	C	B	D

Test 9

1	2	3	4	5
B	D	B	D	D
6	7	8	9	10
B	B	B	A	D

Test 10

1	2	3	4	5
A	C	B	D	B
6	7	8	9	10
A	D	C	D	A

Test 11

1	2	3	4	5
D	B	C	B	D
6	7	8	9	10
B	A	C	B	B

3. Spot the Error

The most common errors in English are of spellings, grammar and usage of words. By regular practice, the errors can be easily spotted and minimised.

COMMON ERRORS WITH NOUNS AND NOUN-PHRASES

	Incorrect	Correct
1.	I have bought new *furnitures.*	I have bought new *furniture.*
2.	The wages of sin *are* death.	The wages of sin *is* death.
3.	She told these *news* to her mother.	She told her mother this *news.*
4.	He took *troubles* to do his work.	He took *trouble* (or pains) over his work.
5.	The *cattles* were grazing.	The *cattle* were grazing.
6.	He showered *many abuses* on me.	He showered *much abuse* on me.
7.	I spent the holidays with my *family members.*	I spent the holidays with my *family.*
8.	There is no *place* in this compartment.	There is no *room* in this compartment.
9.	Write this new *poetry* in your *copy.*	Write this new *poem* in your *note-book.*
10.	He took *insult* at this.	He took *offence* at this.
11.	Put your *sign* here.	Put your *signatures* here.
12.	She is my *cousin sister.*	She is my *cousin.*
13.	*Sunil's* my *neighbour's* house was burgled.	*Sunil* my *neighbour's* house was burgled.
14.	I lost a *ten-rupees* note.	I lost *a ten-rupee* note.
15.	Road closed for *repair.*	Road closed for *repairs.*
16.	His house is out of *repairs.*	His house is out of *repair.*
17.	What is the *reason* of an earthquake?	What is the *cause* of an earthquake?
18.	This building is made of *stones.*	This building is made of *stone.*
19.	I disapprove of *these kinds* of games.	I disapprove of *this kind* of games.
20.	Veena's and Sheela's father is ill.	Veena and Sheela's father is ill.
21.	His *son-in-laws* are doctors.	His *sons-in-law* are doctors.
22.	*Alms* is given to the *poor.*	*Alms* are given to the poor.
23.	He always keeps his words.	He always keeps his *word.*
24.	I carried the *luggages.*	I carried the *luggage.*
25.	*Two-third* of the work is left.	*Two-thirds* of the work is left.

COMMON ERRORS WITH PRONOUNS

	Incorrect	Correct
1.	Both did not go.	Neither went.
2.	We all did not go.	None of us went.
3.	Each of these boys play.	Each of these boys plays.
4.	Whoever does best he will get a prize.	Whoever does best will get a prize.
5.	One should not waste his time.	A man should not waste his time.
6.	I and she are sisters.	She and I are sisters.
7.	He is wiser than me.	He is wiser than I.
8.	Between you and I, Anil is not to be trusted.	Between you and me, Anil is not to be trusted.
9.	Nobody was there but I.	Nobody was there but me.
10.	Who is there ? It is me.	Who is there ? It is I.
11.	Only he and me can use this card.	Only he and I can use this card.
12.	Let you and I go now.	Let you and me go now.
13.	Everyone got one's pay.	Everyone got his pay.
14.	Everyone is frightened when they see a tiger.	Everyone is frightened when he sees a tiger.
15.	These two friends are fond of one another.	These two friends are fond of each other.
16.	I did not like him coming at that hour.	I did not like his coming at that hour.
17.	Who do you think I met?	Whom do you think I met?
18.	You should avail this opportunity.	You should avail yourself this opportunity.
19.	When you have read these books, please return the same to me.	When you have read the books, please return them to me.
20.	They that are humble need fear no fall.	Those that are humble need fear no fall.

COMMON ERRORS WITH ADJECTIVES

	Incorrect	Correct
1.	These all oranges are good.	All these oranges are good.
2.	He held the book in the both hands.	He held the book in both hands.
3.	Both men have not come.	Neither man has come.
4.	That man should do some or other work.	That man should do some work or other
5.	He is elder than I.	He is older than I.
6.	Shakespeare is greater than any other poets.	Shakespeare is greater than any other poet.
7.	He is a coward man.	He is a cowardly man.
8.	Many villagers cannot write his own name.	Many villagers cannot write their own name.
9.	Each of us loves our home.	Each of us loves his home.
10.	Much efforts bring their reward.	Much effort brings its reward.
11.	He found hundred rupees.	He found a hundred rupees.
12.	He had leave of four days.	He had four days leave.

Incorrect	Correct
13. This is a worth seeing sight.	This is a sight worth seeing.
14. He will spend his future life here.	He will spend the rest of his life here.
15. There is a best teacher in that class.	There is a very good teacher in that class.
16. Of the two plans this is the best.	Of the two plans this is the better.
17. He is becoming strong every day.	He is becoming stronger every day.
18. He is worst than I.	He is worse than I.
19. Jaipur is hot than Delhi.	Jaipur is hotter than Delhi.
20 In our library the number of books is less.	In our library the number of books is small.
21. From the three he is more clever.	He is the cleverest of the three.
22. India is the first peace-loving country in the world.	India is the foremost peace-loving country in the world.
23. Verbal instruction will not do.	Oral instruction will not do.
24. Her command over French is most excellent.	Her command over French is excellent.
25. He has not some money with him.	He has not any money with him.
26. I have visited Bombay many a times.	I have visited Bombay many a time.
27. Death is more preferable to dishonour.	Death is preferable to dishonour.
28. I gave him a few books I had.	I gave him the few books I had.
29. If he wants farther help send him to me.	If he wants further help, send him to me.
30. She is so cunning as a fox.	She is as cunning as a fox.

COMMON ERRORS WITH VERBS

Incorrect	Correct
1. He asked had we taken our luggage.	He asked if we had taken our luggage.
2. She asked what are you doing.	She asked what we were doing.
3. Rama asked to Anil why he is angry.	Rama asked Anil why he was angry.
4. He does not care for his money.	He does not take care of his money.
5. He does not care for his work.	He takes no care over his work.
6. No one cared for him after his mother died.	No one took care of him after his mother died.
7. He got angry before I said a word.	He got angry before I had said a word.
8. I met a man who was my tutor 20 years ago.	I met a man who had been my tutor twenty years ago.
9. I had been for walking yesterday.	I went for a walk yesterday.
10 If I shall do this I shall be wrong.	If I do this I shall be wrong.
11. I have left trekking.	I have given up trekking.
12. I came to know as to how he did this.	I learnt how he did this.
13. I came to know why he was sad.	I found out why he was sad.
14. He knows to swim.	He knows how to swim.
15. The criminal's head was cut.	The criminal's head was cut off.

Incorrect	Correct
16. I said to him to go.	I told him to go.
17. I told the teacher to excuse me.	I asked the teacher to excuse me.
18. He is troubling me.	He is giving me trouble.
19. I have got a hurt on my leg.	I have hurt my leg.
20. She gave a speech.	She made a speech.
21. He has given his examination.	He has sat for his examination.
22. He took out his shoes.	He took off his shoes.
23. I have ordered for a new car.	I have ordered a new car.
24. He would not hear me.	He would not listen to me.
25. I struck a blow on his face.	I struck him in the face.
26. He denied to come.	He refused to come.
27. He lived there for a day.	He stayed there for a day.
28. The book is not found.	The book is lost.
29. Shut the light.	Turn off the light.
30. I must revenge my brother.	I must avenge my brother.

COMMON ERRORS IN SUBJECT-VERB AGREEMENT

Incorrect	Correct
1. The owners of this factory *is* very rich.	The owners of this factory *are* very rich.
2. The pleasures of nature that one can experience at Shimla *is* beyond description.	The pleasures of nature that one can experience at Shimla *are* beyond description.
3. There *is* no street lights in our colony.	There *are* no street lights in our colony.
4. He and I *am* entrusted with the job.	He and I *are* entrusted with the job.
5. Rice and curry *are* his favourite dish.	Rice and curry *is* his favourite dish.
6. The honour and glory of our country *are* at stake.	The honour and glory of our country *is* at stake.
7. Time and tide *waits* for none.	Time and tide *wait* for none.
8. All the passengers with the driver *was* killed.	All the passengers, with the driver, *were* killed.
9. The teacher, with her students, *were* going out.	The teacher, with her students, *was* going out.
10. I as well as they *am* tired.	I as well as they *are* tired.
11. Not only the soldiers but their captain also *were* captured.	Not only the soldiers but their captain also *was* captured.
12. Neither you nor I *were* selected.	Neither you nor I *was* selected.
13. Either of these two applicants *are* fit for the job but neither want to accept it.	Either of these two applicants *is* fit for the job but neither wants to accept it.
14. One of these students are sure to stand first.	One of these students *is* sure to stand first.
15. Everyone of these workers want a raise.	Everyone of these workers wants a raise.
16. None of these letters has been answered so far.	None of these letters *have* been answered so far.

	Incorrect	Correct
17.	None of the girls were present at the party.	None of the girls *was* present at the party.
18.	Many a battle were fought on Indian soil.	Many a battle *was* fought on Indian soil.
19.	A lot of work remain to be done.	A lot of work *remains* to be done.
20.	The majority of these girls likes music.	The majority of these girls *like* music.
21.	The number of admissions are encouraging.	The number of admissions *is* encouraging.
22.	A large number of boys was present.	A large number of boys *were* present.
23.	A variety of books was on display.	A variety of books *were* on display.
24.	Variety are the spice of life.	Variety *is* the spice of life.
25.	If my estimates are correct. I will need another hundred rupees.	If my estimate is correct, I will need another hun dred rupees.
26.	Mathematics *are* my favourite subject.	Mathematics *is* my favourite subject.
27.	'Gulliver's Travels' *are* written by Swift.	'Gulliver's Travels' *is* written by Swift.
28.	Ten miles *are* a long distance to cover on foot.	Ten miles *is* a long distance to cover on foot.
29.	A new pair of shoes *are* to be purchased.	A new pair of shoes *is* to be purchased.
30.	The Committee *have* issued its report.	The Committee *has* issued its report.
31.	I, who am your friend, *has* always been on your side,	I, who am your friend, *have* always been on your side.
32.	I am the person who *have* always stood by you.	I am the person who *has* always stood by you.
33.	This is one of the best novels that *has* been published this year.	This is one of the best novels that *have* been published this year.
34.	Less than half the amount *have* been wasted.	Less than half the amount *has* been wasted.
35.	A lot of people *has* turned up for the show.	A lot of people *have* turned up for the show.
36.	Much of their honour *are* un-deserved.	Much of their honour *is* un-deserved.
37.	More than a decade *have* passed since this house was built.	More than a decade *has* passed since this house was built.
38.	Either she or he *are* mistaken.	Either she or he *is* mistaken.
39.	Plenty of information *are* available on the subject.	Plenty of information *is* available on the subject.
40.	Plenty of pamphlets *is* available on the subject.	Plenty of pamphlets *are* available on the subject.

COMMON ERRORS IN USE OF WILL, SHALL, WOULD, SHOULD, MAY, MIGHT, MUST

	Incorrect	Correct
1.	When I shall see him I shall tell him this.	When I *see* him, I shall tell him this.
2.	If I should do wrong, he would punish me.	If I *did* wrong, he would punish me.
3.	Until he will have confessed his fault, he will be kept in prison,	Until he *has* confessed his fault, he will be kept in prison.
4.	She will obey me.	She *shall* obey me.
5.	You would work hard.	You *should* work hard.
6.	You shall find him in the garden.	You *will* find him in the garden.

	Incorrect	Correct
7.	He must have died of exposure, but we cannot be certain.	He *might* have died of exposure, but we cannot be certain.
8.	You might not show disrespect to your elders.	You *must* not show disrespect to your elders.
9.	You may take exercise in order to maintain good health,	You *must* take exercise in order to maintain good health.
10.	He must be a crook for all we know.	He *may* be a crook for all we know.

COMMON ERRORS IN THE USE OF ADVERBS

(Very, Much, Too, Enough, Quite, Hardly, Scarcely, Before, Ago, Since, Yet, Still, etc.)

	Incorrect	Correct
1.	He is very much angry.	He is *very* angry.
2.	She was very good enough to help me.	She was *good enough* to help me.
3.	She runs much fast.	She runs *very* fast.
4.	She runs very faster than Seema.	She runs *much* faster than Seema.
5.	It is bitter cold today.	It is *bitterly* cold today.
6.	He is a much learned man.	He is a very learned man.
7	She is thinking very hardly.	She is thinking very hard.
8.	To tell in brief the film was boring.	*In short* the film was boring.
9.	He told the story in details.	He told the story *in detail.*
10.	I did it anyhow.	I *managed to do* it somehow.
11.	Aeroplanes reach Europe soon.	Aeroplanes reach Europe quickly.
12.	Before long there were dinosaurs on the earth.	*Long ago,* there were dinosaurs on the earth.
13.	This book is too interesting.	This book is *very* interesting.
14.	He lives miserly.	He lives in *a miserly* way.
15.	Just I had gone when she came.	I had just gone when she came.
16.	He sings good.	He sings *well.*
17.	He sings good than I.	He sings *better* than I.
18.	Really speaking it is cold.	*As a matter of fact* it is cold.
19.	He is enough tall to reach the ceiling.	He is *tall enough* to reach the ceiling.
20.	He went directly to his college.	He went *direct* to his college.
21.	He is presently at Delhi	He is at Delhi *at present.*
22.	Last night she returned lately.	Last night she *returned late.*
23.	He was even blamed by his friends.	He was *blamed even* by his friends.
24.	I only employed him for a week.	I employed him for a week only.
25.	I met him four months before.	I met him four *months ago.*

Incorrect	Correct
26. Anil seldom ever goes to school.	Anil *seldom goes* to school.
27. I will wait here until you do not go.	I will wait here until *you go.*
28. I never remember having met her before.	I *do not remember* having met her before.
29. She has not been here too long to have many friends,	She has not *been here long* enough to have many friends.
30. Hardly I have had any rest since one week.	Hardly have *I had* any rest for a week.
31. Scarcely the water crossed the danger level, the warning signals were sounded.	Scarcely *had the* water *crossed the* danger level, when the warning signals were sounded.
32. She is neat but fairly slow.	She is *neat* but rather slow.
33. It is a rather good film.	It is a *fairly good* film.
34. We yet have time to catch the bus.	We *still have* time to catch the bus.
35. She has not still spent all her money.	She has *not yet* spent all her money.

COMMON ERRORS IN THE USE OF CONJUNCTIONS

Incorrect	Correct
1. As he is fat so he runs slowly.	As he is fat *he* runs slowly.
2. If he is fat then he will run slowly.	If he is fat, he will run slowly.
3. Though he is fat still he runs fast.	Though he is fat, *he runs* fast.
4. *As* I pulled the trigger at the sametime he shook my arm.	As I pulled the trigger, he shook my arm.
5. No sooner I had spoken than he left.	No sooner *had* I spoken than he left.
6. Not only he will go, but also he will stay there.	Not only *will he* go, but he *will also* stay there.
7. Neither he comes nor he writes.	Neither *does he* come nor *does he* write.
8. Scarcely he entered the room than the telephone rang.	Scarcely *had* he entered the room *when the* telephone rang.
9. Hardly she had left the house than it began to rain.	Hardly *had she* left the house *when* it began to rain.
10. He is the fastest runner and he comes last.	He is the fastest runner *but* he comes last.
11. She is as innocent as if she looks.	She is as innocent as she looks.
12. Until he does not try he must be punished.	He must be punished unless he tries
13. I want to know as to why you are late.	I want to know why you are late.
14. I am fond of Chinese food as for example sweet and sour prawns.	I am fond of Chinese food, for example, sweet and sour prawns.
15. He was angry therefore I ran away.	He was angry so I ran away.
16. I was trying to work, at that time he was disturbing me.	While I was trying to work, he was disturbing me.
17. Supposing if he is late, what will happen?	Supposing he is late (or if he is late) what will happen?
18. He asked me that why I was late.	He asked me why I was late.

Incorrect	Correct
19. Let us catch a taxi lest we should not get late.	Let us catch a taxi lest we should get late.
20. She dresses herself like the teacher does.	She dresses herself as the teacher does.
21 Wait while I come.	Wait *until* (or *till)* I come.
22. Until, there is corruption in India, there can be little progress.	*As long* as there is corruption in India there can be little progress.
23. I have never told a lie nor cheated anybody.	I have never told a lie *nor have I* cheated anybody.
24. Both Mohan as well as Arun are responsible for this action.	Both Mohan *and* Arun are responsible for this action.
25. Hindus and Muslims both are to blame for the riots.	*Both Hindus* and Muslims are to blame for the riots.
26. I have bought paintings, books, records, and etc.	I have bought paintings, books *and records etc.*
27. He as well as you is a fool.	He as well as you *are* a fool.
28. He is so poor and he cannot save anything.	He is so *poor that* he cannot save anything.
29. Such a' book that you want is not available.	Such a book *as* you want is not available.
30. Such was her condition as everyone was moved to pity.	Such was her condition that everyone was moved to pity.

COMMON ERRORS IN THE USE OF PREPOSITIONS

Incorrect	Correct
1. I will not listen him.	I will not listen *to* him.
2. Copy this word by word.	Copy this word *for* word.
3. He enquired from her where she lived.	He enquired *of* her where she lived.
4. Sign here with ink.	Sign here *in* ink.
5. Has she come in train or by foot?	Has she come *by* train or *on* foot?
6. She said this at his face.	She said this *to* his face.
7. Open the book on page one	Open the book *at* page one.
8. I was invited for lunch.	I was *invited to* lunch.
9. I am ill since three months.	I have been *ill for* three months.
10. This paper is inferior than that.	This paper is inferior *to* that.
11. This resembles to that.	This *resembles* that.
12. My brother is superior than you in strength.	My brother is superior *to* you in strength.
13. He wrote me	He wrote *to* me.
14. I shall explain them this.	I shall explain this *to* them.
15. Send this letter on my address.	Send this letter *to* my address.
16. He suggested me this.	He suggested this *to* me.
17. He goes *on his* work.	He goes *to his* work.
18. He *reached to* Nagpur.	He *reached* Nagpur.
19. He told *to me* to go.	He told *me* to go.

	Incorrect	Correct
20	The term begins *from* July 1st.	The term begins *on* July 1st.
21.	There are many advantages *from* this.	The advantages *of* this are many.
22.	We waste much time *in* trifles.	We waste much time *on* (or *over)* trifles.
23.	He sat *on* a tree.	He sat *in* a tree.
24.	This is a comfortable house to *live.*	This is a comfortable house to *live in.*
25.	This is the road to *go.*	This is the road to *go by.*
26.	He married *with* an Indian lady.	He *married an Indian* lady.
27.	He accompanied *with* his friend.	He *accompanied his* friend.
28.	He went *for doing some* business.	He went away *on* business.
29.	He went for *riding.*	He went *for a ride.*
30.	I *pitied on* him.	I *pitied* him.
31.	When this was searched it was found.	When this was searched *for* it was found.
32.	I shall inform them *this.*	I shall inform them *of* this.
33.	*Due to illness* I cannot go to school.	*Owing* to illness I cannot go to school.
34.	He went *to the back side* of the house.	He went *behind* (or to the back of) the house.
35.	I must go; there is no *help.*	I must go; there is no help *for it.*
36.	I *met with your* friend there.	I *met your* friend there.
37.	The First World War was fought *during* 1914-1918.	The First World War was fought *between* 1914-1918.
38.	England grew prosperous *between* Queen Victoria's reign.	England grew prosperous *during* Queen Victoria's reign.
39.	He asked a holiday.	He asked *for* a holiday.
40.	I am obliged of you for this good turn.	I am obliged *to* you for this good turn.
41.	There is no harm to try.	There is no harm *in trying.*

MISCELLANEOUS ERRORS

(Including Ambiguities and Indianisms)

	Incorrect	Correct
1.	Many *homes* are lying vacant.	Many *houses* are lying vacant.
2.	It is cool in the *shadow* of the tree.	It is cool in the *shade* of the tree.
3.	She *keeps* good health.	She *enjoys* good health.
4.	My leg is *paining.*	*I am feeling pain* in my leg.
5.	*See* this word in the dictionary.	*Look up* this word in the dictionary.
6.	The train will arrive *just now*	The train will arrive *shortly.*
7.	They are *pulling* on well.	They are *getting* on well.
8.	The river has *over flown* its bank.	The river has *over flown* its banks.
9.	He was appointed *on* the post.	He was appointed *to* the post.
10.	Last but not *the least,* we have to discuss the problem of over population.	Last but not *least,* we have to discuss the problem of over population.

Incorrect	Correct
11. *Cities* after *cities* fell.	*City* after *city* fell.
12. What is the use Munir going there?	What is the use of Munir going there?
13. He *did many mischief.*	He *made much mischief.*
14. It is exact five *in* my watch.	It is exact five *by* my watch.
15. I will dine with them on *next Sunday*.	I will dine with them *Sunday next.*
16. Misfortunes when faced bravely and *manly* become less troublesome.	Misfortunes when faced bravely and *manfully* become less troublesome.
17. I am *laid down* with fever.	I am *laid up* with fever.
18. He is habituated to smoking.	He is *addicted* to smoking.
19. *According to my opinion* he is right.	*In my opinion* (or according *to me)* he is right.
20. Could you please *open* this knot?	Could you please *untie* this knot?

MULTIPLE CHOICE QUESTIONS

Directions: *In the following questions some of the sentences have errors and some are correct. Find out which part of a sentence has an error, the number of that part is your answer. If a sentence is free from errors, then your answer is D i.e., No error.*

1. (A) Either Ram or/(B) you is responsible/(C) for this action./(D) No error.

2. (A) The student flatly denied/(B) that he had copied/(C) in the examination hall./(D) No error.

3. (A) By the time you arrive tomorrow/(B) I have finished/(C) my work./(D) No error.

4. (A) The captain with the members of his team/(B) are returning/(C) after a fortnight./(D) No error.

5. (A) After returning from/(B) an all-India tour/(C) I had to describe about it./(D) No error.

6. (A) The teacher asked his students/(B) if they had gone through/(C) either of the three chapters included in the prescribed text./(D) No error.

7. (A) Do you know/(B) how old were you/(C) when you came here?/(D) No error.

8. (A) Beware of/(B) a fair-weather friend/(C) who is neither a friend in need nor a friend indeed./(D) No error.

9. (A) Copernicus proved/(B) that Earth/(C) moves round the Sun./(D) No error.

10. (A) The property/(B) was divided/(C) among the two brothers./(D) No error.

11. (A) I am quite certain/(B) that the lady is not only greedy/(C) but miserly./(D) No error.

12. (A) The brilliant success in the examination/(B) as well as his record in sports/(C) deserves high praise./(D) No error.

13. (A) I cannot find/(B) where has he gone/(C) though I have tried may best./(D) No error.

14. (A) If I was/(B) the Prime Minister of India/(C) I would work wonders/(D) No error.

15. (A) If it weren't/(B) for you,/(C) I wouldn't be alive today./(D) No error.

16. (A) He looked like a lion/(B) baulked from/(C) its prey./(D) No error.

17. (A) Widespread flooding/(B) is affecting/(C) large areas of the villages./(D) No error.

18. (A) If we really set to/(B) we can get the whole house/(C) cleaned in an afternoon./(D) No error.

19. (A) It's arrogant for you/(B) to assume you'll/(C)win every time./(D) No error.

20. (A) The two books are the same/(B) except for the fact that this/(C) has an answer in the back./(D) No error.

21. (A) Your husband doesn't/(B) believe that you are older/(C) than I./(D) No error.

22. (A) I could not/(B) answer to/(C) the question./ (D) No error.

23. (A) Two years passed/(B) since/(C) my cousin died./(D) No error.

24. (A) I am learning English/(B) for ten years/(C) without much effect./(D) No error.

25. (A) Ramesh has agreed/(B) to marry with the girl/(C) of his parent's choice./ (D) No error.

26. (A) When he was arriving./(B) the party was/ (C) in full swing./(D) No error.

27. (A) The most studious boy/(B) in the class/ (C) was made as the captain./(D) No error.

28. (A) I am participating/(B) in the two-miles race/(C) tomorrow morning./(D) No error.

29. (A) When the boy committed a mistake/(B) the teacher made him to do/(C) the sum again./(D) No error.

30. (A) Whenever a person lost anything/(B) the poor folk around/(C) are suspected./(D) No error.

31. (A) It is time/(B) we did something/(C) to stop road accidents./(D) No error.

32. (A) I was there/(B) many a time/(C) in the past./(D) No error.

33. (A) Were you/(B) given a choice/(C) or you had to do it?/(D) No error.

34. (A) At the end of the year/(B) every student who had done adequate work/(C) was automatically promoted./(D) No error.

35. (A) She reluctantly said that/(B) if nobody else was doing it/(C) she will do it./(D) No error.

36. (A) He will end up his work/(B) in the city/(C) by the end of the year./(D) No error.

37. (A) Supposing if/(B) there is no bus,/(C) how will you get there?(D) No error.

38. (A) At the moment the house/(B) was burgled the family/(C) attended a night party in the neighbourhood./(D) No error.

39. (A) On a holiday/(B) Sudha prefers reading/(C) than going out visiting friends./(D) No error.

40. (A) Neither he/(B) nor his father is interested/ (C) in joining the party./(D) No error.

41. (A) A group of friends/(B) want to visit/(C) the new plant as early as possible./(D) No error.

42. (A) May I/(B) know who you want/(C) to see please?/(D) No error.

43. (A) Myself and Gopal/(B) will take care of/(C) the function on Sunday./(D) No error.

44. (A) He is not coming tomorrow/(B) as he is having a pain in the chest/(C) and has to see a doctor./(D) No error.

45. (A) They have been/(B) very close friends/(C) until they quarrelled./(D) No error.

46. (A) The reason why/(B) he was rejected/(C) was because he was too young./(D) No error.

47. (A) Scarcely had/(B) I arrived than/(C) the train left./(D) No error.

48. (A) The students/(B) returned back/(C) home well in time./(D) No error.

49. (A) English should/(B) be make/(C) the national language./(D) No error.

50. (A) Ravi is a/(B) intelligent student/(C) of my school./(D) No error.

ANSWERS

1	2	3	4	5	6	7	8	9	10
B	D	B	B	C	C	D	D	B	C
11	12	13	14	15	16	17	18	19	20
C	D	B	A	C	C	C	A	A	C
21	22	23	24	25	26	27	28	29	30
C	B	A	A	B	A	C	B	B	A
31	32	33	34	35	36	37	38	39	40
D	A	A	D	C	A	A	A	C	D
41	42	43	44	45	46	47	48	49	50
B	B	A	C	A	C	B	B	B	A

4. SENTENCE IMPROVEMENT

One may use the same words in many ways but the best way is only one that makes the perfect usage of the words and conveys the proper meaning of the expression. Try it yourself in this exercise.

MULTIPLE CHOICE QUESTIONS

Directions: *In these questions, a part of the sentence is* ***bold****. Below are given alternatives to the* ***bold*** *part at A, B and C which may improve the sentence. Choose the correct alternative to edit and improve the sentence. In case no improvement is needed, your answer is D.*

1. For most people who exercise **at the** morning, there is no getting around the question: Eat and run? Or run and eat later?
   A. in the
   B. in
   C. at the time of
   D. No Improvement

2. Are ad agencies even attempting to peer into the keyhole of this indulgence sanctum to garner consumer insights **ahead of** the curve?
   A. above
   B. over
   C. within
   D. No Improvement

3. Too many people rush into the world of credit and don't stop to think about how **their actions could affect their** credit score and ability to qualify for credit in the future.
   A. their actions may affect their
   B. their actions might affect their
   C. their actions will affect their
   D. No Improvement

4. According to the report, **number of deal with** vaccines were energized by concerns around avian flu, SARS, and biodefense products, while looming patent expirations led to more deals in generics.
   A. number of deals in
   B. number of deal in
   C. number of deals with
   D. No Improvement

5. This is how the Bombay High Court responded to the state government's purported **moral stand which** dance bars were causing grave harm to society.
   A. moral stand in
   B. moral stand at
   C. moral stand that
   D. No Improvement

6. If you have a high credit limit, use **at least a** third of it.
   A. atleast a
   B. at last a
   C. utmost a
   D. No Improvement

7. Fitness experts will say that **first eating provides** fuel for a proper workout.
   A. eating in the beginning provides
   B. first eat provides
   C. eating first provides
   D. No Improvement

8. One study that examined the claim directly in 2012 found that a group of people did **burned much calories from fat on days** when they exercised on an empty stomach than on days when they had a small breakfast first.
   A. burn more calories from fat on days
   B. burn more calorie from fat on days
   C. burnt more calories from fat on days
   D. No Improvement

9. Carefree children spent their afternoons **to run about barefoot**, their clothes dusty, and telltale twigs of the neighbour's mango tree in their hair.
   A. running barefoot in the sun
   B. run about barefoot in the sun
   C. running about barefoot in the sun
   D. No Improvement

10. A year ago, a 13-year-old girl attempted suicide because her mother **refuses to pay his** mobile bills.

A. refuses to pay her B. refused to pay her
C. refused to pay his D. No Improvement

11. Discreet salience **is extremely important** to create that 'irresistible-yet-unattainable' image for brànds that want to take India seriously

A. was extremely important
B. is mainly important
C. was important extremely
D. No Improvement

12. This, over a designer outfit that he wanted for a friend's party and **that his sensitive** parents refused him.

A. which his sensitive
B. which his insensitive
C. that his insensitive
D. No Improvement

13. Goa was full of non-Goa property hunters **rushing about buying up the place** like tomorrow was an expired lease.

A. rushing in buying up the place
B. rushed about buying up the place
C. rushing about to buy up the place
D. No Improvement

14. Property hunting is a **tired and hungry** making business.

A. is a tiresome and hungry
B. is a tiring and hungry
C. is a tiring and waste
D. No Improvement

15. Cultural differences aside, **till luxury need speaks** in a manner that befits.

A. luxury still needs to speak
B. luxury still need to speak
C. luxury till need to speak
D. No Improvement

16. Indian food – the culinary avatar of the subcontinent's social history presented on a platter – **is without doubt the best food** in the world.

A. is undoubtly the greatest food
B. is without doubt greatest food
C. is best food without doubt
D. No Improvement

17. It must retain the language of poetry. **It needed to create** stories, and not statements.

A. It needed creating B. It needs creating
C. It needs to create D. No Improvement

18. In 2012, Asia-Pacific has become the first region **to reach aggregate profiting** in biotech.

A. to reach aggregated profi-tability
B. to reach aggregate profi-tability
C. to reach aggregate of profit
D. No Improvement

19. India is deviating to embrace the West. If Western luxury brands deviate a little, **albeit selectively**, they will find rich Indian arms open far and wide.

A. though selectively
B. however selectively
C. albeit selectedly
D. No Improvement

20. China and India continued to attract attention and deals, motivated by the desire to increase access to these **largest and growing** drug markets and by the need to lower the costs of drug development.

A. larger and growing B. large and growing
C. larger and grown D. No Improvement

21. Luxury brands are **still above of the** clover curve here, with their elite (small) audiences.

A. still ahead of the B. still in the
C. still far of the D. No Improvement

22. Agencies **hence needed to be** sure of returns before investing, say ad men.

A. hence needs to be B. so needs to be
C. hence need to be D. No Improvement

23. India is still a nascent market and that's the spirit everyone's **looking at it**.

A. looking for it B. looking in it
C. looking with it D. No Improvement

24. Questioning the state's move to allow women to serve liquor but not dance in bars **of the ground that** dancing aroused physical lust

A. on the grounds that
B. of the grounds that
C. over the grounds that
D. No Improvement

25. For England the positives from their crushing series lose come in the shape of James Anderson and Kevin Pietersen, **both of which** have made significant strides up the rankings

A. both of which B. both of whom
C. both of who D. No Improvement

26. International campaigns can work well for luxury here, **but context cannot be** ignored.

A. so context cannot be
B. but context cannot
C. but context couldn't
D. No Improvement

27. For one, the Indian luxury context, **while evolved rapidly**, still has its own meaning, and its own implications.

A. while evolved rapid
B. which evolving rapidly
C. while evolving rapidly
D. No Improvement

28. But too much of availability can compromise a luxury brand or **made it lose** its lustre.

A. make her lose B. make him lose
C. make it lose D. No Improvement

29. Still, it's under-the-upper **layers themselves who** are aspiring for slivers of luxury

A. layers themselves which
B. layer itself who
C. layers themself which
D. No Improvement

30. It is like saying Hindi movies, with skimpily dressed dancers, would **effect public** order

A. effect your B. affect public
C. affected public D. No Improvement

31. The court held that a few women being involved in prostitution was no **justice to deny other** bar girls the right to livelihood

A. justification to declare other
B. justification to deny other
C. justice to let other
D. No Improvement

32. All-rounder Irfan Pathan has also made some progress **over the** player rankings.

A. above the B. at the
C. up the D. No Improvement

33. Former PM on Sunday **joined hands** with suspended Lok Sabha members to float a new political outfit.

A. folded hands
B. walked hand in hand
C. shaked hands
D. No Improvement

34. Pakistan's former PMs will meet in London on Monday **to ask** a strategy to return home from exile.

A. to chalk out B. to negotiate
C. to create D. No Improvement

35. It's a family potboiler, medical thriller and political drama **all in one** – except that it's all too real and all too grim.

A. all 3 in one
B. all coupled into one
C. all rolled into one
D. No Improvement

ANSWERS

1	2	3	4	5	6	7	8	9	10
A	D	C	A	C	D	C	A	C	C
11	**12**	**13**	**14**	**15**	**16**	**17**	**18**	**19**	**20**
D	C	D	B	A	D	C	C	D	B
21	**22**	**23**	**24**	**25**	**26**	**27**	**28**	**29**	**30**
C	C	D	A	C	D	C	C	C	C
31	**32**	**33**	**34**	**35**					
B	C	C	A	C					

5. Reordering Words

The words form a sentence and convey their meaning only when they are arranged in a proper order. One must study and practise it regularly.

MULTIPLE CHOICE QUESTIONS

Directions: *In the following questions, some parts of the sentence have been jumbled up. You are required to rearrange these parts which are labelled P, Q, R and S to produce the correct sentence. Choose the option with proper sequence.*

1. We are doing
P : to the people
Q : to give relief
R : all we can
S : but more funds are needed
The correct sequence should be
A. P Q R S B. R Q P S
C. Q P R S D. S P Q R

2. The man
P : when he was
Q : in the office last evening
R : could not finish
S : all his work
The correct sequence should be
A. P Q R S B. Q R S P
C. R Q P S D. R S P Q

3. The people decided
P : they were going
Q : how much
R : to spend
S : on the construction of the school building
The correct sequence should be
A. Q P R S B. P Q R S
C. P R Q S D. S Q P R

4. The man said that
P : those workers
Q : would be given a raise
R : who did not go on
S : strike last month
The correct sequence should be
A. P Q R S B. P R S Q
C. Q P R S D. R S P Q

5. I think
P : the members
Q : are basically in agreement
R : of the group
S : on the following points.
The correct sequence should be
A. R Q P S B. S Q R P
C. P R Q S D. P Q S R

6. While it was true that
P : I had
Q : to invest in industry
R : some lands and houses
S : I did not have ready cash
The correct sequence should be
A. P Q R S B. P R S Q
C. S Q P R D. Q P R S

7. P : But your help
Q : to finish this work
R : it would not have been possible
S : in time
The correct sequence should be
A. P R Q S B. S P Q R
C. R P Q S D. P Q R S

8. The boy
P : in the competition
Q : who was wearing spectacles
R : won many prizes
S : held in our college

The correct sequence should be
A. P Q R S B. R P S Q
C. Q R P S D. Q P S R

9. About 200 years ago,
P : in the south of India
Q : an old king
R : ruled over a kingdom
S : called Rajavarman.
The correct sequence should be
A. Q S R P B. P Q R S
C. Q P S R D. Q S P R

10. P : his land
Q : a wooden plough
R : the Indian peasant still uses
S : to cultivate.
The correct sequence should be
A. R Q P S B. Q P S R
C. S R Q P D. R Q S P

11. He was a man,
P : even if he had to starve
Q : who would not beg
R : borrow or steal
S : from anyone.
The correct sequence should be
A. P Q R S B. P R Q S
C. Q R S P D. Q P R S

12. P : in the progress of
Q : universities play a crucial role
R : our civilization
S : in the present age.
The correct sequence should be
A. S Q P R B. Q R S P
C. Q R P S D. S Q R P

13. P : far out into the sea
Q : for the next two weeks there were further explosions
R : which hurled
S : ashes and debris.
The correct sequence should be
A. Q R P S B. R S P Q
C. Q R S P D. S R P Q

14. William Shakespeare,
P : in his lifetime
Q : the great English dramatist
R : wrote thirty-five plays
S : and several poems.
The correct sequence should be
A. P Q R S B. R S P Q
C. Q S R P D. Q R S P

15. Whenever I am,
P : with an old friend of mine
Q : in New Delhi
R : to have dinner
S : I always try.
The correct sequence should be
A. S Q P R B. Q S R P
C. R P S Q D. P R Q S

16. P : I don't know
Q : must have thought
R : what people sitting next to me
S : but I came away.
The correct sequence should be
A. R S Q P B. R Q S P
C. P Q R S D. P R Q S

17. P : in estimating the size of the earth
Q : but they were hampered by the lack of instruments of precision
R : ancient astronomers
S : used methods which were theoretically valid
The correct sequence should be
A. R P Q S B. P R Q S
C. R S Q P D. R P S Q

18. P : It is a pity that
Q : by offering a handsome dowry
R : a number of parents think that
S : they will be able to ensure the happiness of their daughters
The correct sequence should be
A. S Q R P B. P R S Q
C. P S R Q D. P R Q S

19. The common man
P : in nurturing
Q : a more active role
R : communal harmony
S : should play
The correct sequence should be
A. P R S Q B. S Q P R
C. S Q R P D. P R Q S

20. The doctor
P : able to find out
Q : what has caused

6. Ordering of Sentences

A Paragraph is formed from sentences, it will convey its true meaning and purpose only when the sentences are arranged in a proper manner. Try and practise it in this exercise.

MULTIPLE CHOICE QUESTIONS

Directions: *A number of sentences are given below which when properly sequenced form a coherent paragraph. Each sentence is labelled as abcdef...... Choose the most logical order of sentences from among the given choices to construct a coherent paragraph:*

1. (a) The leopard was discovered in the servant quarters of a farmhouse.
(b) The injuries appeared to have been caused by the paws of the leopard, and were not teeth wounds.
(c) It took the wild life officials, Delhi Police and Delhi zoo vets eight hours to capture the leopard that had wandered into a factory in south Delhi.
(d) The leopard then jumped into the factory where the workers managed to lock it in a small generator room before calling in the police.
(e) Before its capture, the leopard attacked two women and a man in the farmhouse.

A. aebdc B. bdaec
C. eadbc D. adbec

2. (a) The project has already started on an experimental basis in the west district.
(b) A website is soon going to be launched where application forms can be downloaded and submitted.
(c) Standing in a queue at a government office to submit application form will be a thing of the past.
(d) A unique code will be alloted while submitting the form which will help in finding the status of the application.

A. abcd B. dabc
C. cbda D. badc

3. (a) Police suspect a carpenter working at John's house as he has not reported for work since the day the boy went missing.
(b) John did not return home in the afternoon.
(c) John's mother had herself put the boy on the vehicle in the morning.
(d) John smiled at him and was last seen walking up to him.
(e) His parents called the school and were told John had not been to school at all and had been marked absent.
(f) He was about to enter the school when someone called out his name.

A. cfdbea B. debfca
C. bfdaec D. abcdef

4. (a) A state champion from the past four years, Tushar began swimming at the age of six.
(b) But he has no plans of making swimming a career.
(c) Tushar's passion for swimming is unshakable.
(d) Something that began as a hobby rewarded him with all the fame he has achieved.
(e) His day begins at 4.30 am for a dip at Talkatora Stadium.
(f) He is determined to make a mark in the world of swimming.

A. dbaecf B. bcadef
C. edfbac D. cefadb

5. (a) However, the mayhem over the last few months is deeply shocking.

(b) Yet I do not agree with the prophets of doom who see nothing but disaster ahead.

(c) When I came back to my motherland India after a stay in Switzerland, I felt I was trading a hotbed of intense religious and political violence for peace and quiet.

(d) I think our nation is searching for an identity.

(e) And a new vision of the future will emerge from this.

A. abcde B. cabde
C. cebad D. bedca

6. (a) The universities in a democracy can no longer be content with the limited goal of scholarship.

(b) They are to respond to changed conditions and to new demands.

(c) Universities in the modern world are called upon to play a crucial role in the progress of our civilization.

(d) They have to devise new programmes and take into account the needs of society.

(e) They must not merely display their traditional resourcefulness but also must have the capacity for effective growth.

A. cbdae B. cbead
C. cadbe D. dbaec

7. (a) He decided to enter a new line by investing in some new equipments.

(b) Some of the old machines were to be sold to raise the money.

(c) Ram's business was not prospering.

(d) For this more money had to be found.

(e) He was still short of money and had to borrow some.

A. cadbe B. adebc
C. ebdac D. cbdae

8. (a) Parts of northern region were pounded by heavy rains today,

(b) Vehicular traffic came to a near halt.

(c) As mid and high altitude areas of Himachal Pradesh were in grip of severe cold wave with snow lashing the tribal areas and mid ranges receiving showers.

(d) As the sky remained heavily overcast with dark clouds reducing the visibility considerably.

(e) A large number of tourists were forced to buy heavy woollens and stay indoors due to inclement weather.

A. ecabd B. adecb
C. edabc D. acbde

9. (a) Clearly, age is not a deterrent in one's choice of learning.

(b) Perhaps, it was because of her childhood desire.

(c) When Rachna came to Delhi eight years back, she had not anticipated a career in the field of art.

(d) She has been successful in the various exhibitions that she has been part of in terms of business.

(e) She had got into expressing her thoughts with the help of a brush and colours only because her daughter refused to get initiated into it.

(f) She feels that her use of colour appeals to people.

A. aedcbf B. cdefba
C. cebadf D. acdebf

10. (a) The idea is that students should be able to find employment for themselves after the course.

(b) The Central Board of Secondary Education is planning a revamp of its vocational courses.

(c) For this it is necessary to tie up with the industry as well as mobilise schools for their support.

(d) While others will be made less academic and more in tune with the needs of the industry.

(e) A number of courses have been identified as 'deadwood' and will be done away with.

A. bedac B. abcde
C. acebd D. baced

11. (a) An integrated and combined approach was required to reveal the mystery of the brain – its structure, composition and function.

(b) Since the early 80's, scientists were clear that the brain would be the final frontier to conquer.

(c) The initiative was flagged off and came to be known as the Human Brain Project.

(d) But that wasn't easy because understanding the brain involved completely integrating information from the level of the gene to the level of behaviour.

(e) To fulfill this requirement a group of American scientists from various diciplines decided to work together.

A. acbed B. bdaec
C. abdec D. badec

12. (a) The rehabilitation record has been dismal.
(b) It has been two years years since the earthquake rudely rattled the people of Gujrat.
(c) And since then, life has been a constant struggle.
(d) The quake set Gujrat's clock back by 10 years.
(e) Things changed forever.

A. bedca B. bcade
C. dbace D. edcba

13. (a) In fact, success in exams depended on rote learning from old notes.
(b) when he was studying civil engineering in a college in Gujrat.
(c) He was detained for lack of attendance.
(d) Lectures were soporific, classes rarely worth attending and 80 per cent attendance compulsory.
(e) The college became a trap he hated.
(f) His is a plight many engineers across India would identify with.
(g) He found the going tough.

A. abcdgef B. bgdacef
C. fabcdge D. abcdefg

14. (a) In a country that has close to 600 recognised engineering colleges, there are only seven IITs.
(b) Barring a few exeptions, the academic atmosphere in these is moribund.
(c) The very best students usually get there.
(d) many waste themselves in frustration.
(e) Most of those who get into engineering are good students.
(f) but about 1.25 lakh others and up in the remaining colleges.

A. aecfbd B. abecdf
C. abcdef D. acfbed

15. (a) Whatever the job market, common wisdom says that IIT graduates will find jobs where others have failed.
(b) The IIT brand name is a ticket to success.
(c) When recruiters go headhunting, the IITs are still top of their list.
(d) Its possessor is understood to have an excellent academic record and the will to succeed.
(e) In the job market, that counts.

A. bdeac B. abcde
C. abdce D. dbace

16. (a) It will pave the way ....
(b) signalling a new beginning in strategic ties......
(c) for a tangible Indian economic presence in Iran and Central Asia.
(d) Iran has offered India valuable road linkages to central Asia ......
(e) aimed at promoting peace and economic cooperation in the region.

A. dbeac B. debca
C. acebd D. abced

17. (a) A good college is essential for a successful career and admissions are based on marks.
(b) The marks-based system followed by all the boards in the country recognises only a small percentage of students as successful.
(c) The marks one scores in the crucial board exams dictate the path his life takes.
(d) Anyone scoring below a certain percentage is automatically branded a 'failure'.
(d) So if you cannot make it into the best college, your career is over even before it has started.

A. abcde B. bcdea
C. bdcae D. abdec

18. (a) the pride of their batch.
(b) they're not too far off from taking charge of India's future.
(c) They were the toppers of their class
(d) they may have won accolades, made their schools and families proud, but
(e) Yesterday's toppers have their hands full.
(f) these confident go-getters have had their share of failure too.

A. eacfbd B. eadbfc
C. eadbcf D. cabedf

19. (a) Mistakes or errors should be treated as teacher.
(b) When you make mistake, you should neither feel ashamed nor desperate.
(c) Everybody makes mistakes.
(d) You should be bold enough to accept your mistakes before anybody.
(e) But the only sensible course is to study and analyse why you made that mistake.
(f) Only then you can learn not to make mistakes in future.
A. abfced B. acefbd
C. adbcfe D. cdfbea

20. (a) Our lessons in love and respect make us a tolerant people.
(b) I love Indian culture.
(c) I feel I have to repay my country whatever way I can.
(d) In no other country have I seen so much love and respect.
(e) I was born and brought up in this country and feel I owe everything to it.
A. bcade B. dcbea
C. acdeb D. ecbda

21. (a) To curb bio-terroriom is a difficult task.
(b) To check these attacks and lessen their impact, we need an impartial team of sincere, strong and dedicated men.
(c) The media can play a strong role in stopping this unnecessary spread of panic.
(d) Since Bio-terrorism is not visible or easily detectable, it can be used often.
(e) Men who honour the lives of their fellow countrymen before their own.
A. abcde B. dabce
C. adbec D. acbed

22. (a) He was dying.
(b) No one was ready to touch him as even shifting him from one place to another would lead to profuse bleeding.
(c) He was a five-day old infant, premature and bleeding profusely.
(d) Even if injected one small needle, blood would ooze out and continue to flow for an hour at a stretch.
(e) This small being had haematoma, a thick blood clot in his brain.
A. edbca B. cabde
C. eacdb D. cedba

23. (a) The day I don't treat a patient, I feel ....
(b) I have enough to eat, I crave for blessings now.
(c) But if a financially weak patient gives me only ₹ 50, I don't mind.
(d) Each month I do three to four operations free of cost.
(e) I have lost something in life.
(f) My consultation fee is ₹ 300.
A. fcdeab B. dfcbae
C. fcabde D. bdfcea

24. (a) When he was rushed to the nearby Primary Health Centre after his fall, the doctor referred him to a hospital.
(b) This worsened his injury.
(c) Had a little precaution been exercised after the accident, Tarun would have continued with his gymnastic classes.
(d) He was paralysed from waist downwards when he fell from the vaulting horse while doing gymnastics.
(e) However, the doctor forgot to tell Tarun's parents to take him on a stretcher as he had suffered spinal injuries.
(f) Tarun is wheelchair bound for two years.
A. fdeabc B. abcdef
C. fdcaeb D. fdbcae

25. (a) As the temperature rises, staying hydrated can become a greater challenge for people exercising both indoors and out.
(b) Several things can influence this process, including age, gender, physical conditioning. humidity and a lack of sufficient fluids.
(c) In hot weather, individuals can lose as much as two quarts of sweat per hour.
(d) As we age, we have a lower perceived level of thirst in response to fluid loss and early stages of dehydration.
(e) If not replenished, this can lead to dehydration, heat exhaustion and even heatstroke.
A. abcde B. dbcae
C. cbdea D. acebd

26. (a) Students become passive listeners in the class-room.
(b) Mostly lecturing method is preferred to cover the syllabus.
(c) I feel that there is a lacunae in the teaching techniques adopted by the lecturers in engineering colleges.
(d) Unless the teachers are exposed to different teaching techniques, they will not succeed in imparting knowledge.
(e) Lack of training in teaching can be ascribed to this sorry state of affairs.

A. dbeca B. cadbe
C. chaed D. dceab

27. (a) A product is something that is made in a factory, a brand is something that is bought by a consumer.
(b) The trick therefore, lies in the brand positioning.
(c) For a counsumer, the satisfaction of becoming associated with a name that is the 'best' and the 'leader' is far more important and at times makes him ignore the price factor.
(d) Brands come and go.
(e) Still there are those who manage to stay and develop an affinity with consumers.

A. aebcd B. debac
C. decab D. aecdb

28. (a) Many people fail simply because they make too many wrong decisions.
(b) Over a period of time you make a series of decisions, each seemingly of little consequence.
(c) So do people's lives.
(d) It has been said that history turns on small hinges.
(e) Yet the total of these decisions finally determines the outcome of your life.
(f) A successful life depends upon developing a higher percentage of wisdom than error.

A. acbedf B. adcbef
C. fedcba D. abcdef

29. (a) The younger you are when you discover this mighty power, the more likely you are to live successfully and happily.
(b) Everything you do has some effect upon others, as do their actions upon you.
(c) You are influenced by other people's acts and wishes, by law and custom, by your duties and your responsibilities.
(d) You live in a world filled with outside influences which impinge upon you.
(e) And yet you must find out how to live your own life.

A. abcde B. adebc
C. dcbea D. baedc

30. (a) She had wanted to go to Mars.
(b) Lots of young people talk about how they dream of this or that.
(c) Kalpana Chawla had wanted to make at least one more trip to space.
(d) She is one person who got to live out her dreams.
(e) She had also said that when it was time for her to die, she would like to die in space.

A. bcade B. bdeac
C. caebd D. cbead

ANSWERS

1	2	3	4	5	6	7	8	9	10
A	C	A	D	B	B	A	D	C	A
11	**12**	**13**	**14**	**15**	**16**	**17**	**18**	**19**	**20**
B	A	B	D	A	A	C	D	B	D
21	**22**	**23**	**24**	**25**	**26**	**27**	**28**	**29**	**30**
C	D	B	C	D	C	B	B	C	C

7. SENTENCE COMPLETION

A sentence conveys its meaning effectively only when it is completed in a proper way. Try and practise it in this exercise.

Directions: *In each question, an incomplete statement (Stem) followed by four fillers is given. Pick out the best one which can complete the incomplete stem correctly and meaningfully.*

1. He is so lazy that he .....
A. cannot depend on others for getting his work done.
B. cannot delay the schedule of completing the work.
C. can seldom complete his work on time.
D. dislike to postpone the work that he undertakes to do.

2. He always stammers in public meetings, but his today's speech .....
A. was fairly audible to everyone present in the hall.
B. was not received satisfactorily.
C. could not be understood properly.
D. was free from that defect.

3. In order to raise the company's profit, the employees .....
A. demanded two additional increments.
B. decided to go on paid holidays.
C. requested the management to implement new welfare schemes.
D. offered to work overtime without any compensation.

4. Although, he is reputed for making very candid statements, ...
A. his today's speech was not fairly audible.
B. his promises had always been realistic.
C. his speech was very interesting.
D. his today's statements were very ambiguous.

5. I felt somewhat more relaxed .....
A. but tense as compared to earlier.
B. and tense as compared to earlier.
C. as there was already no tension at all.
D. and tension-free as compared to earlier.

6. With great efforts his son succeeded in convincing him not to donate his entire wealth to an orphanage .....
A. and lead the life of a wealthy merchant.
B. but to a home for the forsaken children.
C. and make an orphan of himself.
D. as the orphange needed a lot of donations.

7. Even though it is a very large house, ...
A. there is a lot of space available in it for children.
B. there is hardly any space available for children.
C. there is no dearth of space for children.
D. the servants take a long time to clean it.

8. Practically, very little work could be completed in the last week as it was .....
A. full of working days.
B. a very hectic week.
C. full of holidays.
D. a very busy week.

9. He tames animals because he .....
A. is fond of them.
B. hates them.
C. is afraid of them
D. wants to set them free

10. He has no money now .....
A. although he was very poor once.
B. as he has given up all his wealth.
C. because he was very rich once.
D. because he has received huge donation.

11. The employer appeared to be in such an affable mood that Rohit .....

A. decided to ask for a raise in his salary.

B. was scared to talk to him about his leave.

C. felt very guilty for his inadvertent slip.

D. promised him that he would not commit mistake again.

12. Since people cannot learn through legitimate channels all that they are anxious to learn .....

A. they resort to ways and means without any ethical or moral considerations.

B. they join academics in order to quench their thirst for learning.

C. they adopt formal ways and means to achieve what they want to.

D. these social service organisations provide them the required input of knowledge.

13. It was an extremely pleasant surprise for the hutment-dweller when the Government officials told him that .....

A. he had to vacate hutment which he had been unauthorisedly occupying

B. he had been gifted with a furnished apartment in a multi-storeyed building.

C. he would be arrested for wrongfully encroaching on the pavement outside his dwelling.

D. they would not accede to his request.

14. Despite his best efforts to conceal his anger .....

A. we could detect that he was very happy.

B. he failed to give us an impression of his agony.

C. he succeeded in camouflaging his emotions.

D. people came to know that he was annoyed.

15. His appearance is unsmiling but .....

A. his heart is full of compassion for others.

B. he looks very serious on most occasions.

C. people are afraid of him.

D. he is uncompromising on matters of task performance.

16. The weather outside was extremely pleasant and hence we decided to .....

A. utilise our time in watching the television.

B. refrain from going out for a morning walk.

C. enjoy a morning ride in the open.

D. employ this rare opportunity for writing letters.

17. The officer who had neglected to file his income tax returns had to .....

A. return the files. B. pay a fine.

C. be rewarded. D. play mischief.

18. In order to help the company attain its goal of enhancing profit, all the employees .....

A. urged the management to grant paid leave.

B. appealed the management to implement new welfare schemes.

C. voluntarily offered to work overtime with lucrative compensation.

D. voluntarily offered to render additional services in lieu of nothing.

19. His behaviour is so unpredictable that he .....

A. never depends upon others for getting his work done.

B. is seldom trusted by others.

C. always finds it difficult to keep his word.

D. always insists on getting the work completed on time.

20. Since it is already midnight, we .....

A. had better leaving.

B. ought to have leave.

C. should take our leave.

D. might as well as leave.

21. It is not easy to remain tranquil when those around you .....

A. behave in a socially acceptable manner.

B. exhibit pleasant mannerism.

C. are losing their heads.

D. agree to whatever you say.

22. Although initial investigations pointed towards him, ...

A. the preceding events corroborated his involvement in the crime.

B. the additional information confirmed his guilt.

C. the subsequent events established that he was guilty.

D. the subsequent events proved that he was innocent.

23. Because he believes in democratic principles, he always .....

A. decides all the matters himself.

B. listens to others' views and enforces his own.

C. shown respect to others' opinions if they match his own.

D. reconciles with the majority's views and gives us his own.

24. Owing to the acute power shortage, the people of our locality have decided to .....

A. dispense with other non-conventional energy sources.

B. resort to abundant use of electricity for illumination.

C. off-switch the electrical appliance while not in use.

D. resort to use of electricity only when it is inevitable.

25. She never visits any zoo because she is a strong opponent of the idea of .....

A. setting the animals free into the forest.

B. feeding the animals while others are watching.

C. watching the animals in their natural abode.

D. holding the animals in captivity for our joy.

26. Unless you work harder you will fail, means .....

A. if you fail you will work harder.

B. you must at least plan well than you will not fail.

C. hardly you will fail if you do not desire so.

D. if you do not put more efforts, then you will fail.

27. Even if it rains I shall come, means .....

A. if I come it will not rain.

B. if it rains I shall not come.

C. I will certainly come whether it rains or not.

D. whenever there is rain I shall come.

28. Dinesh is as stupid as he is lazy means .....

A. Dinesh is stupid because he is lazy.

B. Dinesh is lazy because he is stupid.

C. Dinesh is either stupid or lazy.

D. Dinesh is equally stupid and lazy.

29. Mahesh needn't have purchased the bag, means .....

A. it was not necessary for Mahesh to purchase the bag but he has purchased it.

B. it was necessary for Mahesh to purchase the bag and he has not purchased it.

C. it was not necessary for Mahesh to purchase the bag and he has not purchased it.

D. it was necessary for Mahesh to purchase the bag but he has not purchased it.

30. The Manager would like you to help Dhiraj, means .....

A. the Manager would like you if you help Dhiraj.

B. the Manager desires you to help Dhiraj.

C. the Manager likes you because you help Dhiraj.

D. Dhiraj expects the Manager to tell you to help him.

ANSWERS

1	2	3	4	5	6	7	8	9	10
C	D	D	D	D	C	B	C	A	B
11	**12**	**13**	**14**	**15**	**16**	**17**	**18**	**19**	**20**
C	A	B	D	A	C	B	D	B	D
21	**22**	**23**	**24**	**25**	**26**	**27**	**28**	**29**	**30**
C	D	D	D	D	D	C	D	A	B

8. NOUNS, NUMBERS & PRONOUNS

NOUN

A word which denotes a place, a thing, an animal or a person is said to be a noun.

1. Note the plurals of the following nouns:

Singular	*Plural*	*Singular*	*Plural*
copy	copies	cry	cries
baby	babies	duty	duties
body	bodies	country	countries
family	families	diary	diaries
fly	flies	fairy	fairies
city	cities	spy	spies
army	armies	storey	storeys
bay	bays	monkey	monkeys

2. The following nouns do not undergo any change in plural form, in general.

Singular	*Plural*	*Singular*	*Plural*
deer	deer	sheep	sheep
thousand	thousand	pair	pair
hundred	hundred	score	score
dozen	dozen	gross	gross

Note: We can write—
(*a*) thousands of men; (*b*) two pairs of shoes; (*c*) dozens of mangoes; (*d*) scores of people. etc. But—
(*a*) two thousand rupees; (*b*) three hundred men; (*c*) five dozen eggs, etc.

3. The following nouns are usually used in plural forms. They take a plural verb after them—

eatables	fetters	surroundings
riches	alms	spectacles
trousers	pants	scissors
premises	thanks	annals
congratulations	goods	shorts
tongs	pains	arms
breeches	(for troubles)	

4. The following are the nouns which are plural in appearance but are usually used in singular number. They are followed by a singular verb—

news	politics	physics
mathematics	economics	ethics
politics	classics	gallows
statistics	athletics	innings
mechanics	swnmons	mumps

5. Collective nouns often used as plurals—

public	police	cattle
audience	clergy	folk
people	poultry	nation
elite	gentry	glitterati

6. The nouns that are usually used in singular forms—

advice	hair	rice
fuel	alphabet	machinery
offspring	issue	furniture
mischief	stationery	luggage
bedding	information	abuse

7. Material nouns are always used in singular number—

gold	copper	milk
water	silk	wool

Note: They may be used in plural with a different meaning.

copper coins (coppers), chains or fetters (irons), cans made of tin (tins).

Formation of Feminine Gender from Masculine Gender

(*a*) By adding 'ess'/ 'trix'/ 'a' / 'sne' etc.
e.g., lion into lioness

(*b*) Placement of a word before or after noun
e.g., Servant into Maid-Servant; Milkman into Milkmaid

(*c*) A masculine noun containing vowel *e.g.,* Actor Avoid vowel and add 'ess' *i.e.,* Actress

(*d*) No specific note will be applied in some nouns (while changing into feminine gender) *e.g.,* Monk into Nun, Drone into Bee, Drake into Duck, Dog into Bitch.

THE PRONOUN

A pronoun is a word which is used in place of noun.

Kinds of Pronouns

(i) **Personal Pronoun:** I, we, my, mine, our, ours, you, he, she, they, him, her etc.

(ii) **Reflexive Pronoun:** Herself, himself, myself, yourself, themselves etc.

(iii) **Emphatic Pronoun:** I myself, we ourselves.

(iv) **Demonstrative Pronoun:** This, that, there, those etc.

(v) **Indefinite Pronoun:** Somebody, nobody, many, none, someone, few etc.

(vi) **Interrogative Pronoun:** What, who, whose, which, whom etc.

(vii) **Distributive Pronoun:** Neither, each, either, every, none, both etc.

(viii) **Relative Pronoun:** Who, which, whom etc.

MULTIPLE CHOICE QUESTIONS

Directions: *In the following questions choose the correct options to fill the blanks.*

1. The place was so dirty that ..... wished to run away from there.
A. everbody B. anybody
C. few D. some

2. ..... was there to help me.
A. Something B. Anything
C. Anybody D. Nobody

3. Is there .... to eat?
A. some B. something
C. any D. few

4. ..... of the students were making a great noise.
A. Anyone B. Somebody
C. Many D. Nobody

5. ..... of the students can solve this sum.
A. Someone B. Anybody
C. Somebody D. None

6. ...... of us should try our best to make India a heaven.
A. Any B. Somebody
C. Anybody D. All

7. ...... of us do not know the real meaning of our lives.
A. Any B. Something
C. Several D. Many

8. She presented me a .... of flowers.
A. troup B. galaxy
C. bouquet D. cluster

9. There was a .... of eggs floating on the dirty water of the ditch.
A. clump B. shoal
C. clutch D. pile

10. A ...... of dancers was dancing on the stage.
A. troupe B. galaxy
C. herd D. clump

11. To save the drowning man, a .... of sailors came out on the boats.
A. troop B. crew
C. band D. gang

12. A .... (of stars) consists of millions of stars.
A. group B. herd
C. stack D. galaxy

13. Mr. Peter Cash was arranging a .... of bricks near his house.
A. group B. band
C. herd D. stack

14. A .... of geese was swimming in the water.
A. group B. gaggle
C. troupe D. bunch

15. There was a .... of mosquitoes hovering over the slum area.
A. swarm B. group
C. gang D. herd

16. Last night a .... of burglars broke into my house.

A. group	B. cluster
C. clump	D. gang

17. Devika lost her .... of keys.

A. bunch	B. branch
C. band	D. gang

18. I have some .... for you to do.

A. working	B. worker
C. work	D. works

19. They highly admire the .... of Kashmir.

A. scenery	B. sceneries
C. scene	D. scenes

20. I can easily read and write the English ....

A. alphabets	B. alphabetic
C. alphabet	D. alphabetical

21. I have met her many a ....

A. times	B. timing
C. time	D. timings

22. She has written many ....

A. poetry	B. poetries
C. poem	D. poems

23. One is supposed to do ....

A. our duty	B. their duty
C. one's duty	D. his duty

24. He is .... faithful partner.

A. Yours	B. You
C. Your	D. Your's

25. Ajay is more smart than ....

A. her	B. hers
C. herself	D. she

26. The ..... of the Minister's statement cannot be verified by people who have no access to official records.

A. veracity	B. verbosity
C. ambiguity	D. validity

27. Life is to death as pleasure is to ......

A. poverty	B. suffering
C. anguish	D. pain

28. 'Please' and 'Thank you' are the little courtesies by which we keep the ..... of life oiled and running smoothly.

A. path .	B. machine
C. garden	D. river

29. Catching the earlier train will give us the ..... to do some shopping.

A. chance	B. luck
C. possibility	D. occasion

30. Leave a two-inch ..... on each page for the teacher's remarks.

A. border	B. margin
C. blank	D. gap

31. What is the ..... for an airletter?

A. fare	B. value
C. postage	D. stamp

32. The manner in which bombs exploded in five trains within a short span of time suggests that it is a part of a .....

A. game	B. conspiracy
C. villainy	D. sabotage

33. Some regions of our country still remain ..... to the average man.

A. inaccessible	B. impossible
C. impermeable	D. impenetrable

34. The old 'Nature Versus .....' debate regarding crime continues even today.

A. Man	B. Universe
C. Culture	D. Nurture

ANSWERS

1	2	3	4	5	6	7	8	9	10
A	D	B	C	D	D	D	C	C	A
11	**12**	**13**	**14**	**15**	**16**	**17**	**18**	**19**	**20**
B	D	D	B	A	D	A	C	A	C
21	**22**	**23**	**24**	**25**	**26**	**27**	**28**	**29**	**30**
C	D	C	C	D	A	D	B	A	B
31	**32**	**33**	**34**						
C	B	A	A						

9. Prepositions

A Preposition is a word which comes before a Pronoun or a Noun and expresses the relationship between Noun or Pronoun and some part of the remaining sentence.

(*a*) He is busy **with** his work.
(*b*) The boy jumped **into** the river.
(*c*) The birds are chirping *in* the trees.

In these sentences the words **with**, **into** and **in** show the relationship between the verbs **busy**, **jumped** and **chirping** with the nouns **work**, **river** and **trees** respectively.

Position of the Preposition

1. A Preposition usually precedes its object.

(*i*) He laughs **at** the poor.
(*ii*) He is angry **with** you.
(*iii*) She agrees **with** me.

2. In the case of Relative Pronouns it comes after the subject.

(*i*) This is the boy whom I was looking **for**.
(*ii*) That is the pen whose mention I was making **of**.

3. In the following cases, the Preposition comes after its object.

(*i*) Where is the boy you were complaining **against**?
(*ii*) What things are there you are looking **for**?
(*iii*) Who is there, you are waiting **for**?

Omission of the Preposition

In many cases when the sentences contain Nouns of Time or Place, the Prepositions **from**, **in** and **for** are often omitted.

(*i*) He walked many kilometres.
(*ii*) He came to see me last year.
(*iii*) As I could not find my puppy anywhere, I looked here and there.

Prepositions are small words that show the relationship between one word and another. Prepositions in the following sentences show the position of the paper in relation to the desk, the book, his hand and the door.

The paper is **on** the desk.
The paper is **under** the book.
The paper is **in** his hand.
The paper is **by** the door.

Common Prepositions

about	at	by
in	onto	toward
above	before	concerning
inside	out	under
across	behind	despite
into	over	until
after	below	down
like	since	up
against	beneath	during
near	through	upon
along	beside	except
of	throughout	with
amid	between	for
off	till	within
among	beyond	from
on	to	without

MULTIPLE CHOICE QUESTIONS

Directions: *Tick the correct Preposition for the blank in each of the following sentences.*

1. He applied ...... the manager.
A. for B. to
C. with D. by

2. Trust ...... God and do the right.
A. in B. for
C. to D. with

3. She is worthy ...... a prize.
A. with B. for
C. to D. of

4. Mr. Gomes has no taste ...... music.
A. of B. for
C. with D. to

5. You are hard ...... hearing.
A. at B. of
C. with D. for

6. He is sure ...... his success
A. for B. with
C. on D. of

7. Preeti was warned ...... the danger ahead.
A. for B. at
C. of D. about

8. I am thankful ...... you for a good advice.
A. for B. with
C. to D. from

9. Deepak would not surrender ...... the police.
A. with B. to
C. for D. on

10. The small plant in your lawn is very sensitive ...... touch.
A. on B. with
C. to D. for

11. Divya was sure to succeed ..... the examination.
A. for B. in
C. to D. with

12. Geeta was jealous ...... Ravina's beauty.
A. to B. with
C. for D. of

13. He was ignorant ..... what was happening there.
A. for B. of
C. to D. with

14. Your pen is inferior ...... mine.
A. than B. with
C. from D. to

15. Reenu is no match ...... Meenu.
A. to B. for
C. with D. upon

16. It is necessary ...... you to apply for this job.
A. on B. with
C. for D. to

17. Be loyal ...... your country.
A. for B. to
C. on D. with

18. Mukesh is junior ...... me.
A. than B. to
C. from D. of

19. Deepika was innocent ...... the crime.
A. of B. with
C. from D. to

20. I am desirous.... joining the Indian cricket team.
A. for B. of
C. to D. on

21. Pradeep is not eligible ...... the post.
A. to B. on
C. upon D. for

22. Does she believe ...... God?
A. to B. for
C. in D. over

23. Mr. Posh was charged..... the murder of his aunt.
A. for B. with
C. on D. to

24. Tagore is famous (or popular) ...... Indians.
A. for B. with
C. to D. towards

25. Kalidasa is famous ...... his drama the *Shakuntalam*.
A. for B. with
C. on D. about

26. He applied ...... the post of a teacher.
A. to B. on
C. for D. at

27. I differ ...... you in this matter.
A. from B. with
C. for D. above

28. My pen differs ...... yours.
A. with B. from
C. for D. upon

29. The air escaped out ...... the balloon.
A. from B. of
C. to D. under

30. I am confident ...... success.
A. of B. to
C. from D. about

31. He was deprived ...... his share and property.
A. of B. with
C. from D. about

32. He complains ...... headache.
A. about B. to
C. of D. in

33. My father deals ...... sugar.
A. with B. to
C. in D. about

34. His services were dispensed ......
A. for B. to
C. with D. of

35. Mohinder was born ...... a noble famly.
A. with B. about
C. towards D. in

36. He was born ...... poor parents.
A. of B. to
C. in D. on

37. A son was born ...... him.
A. to B. for
C. in D. upon

38. I was aware ...... the matter.
A. to B. of
C. in D. upon

39. He was absorbed ...... study.
A. in B. into
C. of D. under

40. The boy jumped ...... the river.
A. in B. under
C. below D. into

41. I agree ...... you.
A. upon B. to
C. with D. None of these

42. Wolves abound ...... this forest.
A. for B. in
C. with D. to

43. She did not agree ...... your proposal.
A. with B. in
C. to D. None of these

44. I was angry ...... his misconduct.
A. with B. to
C. at D. on

45. He is bent ...... mischief.
A. on B. of
C. to D. for

ANSWERS

1	2	3	4	5	6	7	8	9	10
B	A	D	B	B	D	C	C	B	D
11	**12**	**13**	**14**	**15**	**16**	**17**	**18**	**19**	**20**
B	D	B	D	B	D	B	B	A	B
21	**22**	**23**	**24**	**25**	**26**	**27**	**28**	**29**	**30**
D	C	B	B	A	C	B	B	A	A
31	**32**	**33**	**34**	**35**	**36**	**37**	**38**	**39**	**40**
A	C	C	C	D	A	A	B	A	D
41	**42**	**43**	**44**	**45**					
D	B	C	D	A					

10. ADJECTIVES, ADVERBS & DEGREE OF COMPARISON

Some words tell more about another word they are called *modifiers*. There are two main kinds of modifiers: *adjectives* and *adverbs*.

Adjectives

An *adjective* modifies—tells more about—a noun or pronoun. It tells *what kind, how many,* or *which one*.

Example: *beautiful* music, *blue* sky, *large* room.

Adjectives are usually found right before a noun, right after a noun, or after a linking verb.

Note: Some adjectives, such as articles, numbers, and possessive adjectives, usually come before the noun.

Adverb

An *adverb* modifies—tells more about—a verb, adjective, or another adverb. It tells *how, when, where,* or *to what extent.*

Comparison and Adjectives

Adjectives and adverbs have three forms that show a greater or lesser degree of the characteristic of the basic word: the positive, the comparative, and the superlatives.

Use the comparative to compare two things:

1. Mary is the more lazy of the two.
2. I've tasted creamier cheese than this.
3. James is the shorter of the two boys.

Use the superlative to compare more than two things:

1. Mary is the laziest girl I know.
2. This is the creamiest cheese I've ever tasted.
3. James is the shortest boy in the class.

There are some words to which comparison does not apply, since they already indicate the highest degree of a quality.

Here are some examples:

Immediately	Superlative	First
Last	very	unique
Uniquely	universally	perfect
Perfectly	exact	complete
Correct	dead	deadly
Preferable	round	perpendicularly
Square	third	supreme
Totally	infinitely	immortal

Errors to Avoid in Comparison

Do not combine two superlatives:

Incorrect: That was the most bravest thing he ever did.

Correct: That was the bravest thing he ever did.

Incorrect: He grew up to be the most handsomest boy in the town.

Correct: He grew up to be the most handsome boy in the town.

Do not combine two comparatives:

Incorrect: Mary was more friendlier than Susan.

Correct: Mary was friendlier than Susan.

Incorrect: The puppy was more timider last week.

Correct: The puppy was more timid last week.

MULTIPLE CHOICE QUESTIONS

Directions: *In the following questions choose the correct option to fill the blank.*

1. The girl whom you met is the .... sister of Ravi.
   A. eldest B. elder
   C. older D. oldest
2. The historical place is ....
   A. seeing worth B. worthy of seeing
   C. worth seeing D. worthy seeing
3. These flowers smell ....
   A. sweet B. sweetly
   C. more sweetly D. most sweetly
4. .... aspirant can not pass the UPSC examination.
   A. Each B. Every
   C. All D. No
5. Harivansh Rai .... second Shakespeare.
   A. is a B. is
   C. is the D. is another
6. .... student in the class got prizes.
   A. Each and every B. Every and each
   C. Every D. Never
7. It is .... picture than the one we saw last Monday.
   A. interesting B. much interesting
   C. more interesting D. most interesting
8. She is clever ....
   A. that her mother B. as her mother
   C. so her mother D. than her mother
9. They will get ....
   A. Red, green and black paper
   B. Red, green black paper
   C. Red and green and black paper
   D. Either B or C
10. Health is .... wealth.
    A. preferable to
    B. more preferable than
    C. more preferable to
    D. most preferable then
11. .... water that was in the jug evaporated.
    A. Little B. The little
    C. Small D. A small
12. He has not sung .... songs.
    A. much B. most
    C. more D. many
13. Srishti has searched .... office.
    A. whole the B. the whole
    C. a whole D. some whole
14. K.R. Dhiraj was .... best and .... famous writer.
    A. a, the most B. the, a most
    C. the, more D. the, the most
15. Willam Shakespeare is famous as ....
    A. a poet and a dramatist
    B. a poet and dramatist
    C. the poet and the dramatist
    D. the poet and a dramatist
16. What does .... leader suggest?
    A. other B. another
    C. others D. anothers
17. He .... money
    A. has few B. have few
    C. has little D. have little
18. The .... boys are rewarded.
    A. first two B. two first
    C. firsts two D. two's first
19. He is .... brave.
    A. strong B. stronger
    C. more strong D. strong and
20. No sooner said ....
    A. so done B. and done
    C. then done D. but done

ANSWERS

1	2	3	4	5	6	7	8	9	10
A	C	A	B	A	C	C	D	A	A
11	**12**	**13**	**14**	**15**	**16**	**17**	**18**	**19**	**20**
B	D	B	D	B	A	C	A	D	C

11. Determiners & Articles

Determiners are actually Adjectives. They are always followed by nouns.

Determiners are of the following kinds:

(A) Demonstrative Determiners
this, that, these, those etc.

(B) Possessive Determiners
my, our, your, his, her, its, their etc.

(C) Quantitative Determiners
some, any, much, enough, sufficient, whole, a little, the little, little, all, both etc.

(D) Numerical Determiners
a few, some, few, the few, any, several, many, no, etc.
One, two, three .... (Cardinals)
First, second, third .... (Ordinals)

(E) Distributive Determiners
either, neither etc.

(F) Articles
Indefinite: a, an
Definite: the

MULTIPLE CHOICE QUESTIONS

Directions: *In the following questions choose the correct options to fill the blanks.*

1. Give me .... rice.
A. some B. few
C. a few D. any

2. .... sheep grazing on the slope of the hill had gone away.
A. Any B. The few
C. This D. Much

3. Have you got .... magazines to read?
A. all B. much
C. some D. little

4. I have .... money that I want to spend on shares.
A. any B. much
C. less D. some

5. There is .... owl on the branch of the tree.
A. a B. the
C. an D. some

6. My brother is .... MBA.
A. a B. an
C. the D. any

7. Have you got .... cheese?
A. some B. many
C. a few D. few

8. No, I haven't got .... cheese.
A. many B. few
C. any D. some

9. There is only .... milk left in the bottle.
A. enough B. few
C. much D. a little

10. There is .... hope of his recovery.
A. any B. little
C. many D. few

11. .... dogs were barking at the strangers.
A. some B. any
C. much D. less

12. The girl bought her father .... juice.
A. few B. some
C. any D. many

13. You should take .... honey everyday.
A. any B. many
C. a little D. a few

14. .... boy was punished by the teacher.
A. Either B. All
C. Any D. Many

15. .... girl was asked to join the army.
A. None B. Neither
C. All D. Any

16. .... water in the jug has been drunk by Mohan.
A. The little B. The few
C. A few D. Few

17. I shall play .... piano at the party.
A. some B. any
C. the D. few

18. .... labourers were found dead in the mine.
A. Any B. Fewer
C. Many D. Less

19. Could I borrow .... umbrella?
A. our B. your
C. yours D. my

20. My brother is standing in the .... row.
A. any B. many
C. some D. first

21. Do you want .... tea?
A. any B. more
C. much D. few

22. He can fly .... aeroplane.
A. a B. an
C. some D. many

23. .... students were asked to bring their birth certificates.
A. Many B. Any
C. Much D. Less

24. .... gun needs oiling.
A. It B. This
C. These D. Those

25. .... shirts are mine.
A. These B. This
C. It D. That

26. .... child was allowed to enter the kitchen.
A. The B. All
C. Many D. A few

27. I have been waiting for you for .... hour.
A. a B. an
C. the D. a few

28. You must pay .... visit to your brothers.
A. the B. an
C. a few D. a

29. Why are you making .... noise?
A. your B. enough
C. a D. whole

30. He is .... honourable man.
A. a B. the
C. an D. much

31. .... shirts are mine.
A. These B. That
C. This D. It

32. .... glasses belong to Mr. Jack.
A. This B. That
C. Those D. It

33. .... birds have colourful wings.
A. That B. These
C. This D. It

34. I want a car. I'll get ....one.
A. these B. this
C. those D. it

35. I need a camera. I'll get .... now.
A. it B. these
C. this D. those

ANSWERS

1	2	3	4	5	6	7	8	9	10
A	B	C	D	C	B	A	C	D	B
11	12	13	14	15	16	17	18	19	20
A	B	C	A	B	A	C	C	B	D
21	22	23	24	25	26	27	28	29	30
B	B	A	B	A	A	B	D	C	C
31	32	33	34	35					
A	C	B	B	A					

12. CONJUNCTIONS

A word which joins either two or more than two words/sentences is known as conjunction. e.g.,

Neither .... nor (in negative sense)
Either .... or (in affirmative sense)
Both .... and
Hardly .... when/before
No sooner .... than
Scarcely .... when/before
Though .... yet

Some illustrations based on above guidelines
Illustration:

(i) Yashwant is neither good nor bad.

(ii) It is both cheap and good.

(iii) No sooner did Ashok see the police than he ran away.

MULTIPLE CHOICE QUESTIONS

Directions: *In the following questions choose the correct options to fill the blanks.*

1. Neither he .... his friend is good.
A. or B. and
C. but D. nor

2. The officer asked the peon .... why he was late.
A. that B. if
C. but D. No word

3. Both Ajay .... Vijay are intelligent.
A. or B. nor
C. and D. No word

4. No sooner did the thief see the public .... he ran away.
A. then B. and
C. but D. than

5. Abhinav .... his brothers was going to Mumbai.
A. but B. yet
C. no word D. together

6. He behaves .... he were the captain of the team.
A. as if B. as
C. no word D. that

7. Either Rupali .... Sonali is going to attend the meeting.
A. and B. but
C. nor D. or

8. Neither Nirmal .... Ashwinee is going to listen the speech of the minister.
A. and B. but
C. nor D. or

9. Ravi .... Prakash are going to Kolkata.
A. or B. nor
C. but D. and

10. Rice .... curry is my usual breakfast.
A. and B. but
C. then D. than

11. Hardly had he left .... his brother came.
A. then B. than
C. when D. that

12. I would rather have a copy .... a book.
A. then B. than
C. when D. that

13. He is no other .... my friend.
A. then B. than
C. when D. but

14. He saw a snake ....he awoke.
A. then B. when
C. than D. No word

15. Ten years have passed .... my grandmother died.
A. since B. when
C. then D. than

16. She is .... good .... bad.
A. either, not B. neither, or
C. neither, nor D. neither, than

17. The cellphone is both cheap .... best.
A. than B. and
C. then D. or

18. No sooner did the thief see the police .... he ran away.
A. then B. than
C. so D. because

19. Srishti will go .... Sanju goes.
A. if B. than
C. then D. although

20. She is wise .... timid.
A. and B. yet
C. but D. however

21. Make hay .... the sun shines.
A. though B. while
C. after D. before

22. He is so weak .... he cannot walk.
A. but B. that
C. then D. so

23. Although he is rich, ... he is unhappy.
A. but B. yet
C. so D. still

24. Wait here .... I come back.
A. till B. until
C. before D. after

25. He is my friend .... I shall help him.
A. so B. hence
C. that is why D. therefore

26. He must go away .... he will be beaten.
A. otherwise B. and
C. or D. else

27. God loves good men .... good men love God.
A. and B. or
C. that D. those

28. He was late .... he was not punished.
A. but B. yet
C. still D. therefore

29. Walk slowly ...., you may fall.
A. and B. or
C. so D. otherwise

30. Work hard, ... you will fail.
A. and B. or
C. otherwise D. else

ANSWERS

1	2	3	4	5	6	7	8	9	10
D	D	C	D	D	A	D	C	D	A
11	**12**	**13**	**14**	**15**	**16**	**17**	**18**	**19**	**20**
C	B	B	B	A	C	B	B	A	C
21	**22**	**23**	**24**	**25**	**26**	**27**	**28**	**29**	**30**
B	B	B	A	B	C	A	C	D	D

13. TENSES & VERBS

1. Tense indicates a point in time or period of time in the past, present, or future tense.
2. The verb may consist of a single word, or a main verb and one or more auxiliary words. The key point is that tense is related to the form of verb. There are normally three forms of the verb, say, V_1, V_2, V_3 and for convenience a fourth form V_4 as verb+ing may be assumed.

A Comparative Chart Regarding Tenses and Verbs

Simple Present	**Simple Past**	**Simple Future**
V_1	V_2	shall/will + V_1
Present Continuous	**Past Continuous**	**Future Continuous**
is/am/are + V_4	was/were + V_4	shall/will + be + V_4
Present Perfect	**Past Perfect**	**Future Perfect**
has/have + V_3	had + V_3	shall/will + have + V_3
Present Perfect Cont.	**Past Perfect Cont.**	**Future Perfect Cont.**
has/have + been + V_4	had + been + V_4	shall/will + have been + V_4

SIMPLE PRESENT:

A. A present state of affairs. — A. My sister lives in Nagpur.
B. A general fact. — B. The sun rises in the east.
C. Habitual actions. — C. I listen to the radio in the mornings.
D. Future time-tables. — D. My flight leaves at 10:00.

PRESENT CONTINUOUS:

A. A specific action that is occurring. — A. Arvind is watching TV (right now).
B. A general activity that takes. — B. These days, I'm taking it easy.
C. Future arrangements. — C. I'm inviting Hari to the party on Friday.

SIMPLE PAST:

A. An action that began and ended at a particular time in the past. — A. The mail came early this Morning.
B. An action that occurred over a period of time but was completed in the past. — B. Dad worked in advertising in the past.
C. An activity that took place regularly in the past. — C. We jogged every morning before class.

PAST CONTINUOUS:

A. Interrupted Actions. — A. I was sewing when the telephone rang.

B. A continuous state over a period of time but was completed in the past.	B. She was looking very ill. I was meeting lots of people at that time.
C. Events planned in the past.	C. Neetu was leaving for Kolkata but had to make a last minute change
D. Expressing a future intent.	D. Jyoti is going to bring her sister tonight.
E. Predicting an event.	E. You are going to pass the test. Don't worry.

SIMPLE FUTURE:

A. Making a future decision.	A. I will call you after lunch.
B. Predicting a future event.	B. You will pass the test. Don't worry.
C. Indicating willingness to do something.	C. If I don't feel better soon, I will go to to the doctor.

FUTURE CONTINUOUS:

A. An action that will be going at a particular time in the future.	A. At noon tomorrow, I will be taking the children to their piano lessons.
B. Future actions which have already been decided.	B. I will be wearing my black dress to the dinner.

PRESENT PERFECT:

A. An action that happened at an unspecified time.	A. She has never climbed a mountain. I'm sorry. I have forgotten your Name.
B. An action that has recently occurred.	B. He's just gone to sleep.
C. An action that began in the past and continues up to the present (often used with "for" or "since").	C. Jack has lived in Chennai all his life. I have been here since Monday. He has known her for two weeks.
D. An action that happened repeatedly before now.	D. We have flown across the Pacific four times. I've failed my driver's test twice.

PRESENT PERFECT CONTINUOUS:

A. An action that began in the past and has just recently ended.	A. Have you been ringing the Bell?
B. An action that began in the past and continues in the present.	B. Lokesh has been studying for two hours.
C. An action repeated over a period of time in the past and continuing in present.	C. Suresh has been smoking since he was fifteen.

PAST PERFECT:

A. An action that occurred before another past action.	A. Tarun had left hours before we got there.
B. An action that was expected to occur in the past.	B. I had hoped to know about the job before now.

PAST PERFECT CONTINUOUS:

A. An action that occurred before another past action.	A. His eyes hurt because he had been Reading for eight hours.
B. An action that was expected to occur in the past.	B. I had been expecting a change in his attitude.

D. The police officer requested the criminal to speak as he told him.

8. The preacher said to me, "May God help you!"

A. The preacher prayed that God might help me.

B. The preacher prayed that God might help him.

C. The preacher requested that God might help me.

D. The preacher requested the God might help them.

9. She said to me, "Happy Diwali!"

A. She blessed me a happy Diwali.

B. She wished me a happy Diwali.

C. She prayed a happy Diwali.

D. She said to me a very happy Diwali.

10. He said, "Shall I open the gate?"

A. He asked that he should open the gate.

B. He asked if he should open the gate.

C. He ordered that he should open the gate.

D. He requested that he should open the gate.

11. I told Ravi, "Do have a cup of tea".

A. I ordered Ravi to have a cup of tea.

B. I advised Ravi to had a cup of tea.

C. I requested Ravi to have a cup of tea.

D. I said Ravi to have a cup of cold tea.

12. He told me, "Shall I go to the picture?"

A. He asked that he should go to the picture.

B. He asked me if he shall go to the picture.

C. He asked me if he should go to the picture.

D. He requested me to go to the picture.

13. The teacher says, "Two and two makes four".

A. The teacher says that two and two made four.

B. The teacher wishes that two and two makes four.

C. The teacher advises that two and two makes four.

D. The teacher says that two and two makes four.

14. Baby said, "I will go".

A. Baby said that she will go.

B. Baby said that she could go.

C. Baby say that she will go.

D. Baby said that she would go.

15. I said to my sister, "Please, give me more money".

A. I requested my sister to give me more money.

B. I ordered my sister to give me more money.

C. I advised my sister to gave me more money.

D. I requested my sister to give her more money.

16. He said, ''Bring a chair at once''.

A. He ordered to bring a chair at once.

B. He requested to bring a chair at once.

C. He told to bring a chair at once.

D. He says to bring a chair at once.

17. The teacher said, ''Don't make a noise''.

A. The teacher says to us not to make a noise.

B. The teacher asked us not to make a noise.

C. The teacher requested us not to make a noise.

D. The teacher asked us not to made a noise.

18. My father said, ''The earth is round''.

A. My father said that the earth was round.

B. My father says that the earth is round.

C. My father said that the earth is round

D. My father ordered that the earth is round.

19. We said, ''What a place it is!''

A. We said that it was a very fine place.

B. We said that is a very fine place.

C. We said that the place is fine.

D. We exclaimed with joy that the place was very fine.

20. She said, ''Shall I thread the needle?''

A. She asked if she should thread the needle.

B. She asked if she shall thread the needle.

C. She requested if she should thread the needle.

D. She says that if she would thread the needle.

ANSWERS

1	2	3	4	5	6	7	8	9	10
B	B	A	D	C	C	A	A	B	B
11	**12**	**13**	**14**	**15**	**16**	**17**	**18**	**19**	**20**
C	C	D	D	A	A	B	C	D	A

15. Active & Passive Voice

An active sentence focuses on the person or thing doing the action. A passive sentence focuses on the person or thing affected by the action.

e.g., The tower was built. (Active voice)

Someone built the tower. (Passive voice)

Transformation of Voice

i.e., Active voice to Passive voice & vice versa.

- Voice and Tense are closely associated with each other.
- Tense plays an important role while transforming the voice.

MULTIPLE CHOICE QUESTIONS

Directions: *In these questions, the sentences have been given in Active/Passive voice. From the given options, choose the one which best expresses the given sentence in Passive/Active voice.*

1. Help the poor.
A. The poor should be helped.
B. The poor would be helped.
C. The poor must be helped.
D. The poor will be helped.

2. Bring a glass of water.
A. A glass of water will be brought.
B. A glass of water should be brought.
C. Let a glass of water be brought.
D. Let a glass of water will be brought.

3. He gave me a beautiful flower pot.
A. A beautiful flower pot was given to me by him.
B. A beautiful flower pot had given to me by him.
C. A beautiful flower pot had been giving by him.
D. I was giving him a beautiful flower pot.

4. Is he answering the question?
A. The question is answered by him.
B. The question is being answered by him.
C. Is the question being answered by him?
D. Is the question being answering by him?

5. Who gave you this letter?
A. This letter was given to you by whom?
B. This letter had given to you by whom?
C. Was this letter given to you?
D. By whom was this letter given to you?

6. The professor teaches students.
A. Students are being taught by the professor.
B. Students are taught by the professor.
C. The professor is being taught by students.
D. Students being taught by the professor.

7. M.S. Dhoni has created a world record.
A. A world record has been created by M.S. Dhoni.
B. A world record has created by M.S. Dhoni.
C. A world record is created by M.S. Dhoni.
D. A world record is being created by M.S. Dhoni.

8. Srishti sings a lovely song.
A. A lovely song had sung by Srishti.
B. A lovely song was sung by Srishti.
C. A lovely song is sung by Srishti.
D. A lovely song is sang by Srishti.

9. He was drawing a picture.
A. A picture was drawn by him.
B. A picture was being drawn by him.
C. A picture was drawing by him.
D. A picture was drew by him.

10. We made him leader.
A. He was made leader by us.

B. He was maded leader.
C. He made leader by us.
D. He was made leader.

11. There is no time to waste.
A. There is no time to be wasted.
B. No time to be wasted there.
C. No time to be wasted by there.
D. No time is to be wasted.

12. Take medicine in time.
A. In time medicine to be taken.
B. Medicine should be taken in time.
C. Medicine in time will be taken.
D. Medicine has to be in time taken.

13. He reads a novel.
A. A novel was read by him.
B. A novel has read by him.
C. A novel is being read by him.
D. A novel is read by him.

14. They had cleared the dues.
A. The dues had been cleared by them.
B. The dues had cleared by them.
C. The dues are being cleared.
D. The dues is cleared.

15. I invite you on the dinner.
A. On the dinner you have been invited.
B. On the dinner you are inviting.
C. You are inviting by me on the dinner.
D. You are invited by me on the dinner.

16. We chose him our leader.
A. He was chosen our leader.
B. He has been chosen our leader.
C. He had chosen our leader.
D. He have been chosen our leader.

17. Who made a maiden century?
A. By whose was a maiden century made?
B. By whom was a maiden century make?
C. By whom was a maiden century made?
D. By whom had a maiden century made?

18. I may help her in her project.
A. She might be helped by me in her project.
B. She may be helped by me in her project.
C. She might be helped in her project by me.
D. In her project, she may be help by me.

19. Take medicine in time.
A. Medicine should be taken in time.
B. Medicine will be taken in time.
C. Medicine will be took in time.
D. Medicine shall take in time.

20. I am solving the questions.
A. The questions are being solved by me.
B. The questions have been solved by me.
C. The questions are to be solved by me.
D. The question are solved by me.

21. May I take this pen?
A. May this pen will be taken by me?
B. May this pen shall be taken by me?
C. May this pen should be taken by me?
D. May this pen be taken by me?

22. Can we send it by air?
A. Can this be sent by air?
B. Can it be sent by air?
C. Can it go by air?
D. Can it be send by air?

23. Who wrote this book?
A. By whom was this book written?
B. By whom is this book written?
C. By whom was this book being written?
D. By whom is this book being written?

24. What did you buy?
A. What is bought by you?
B. What is being bought by you?
C. What was bought by you?
D. What was being bought by you?

25. Whom do you want?
A. Who is wanted by you?
B. Who is being wanted by you?
C. You are wanted by whom?
D. You are being wanted by whom?

ANSWERS

1	2	3	4	5	6	7	8	9	10
A	C	A	C	D	B	A	C	B	A
11	**12**	**13**	**14**	**15**	**16**	**17**	**18**	**19**	**20**
A	B	D	A	D	A	C	B	A	A
21	**22**	**23**	**24**	**25**					
D	B	A	C	A					

16. Synonyms, Antonyms & Homonyms

Synonym: A word or phrase that means the same as another word or phrase.
Antonym: A word or phrase that means the opposite of another word or phrase.
Homonyms: Two or more words having the same spelling or pronunciation but different meanings.

MULTIPLE CHOICE QUESTIONS

Directions: *In the following questions choose the word which best expresses the meaning of the given word.*

1. INDICT
A. Condemn B. Reprimand
C. Accuse D. Allege

2. SCINTILLATING
A. Smouldering B. Gilittering
C. Touching D. Warming

3. REFECTORY
A. Restaurant B. Parlour
C. Living Room D. Dining Room

4. DISTINCTION
A. Diffusion B. Disagreement
C. Different D. Degree

5. IMPROVEMENT
A. Advancement B. Betterment
C. Promotion D. Preference

6. ADVERSITY
A. Failure B. Helplessness
C. Misfortune D. Crisis

7. TURN UP
A. Land up B. Show up
C. Crop up D. Come up

8. DEIFY
A. Flatter B. Challenge
C. Worship D. Face

9. ERROR
A. Misadventure B. Misgiving
C. Ambiguity D. Blunder

10. SHALLOW
A. Artificial B. Superficial
C. Foolish D. Worthless

11. MASSACRE
A. Murder B. Stab
C. Assassinate D. Slaughter

12. COMBAT
A. Conflict B. Quarrel
C. Feud D. Fight

13. VORACIOUS
A. Wild B. Hungry
C. Angry D. Quick

14. IMPROMPTU
A. Offhand B. Unimportant
C. Unreal D. Effective

15. RABBLE
A. Mob B. Noise
C. Roar D. Rubbish

16. TEPID
A. Hot B. Warm
C. Cold D. Boiling

17. MAYHEM
A. Jubilation B. Havoc
C. Excitement D. Defeat

18. TIMID
A. Fast B. Slow
C. Medium D. Shy

19. CANTANKEROUS
A. Quarrelsome B. Rash
C. Disrepectful D. Noisy

20. PRECARIOUS
A. Cautious B. Critical
C. Perilous D. Brittle

Directions: *In the following questions choose the word which best expresses the opposite of the given word.*

21. DEAR
A. Priceless B. Free
C. Worthless D. Cheap

22. FLAGITIOUS
A. Innocent B. Vapid
C. Ignorant D. Frivolous

23. LIABILITY
A. Property B. Assets
C. Debt D. Treasure

24. VIRTUOUS
A. Wicked B. Corrupt
C. Vicious D. Scandalous

25. ENCOURAGE
A. Dampen B. Disapprove
C. Discourage D. Warn

26. MORTAL
A. Divine B. Immortal
C. Spiritual D. Eternal

27. LEND
A. Borrow B. Cheat
C. Pawn D. Hire

28. COMIC
A. Emotional B. Tragic
C. Fearful D. Painful

29. ADDITION
A. Division B. Enumeration
C. Subtraction D. Multiplication

30. MINOR
A. Big B. Major
C. Tall D. Heavy

31. REPEL
A. Attend B. Concentrate
C. Continue D. Attract

32. ARTIFICIAL
A. Red B. Natural
C. Truthful D. Solid

33. CAPACIOUS
A. Limited B. Caring
C. Foolish D. Changeable

34. PROVOCATION
A. Vocation B. Pacification
C. Peace D. Destruction

35. METICULOUS
A. Mutual B. Shaggy
C. Meretricious D. Slovenly

36. Choose the correct homonym for the word 'been'.
A. done B. being
C. bean D. covered

37. Choose the correct homonym for the word 'dose'?
A. doze B. does
C. douse D. dyes

38. Choose the correct homonym for the word 'would':
A. could B. weed
C. wood D. hold

39. Choose the correct homonym for the word 'load':
A. loud B. laud
C. lead D. lode

40. Choose the correct homonym for the word 'loan':
A. lawn B. lean
C. lone D. long

ANSWERS

1	2	3	4	5	6	7	8	9	10
C	B	D	C	B	C	B	C	D	B
11	**12**	**13**	**14**	**15**	**16**	**17**	**18**	**19**	**20**
D	D	B	A	A	B	B	D	A	B
21	**22**	**23**	**24**	**25**	**26**	**27**	**28**	**29**	**30**
D	A	B	C	C	B	A	B	C	B
31	**32**	**33**	**34**	**35**	**36**	**37**	**38**	**39**	**40**
D	B	A	B	D	C	A	C	D	C

17. ONE WORD SUBSTITUTION

There are many words in English language which can be perfectly used for a number of words. These words help in expressing ideas in a short and correct manner for the right occasion. Such words not only increase the vocabulary but also enable you to economise in the use of words to a great extent.

MULTIPLE CHOICE QUESTIONS

Directions: *In questions given below out of the four alternatives choose the one which can be substituted for the given words/sentence.*

1. Something that relates to everyone in the world
A. General B. Common
C. Usual D. Universal

2. An expression of mild disapproval
A. Warning B. Denigration
C. Impertinence D. Reproof

3. One who is not easily pleased by anything
A. Maiden B. Medieval
C. Precarious D. Fastidious

4. Murder of a king
A. Infanticide B. Matricide
C. Genocide D. Regicide

5. A remedy for all diseases
A. Stoic B. Marvel
C. Panacea D. Recompense

6. A dramatic performance
A. Mask B. Mosque
C. Masque D. Mascot

7. Study of birds
A. Orology B. Optology
C. Ophthalmology D. Ornithology

8. Ready to believe
A. Credulous B. Credible
C. Creditable D. Incredible

9. Incapable of being seen through
A. Ductile B. Opaque
C. Obsolete D. Potable

10. One who eats everything
A. Omnivorous B. Omniscient
C. Irresistible D. Insolvent

11. A place where bees are kept is called
A. An apiary B. A mole
C. A hive D. A sanctuary

12. One who cannot be corrected
A. Incurable B. Incorrigible
C. Hardened D. Invulnerable

13. One who is in charge of a museum
A. Curator B. Supervisor
C. Caretaker D. Warden

14. Continuing fight between parties, families, clans, etc.
A. Enmity B. Feud
C. Quarrel D. Skirmish

15. A voice loud enough to be heard
A. Audible B. Applaudable
C. Laudable D. Oral

16. A paper written by hand
A. Handicraft B. Manuscript
C. Handiwork D. Thesis

17. Habitually silent or talking little
A. Serville B. Unequivocal
C. Taciturn D. Synoptic

18. To slap with a flat object
A. Chop B. Hew
C. Gnaw D. Swat

19. A person who speaks many languages
A. Linguist B. Monolingual
C. Polyglot D. Bilingual

20. A light sailing-boat built specially for racing
A. Canoe B. Yacht
C. Frigate D. Dinghy

21. A fixed orbit in space in relation to earth
A. Geological B. Geo-synchronous
C. Geo-centric D. Geo-stationary

22. A style in which a writer makes a display of his knowledge
A. Pedantic B. Verbose
C. Pompous D. Ornate

23. A religious discourse
A. Preach B. Stanza
C. Sanctorum D. Sermon

24. A place that provides refuge
A. Asylum B. Sanatorium
C. Shelter D. Orphanage

25. Detailed plan of a journey
A. Travelogue B. Travelkit
C. Schedule D. Itinerary

26. A person who insists on something
A. Disciplinarian B. Stickler
C. Instantaneous D. Boaster

27. A drawing on transparent paper
A. Red print B. Blue print
C. Negative D. Transparency

28. One who believes that all things and events in life are predetermined is a
A. Fatalist B. Puritan
C. Egoist D. Tyrant

29. A school boy who cuts classes frequently is a
A. Defeatist B. Sycophant
C. Truant D. Martinet

30. The act of violating the sanctity of the church is
A. Blasphemy B. Heresy
C. Sacrilege D. Desecration

31. A place where monks live as a secluded community
A. Cathedral B. Diocese
C. Convent D. Monastery

32. One who is fond of fighting
A. Bellicose B. Aggressive
C. Belligerent D. Militant

33. Tending to move away from the centre or axis
A. Centrifugal B. Centripetal
C. Axiomatic D. Awry

34. A person of good understanding, knowledge and reasoning power
A. Expert B. Intellectual
C. Snob D. Literate

35. One absorbed in his own thoughts and feelings rather than in things outside
A. Scholar B. Recluse
C. Introvert D. Intellectual

36. One who does not marry, especially as a religious obligation
A. Bachelor B. Celibate
C. Virgin D. Recluse

37. A person who tries to deceive people by claiming to be able to do wonderful things.
A. Trickster B. Impostor
C. Magician D. Mountebank

38. To take secretly in small quantities
A. Robbery B. Pilferage
C. Theft D. Defalcation

39. Policemen riding on motorcycles as guards to a VIP.
A. Outriders B. Servants
C. Commandos D. Attendants

40. The part of a government which is concerned with making of rules.
A. Court B. Tribunal
C. Bar D. Legislature

ANSWERS

1	2	3	4	5	6	7	8	9	10
D	D	D	D	C	C	D	A	B	A
11	12	13	14	15	16	17	18	19	20
A	B	A	B	A	B	C	D	A	B
21	22	23	24	25	26	27	28	29	30
D	A	D	A	D	B	D	A	C	C
31	32	33	34	35	36	37	38	39	40
D	A	A	B	C	B	A	B	A	D

18. Idioms, Phrases & Proverbs

An idiom is a group of words established by usage as having a meaning different from the individual words.
A phrase is a small group of words standing together as an idiomatic expression.
A proverb is a short pithy saying in general use, stating a general truth or piece of advice.

MULTIPLE CHOICE QUESTIONS

Directions: *Some idioms/phrases are given below with their meanings. Choose their correct meanings.*

1. **To beg the question**
   A. To refer to
   B. To take for granted
   C. To raise objections
   D. To be discussed
2. **To drive home**
   A. To find one's roots
   B. To return to place of rest
   C. Back to original position
   D. To emphasise
3. **To hit the right nail on the head**
   A. To do the right thing
   B. To destroy one's reputation
   C. To announce one's fixed views
   D. To teach someone a lesson
4. **To pick holes**
   A. To find some reason to quarrel
   B. To destory something
   C. To criticise someone
   D. To cut some part of an item
5. **To smell a rat**
   A. To see signs of plague epidemic
   B. To get bad smell of a dead rat
   C. To suspect foul dealings
   D. To be in a bad mood
6. **A black sheep**
   A. An unlucky person
   B. A negro
   C. An ugly person
   D. A disgraced member
7. **To catch a tarter**
   A. To trap wanted criminal with great difficulty
   B. To catch a dangerous person
   C. To meet with disaster
   D. To deal with a person who is more than one's watch
8. **To be above board**
   A. To have a good height
   B. To be honest in any business deal
   C. To have no debts
   D. To try to be beautiful
9. **To keep one's temper**
   A. To become angry
   B. To be in good mood
   C. To preserve one's energy
   D. To be aloof from
10. **To have an axe to grind**
    A. A private end to serve
    B. To fail to arouse interest
    C. To have no result
    D. To work for both sides
11. **To cry wolf**
    A. To listen eagerly
    B. To give false alarm
    C. To turn pale
    D. To keep off starvation
12. **A man of straw**
    A. A man of no substance
    B. A very active person
    C. A worthy fellow
    D. An unreasonable person

13. To make clean breast of
A. To gain prominence
B. To praise oneself
C. To confess without reserve
D. To destroy before it blooms

14. To end in smoke
A. To make completely understand
B. To ruin oneself
C. To excite great applause
D. To produce no result

15. To leave someone in the lurch
A. To come to compromise with someone
B. Constant source of annoyance to someone
C. To put someone at ease
D. To desert someone in his difficulties

16. To play second fiddle
A. To be happy, cheerful and healthy
B. To reduce importance of one's senior
C. To support the role and view of another person
D. To do back seat driving

17. To set one's face against
A. To oppose with determination
B. To judge by appearance
C. To get out of difficulty
D. To look at one steadily

18. To put one's hand to the plough
A. To take up agricultural farming
B. To take a difficult task
C. To get entangled into unnecessary things
D. Take interest in technical work

19. To join issue with
A. To cooperate with others for a cause
B. To join any voluntary organisation for good purpose
C. To resolve dispute and restore peace
D. To enter into argument over any issue

20. To do oneself justice
A. To dispense justice on our own
B. To treat others with due respect
C. To defend one's point of view
D. To perform and be able

21. Once in a blue moon
A. Once in a while
B. Often
C. At a short interval
D. At a particular time

22. Necessity is the mother of invention
A. The mother of a girl named 'Necessity' made an invention.
B. She who can make some invention should be called 'mother'.
C. Your mother will feel happy if you make some invention.
D. A difficult problem compels people to think about its solution.

23. No pain, no gain
A. It is useless to suffer so much pain just for a little gain.
B. If you want to achieve something, you have to suffer to some extent.
C. Unless you have pain in your body, no doctor will care for you.
D. If you get injured in a competition, you will be allowed to get the prize.

24. Beauty is only skin deep
A. The real beauty of a person lies in his character and not in his outer appearance.
B. Only the quality of skin makes a person really beautiful.
C. If you want to be beautiful, give attention to your skin.
D. Rub cosmetics below the skin to get really beautiful.

25. Beggars cannot be choosers
A. Beggars are not allowed at all places.
B. Begging is prohibited by law.
C. It is not easy even to become a beggar.
D. Beggars have to accept (without choice) whatever is given to them.

ANSWERS

1	2	3	4	5	6	7	8	9	10
B	D	A	C	C	D	B	B	B	A
11	**12**	**13**	**14**	**15**	**16**	**17**	**18**	**19**	**20**
B	A	C	D	D	C	A	B	B	D
21	**22**	**23**	**24**	**25**					
A	D	B	A	D					

19. Modals & Auxiliaries

AUXILIARY VERBS

Modals are actually helping verbs. They help the finite verbs in framing sentences:

She **was** cooking food.
I **shall** guide you.

Kinds of Auxiliary Verbs

Auxiliary verbs are of two kinds:

A. Primary Auxiliaries (Modals)
B. Modal Auxiliaries (Auxiliary Modals)

A. Primary Modals

Primary modals work both as Helping Verbs and Finite Verbs.

Be = is, am, are, was, were, being, been
Have = has, have, had, having
Do = do, does, did, done, doing

(*a*) **Usage of be/have/do as Helping verbs:**
She **is** making a cane basket.
I **have** finished my homework.
She **does** know French.

(*b*) **Usage of be/have/do as Finite verbs:**
She **was** happy.
I **have** an expensive pen.
She **is doing** her homework.

B. Modal Auxiliaries

Shall, should, will, would, can, could, may, might, must, ought to, used to, have to, had to, dare, daren't, need needn't, mustn't are modal Auxiliaries.

Shall

'Shall' is used in the following ways:

(*a*) **With first Person Pronouns (I/we)**
I shall lend you my book.
We shall go to school together.

(*b*) **to express a suggestion**
Shall we go out for a walk?
Shall we meet the officer tomorrow?

Sometimes 'Shall' is used with Second and Third Person Pronouns as under:

(*a*) **to express a command**
You shall not tell a lie.
You shall not disturb us.

(*b*) **to express prohibition**
You shall not smoke here.
You shall not drink here.

(*c*) **to express a legal obligation**
You shall submit your sales tax return before the end of this month.

Should

'Should' is used in the following ways:

(*a*) **As Past Tense of 'shall'**
She said that she **should** settle in America.

(*b*) **to express duty and obligation**
You should do your duty honestly.

(*c*) **to express advice**
You should reach the station before time.

(*d*) **to express guess**
It should be 9 o'clock now.

(*e*) 'Should' is used with lest to express purpose.
Walk fast lest you should miss the train.

Will

'Will' is used in the following ways:

(*a*) **With Second and Third person Pronouns:**
You will dance at the party.
He will sing a song.

(*b*) **to express (Invitation/offer)**
Will you dine with [illegible]

(*c*) **to express an order**
Will you shut your big mouth?

(*d*) **to express probability**
He will come to see me tomorrow.

Sometimes 'Will' is used with 'I'

(*a*) **Determination**
I will win the first position.

(*b*) **A threat**
I will punish you.

(*c*) **A promise**
I will lend you Rs. 500/- tomorrow.

Would

'Would' is used in the following ways:

(*a*) **As Past Tense of 'will'**
He said that they would be attending the meeting the next day.

(*b*) **to express a desire or wish**
Would that I were a king!

(*c*) **to express a polite invitation**
Would you like some biscuits?

(*d*) **The usage of would in conditional sentences**
You would get good marks if you worked hard.
You would have won the race if you had run fast.

(*e*) **to express a piece of advice**
I would not meet him if I were you.

Can

'Can' is used in the following ways:

(*a*) **to express ability**
He can speak English fluently.

(*b*) **to grant permission**
You can go now.

(*c*) **to express impossibility**
Who can defeat his fate?

(*d*) **to make a request**
Can I use your motorbike?

Could

'Could' is used in the following ways:

(*a*) **As Past Tense of 'can'**
She said that she could see the sun rising.

(*b*) **to express past ability**
I could sing and dance when I was young.

(*c*) **to express a request**
Could I use your phone?

May

'May' is used in the following ways:

(*a*) **to express a request**
May I use your bicycle?

(*b*) **to seek and allow permission**
May I come in, sir?
Yes, you may.

(*c*) **to express possibility**
It may rain tonight.

(*d*) **In optative sentences**
May you live long!

Might

'Might' is used in the following ways:

(*a*) **As past tense of 'may'**
She said that her brother might come back home.

(*b*) **to express less possibility**
It might rain tonight.

(*c*) **to give and seek permission**
Might I come in, sir?
You might go home now.

Must

'Must' is used in the following ways:

(*a*) **to express duty**
You must serve your motherland.

(*b*) **to express obligation**
We must obey our elders.

(*c*) **to express advice**
You must take an umbrella before going to office.

(*d*) **to express probability**
'Must' expresses a stronger probability than may.
It must rain tonight.

Ought to

'Ought to' is used in the following ways:

(*a*) **to express obligation**
We ought to respect our teachers.

(*b*) **to express advice**
You ought to help the poor.

Used to

'Used to' is used in the following ways:
(*a*) **to express past habits**
He used to smoke.
(*b*) **to express past existence of something**
There used to be a five star hotel in this city.

Have to

'Have to' expresses compulsion in the present tense.
You have to sign the documents.

Had to

'Had to' expresses compulsion in the past time.
She had to join the office again.

Dare

'Dare' is used as a Modal only in Interrogative sentences.
How dare you touch my bag?

Dare not (Daren't)

'Dare not (Daren't)' is used in negative sentences.
She daren't complain against me.

Need

'Need' expresses an obligation/compulsion. It is used in Interrogative Sentences.
Need I say more?

Need not (Needn't)

'Need not (Needn't)' is used in negative sentences.
You needn't come here again.

Must not (Mustn't)

'Must not (Mustn't)' is the negative form of must.
You mustn't follow us.

MULTIPLE CHOICE QUESTIONS

Directions: *In the following questions choose the correct options to fill in the blanks:*

1. Work hard lest you .... fail.
A. should B. may
C. can D. must

2. .... I come in, madam?
A. Can B. May
C. Will D. Must

3. It ...... rain tonight.
A. shall B. will
C. may D. can

4. You ...... love your countrymen.
A. need to B. have to
C. had to D. ought to

5. .... you like some pastries?
A. Should B. Would
C. Could D. Will

6. ...... that I were an actor!
A. Would B. Should
C. Could D. Will

7. Had you made one more effort you ...... have won the race.
A. will B. may
C. would D. shall

8. I ...... solve any sum.
A. may B. am
C. must D. can

9. ...... I smoke here?
A. Can B. Will
C. Could D. Must

10. The passengers .... keep watch on their luggage.
A. has B. have
C. should D. had

11. You .... submit your file to the authorities within a week.
A. have B. had
C. should D. would

12. ...... I use your phone?
A. Have B. Could
C. Would D. Had

13. ..... you give me your pen?
A. May B. Can
C. Must D. Dare

14. There ...... be an hospital at this place.
A. have to B. may
C. used to D. might

15. He ...... read and write when he was young.
A. would B. could
C. should D. can

16. He said that he ..... sing a song at the party.
A. should B. would
C. can D. will

17. She asked if he ...... help her.
A. should B. can
C. must D. would

18. We .... respect our elders.
A. need to B. have to
C. ought to D. had to

19. Nothing .... be done under such circumstances.
A. can B. used to
C. must D. have to

20. She ..... not ask about it.
A. has B. have
C. had D. dare

21. You .... not bring the child here.
A. have B. had
C. need D. would

22. ..... you live long!
A. Will B. May
C. Shall D. Can

23. ..... God help you!
A. Can B. Will
C. May D. Shall

24. ..... that I were a leader!
A. Would B. Should
C. Could D. Will

25. It ...... be ten o'clock now.
A. could B. would
C. should D. will

26. He ..... have reached the station by now.
A. shall B. will
C. would D. should

27. Being a receptionist, she will .... type a letter.
A. has to B. have to
C. need to D. must

28. The birds ...... fly high in the sky.
A. may B. should
C. can D. would

29. ...... I open the main gate?
A. Should B. Would
C. Could D. Must

30. If you played well, we ...... win the match.
A. would B. should
C. must D. need

31. If I were you I ... not attend the meeting.
A. can B. would
C. could D. should

32. She ...... smoke in those days.
A. used to B. could
C. would D. had to

33. You ...... take the child to an intelligent doctor.
A. shall B. will
C. ought to D. would

34. ..... I sit here for some time?
A. Can B. Shall
C. Will D. Must

35. I think you .... not mind my reciting the poem loudly.
A. should B. could
C. may D. would

ANSWERS

1	2	3	4	5	6	7	8	9	10
A	B	C	D	B	A	C	D	A	C
11	12	13	14	15	16	17	18	19	20
A	B	B	C	B	B	D	C	A	D
21	22	23	24	25	26	27	28	29	30
C	B	C	A	C	B	B	C	A	A
31	32	33	34	35					
B	A	C	A	D					

20. Non Finites

Read the following sentences:

1. She has decided to resign.
2. I see a thief running.
3. She insists on my sitting beside her.

In the above sentences, the underlined words are non-finites because they are not changed with the change of the subject, *e.g.*,

They have decided to resign.
She sees a thief running.
You insist on my sitting beside you.

Non-finites are of three kinds:

1. The Infinitives (to + v_1)
2. The Participles (v_1 + ing)
3. The Gerund (v_1 + ing)

1. THE INFINITIVE

To plus first form of the verb is called an Infinitive. It is often used as a Noun.

Uses of the Infinitive

(*a*) Subject of a sentence.
To laugh loudly is good for health.
To steal is bad.

(*b*) After a transitive verb.
He loves **to eat** sweets.
She likes **to play** tennis.

(*c*) After a preposition.
They are about **to leave.**

(*d*) As a complement after the verb 'be'.
Her ambition is **to be** a teacher.
His immediate aim is **to help** her.

(*e*) As an object.
He made me **weep.**
I saw him **go.**

(*f*) After an adjective.
Honey is sweet **to taste.**
He was ashamed **to talk** to his criminal friend.

(*g*) After a noun. (often in passive)
Here is a book **to be** read carefully.

Bare Infinitive

Some Infinitives are used without 'to' and are called Bare Infinitives.

You had better **go** home.
I saw him **go.**
I heard him **sing.**
He would rather **rest** than **play.**
I can **solve** this sum.
I watched him **steal** your purse.
I watched him **open** the safe.
Let him **come** in.
You had sooner **read** your book than **play.**

Note: Bare Infinitives are usually used after 'causal' (or 'causative') verbs and 'modals'.

2. THE PARTICIPLE

Participles serve the purpose of Adjectives.

I heard him **singing.**
I saw him **going.**

Kinds of Participles

Participles are of the following kinds:

I. Present Participle

I watched the boy **stealing** your purse.
I saw him **climbing** the hill.
She smelt something **burning.**
Don't let me catch you **smoking.**

II. Past Participle

I got the house **painted** last week.
I had my hair **cut.**
The rose has **faded.**

33. He is reported (be) dead.
A. be to B. to be
C. to being D. to been

34. You are ordered (bring) the file number 100.
A. bringing B. to bringing
C. bring to D. to bring

35. You are advised (take) part in sports.
A. taking to B. to taking
C. to take D. take to

36. He appeared (have) cast his vote in favour of us.
A. having B. to having
C. to have D. have to

37. His ambition is (become) a doctor.
A. becoming B. to becoming
C. to become D. become to

38. We are asked (be) there in the main hall.
A. being B. been
C. to be D. be to

39. Our immediate aim is (provide) financial help to the needy.
A. provide to B. providing to
C. to providing D. to provide

40. We read and write (become) civilized.
A. becoming B. becoming to
C. to become D. become to

41. You need (improve) your health.
A. improving B. improvinto to
C. to improve D. improve to

42. You are allowed (paint) this door.
A. painting B. painting to
C. to paint D. paint to

43. Remind me (post) this letter.
A. posting B. posting to
C. to post D. post to

44. The teacher forgot (bring) the roll call register.
A. bringing B. to bringing
C. bring to D. to bring

45. He was appointed (keep) a check on the accounts.
A. keep to B. keeping to
C. to keep D. keeping

46. Your activities are (be) noticed.
A. being B. been
C. to be D. be to

47. Stop (talk), please.
A. talk to B. talking
C. to talk D. to talking

48. He does not bother (listen to) anybody.
A. listen to B. to listen to
C. listening D. listening to

49. He is not accustomed to (have) soup before meal.
A. have to B. to have
C. having D. to having

50. She is glad (be) in the company of children.
A. being B. been
C. to be D. be to

ANSWERS

1	2	3	4	5	6	7	8	9	10
B	C	B	D	A	B	B	C	B	B
11	12	13	14	15	16	17	18	19	20
C	B	A	B	C	C	A	B	D	B
21	22	23	24	25	26	27	28	29	30
C	C	C	C	C	D	B	C	D	D
31	32	33	34	35	36	37	38	39	40
A	B	B	D	C	C	C	C	D	C
41	42	43	44	45	46	47	48	49	50
C	C	C	D	C	A	B	B	D	C

21. Commonly Confusing Words

There are many words in English which may look or sound similar but there is lot of difference in their meanings and usage. Learn more about such words in this exercise.

MULTIPLE CHOICE QUESTIONS

Directions: *In the following questions choose the correct word to fill the blank. Two words at A and B are provided for choice. If either of the words can be filled, mark C and if none of the word can be filled then mark D as your choice.*

1. She comes of a .... family.
A. respectable B. respectful
C. Any one of these D. None of these

2. It began to .... as I reached my office.
A. reign B. rain
C. Any one of these D. None of these

3. The teacher told the students to be ....
A. quiet B. quite
C. Any one of these D. None of these

4. The .... has gone to attend the meeting.
A. principle B. principal
C. Any one of these D. None of these

5. .... makes a man perfect.
A. Practice B. Practise
C. Any one of these D. None of these

6. Uttar Pradesh is the most .... state of India.
A. popular B. populous
C. Any one of these D. None of these

7. The bird had a .... of bread with beak.
A. piece B. peace
C. Any one of these D. None of these

8. As she read the letter, her face turned ....
A. pail B. pale
C. Any one of these D. None of these

9. Man is the maker of his own ....
A. destination B. destiny
C. Any one of these D. None of these

10. Try this medicine, it will prove ....
A. effectual B. effective
C. Any one of these D. None of these

11. Maninder has employed an .... boy for his office works.
A. errand B. errant
C. Any one of these D. None of these

12. The soldiers wanted to .... over their victory in the battle.
A. exalt B. exult
C. Any one of these D. None of these

13. When I asked him to accompany us, he .... illness.
A. fained B. feigned
C. Any one of these D. None of these

14. The books are lying on the .... piece.
A. mantal B. mantle
C. Any one of these D. None of these

15. Sohan lives a .... life.
A. luxurious B. luxuriant
C. Any one of these D. None of these

16. She is a lady of .... birth.
A. lowly B. low
C. Any one of these D. None of these

17. We should not be ....of other's wealth.
A. jealous B. zealous
C. Any one of these D. None of these

18. It is two days .... from Delhi to Kerala by train.
A. journey B. voyage
C. Any one of these D. None of these

28. A. Ocasion B. Occassion
C. Occasion D. Ocassion

29. A. Boquet B. Bouquet
C. Bouquete D. Bouquette

30. A. Chettering B. Chaterring
C. Chattering D. Chatering

31. A. Discourage B. Disscourage
C. Discourege D. Discaurage

32. A. Curageous B. Courageous
C. Courrageous D. Couregeous

33. A. Abandon B. Abanddon
C. Abendon D. Abbandon

34. A. Embarassment B. Emberrassement
C. Embarrassment D. Embbaresment

35. A. Eccintric B. Eccentrie
C. Eccentric D. Eccintrie

36. A. Occasional B. Occassional
C. Occesional D. Occessional

37. A. Querrel B. Querral
C. Quarrel D. Quarel

38. A. Contrebuticn B. Contribution
C. Contributtion D. Conterbution

39. A. Desgrace B. Disgrece
C. Disgrice D. Disgrace

40. A. Harassment B. Herassment
C. Harasment D. Harassmient

41. A. Imaginative B. Imeginative
C. Imagenative D. Imaginetive

42. A. Suficient B. Suficiant
C. Sufficient D. Sufficiant

43. A. Adequate B. Edequate
C. Adaquete D. Edaquete

44. A. Exparienced B. Experianced
C. Experienced D. Experrienced

45. A. Flatering B. Fletering
C. Flattering D. Fletaring

46. A. Cuttiveted B. Culltrivated
C. Cultivated D. Caltivated

47. A. Praiceworthy B. Peiseworthy
C. Praiseworthy D. Praisaworthy

48. A. Profesional B. Professionel
C. Professional D. Profissional

49. A. Ameteur B. Amateur
C. Amataur D. Amateor

50. A. Unfevourable B. Unfevaurable
C. Unfavourable D. Unfivourable

ANSWERS

1	2	3	4	5	6	7	8	9	10
A	C	A	B	B	A	B	B	D	C
11	**12**	**13**	**14**	**15**	**16**	**17**	**18**	**19**	**20**
A	B	A	A	C	A	A	A	C	A
21	**22**	**23**	**24**	**25**	**26**	**27**	**28**	**29**	**30**
B	B	B	D	B	C	A	C	B	C
31	**32**	**33**	**34**	**35**	**36**	**37**	**38**	**39**	**40**
A	B	A	C	C	A	C	B	D	A
41	**42**	**43**	**44**	**45**	**46**	**47**	**48**	**49**	**50**
A	C	A	C	A	C	C	C	B	C

23. PUNCTUATION

Punctuation marks help us to make grammatically correct sentences.

The following pairs of sentences will bring home to you the importance of punctuation marks:

(*a*) Jack, my neighbour, is going abroad.

(*b*) Jack, my neighbour is going abroad.

The sentence (*a*) means 'Jack' is my neighbour and he is going abroad. The sentence (*b*) means that I'm telling Jack that my neighbour is going abroad.

Learn and practise the correct usage of punctuation marks.

The following are some most commonly used punctuation marks:

(*i*)	Full Stop	(.)
(*ii*)	Note of Interrogation	(?)
(*iii*)	Note of Exclamation	(!)
(*iv*)	Comma	(,)
(*v*)	Inverted commas	(" ")
(*vi*)	Apostrophe	(')
(*vii*)	Capital Letters	(A)
(*viii*)	Colon	(:)
(*ix*)	Semicolon	(;)
(*x*)	Dash	(–)
(*xi*)	Oblique	(/)
(*xii*)	Parentheses	( )
(*xiii*)	Hyphen	(-)

MULTIPLE CHOICE QUESTIONS

Directions: *In the questions given below, which one alternative out of four has been applied with correct punctuation marks?*

1. When mankind passed through the grunt-and-groan stage and language had been invented everyone was happy

A. When mankind passed through the grunt-and-groan stage, and language had been invented, everyone was happy.

B. When, mankind passed through the grunt-and-groan stage, and language had been invented everyone was happy.

C. When mankind passed, through the grunt-and-groan stage and language had been invented everyone was happy.

D. When mankind, passed through the grunt-and-groan stage and language had been invented everyone was happy.

2. Communication has been established they said and now we can understand each other

A. Communication has been established, they said and now, we can understand each other.

B. ''Communication has been established,'' they said, ''and now we can understand each other.''

C. Communication has been established, they said, "and now we can understand, each other."

D. "Communication has been established" they said and now we can understand each other.

3. Then writing was developed so that words could be given some durability

A. Then, writing was developed so that words could be given some durability.

B. Then writing was developed, so that words could be given some durability.

C. Then writing was developed so that words could be given some durability.
D. Then writing was developed, so that words could be given, some durability.

4. How wonderful everyone exclaimed now we can read and write
A. How wonderful! everyone exclaimed, now we can read and write.
B. How wonderful everyone exclaimed! now we can read and write.
C. "How wonderful everyone exclaimed!" now we can read and write.
D. ''How wonderful!'' everyone exclaimed, ''Now we can read and write.''

5. But then they began to have difficulty understanding what was written down because everything seemed to run together
A. But then they began to have difficulty understanding what was written down, because everything seemed to run together.
B. But, then they began to have difficulty understanding, what was written down? because everything seemed to run together.
C. But then, they began to have difficulty understanding–what was written down? because everything seemed to run together.
D. But then they began to have difficulty, understanding what was written down because, everything seemed to run together.

6. How confusing they complained
A. "How confusing, they complained!"
B. "How confusing!" they complained.
C. "How confusing" they complained.
D. "How confusing?" they complained.

7. So they invented sentences phrases clauses and punctuation
A. So, they invented sentences phrases clauses and punctuation.
B. So they, invented sentences phrases clauses and punctuation.
C. So they invented sentences, phrases, clauses and punctuation.
D. So they invented, sentences, phrases, clauses and punctuation.

8. Now they stated gleefully we can set our thoughts down read them and understand just what is meant
A. Now, they stated gleefully, "we can set our thoughts down, read them and understand just what is meant.
B. Now, they stated, "gleefully we can set our thoughts down read them and understand just what is meant."
C. Now they stated gleefully, "we can set our thoughts down read them and understand," just what is meant.
D. ''Now,'' they stated gleefully, ''we can set our thoughts down, read them and understand just what is meant.''

9. Will you lend me ten rupees said sarla yes i will promila replied
A. "Will you lend me ten rupees?" said Sarla. "Yes, i will," promila replied.
B. "Will you lend me ten rupees," said Sarla. 'Yes, I will' Promila replied.
C. 'Will you lend me ten rupees?' said Sarla 'Yes, I will,' Promila replied.
D. "Will you lend me ten rupees?" said Sarla. "Yes, I will," Promila replied.

10. You are a thief policeman said the thief you asked for a bribe
A. "You are a thief!" policeman said, the thief, "You asked for a bribe."
B. "You are a thief policeman!" said the thief, You asked for a bribe.
C. "You are a thief policeman!" said, the thief, 'you asked for a bribe.'
D. "You are a thief, policeman!" said the thief, "You asked for a bribe."

ANSWERS

1	2	3	4	5	6	7	8	9	10
A	B	C	D	A	B	C	D	D	D

24. Word Analogy

Like different people words also have different relationships in comparison to each other. This is called word analogy. Try and master it in the following questions.

MULTIPLE CHOICE QUESTIONS

Directions (Qs. 1 to 25): *Each question consists of two words which have a certain relationship to each other followed by four pairs of related words. Select the pair which has the same relationship.*

1. Lunatic : Asylum

A. The poor : palace
B. Soldiers : barracks
C. Flowers : fields
D. Crops : garden

2. Soldier : Rifle

A. Blacksmith : anvil
B. Thief : ladder
C. Watchman : uniform
D. Barber : hair

3. Frog : Tadpoles

A. Man : sons
B. Woman : daughters
C. Cat : kids
D. Elephant : calves

4. Lizards : Reptiles

A. Frogs : amphibians
B. Tree : fruit
C. Earth : moon
D. Man : woman

5. Earthworm : Segments

A. Tree : wood
B. Crocodiles : scales
C. Apple : juice
D. Earth : moisture

6. Mosquito : Malaria

A. Rabid dog : rabies
B. House fly : AIDS
C. Cockroach : influenza
D. Virus : diabetes

7. Fish : Water

A. Man : air
B. Cat : mouse
C. Lion : flesh
D. Tree : roots

8. Impulsive : Cautious

A. Liberty : bondage
B. Tyrant : bully
C. Tremble : quake
D. Vulgar : indecent

9. Weighty : Voluminous

A. Jolly : dismal
B. Loyalty : perfidy
C. Wealth : opulence
D. Odd : normal

10. Innocent : Guilty

A. Kill : produce
B. Suspect : doubt
C. Depress : discourage
D. Contract : condense

11. Useless : Cheap

A. Late : unpunctual
B. Real : illusive
C. Just : unfair
D. Humble : proud

12. Loyal : Faithful
A. Treacherous : devoted
B. Just : fair
C. Yield : suppress
D. Uncertain : sure

13. Cancel : Confirm
A. Certain : ambiguous
B. Vulgar : crude
C. Reliable : trustworthy
D. Obscure : anonymous

14. Gloomy : Bright
A. Pleasant : delightful
B. Funny : comic
C. Condemn : blame
D. Hard : flexible

15. Modern : Ancient
A. Happy : joyful
B. Service : slavery
C. Mild : harsh
D. assumed : unreal

16. Dexterous : Clumsy
A. Cheap : worthless
B. Usual : common
C. Zenith : acme
D. True : false

17. Luscious : Sweet
A. Above : below
B. Absolve : penalise
C. Lucrative : profitable
D. Adopt : abandon

18. Fraud : Duplicity
A. Inferior : cheap
B. Delicious : abhorrent
C. Desire : detest
D. Diligent : lackadiasical

19. Weired : Ordinary
A. Vacant : void
B. Vivid : clear
C. Vivid : dim
D. Wicked : unvirtuous

20. Build : Demolish
A. Abide : persist
B. Compel : coax
C. Odious : hateful
D. Claim : demand

21. Passionate : Impassive
A. Deter : discourage
B. Folly : stupidity
C. Polite : rude
D. Fanciful : whimsical

22. Gauche : Attractive
A. True : exact
B. Tough : hard
C. Tasteful : palatable
D. Insipid : delicious

23. Existence : Life
A. Silence : noise
B. Risk : shield
C. Enormous : immense
D. Rural : urban

24. Belief : Suspicion
A. Unravel : unweave
B. Profuse : insufficient
C. Urge : spur
D. Use : occupy

25. Violent : Calm
A. Tranquil : peaceful
B. Reticent : quiet
C. Even : smooth
D. Disdain : reverence

ANSWERS

1	2	3	4	5	6	7	8	9	10
B	A	D	A	B	A	A	A	C	A
11	**12**	**13**	**14**	**15**	**16**	**17**	**18**	**19**	**20**
A	B	A	D	C	D	C	A	C	B
21	**22**	**23**	**24**	**25**					
C	D	C	B	D					

25. Figures of Speech

It is a common saying that a picture is worth a thousand words. Same goes with the figures of speech as they elaborate the meaning of words.

There are four common types of figures of speech:

- Simile
- Metaphor
- Hyperbole
- Oxymoron

Simile

A simile is a figure of speech that says that one thing is like another different thing. We can use similes to make descriptions more emphatic or vivid.

We often use the words as....as and like with similes.

Common patterns for similes, with example sentences, are:

- Something AS adjective AS something
  His skin was as cold as ice.
  It felt as hard as rock.
  She looked as gentle as a lamb.
- Something LIKE something
  My love is like a red, red rose.
  These cookies taste like garbage.
  He had a temper (that was) like a volcano.
  Something LIKE something
  He eats like a pig.
  He smokes like a chimney.
  They fought like cats and dogs.

Metaphor

A metaphor is a figure of speech that says that one thing is another different thing. This allows us to use fewer words and forces the reader or listener to find the similarities.

The word metaphor comes from the Greek word *metapherin* (meaning "transfer").

The simplest form of metaphor is : "The [first thing] is a [second thing]."

Look at this example :

Her home was a prison.

In the above sentence, we understand immediately that her home had some of the characteristics of a prison. Mainly, we imagine, she could not leave her home. She was trapped inside. In this sentence, "prison" is a metaphor.

Look at another example :

George is a sheep.

What is one characteristic of sheep? They follow each other. So we can imagine that George is a follower, not a leader. In this sentence "sheep" is a metaphor.

Metaphors are very common in everyday language.

Difference Between Metaphor and Simile

Both similes and metaphors link one thing to another. A simile usually uses "as" or "like". A metaphor is a condensed simile, a shortcut to meaning, which omits "as" or "like". A metaphor creates a relationship directly and leaves more to the imagination. With simile, A is like B. With metaphor, A is B.

Simile	Metaphor
Your eyes are like the sun.	You are my sunshine.
He eats like a pig.	He is a pig.
He lives like a pig.	He is a pig.

Hyperbole

Hyperbole is a figure of speech that uses an exaggerated or extravagant to create a strong emotional response. As a figure of speech it is not intended to be taken literally. Hyperbole is frequently used for humour. Examples of hyperbole are :

- They ran like greased lightning.
- He's got tons of money.
- Her brain is the size of a pea.
- He is older than the hills.
- I will die if she asks me to dance.
- She is as big as an elephant!
- I'm so hungry I could eat a horse.
- I have told you a million times not to lie!

The media and the advertising industry often use hyperbole (which may then be described as hyper or media hype).

Oxymoron

An oxymoron is a figure of speech that deliberately uses two contradictory ideas. This contradiction creates a paradoxical image in the reader or listener's mind that generates a new concept or meaning for the whole. Some typical oxymorons are :

- a living death
- sometimes you have to be cruel to be kind
- a deafening silence
- bitter-sweet

The following are the other major Figures of Speech :

1. **Personification**—"In Personification inanimate objects and abstract notions are spoken of as having life or intelligence."
2. **Onomatopoeia**—"Onomatopoeia is that artifice of language by which the sound of words is made to suggest or echo the sense."
3. **Apostrophe**—"An Apostrophe is a direct address to the dead, to the absent, or to a personified object or idea."
4. **Alliteration**—"Alliteration consists in the repetition of the same sound or syllable at the beginning of two or more words."
5. **Irony**—"Irony is a mode of speech in which the real meaning is exactly the opposite of that which is literally conveyed."
6. **Pun**—"This consists in a play on the various meanings of a word, and is seldom used except as a joke."
7. **Metonymy**—"In Metonymy an object is designated by the name of something which is generally associated with it."
8. **Synecdoche**—"In Synecdoche a part is used to designate the whole, or the whole to designate a part."
9. **Antithesis**—"In Antithesis a striking opposition or contrast of words or sentiments is made in the same sentence. It is employed to secure emphasis."
10. **Transferred Epithet**—"In this figure an epithet is tranferred from its proper word to another that is closely associated with it in the sentence."

MULTIPLE CHOICE QUESTIONS

Directions (Qs. 1 to 25) : *Fill in the blanks with the correct similes.*

1. As black as ....

A. coal B. colour
C. coat D. cloud

2. As blind as a ....

A. cat B. rat
C. dog D. bat

3. As bold as ....

A. grass B. brass
C. ass D. gas

4. As brave as a ....

A. horse B. elephant
C. lion D. bull

5. As busy as a ....

A. man B. animal
C. bird D. bee

6. As cheap as ....
A. dirt B. shirt
C. trouser D. shoes

7. As clear as ....
A. shirt B. picture
C. crystal D. sky

8. As cold as ....
A. ice B. water
C. milk D. breeze

9. As cunning as a ....
A. ox B. fox
C. crow D. man

10. As dead as ....
A. button B. air
C. water D. mutton

11. As deaf as a ....
A. man B. bird
C. stone D. animal

12. As dry as ....
A. cloth B. bone
C. air D. sand

13. Rivers of blood flowed on the battlefied :
A. Simile B. Metaphor
C. Hyperbole D. Alliteration

14. Camel is the ship of the desert :
A. Metaphor B. Simile
C. Pun D. Personification

15. 'O my love's liek a red, red rose, that's newly sprung in June':
A. Alliteration B. Metaphor
C. Simile D. Hyperbole

16. "Opportunity knocks at the door but once."
A. Hyperbole B. Metaphor
C. Antithesis D. Personification

17. "Death lays his icy hand on Kings" :
A. Personification B. Antithesis
C. Metaphor D. Oxymoron

18. "The murmurous haunt of flies on summer eves."
A. Hyperbole B. Alliteration
C. Onomatopoeia D. Personification

19. "Milton! thou should'st be living at this hour. "
A. Personification B. Apostrophe
C. Alliteration D. Irony

20. How high his honour holds his haughty head!
A. Oxymoron B. Personification
C. Alliteration D. Irony

21. "Yet Brutus says he was ambitious. And Brutus is an honourable man."
A. Irony B. Oxymoron
C. Apostrophe D. Pun

22. Is life worth living? That depends upon the liver.
A. Pun B. Alliteration
C. Irony D. Metaphor

23. The pen is mightier than the sword.
A. Simile B. Metaphor
C. Metonymy D. Irony

24. A reeling road, a rolling road, that rambles round the shire.
A. Alliteration B. Metonymy
C. Personification D. Apostrophe

25. "The ploughman homeward plods his weary way."
A. Oxymoron B. Synecdoche
C. Transferred Epithet D. Pun

ANSWERS

1	2	3	4	5	6	7	8	9	10
A	D	B	C	D	A	C	A	B	D
11	**12**	**13**	**14**	**15**	**16**	**17**	**18**	**19**	**20**
C	B	C	A	C	D	A	C	B	C
21	**22**	**23**	**24**	**25**					
A	A	C	A	C					

26. Literary Terms

Abridged edition: Condensed or shortened version of a work.

Acrostic : Poem in which the initial letters of the word of each line make a word or words when read downwards.

Act: Major division in a dramatic work.

Adage: Maxim or proverb.

Addendum: Addition or appendix to a book.

Allegory: Story or tale in which characters and events have a second, symbolic, meaning.

Alliteration: Figure of speech where consonants at the beginning of words, or stressed syllables, are repeated.

Almanac: Book or table comprising a calendar of days, weeks and months indicating special occasions or events.

Anagram: Letters or word or phrase which, when re-arranged, form a new word.

Anecdote: Brief account or story about an individual.

Annotation: Textual comment on a book.

Anthology: Collection of poetry or prose from diverse sources.

Antithesis: In Antithesis a striking opposition or contrast of words or sentiments is made in the same sentence. It is employed to secure emphasis.

Aphorism: Short statement of a truth or dogma couched in memorable terms.

Apostrophe: An Apostrophe is a direct address to the dead, to the absent, or to a personified object or idea.

Argot: Slang or coarse vernacular language.

Assonance: Repetition of similar vowel sounds in speech or writing to achieve a particular effect.

Autobiography: An account of a person's life by himself or herself.

Avant-garde: Advanced (in style or thought); ahead of its time.

Ballad: Story in verse, a narrative song, usually treating a single event.

Belles lettres: Essays on literary studies and the aesthetics of literature.

Bibliography: List of works on a particular subject or author.

Biography: An account of a person's life.

Blank verse: Poetry with unrhymed line endings (usually written in iambic pentameters).

Blurb: Brief description of a book printed on the dust cover or jacket.

Bound verse: Verse based on metrical pattern.

Bowdlerize: To 'cleanse' a work by omitting or cutting out indecent passages, phrases or words.

Cadence: Rhythm and phrasing of language.

Caesura: Pause in line of verse.

Canon: Collection of works established as genuine.

Canto: Division of an epic or narrative poem.

Caption: Short description accompanying an illustration.

Catalogue: List of books or works.

Chronicle: A compilation of events in sequence, either actual or fictional.

Cipher: Writing that employs substitution or transposition of letters.

Cliche: Over-used expression that has become trite.

Colloquialism: Word, phrase or expression in everyday use.

Comedy: Humorous dramatic piece; *high comedy* has welldrawn characterization and witty dialogue; *low comedy*, or *slapstick* has absurd situations and boisterous action; *farce* is exaggerated comedy; *tragi-comedy* is a blend of the tragic and comic; *satire* uses sarcasm and wit to ridicule people's follies and vices (originally in verse).

Concordance: Alphabetical index of words in a work, or works by a single author.

Copyright: Protective law to prevent pirating or plagiarism of an author's work.

Couplet: Two successive rhyming lines in poetry.

Cycle: Group of works united by an overall theme.

Denouement: Final unwinding of complex plot.

Dialect: Manner of speaking pertaining to a particular class or geographical region.

Dialogue: The speech of characters in a story or play; part of work in which characters speak.

Diary: Sequential private record of personal and other events kept by an individual.

Dictionary: Book containing the words of a language, and their definitions, alphabetically; two-language dictionaries contain the corresponding words of both languages and their meanings, also alphabetically; any book that gives words and phrases about a particular subject, arranged alphabetically.

Digest: Publication where works are abridged.

Documentary: Form of fiction or drama based on documentary evidence provided by newspapers, recent historical reports or other contemporary or recent factual evidence.

Doggerel: Rough, ill-constructed verse.

Double entendre: Ambiguity in a word or expression, one of whose meanings is usually bawdy or frivolous.

Drama: Work to be performed on a stage by actors.

Dramatic irony: Situation or remark that has a significance unperceived by the character involved.

Dramatis Personae: Characters in a play.

Duologue: Conversation between two characters in a play, story or poem.

Edition: Total number of copies of a book printed from unchanged set of type.

Elegy: Serious meditative poem; often lamenting death.

Encyclopedia: Comprehensive work encompassing and describing many aspects of knowledge; specialist work covering comprehensively a subject or discipline.

Epic: Long narrative poem incorporating myth, legend, folklore and history, about the deeds of heroes, warriors, important people; a grandiose treatment of an individual's or nation's story.

Epigram: Short witty statement in verse or prose.

Epistle: Direct address to another person, a 'letter' in the form of verse.

Epitaph: Valediction to dead person or persons; inscription on a tomb or grave.

Eponymous: Person whose name becomes the title of the work.

Essay: Short composition, usually in prose, discussing a topic or variety of topics.

Euphemism: Substitution of a bland expression for a harsh or blunt one.

Exposition: Summary of plot and events given at the beginning of play.

Fable: A short narrative in prose or verse, often with animals, that points a moral.

Fiction: General term for an imaginative work, usually in prose.

First person: Style of novel, etc., in which narrator is a character.

Folk tale: Story handed down by word of mouth from generation to generation.

Foot: In poetry, rhythmic unit of two or three syllables.

Foreword: Short introduction to a work.

Free verse (*vers libre*): Poetry free from mechanical restrictions such as metre and rhyme, cadenced according to meaningful stress.

Gazetteer: Geographical dictionary or index.

Ghost writer: Person who undertakes literary work for another who takes the credit.

Glossary: Alphabetical list of unfamiliar or uncommon words, usually appended to work in which they appear.

Haiku: Japanee verse form composed of 17 syllables (5, 7, 5).

Heroic Couplet: Rhymed couplet in *horoic lines* (iambic pentameters).

Heroic verse : That used in *epic poetry.*

Hyperbole: Figure of speech that contains exaggeration for emphasis.

Idiom: Form of expression of phrase peculiar to its language and possessing a meaning other than its literal one.

Idyll: Short pastoral poem conveying mood of happy innocence.

Imagism: School of poetry (early 1900s) concerned with precise language, direct treatment, and freedom of form.

Introduction: Essay stating author's intention to reader.

Irony: Irony is a mode of speech in which the real meaning is exactly the opposite of that which is literally conveyed.

Jingle: Verse or verses with strong rhyme and rhythm.

Journal: Paper, periodical or magazine.

Legend: Story about a particular person containing myth and historical fact; explanation of symbols on a map or chart.

Lexicon: Dictionary, especially for Classical and Middle Eastern languages.

Limerick: Humorous verse form of five lines rhyming *a-a-b-b-a* (*a* in trimeter, *b* in diameter).

Linguistics: The scientific study of language.

Lyric: Usually short, song-like poem in which the poet expresses personal feelings.

Manuscript: Book or work written by hand.

Maxim: Short statement or even sentence containing a general truth about human conduct and human nature.

Melodrama: Exaggeratedly and emotionally written story, usually tragic.

Metaphor: Figure of speech in which one thing is described in terms of another by implication.

Meter: Patterns of stressed and unstressed syllables in verse.

Metonymy: In Metonymy an object is designated by the name of something which is generally associated with it.

Monologue: Single person addressing an audience alone, in drama, verse or prose. *Interior monologue*: unspoken but thought speech in verse or prose.

Myth: Non-factual story that embodies explanation of how something comes to exist, usually involving supernatural or superhuman creatures.

Narrative: Story or tale in prose or verse.

Neoclassicism: Movement of late 17th and 18th century reviving classical values in English literature, emphasizing discipline, reason and clarity.

Neologism: Newly-coined word.

New Wave (*la Nouvelle Vague*): Movement in literature and cinema originating in France in late 1950s that attempted to eschew fixed values, revealing a character by the way he experienced objects and events, which were often meticulously described.

Nom de plume: Term used to indicate a fictitious name used by a writer to represent his work.

Novel: Extended piece of prose fiction.

Novelette: Long short story of some 15,000 words.

Novella: Prose fiction longer than a short story, shorter than a novel (about 30,000 words), concentrating upon a single event.

Ode: Lyric poem describing an event or feelings about a person, object or event. *Pindaric Ode* (Greece) written for choral recitation in units of three stanzas; *Horatian Ode* (Rome) consisted of succession of stanzas following pattern of first one.

Onomatopoeia: Onomatopoeia is that artifice of language by which the sound of words is made to suggest or echo the sense.

Parable: A story which conveys a moral lesson is known as a parable, as for instance, the biblical parables.

Paradox: Apparently self-contradicting statement that, on closer examination, is found to contain a truth reconciling the two opposites.

Parody: Comic imitation of serious words, style, sense, subject of a writer to make them appear ridiculous.

KNOWLEDGE OF COMPUTER

A Brief History of Computers

INTRODUCTION OF COMPUTER

Computer is the most amazing machine man has ever created. Today computers are used in almost all walks of life: bank, hospitals, schools, publishing, manufacturing, entertainment, shops, libraries, factories, games, elections, security services etc. A computer is basically a programmable computing machine. In this chapter we will discuss the various parts of the computer which make the fast and better computation. We will provide a better solution to the problems related to the organization of computer.

GENERATIONS OF COMPUTERS

The first Generation: Vacuum Tubes

ENIAC

The ENIAC (Electronic Numerical Integrator And Computer), designed by and constructed under the supervision of John Mauchly and John Presper Eckert at the University of Pennsylvania, was the world's first general-purpose electronic digital computer. The project was a response to U.S. wartime needs. Mauchly, a professor of electrical engineering at the University of Pennsylvania and Eckert, one of his graduate students, proposed to build a general-purpose computer using vacuum tubes. In 1943, this proposal was accepted by the Army, and work began on the ENIAC. The resulting machine was enormous, weighing 30 tons, occupying 15,000 square feet of floor space, and containing more than 18,000 vacuum tubes. When operating, it consumed 140 kilowatts of power. It was also substantially faster than any electronic-mechanical computer, being capable of 5000 additions per second.

The ENIAC was decimal rather than a binary machine. That is, numbers were represented in decimal form and arithmetic was performed in the decimal system. Its memory consisted of 20 "accumulators", each capable of holding a 10-digit decimal number. Each digit was represented by a ring of 10 vacuum tubes. At any time, only one vacuum tube was in the ON state, representing one of the 10 digits. The major drawback of the ENIAC was that it had to be programmed manually by setting switches and plugging and unplugging cables.

The ENIAC was completed in 1946, too late to be used in the war effort. Instead, its first task was to perform a series of complex calculations that were used to help determine the feasibility of the H-bomb. The ENIAC continued to be used until 1955.

The Von Neumann Machine

The programming process could be facilitated if the program could be represented in a form suitable for storing in memory alongside the data. Then, a computer could get its instructions by reading them from memory, and a program could be set of altered by setting the values of a portion of memory.

This idea, known as the Stored-program concept, is usually attributed to the ENIAC designers, most notably the mathematician John Von Neumann, who was a consultant on the ENIAC project. The idea was also developed at about the same time by Turing. The first publication of the idea was in a 1945 proposal by Von Neumann for a new computer, the EDVAC (Electronic Discrete Variable Computer).

In 1946, von Neumann and his colleagues began the design of a new stored-program computer, referred to as the IAS computer, at the Princeton

Institute for Advanced Studies. The IAS computer, although not completed until 1952, is the prototype of all subsequent general-purpose computers. Figure below shows the general structure of the IAS computer. It consists of:

- A main memory, which stores both data and instructions.
- An arithmetic-logical unit (ALU) capable of operating on binary data.
- A control unit, which interprets the instructions in memory and causes them to be executed.
- Input and output (I/O) equipment operated by the control unit.

Commercial Computers

The 1950's saw the birth of the computer industry with two companies, Sperry and IBM, dominating the marketplace.

In 1947, Eckert and Mauchly formed the Eckert-Mauchly Computer Corporation to manufacture computers commercially. Their first successful machine was the UNIVAC I (Universal Automatic Computer), which was commissioned by the Bureau of the Census for the 1950 calculations. The Eckert-Mauchly Computer Corporation became part of the UNIVAC division of Sperry-Rand Corporation, which went on to build a series of successor machines.

The UNIVAC II, which had greater memory capacity and higher performance than the UNIVAC I, was delivered in the late 1950's and illustrates several trends that have remained characteristic of the computer industry. First, advances in technology allow companies to continue to build larger, more powerful computers. Second, each company tries to make its new machines upward compatible with the older machines. This means that the programs written for the older machines can be executed on the new machine. This strategy is adopted in the hopes of retaining the customer base; that is, when a customer decides to buy a newer machine, he is likely to get it from the same company to avoid losing the investment in programs.

The UNIVAC division also began development of the 1100 series of computers, which was to be its bread and butter. This series illustrates a distinction that existed at one time. The first model, the UNIVAC 1103, and its successors for many years were primarily intended for scientific applications, involving long and complex calculations. Other companies concentrated on business applications, which involved processing large amounts of text data. This split has largely disappeared but it was evident for a number of years.

IBM, which was then the major manufacturer of punched-card processing equipment, delivered its first electronic stored-program computer, the 701, in 1953. The 701 was intended primarily for scientific applications. In 1955, IBM introduced the companion 702 product, which had a number of hardware features that suited it to business applications. These were the first of a long series of 700/7000 computers that established IBM as the overwhelmingly dominant computer manufacturer.

The Second Generation: Transistors

The first major change in the electronic computer came with the replacement of the vacuum tube by the transistor. The transistor is smaller, cheaper, and dissipates less heal than a vacuum tube but can be used in the same way as a vacuum tube to construct computers. Unlike the vacuum tube, which requires wires, metal plates, a glass capsule, and a vacuum, the transistor is a solid-state device, made from silicon. The transistor was invented at Bell Labs in 1947 and by the 1950's had launched an electronic revolution. It was not until the late 1950s, however, that fully transistorized computers were commercially available. IBM again was not the first company to deliver the new technology. NCR and more successfully RCA were the front-runners with some small transistor machines. IBM followed shortly with the 7000 series.

The use of the transistor defines the second generation of computers. It has become widely accepted to classify computers into generations based on the fundamental hardware technology employed. Each new generation is characterized by greater processing performance, larger memory capacity, and smaller size than the previous one.

The Third Generation: Integrated Circuits

A single, self-contained transistor is called a discrete component. Throughout the 1950s and early 1960s, electronic equipment was composed largely of discrete components—transistors, resistors, capacitors, and so on. Discrete components were manufactured separately, packaged in their own containers, and soldered or wired together onto circuit boards, which were then installed in computers, oscilloscopes, and other electronic equipment. Whenever an electronic device called for a transistor, a little tube of metal containing a pinhead-sized piece of silicon had to be soldered to a circuit board. The entire manufacturing process, from transistor to circuit board, was expensive and cumbersome.

These facts of life were beginning to create problems in the computer industry. Early second-generation computers contained about 10,000 transistors. This figure grew to the hundreds of thousands, making the manufacture of newer, more powerful machines increasingly difficult. In 1958 came the achievement that revolutionized electronics and started the era of microelectronics: the invention of the integrated circuit. It is the integrated circuit that defines the third generation of computers. Perhaps the two most important members of the third generation are the IBM System/360 and the DEC PDP-8.

Later Generations

Beyond the third generation there is less general agreement on defining generations of computers. There have been a fourth and a fifth generation, based on advances in integrated circuit technology. With the introduction of large-scale integration (LSI), more than 1000,000 components can be placed on a single integrated circuit chip.

The Summary of Generations of Computer

- Vacuum tube - 1946-1957
- Transistor - 1958-1964
- Small scale integration: 1965

  Up to 100 devices on a chip
- **Medium scale integration: -1971**

  100-3,000 devices on a chip
- **Large scale integration :1971-1977**

  3,000 - 100,000 devices on a chip
- **Very large scale integration: 1978 -1991**

  100,000 - 100,000,000 devices on a chip
- **Ultra large scale integration : 1991**

  Over 100,000,000 devices on a chip

FUNCTIONAL UNITS OF COMPUTER

Computer allocates the task between its various functional units. The computer system is divided into three separate functional units for its operation. They are:

- Central Processing Unit (CPU)
- Arithmetic Logical Unit (ALU)
- Control Unit (CU)

Central Processing Unit (CPU)

The ALU and the CU of a computer system are jointly known as the Central Processing Unit. You may call CPU as the brain of any computer system. It is just like brain that takes all major decisions, makes all sorts of calculations and directs different parts of the computer functions by activating and controlling the operations.

Arithmetic Logical Unit (ALU)

After you enter data through the input device it is stored in the Primary storage unit. The actual processing of the data and instruction are performed by Arithmetic Logical Unit. The major operations performed by the ALU are addition, subtraction, multiplication, division, logic and comparison. Data is transferred to ALU from storage unit when required. After processing the output is returned back to storage unit for further processing or getting stored.

Control Unit (CU)

The next component of computer is the Control Unit, which acts like the supervisor seeing that things are done in proper fashion. The control unit determines the sequence in which computer programs and instructions are executed. Things like processing of programs stored in the main memory, interpretation of the instructions and issuing of signals for other units of the computer to execute them. It also acts as a switch board operator when several users access the computer simultaneously. Thereby it coordinates the activities of computer's peripheral as they perform the input and output.

PARTS OF THE COMPUTER

There is basically two parts of the computer:

(a) Hardware
(b) Software

(a) Hardware

Hardware is best described as a device that is physically connected to your computer or something that can be physically touched. A CD-ROM, Monitor, Printer, and video card are all examples of computer hardware. Without any hardware your computer would not exist and software would have nothing to run on. The image to the right is of a web cam, an example of an external hardware peripheral that allows users to make basic videos, transmit videos of themselves over the Internet, and take pictures.

Computer hardwares are:

- **Central Processing Unit (CPU):** The "microprocessor" brain of the computer system is called the central processing unit. Everything that a computer does is overseen by the CPU.
- **Memory:** This is very fast storage used to hold data. It has to be fast because it connects directly to the microprocessor. There are several specific types of memory in a computer.
- **RAM (Random Access Memory):**It is used to temporarily store information that the computer is currently working with.
- **ROM (Read Only Memory):** A permanent type of memory storage used by the computer for important data that does not change.
- **Keyboard:** Generally used to type or select an option on the screen. It is an input device.
- **Mouse:** It is an input device which is used to point and select some option on VDU.
- **VDU (Visual Display Unit):** It is an output device where the output of any command is displayed *i.e.*, The screen.
- **Printer:** It is the output device. Different types of printer are:
  1. Dot matrix printer
  2. Inkjet Printer
  3. Laser Printer etc.
- **Floppy Disk Drives:** It is a common form of removable storage. Floppy disk are extremely inexpensive and easy to save information.
- **Scanner:** It is an input device. A scanner scans an image and transform the image to ASCII Graphics. These codes can be edited, manipulated & then printed.
- **CD-ROM Drive:** It is an input device. To read a CD-ROM disk a CD-ROM drive is required. One can only read from it and cannot write on it.
- **DVD-ROM:** DVD-ROM is similar to Cd-Rom but is capable of holding much more information.
- **CD-Writer:** It is input device. To write from other CD to your CD, writer is used.

(b) Software

Software is a collection of commands that help users to communicate with the computer or help the computer perform specific tasks for them. Without any type of software the computer would be of no use.

Examples of software **programs** or **applications** would be the **Operating System** (DOS, Windows, UNIX, MacOS and various others), **Wordprocessor** (typing letters), **Spreadsheet** (financial info), **Database** (inventory control and address book), **Graphics program**, **Internet Browser**, **Email** and many others.

Software is capable of performing specific tasks, as opposed to hardware which only perform mechanical tasks that they are mechanically designed for. Practical computer systems divide software systems into three major groups:

System Software

System software is a program that manages and supports the computer resources and operations of a computer system while it executes various tasks such as processing data and information, controlling hardware components, and allowing users to use application software. That is, systems software functions as a *bridge* between computer system hardware and the application software. System software is made up of many control programs, including the operating system, communications software and database manager. Computer software includes operating systems, device drivers, diagnostic tools and more.

Systems software consists of three kinds of programs. The system management programs, system support programs, and system development programs. These are explained briefly.

System Management Programs

These are programs that manage the application software, computer hardware, and data resources of the computer system. These programs include operating systems, operating environment programs, database management programs, and telecommunications monitor programs. Among these, the most important system management programs are operating systems. The operating systems are needed to study more details. There are two reasons. First, users need to know their functions first. For the second, there are many kinds of operating systems available today.

Telecommunications monitor programs are additions of the operating systems of microcomputers. These programs provide the extra logic for the computer system to control a class of communications devices.

System Support Programs

These are the programs that help the operations and management of a computer system. They provide a variety of support services to let the computer hardware and other system programs run efficiently. The major system support programs are system utility programs, system performance monitor programs, and system security monitor programs (virus checking programs).

System Development Programs

These are programs that help users develop information system programs and prepare user programs for computer processing. These programs may analyze and design systems and program itself. The main system development programs are programming language translators, programming environment programs, computer-aided software engineering packages.

Programming Software

Software that assists a programmer in writing computer programs.

Application Software

Allows users to accomplish one or more tasks. Application software utilizes the capacities of a computer directly for a dedicated task. Application software is able to manipulate text, numbers and graphics. It can be in the form of software focused on a certain single task like word processing, spreadsheet or playing of audio and video files. Here, we look at the application software types along with some examples of application software of each type.

Different Types of Application Software

- **Word Processing Software:** This software enables users to create and edit documents. The most popular examples of this type of software are MS-Word, WordPad and Notepad among other text editors.
- **Database Software:** Database is a structured collection of data. A computer database relies on database software to organize data and enable database users to perform database operations. Database software allows users to store and retrieve data from databases. Examples are Oracle, MSAccess, etc.

- **Spreadsheet Software:** Excel, Lotus 1-2-3 and Apple Numbers are some examples of spreadsheet software. Spreadsheet software allows users to perform calculations using spreadsheets. They simulate paper worksheets by displaying multiple cells that make up a grid.
- **Multimedia Software:** They allow users to create and play audio and video files. They are capable of playing media files. Audio converters, audio players, burners, video encoders and decoders are some forms of multimedia software. Examples of this type of software include Real Player and Media Player.
- **Presentation Software:** The software that is used to display information in the form of a slide show is known as presentation software. This type of software includes three functions, namely, editing that allows insertion and formatting of text, methods to include graphics in the text and a functionality of executing slide shows. Microsoft PowerPoint is the best example of presentation software.
- **Enterprise Software:** It deals with the needs of organization processes and data flow. Customer relationship management or the financial processes in an organization are carried out with the help of enterprise software.
- **Information Worker Software:** Individual projects within a department and individual needs of creation and management of information are handled by information worker software. Documentation tools, resource management tools and personal management systems fall under the category of this type of application software.
- **Educational Software:** It has the capabilities of running tests and tracking progress. It also has the capabilities of a collaborative software. It is often used in teaching and self-learning. Dictionaries like Britannica and Encarta, mathematical software like Matlab and others like Google Earth and NASA World Wind are some of the well-known names in this category.
- **Simulation Software:** It is used to simulate physical or abstract systems. Simulation software finds applications in both, research and entertainment. Flight simulators and scientific simulators are examples of simulation software.
- **Content Access Software:** It is used to access content without editing. Common examples of content access software are web browsers and media players.
- **Application Suites:** An application suite is an important type of application software. It consists of a group of applications combined to perform related functions. OpenOffice.org and Microsoft Office are the best examples of this type of application software. These application suites, as you know, come as bundles of applications like word processors, spreadsheets, presentation software, etc. Applications in the suite can work together or operate on each other's files.

Utility Software

Utility software is system software designed to help analyze, configure, optimize or maintain a computer. A single piece of utility software is usually called a utility or tool.

Utility software usually focuses on how the computer infrastructure (including the computer hardware, operating system, application software and data storage) operates. Due to this focus, utilities are often rather technical and targeted at people with an advanced level of computer knowledge - in contrast to application software, which allows users to do things like creating text documents, playing games, listening to music or viewing websites.

Utility Software Examples

- **Anti-virus** utilities scan for computer viruses.
- **Backup** utilities can make a copy of all information stored on a disk, and restore either the entire disk (e.g. in an event of

disk failure) or selected files (e.g. in an event of accidental deletion).

- **Data compression** utilities output a shorter stream or a smaller file when provided with a stream or file.
- **Disk cleaners** can find files that are unnecessary to computer operation, or take up considerable amounts of space. Disk cleaner helps the user to decide what to delete when their hard disk is full.
- **Disk compression** utilities can transparently compress/uncompress the contents of a disk, increasing the capacity of the disk.
- **Disk defragmenters** can detect computer files whose contents are broken across several locations on the hard disk, and move the fragments to one location to increase efficiency.
- **Disk partitions** can divide an individual drive into multiple logical drives, each with its own file system which can be mounted by the operating system and treated as an individual drive.
- **Disk space analyzers** for the visualization of disk space usage by getting the size for each folder (including sub folders) & files in folder or drive, showing the distribution of the used space.
- **Archive** utilities output a stream or a single file when provided with a directory or a set of files. Archive utilities, unlike archive suites, usually do not include compression or encryption capabilities. Some archive utilities may even have a separate un-archive utility for the reverse operation.
- **File managers** provide a convenient method of performing routine data management tasks, such as deleting, renaming, cataloging, uncataloging, moving, copying, merging, generating and modifying data sets.
- **Memory testers** check for memory failures.
- **Network utilities** analyze the computer's network connectivity, configure network settings, check data transfer or log events.
- **Registry cleaners** clean and optimize the Windows registry by removing old registry keys that are no longer in use.
- **Screensavers** were desired to prevent phosphor burn-in on CRT and plasma computer monitors by blanking the screen or filling it with moving images or patterns when the computer is not in use. Contemporary screensavers are used primarily for entertainment or security.

Firmware

Firmware is a program for the hardware. It is an embedded coded (program) for the hardware. So, it can perform its function specifically for which device is made. Every device has inbuilt firmware that gives the device ability to perform its work. There are lots of devices that use a screen and buttons. The device consists of firmware that instruct the device to perform certain functions on given command. Examples are a video card and sound card.

COMPUTER FUNDAMENTAL

COMPUTER

Computer is an advanced electronic device that takes raw data as input from the user and processes these data under the control of set of instructions (called program) and gives the result (output) and saves output for the future use. It can process both numerical and non-numerical (arithmetic and logical) calculations.

A computer has four functions:

(*a*) accepts data	**Input**
(*b*) processes data	**Processing**
(*c*) produces output	**Output**
(*d*) stores results	**Storage**

- Laser printers use the same technology as a photocopier using heat to transfer toner onto paper.

Modem

A modem is used to translate information transferred through telephone lines, cable, satellite or line-of-sight wireless.

The term stands for **modulate and demodulate** which changes the signal from **digital**, which computers use, to **analog**, which telephones use and then back again. **Digital modems** transfer digital information directly without changing to analog.

Modems are measured by the speed that the information is transferred. The measuring tool is called the **baud rate**. Originally modems worked at speeds below 2400 baud but today analog speeds of 56,000 baud are standard. Cable, wireless or digital subscriber lines can transfer information much faster with rates of 300,000 baud and up.

Modems also use **Error Correction** which corrects for transmission errors by constantly checking whether the information was received properly or not and Compression which allows for faster data transfer rates. Information is transferred in **packets**. Each packet is checked for errors and is re-sent if there is an error.

Anyone who has used the Internet has noticed that at times the information travels at different speeds. Depending on the amount of information that is being transferred, the information will arrive at it's destination at different times. The amount of information that can travel through a line is limited. This limit is called **bandwidth**.

There are many more variables involved in communication technology using computers, much of which is covered in the section on the Internet.

Scanners

Scanners allow you to transfer pictures and photographs to your computer. A scanner 'scans' the image from the top to the bottom, one line at a time and transfers it to the computer as a series of bits or a bitmap. You can then take that image and use it in a paint program, send it out as a fax or print it. With optional **Optical Character Recognition** (OCR) software you can convert printed documents such as newspaper articles to text that can be used in your word processor. Most scanners use **TWAIN** software that makes the scanner accessable by other software applications.

Digital cameras allow you to take digital photographs. The images are stored on a memory chip or disk that can be transferred to your computer. Some cameras can also capture sound and video.

Case

The case houses the microchips and circuitry that run the computer. Desktop models usually sit under the monitor and tower models beside. They come in many sizes, including desktop, mini, midi, and full tower. There is usually room inside to expand or add components at a later time. By removing the cover off the case you may find plate covered, empty slots that allow you to add cards. There are various types of slots including IDE, ASI, USB, PCI and Firewire slots.

Depending on the type notebook computers may have room to expand. Most Notebooks also have connections or ports that allows expansion or connection to exterior, peripheral devices such as monitor, portable hard-drives or other devices.

Cards

Cards are components added to computers to increase their capability. When adding a peripheral device make sure that your computer has a slot of the type needed by the device.

Sound cards allow computers to produce sound like music and voice. The older sound cards were 8 bit then 16 bit then 32 bit. Though the human ear can't distinguish the fine difference between sounds produced by the more powerful sound card they allow for more complex music and music production.

Colour cards allow computers to produce colour (with a colour monitor of course). The first colour cards were 2 bit which produced 4 colours [CGA]. It was amazing what could be done with those 4 colours. Next came 4 bit allowing for 16

[EGA and VGA] colours. Then came 16 bit allowing for 1064 colours and then 24 bit which allows for almost 17 million colours and now 32 bit and higher allow monitors to display almost a billion separate colours.

Video cards allow computers to display video and animation. Some video cards allow computers to display television as well as capture frames from video. A video card with a digital video camera allows computers users to produce live video. A high speed connection is required for effective video transmission.

Network cards allow computers to connect together to communicate with each other. Network cards have connections for cable, thin wire or wireless networks for more information.

Cables connect internal components to the **Motherboard**, which is a board with series of electronic path ways and connections allowing the CPU to communicate with the other components of the computer.

Memory

Memory can be very confusing but is usually one of the easiest pieces of hardware to add to your computer. It is common to confuse **chip memory** with disk storage. An example of the difference between memory and storage would be the difference between a table where the actual work is done (memory) and a filing cabinet where the finished product is stored (disk). To add a bit more confusion, the computer's hard disk can be used as **temporary memory** when the program needs more than the chips can provide.

Random Access Memory or **RAM** is the memory that the computer uses to temporarily store the information as it is being processed. The more information being processed the more RAM the computer needs.

One of the first home computers used 64 kilobytes of RAM memory (Commodore 64). Today's modern computers need a minimum of 64 Mb (recommended 128 Mb or more) to run Windows or OS 10 with modern software. RAM memory chips come in many different sizes and speeds and can usually be **expanded**. Older computers came with 512 Kb of memory which could be expanded to a maximum of 640 Kb. In most modern computers the memory can be expanded by adding or replacing the memory chips depending on the processor you have and the type of memory your computer uses. Memory chips range in size from 1 Mb to 4 Gb. As computer technology changes the type of memory changes as well making old memory chips obsolete. Check your computer manual to find out what kind of memory your computer uses before purchasing new memory chips

MULTIPLE CHOICE QUESTIONS

1. Android is a mobile operating system designed primarily for touchscreen mobile devices such as smartphones and tablets. Which among the following was the first Android Operating System?

A. Cupcake B. Alpha
C. Gingerbread D. Doughnut
E. Eclair

2. Which among the following key combinations can be used to search in Windows Explorer?

A. Ctrl + F B. Ctrl + S
C. Ctrl + G D. Alt + S
E. None of the above

3. A router is a networking device that forwards data packets and is connected to two or more data lines from different networks. Which among the following was the earliest device which had almost the same functionality as that of a router?

A. Interface Delay Device
B. Interface Traffic Manager
C. Interface Routing Processor
D. Interface Message Processor
E. Interface Data Manager

4. A vacuum tube (also called a VT, electron tube or, in the UK, a valve) is a device sometimes used to amplify electronic signals. Vacuum Tubes were used in which generation of Computers?
A. 1st Generation B. 2nd Generation
C. 3rd Generation D. 4th Generation
D. 5th Generation

5. In Computer programming API is a set of subroutine definitions, protocols, and tools for building software and applications. Which among the following is an application programming interface for the programm-ing language Java, which defines how a client may access a database?
A. J2EE B. JDK
C. JAVA SE D. JDBC
E. JSX

6. Which of the following errors occurs when software tries to access protected memory?
A. Segmentation Fault
B. Displaytime Error
C. IO Error
D. Runtime Error
E. Zero Division Error

7. Which among the following is a term representing unit of data storage in computer memory?
A. Pixel B. Decimal
C. Octet D. Point
E. Fragment

8. Microsoft PowerPoint is a slide show presentation program for use on both Microsoft and Apple Macintosh operating systems. In MS PowerPoint Broadcast is a feature available in which tab?
A. File B. View
C. Slide Show D. Transitions
E. Review

9. Which among the following carries signals that control the actions of the computer?
A. Control Bus B. Data Bus
C. Memory Unit D. NIC
E. Address Bus

10. Which among the following is not a secondary memory?
A. Cache B. Pen Drive
C. Hard Disk D. Memory Card
E. Memory Stick

11. Which among the following is a cloud computing platform and infrastructure created by Microsoft?
A. Simple Storage Service
B. Atmos
C. Openstack Swift
D. OceanStore
E. Azure

12. After a credit card transaction has been authorized by the issuing bank by sending an authorization code to the merchant, the settlement stage of the process begins. Which of the following is a system type used to process such statements?
A. Multi-tasking B. Memory Processing
C. Level Processing D. Batch Processing
E. Online Processing

13. Assembly is a _______ based low-level language replacing binary machine-code instructions, which are very hard to remember, it is the classic and uncontroversial example of a low level language.
A. Memory B. High Level
C. Key D. Mnemonic
E. FORTRAN

14. China now has more of the world's fastest supercomputers than other countries. Which among the following is a Chinese super-computer?
A. BlueGene/Q system
B. Cray XC30
C. Shaheen II
D. Fujitsu's K
E. Tianhe-2

15. Which among the following is an important circuitry in a computer system that does the arithmetic and logical processing?
A. Memory B. ALU
C. Flag Register D. CU
E. Calculator

16. Which among the following is not a mobile Operating System?

A. Bada B. Safari
C. Symbian D. MeeGo
E. WebOS

17. Which among the following key can be used as a shortcut to rename a folder in Microsoft Windows 8 and higher versions?

A. F2 B. F4
C. F6 D. F9
E. F11

18. AT & T designed its first commercial modem, specifically for converting digital computer data to analog for transmission across its long distance network. What is the name of the modem?

A. Telex B. Memex
C. CompuServe D. Bell 103 dataset
E. Dataphone

19. Integrated Chips or IC's were started to be in use from which generation of computers?

A. 1st Generation B. 2nd Generation
C. 3rd Generation D. 4th Generation
E. 5th Generation

20. In Computer programming there is a set of subroutine definitions, protocols, and tools for building software and applications. Which among the following is a term for sets of requirements that govern how one application can talk to another?

A. UPS B. API
C. CGI D. J2EE
E. OLE

21. When you first turn on a computer, the COU is preset to execute instructions stored in ....

A. RAM B. Flash memory
C. ROM D. The CD-ROM
E. The ALU

22. Which of the following is **not** a function of the control unit?

A. Read instructions
B. Interpret instructions
C. Execute instructions
D. Direct operations
E. Provide control signals

23. What are .bas, .doc, .htm examples of in computing?

A. Extensions
B. Protocols
C. Databases
D. Other than those given as options
E. Domains

24. Documents converted to .... can be published to the web.

A. a doc file
B. http
C. Other than those given as options
D. machine language
E. HTML

25. What kind of software would you most likely use to keep track of a billing account?

A. Web authoring
B. electronic publishing
C. spreadsheet
D. word processing
E. Power point

26. A computer virus normally attaches itself to another computer program known as a ....

A. host program
B. target program
C. backdoor program
D. Bluetooth
E. Trojan horse

27. When a file contains instructions that can be carried out by the computer. It is often called a(n) .... file.

A. Other than those given as options
B. information
C. application
D. executable
E. data

28. Data duplication wastes the space, but also promotes a more serious problem called ....

A. Isolated data
B. Data inconsistency
C. Other than those given as options
D. Program dependency
E. Separated data

29. Which of the following is **not** a version of the Windows operating system software for the PC?

A. ME
B. 98
C. XP
D. 10
E. 95

30. The main directory of a disk is called the .... directory.

A. network
B. folder
C. root
D. File
E. Other than those given as options

31. Which of the following is **not** an example of application software?

A. Word processing software
B. Spreadsheet software
C. Operating system software
D. Database software
E. Graphics software

32. Which of the following is **not** true about RAM?

A. RAM is the same as hard disk storage
B. RAM is a temporary storage area
C. RAM is volatile
D. RAM is a primary memory
E. All are true

33. The data storage hierarchy consists of ....

A. Bits, Bytes, Records, Fields, files and databases
B. Characters, fields, records, files and databases
C. Bytes, bits, fields, records, files and databases
D. Bits, bytes, fields, records, files and databases
E. Other than those given as options

34. = Sum (B1 B0) is an example of a ....

A. function
B. cell address
C. formula
D. value
E. Other than those given as options

35. .... are often delivered to a PC through an email attachment and are often designed to do harm.

A. Portals
B. Spam
C. Viruses
D. Other than those given as options
E. E-mail messages

36. Decreasing the amount of space required to store data and programs is accomplished by ....

A. Crashing
B. Disk caching
C. RAID
D. file compression
E. Other than those given as options

37. What is the difference between a CD-ROM and CD-RW?

A. They are the same –just two different terms used by different manufacturers
B. A CD-Rom can be written to and a CD-RW cannot
C. Other than those given as options
D. A CD-ROM holds more information than a CD-RW
E. A CD-RW can be written to but a CD-ROM can only be read from

38. Computer program are written in a high-level programming language, however, the human readable version of a program is called ....

A. word size
B. source code
C. instruction set
D. Read & Write code
E. None of these

39. The clock rate of a processor is measured in ....

A. megabytes or gigabytes
B. milliseconds
C. megahertz or gigahertz
D. nanoseconds
E. micro hertz

40. When cutting and pasting, the item cut is temporarily stored in the ....

A. dashboard
B. ROM
C. hard drive
D. Diskette
E. clipboard

41. Copying the Excel 2007 formula = SUM (A1:A5) from cell A6 to cell B6 will result in what formula for cell B6?

A. = SUM (B6:A6)
B. < SUM (A1:B6)
C. = SUM (B1:A5)

D. > SUM (B1:B5)
E. Other than those given as options

42. RAM is used as a short memory because it—
A. has small capacity B. is very expensive
C. is programmable D. volatile
E. not very useful

43. The Num Lock Key and Caps Lock Key are considered .... because their function changes each time you press them.
A. toggle B. dual
C. function D. cursor control
E. control

44. OLE stands for—
A. Offline Linking and Embedding
B. Online Link Emulation
C. Object Link Export
D. Object Linking and Embedding
E. Online Link Embedding

45. Microsoft Word is an example of—
A. Application software
B. An input device
C. System software
D. A processing system
E. An operating system

46. Which of the following is not an example of an output device?
A. Speaker B. Plotter
C. Microphone D. Printer
E. Monitor

47. The digital telecommunications, termed as ISDN is an abbreviation for—
A. Interactive Standard Dynamic Networks
B. Integrated Standard Digital Networks
C. Internet Services Data Network
D. International Services Data Network
E. Integrated Services Digital Network

48. Which of the following places the common data elements in order to the smallest from the largest?
A. Character, file, field, record, database
B. Character, field, record, file, database
C. Character, record, field, database, file
D. Character, file, record, field, database
E. Character, field, record, database, file

49. Software made freely available to the public by the publisher is called—
A. Fair use
B. Compact disc
C. Freeware
D. Process ware
E. Copyright

50. A web site's own unique Internet address that no other web site can use is its—
A. Search Engine B. FTP
C. URL D. WWW
E. IP v 6

51. The windows shortcut to delete an item permanently is—
A. Shift + Delete B. Shift + F1
C. Ctrl + F1 D. Ctrl + F2
E. Shift + F2

52. WAN is a type of computer network. It stands for—
A. Wireless Array Network
B. Wild Area Network
C. Wide Access Network
D. Wide Area Network
E. Wireless Area Network

53. Which of the following is a type for intercepting computer communications?
A. Hacking B. Sniffing
C. Pretexting D. Spoofing
E. Phishing

54. Which key allows movement from one cell of a table to the next?
A. Shift B. CTRL
C. Esc D. Tab
E. ALT

55. Pressing the .... key will make the number pad act as directional arrows.
A. Caps lock B. Arrow lock
C. Shift D. Esc
E. Num lock

56. The most widely used device in communication is a —
A. Coprocessor B. Channel
C. Bus D. Modem
E. Scanner

85. Fourth-generation mobile technology provides enhanced capabilities allowing the transfer of both .... data, including full-motion video, high-speed internet access, and video-conferencing.
A. video data and information
B. voice and nonvoice
C. music and video
D. video and audio
E. None of these

86. .... is a form of denial of service attack in which a hostile client repeatedly sends SYN packets to every port on the server using fake IP addresses.
A. Cybergaming crime
B. Memory shaving
C. Syn flooding
D. Software piracy
E. None of these

87. Which of these is a point-and-draw device?
A. mouse B. scanner
C. printer D. CD-ROM
E. keyboard

88. The letter and number of the intersecting column and row is the—
A. cell location
B. cell position
C. cell address
D. cell coordinates
E. cell contents

89. A set of rules for telling the computer what operations to perform is called a—
A. procedural language
B. structures
C. natural language
D. command language
E. programming language

90. A detailed written description of the programming cycle and the program, along with the test results and a printout of the program is called—
A. documentation B. output
C. reporting D. spec sheets
E. Directory

91. Forms that are used to organize business data into rows and columns are called—
A. transaction sheets B. registers
C. business forms D. sheet-spreads
E. spreadsheets

92. In Power Point, the Header & Footer button can be found on the Insert tab in what group?
A. Illustrations group B. Object group
C. Text group D. Tables group
E. None of these

93. A(n) .... is a set of programs designed to manage the resources of a computer, including starting the computer, managing programs, managing memory and coordinating tasks between input and output devices.
A. application suite
B. compiler
C. input/output system
D. interface
E. operating system (OS)

94. A typical slide in a slide presentation would **not** include—
A. photo images charts and graphs
B. graphs and clip art
C. clip art and audio clips
D. full-motion video
E. content templates

95. The PC productivity tool that manipulates data organized in rows and columns is called a—
A. spreadsheet
B. word processing document
C. presentation mechanism
D. database record manager
E. EDI creator

96. In the absence of parentheses, the order of operation is —
A. Exponentiation, addition or subtraction, multiplication or division
B. Addition or subtraction, multiplication or division, exponentiation
C. Multiplication or division, exponentiation, addition or subtraction
D. Exponentiation, multiplication or division, addition or subtraction
E. Addition or subtraction, exponentiation, Multiplication or division

97. To find the Paste Special option, you use the Clipboard group on the ...... tab of PowerPoint.
A. Design B. Slide Show
C. Page Layout D. Insert
E. Home

98. Which view display miniature images of photographs within a folder?
A. Tiles view and Icons view
B. Thumbnails view and Filmstrip view
C. Details view and List view
D. All views display a miniature image
E. None of these

99. Usually downloaded into folders that hold temporary internet files, ... are written to your computer's hard disk by some of the Web sites you visit.
A. anonymous files B. behaviour files
C. banner ads D. large files
E. cookies

100. What is the easiest way to change the phrase, revenues, profits, gross margin, to read revenues, profit and gross margin?
A. Use the insert mode, position the cursor before the g in gross, then type the word and followed by a space
B. Use the insert mode, position the cursor after the g in gross, then type the word and followed by a space
C. Use the overtype mode, position the cursor before the g in gross, then type the word and followed by a space
D. Use the overtype mode, position the cursor after the g in gross, then type the word and followed by a space
E. None of these

101. A program, either talk or music, that is made available in digital format for automatic download over the internet is called a —
A. wiki B. broadcast
C. vodcast D. blog
E. podcast

102. Which PowerPoint view displays each slide of the presentation as a thumbnail and is useful for rearranging slides?
A. Slide Sorter B. Slide Show
C. Slide Master D. Notes Page
E. Slide Design

103. Different components on the motherboard of a PC unit are linked together by sets of parallel electrical conducting lines. What are these lines called?
A. Conductors B. Buses
C. Connectors D. Consecutives
E. None of these

104. What is the name given to those applications that combine text, sound, graphics, motion video, and/or animation?
A. motionware B. anigraphics
C. videoscapes D. multimedia
E. maxomedia

105. A USB communication device that supports data encryption for secure wireless communication for notebook users is called a—
A. USB wireless network adapter
B. wireless switch
C. wireless hub
D. router
E. None of these

106. A(n) .... language reflects the way people think mathematically.
A. cross-platform programming
B. 3GL business programming
C. event-driven programming
D. functional
E. None of these

107. When entering text within a document, the Enter key is normally pressed at the end of every—
A. Line B. Sentence
C. Paragraph D. Word
E. File

108. When a real-time telephone call between people is made over the Internet using computers, it is called—
A. a chat session
B. an e-mail
C. an instant message
D. Internet telephony
E. None of these

133. A device that connects to a network without the use of cables is said to be ....
A. distributed B. free
C. centralized D. open source
E. None of these

134. Non-physical components of the computer are referred to as
A. CPU B. software
C. hardware D. program
E. None of these

135. The most common type of storage devices are ....
A. persistent B. optical
C. magnetic D. flash
E. steel

136. Codes consisting of lines of varying widths or lengths that are computer-readable are known as–
A. an ASCII code
B. a magnetic tape
C. an OCR scanner
D. a bar code
E. None of these

137. A Web site's main page is called its–
A. Home Page
B. Browser Page
C. Search Page
D. Bookmark
E. None of these

138. Part number, part description, and number of parts ordered are examples of–
A. control B. output
C. processing D. feedback
E. input

139. To access properties of an object, the mouse technique to use is–
A. dragging B. dropping
C. right-clicking D. shift-clicking
E. None of these

140. Computers use the .... number system to store data and perform calculations.
A. binary B. octal
C. decimal D. hexadecimal
E. None of these

141. .... are attempts by individuals to obtain confidential information from you by falsifying their identity.
A. Phishing trips B. Computer viruses
C. Spyware scams D. Viruses
E. Phishing scams

142. Why is it unethical to share copyrighted files with your friends?
A. It is not unethical, because it is legal.
B. It is unethical because the files are being given for free.
C. Sharing copyrighted files without permission breaks copyright laws.
D. It is not unethical because the files are being given for free.
E. It is not unethical—anyone can access a computer.

143. Which of the following can be used to select the entire document?
A. CTRL + A B. ALT + F5
C. SHIFT + A D. CTRL + K
E. CTRL + H

144. To instruct Word to fit the width of a column to the contents of a table automatically, click the .... button and then point to AutoFit Contents.
A. Fit to Form B. Format
C. Autosize D. Contents
E. AutoFit

145. The simultaneous processing of two or more programs by multiple processors is–
A. multiprogramming B. multitasking
C. time-sharing D. multiprocessing
E. None of these

146. A disk's content that is recorded at the time of manufacture and that cannot be changed or erased by the user is–
A. memory-only B. write-only
C. once-only D. run-only
E. read-only

147. What is the permanent memory built into your computer called?
A. RAM B. Floppy
C. CPU D. CD-ROM
E. ROM

148. The default view in Excel is .... view.
A. Work B. Auto
C. Normal D. Roman
E. None of these

149. What displays the contents of the active cell in Excel?
A. Namebox B. RowHeadings
C. Formulabar D. Taskpane
E. None of these

150. In Word you can force a page break–
A. By positioning your cursor at the appropriate place and pressing the F1 key
B. By positioning your cursor at the appropriate place and pressing Ctrl+Enter
C. By using the Insert/Section Break
D. By changing the font size of your document
E. None of these

151. Grouping and processing all of a firm's transactions at one time is called–
A. a database management system
B. batch processing
C. a real-time system
D. an on-line system
E. None of these

152. Help Menu is available at which button?
A. End B. Start
C. Turn off D. Restart
E. Reboot

153. You can keep your personal files/folders in–
A. My Folder B. My Documents
C. My Files D. My Text
E. None of these

154. A central computer that holds collections of data and programs for many PCs, workstations, and other computers is a(n) –
A. supercomputer B. minicomputer
C. laptop D. server
E. None of these

155. When you save to this, your data will remain intact even when the computer is turned off–
A. RAM
B. motherboard
C. secondary storage device
D. primary storage device
E. None of these

156. The .... folder retains copies of messages that you have started but are not yet ready to send.
A. Drafts B. Outbox
C. Address Book D. Sent Items
E. Inbox

157. You can..........a search by providing more information the search engine can use to select a smaller, more useful set of results.
A. refine B. expand
C. load D. query
E. slowdown

158. The contents of .... are lost when the computer turns off.
A. storage B. input
C. output D. memory
E. None of these

159. The .... enables you to simultaneously keep multiple Web pages open in one browser window.
A. tab box B. pop-up helper
C. tab row D. address bar
E. Esc key

160. A DVD is an example of a(n) –
A. hard disk
B. optical disc
C. output device
D. solid-state storage device
E. None of these

161. The basic unit of a worksheet into which you enter data in Excel is called a ....
A. tab B. cell
C. box D. range
E. None of these

162. .... is the process of dividing the disk into tracks and sectors.
A. Tracking
B. Formatting
C. Crashing
D. Allotting
E. None of these

163. Which ports connect special types of music instruments to sound cards?
A. BUS B. CPU
C. USB D. MIDI
E. MINI

164. The process of transferring files from a computer on the Internet to your computer is called ....
A. downloading B. uploading
C. FTP D. JPEG
E. downsizing

165. In Excel, ... allows users to bring together copies of work books that other users have worked on independently.
A. Copying B. Merging
C. Pasting D. Compiling
E. None of these

166. If you want to connect to your own computer through the Internet from another location, you can use–
A. e-mail B. FTP
C. instant message D. Telnet
E. None of these

167. To reload a Web page, press the .... button.
A. Redo B. Reload
C. Restore D. Ctrl
E. Refresh

168. Mobile Commerce is best described as–
A. The use of Kiosks in marketing
B. Transporting products
C. Buying and selling goods/services through wireless handheld devices
D. Using notebook PC's in marketing
E. None of the above

169. Video processors consist of .... and ...., which store and process images.
A. CPU and VGA B. CPU and memory
C. VGA and memory D. VGI and DVI
E. None of these

170. ...., are words that a programming language has set aside for its own use.
A. Control words B. Control structures
C. Reserved words D. Reserved keys
E. None of these

171. What is the process of copying software programs from secondary storage media to the hard disk called?
A. configuration B. download
C. storage D. upload
E. installation

172. This first step in the transaction processing cycle captures business data through various modes such as optical scanning or at an electronic commerce website–
A. Document and report generation
B. Database maintenance
C. Transaction·processing start-up
D. Data Entry
E. None of these

173. When the pointer is positioned on a ...., it is shaped like a hand.
A. Grammar error B. Formatting error
C. ScreenTip D. Spelling error
E. Hyperlink

174. The computer abbreviation KB usually means–
A. Key Block B. Kernel Boot
C. Key Byte D. Kit Bit
E. Kilo Byte

175. Which of the following are advantages of CD-ROM as a storage media?
A. CD-ROM is an inexpensive way to store large amount of data and information
B. CD-ROM disks retrieve data and information more quickly than magnetic disks do
C. CD-ROMs make less errors than magnetic media
D. All of the above
E. None of the above

176. A(n) ....is a special visual and audio effect applied in PowerPoint to text or content.
A. animation B. flash
C. wipe D. dissolve
E. None of these

177. Which of the following is a storage device that uses rigid, permanently installed magnetic disks to store data/information–
A. floppy diskette B. hard disk

C. permanent disk D. optical disk
E. None of these

178. The piece of hardware that converts your computer's digital signal to an analog signal that can travel over telephone lines is called a–
A. red wire B. blue cord
C. tower D. modem
E. None of these

179. Personal computers can be connected together to form a–
A. server B. supercomputer
C. network D. enterprise
E. None of these

180. A .... is the term used when a search engine returns a Web page that matches the search criteria.
A. blog B. hit
C. link D. view
E. success

181. What type of resource is most likely to be a shared common resource in a computer network?
A. Printers
B. Speakers
C. Floppy disk drives
D. Keyboards
E. None of these

182. Example of non-numeric data is ....
A. Employee address B. Examination score
C. Bank balance D. All of these
E. None of these

183. ....represents raw facts, whereas .... is data made meaningful.
A. Information, reporting
B. Data, information
C. Information, bits
D. Records, bytes
E. Bits, bytes

184. A word in a web page that, when clicked, opens another document ....
A. Anchor B. URL
C. Hyperlink D. Reference
E. None of these

185. A computer cannot "boot" if it does not have the ....
A. Compiler B. Loader
C. Operating System D. Assembler
E. None of these

186. What characteristic of read-only memory (ROM) makes it useful?
A. ROM information can be easily updated
B. Data in ROM is nonvolatile, that is, it remains there even without electrical power
C. ROM provides very large amounts of inexpensive data storage
D. ROM chips are easily swapped between different brands of computers
E. None of these

187. Which of the following refers to a small, single-site network?
A. LAN B. DSL
C. RAM D. USB
E. CPU

188. Which keystroke will take you at the beginning or the end of a long document?
A. Ctrl + PageUp and Ctrl + PageDown
B. Shift + Home and Shift + End
C. Ctrl + Home and Ctrl + End
D. The only way is by using the right scroll bar
E. None of these

189. Coded entries which are used to gain access to a computer system are called ....
A. Entry codes B. Passwords
C. Security commands D. Code words
E. None of these

190. In Word you can force a page break ....
A. By positioning your cursor at the appropriate place and pressing the F1 key
B. By using the Insert/Section Break
C. By positioning your cursor at the appropriate place and pressing Ctrl+Enter
D. By changing the font size of your document
E. None of these

ANSWERS

1	2	3	4	5	6	7	8	9	10
B	A	D	A	D	A	C	C	A	A
11	12	13	14	15	16	17	18	19	20
E	D	D	E	B	B	A	E	C	B
21	22	23	24	25	26	27	28	29	30
C	D	A	E	C	E	D	B	A	C
31	32	33	34	35	36	37	38	39	40
C	A	D	C	C	D	E	B	C	E
41	42	43	44	45	46	47	48	49	50
A	D	A	D	A	C	E	B	C	C
51	52	53	54	55	56	57	58	59	60
A	D	B	D	B	D	E	B	A	B
61	62	63	64	65	66	67	68	69	70
D	A	A	D	B	B	A	D	C	A
71	72	73	74	75	76	77	78	79	80
C	B	B	D	D	C	B	A	C	B
81	82	83	84	85	86	87	88	89	90
C	E	C	A	B	C	A	C	E	A
91	92	93	94	95	96	97	98	99	100
E	C	E	E	A	D	E	B	E	A
101	102	103	104	105	106	107	108	109	110
E	A	B	D	A	D	C	D	C	B
111	112	113	114	115	116	117	118	119	120
D	B	D	E	B	A	D	B	C	A
121	122	123	124	125	126	127	128	129	130
E	B	B	E	C	C	C	B	A	A
131	132	133	134	135	136	137	138	139	140
A	A	E	B	C	D	A	E	C	A
141	142	143	144	145	146	147	148	149	150
A	C	A	A	D	E	E	C	C	B
151	152	153	154	155	156	157	158	159	160
C	B	B	D	D	A	A	B	C	B
161	162	163	164	165	166	167	168	169	170
B	B	C	A	B	D	E	C	C	C
171	172	173	174	175	176	177	178	179	180
E	D	C	E	D	A	B	D	C	C
181	182	183	184	185	186	187	188	189	190
A	A	B	C	C	B	A	A	B	C

●●●

GENERAL AWARENESS

1. OUR INDIA

INDIA : AT A GLANCE

Population (2011)	:	1,21,08,54,977
Capital	:	New Delhi
Area	:	32,87,263 sq km
Geographic Location	:	Between 8°4' and 37°6' north latitudes
	:	Between 68°7' and 97°25' east longitudes
Coastline Length	:	7,516.6 km including the coastline of Lakshadweep, Andaman & Nicobar Islands.
Major Languages	:	22
National Anthem	:	Jana Gana Mana
National Currency	:	Rupee (₹)
National Animal	:	Tiger
National Aquatic Animal	:	Dolphin
National Bird	:	Peacock
National River	:	Ganga
Characteristics of Indian	:	Socialist, Secular, Democratic, Republic
Legislature	:	Bicameral Legislature at the Centre
	:	Uni/Bicameral Legislatures in States
Executive	:	President, Vice-President and Council of Ministers at the Centre Governor and Council of Ministers in States
Judiciary	:	Independent from Executive with Supreme Court at the apex of the hierarchy
Total Road Length	:	66.7 lakh kilometres (March 2024)

2011 CENSUS OF INDIA : POPULATION DISTRIBUTION, POPULATION DENSITY AND LITERACY RATE

S. No.	State/ Union Territories*	Population 2011			Population Density (per sq. km.)	Literacy Rate 2011		
		Persons	Males	Females	2011	Persons	Males	Females
	INDIA	**1,21,08,54,977**	**62,32,70,258**	**58,75,34,719**	**382**	**73.0**	**80.9**	**64.6**
1.	Jammu and Kashmir	1,25,41,302	66,40,662	59,00,640	124	67.2	76.8	56.4
2.	Himachal Pradesh	68,64,602	34,81,873	33,82,729	123	82.8	89.5	75.9
3.	Punjab	2,77,43,338	1,46,39,465	1,31,03,873	551	75.8	80.4	70.7
4.	Chandigarh	10,55,450	5,80,663	4,74,787	9,258	86.0	90.0	81.2
5.	Uttarakhand	1,00,86,292	51,37,773	49,48,519	189	78.8	87.4	70.0
6.	Haryana	2,53,51,462	1,34,94,734	1,18,56,728	573	75.6	84.1	65.9
7.	Delhi	1,67,87,941	89,87,326	78,00,615	11,320	86.2	90.9	80.8
8.	Rajasthan	6,85,48,437	3,55,50,997	3,29,97,440	200	66.1	79.2	52.1
9.	Uttar Pradesh	19,98,12,341	10,44,80,510	9,53,31,831	829	67.7	77.3	57.2
10.	Bihar	10,40,99,452	5,42,78,157	4,98,21,295	1,106	61.8	71.2	51.5
11.	Sikkim	6,10,577	3,23,070	2,87,507	86	81.4	86.6	75.6
12.	Arunachal Pradesh	13,83,727	7,13,912	6,69,815	17	65.4	72.6	57.7
13.	Nagaland	19,78,502	10,24,649	9,53,853	119	79.6	82.8	76.1
14.	Manipur	28,55,794	14,38,586	14,17,208	115	79.2	86.1	72.4
15.	Mizoram	10,97,206	5,55,339	5,41,867	52	91.3	93.3	89.3
16.	Tripura	36,73,917	18,74,376	17,99,541	350	87.2	91.5	82.7
17.	Meghalya	29,66,889	14,91,832	14,75,057	132	74.4	76.0	72.9
18.	Assam	3,12,05,576	1,59,39,443	1,52,66,133	398	72.2	77.8	66.3
19.	West Bengal	9,12,76,115	4,68,09,027	4,44,67,088	1,028	76.3	81.7	70.5
20.	Jharkhand	3,29,88,134	1,69,30,315	1,60,57,819	414	66.4	76.8	55.4
21.	Odisha	4,19,74,218	2,12,12,136	2,07,62,082	270	72.9	81.6	64.0
22.	Chhattisgarh	2,55,45,198	1,28,32,895	1,27,12,303	189	70.3	80.3	60.2
23.	Madhya Pradesh	7,26,26,809	3,76,12,306	3,50,14,503	236	69.3	78.7	59.2
24.	Gujarat	6,04,39,692	3,14,91,260	2,89,48,432	308	78.0	85.8	69.7
25.	Daman and Diu	2,43,247	1,50,301	92,946	2,191	87.1	91.5	79.5
26.	Dadra & Nagar Haweli	3,43,709	1,93,760	1,49,949	700	76.2	85.2	64.3
27.	Maharashtra	11,23,74,333	5,82,43,056	5,41,31,277	365	82.3	88.4	75.9
28.	Andhra Pradesh	4,93,86,799	2,47,38,068	2,46,48,731	308	67.4	74.8	60.0
29.	Karnataka	6,10,95,297	3,09,66,657	3,01,28,640	319	75.4	82.5	68.1
30.	Goa	14,58,545	7,39,140	7,19,405	394	88.7	92.6	84.7
31.	Lakshadweep	64,473	33,123	31,350	2,149	91.8	95.6	87.9
32.	Kerala	3,34,06,061	1,60,27,412	1,73,78,649	860	94.0	96.1	92.1
33.	Tamil Nadu	7,21,47,030	3,61,37,975	3,60,09,055	555	80.1	86.8	73.4
34.	Puducherry	12,47,953	6,12,511	6,35,442	2,547	85.8	91.3	80.7
35.	Andaman & Nicobar Island	3,80,581	2,02,871	1,77,710	46	86.6	90.3	82.4
36.	Telangana	3,51,93,978	17,704,078	17,489,900	308	66.5	75.0	57.9

* * * * *

2. NATIONAL SYMBOLS

State Emblem: The State Emblem of India is an adaptation from the Sarnath Lion Capital of Ashoka. It was adopted by the Government of India on January 26, 1950. In the adapted form, only three lions are visible, the fourth being hidden from the view. The wheel (Dharma Chakra) appears in relief in the centre of the abacus with a bull on the right and a horse on the left. The bell-shaped lotus has been omitted. The words "Satyameva Jayate" meaning "Truth alone triumphs" are inscribed below the Emblem in Devanagari script.

National Flag: The National Flag of India is a horizontal tricolour of deep saffron (Kesari), white and dark green in equal proportion. In the centre of the white band there is a wheel in navy blue colour. It has 24 spokes. The ratio of the length and the breadth of the flag is 3 : 2. Its design was adopted by the Constituent Assembly of India on July 22, 1947.

National Anthem: Rabindranath Tagore's song 'Jana-gana-mana' was adopted by the Constituent Assembly as the National Anthem of India on January 24, 1950.

Jana-gan-mana-adhinayaka jaya he,
Bharata-bhagya-vidhata
Punjab-Sindh-Gujarat-Maratha-Dravida-
Utkala-Banga
Vindhya-Himachala-Yamuna-Ganga Uchhala-
jaladhi-taranga.
Tava subha name jage, Tava subha asisa mange,
Gahe tava jaya gatha,
Jana-gana-mangala-dayak, jaya he Bharata
bhagya vidhata,
Jaya he, jaya he, jaya he, Jaya jaya jaya,
jaya he.

National Song: Bankim Chandra Chatterji's 'Vande Mataram' which was a source of inspiration to the people in their struggle for freedom, has been adopted as National Song. It has an equal status with the National Anthem.

Vande Mataram

Sujalam, suphalam, malayaja-shitalam,
Shasya shyamalam, Mataram
Shubhrajyotsna,pulkita yaminim,
Phulla kusumita drumadalashobhinim,
Subhasinim sumadhura—bhashinim,
Sukhadam, Varadam, Mataram.

National Bird and Animal of India: Peacock and Tiger; **National Aquatic Animal:** Dolphin; **National Flower:** Lotus; **National Calendar:** It was adopted on March 22, 1957. It has 365 days in the year and the first month of the year is Chaitra.

Months of the National Calendar

(1) Chaitra, (2) Vaishakha, (3) Jaishtha, (4) Ashadha, (5) Shravan, (6) Bhadra, (7) Ashvina, (8) Kartika, (9) Marga-Shirsha, (10) Pausha, (11) Magha, (12) Phalguna.

*****

Range	Location	Length (km)
Great Dividing Range	East Australia	3,600
Atlas	North West Africa	1,930
Western Ghats	Western India	1,610
Caucasus	Europe	1,200
Alaska	USA	1,130
Alps	Europe	1,050

Largest Deserts of the World

Subtropical	
Sahara, North Africa	94,00,000 sq. km.
Kalahari, Southern Africa	9,00,000 sq. km.
Thar, India/Pakistan	2,00,000 sq. km.
Great Sandy, Australia	4,00,000 sq. km.
Cool Coastal	
Atacama, Chile S.A.	1,40,000 sq. km
Cool Winter	
Gobi, China	13,00,000 sq. km.
Colorado, Western USA (also called the painted desert)	3,37,000 sq. km.

Atmosphere

Composition of Gases in Atmosphere

Nitrogen	78.03%
Oxygen	20.99%
Argon	0.93%
Carbon dioxide	0.03%
Hydrogen	0.01%
Neon	0.0018%
Helium	0.0005%
Crypton	0.0001%
Xenon	0.000,005%
Ozone	0.000,0001%

World Important Local Winds

Chinoon: A warm day wind frequently experienced on the eastern side of the Rocky Mountains.

Fohn: A warm dry wind descending a mountain, as on the north side of the Alps.

Haboob: A sand storm or a dust storm in north and north-east Sudan near Khartoum.

Bagrrio: It is the tropical cyclone of the Philippine Island.

Loo: A hot wind which blows in summer season in Indian sub-continent.

Papasago: A cold northerly wind sometimes felt on the Mexico plateau.

Bora: It is the name given to the cold dry wind experienced particularly in winter along the eastern coast of the Atlantic Ocean and in northern Italy.

Black Toller: A hot dust wind which blows in the vast plain of North America.

Principal Mountain Peaks of the World

Mountains	Height in Metres	Range	Date of First Ascent
1. Mount Everest	8,848	Himalayas	May 29, 1953
2. K-2 (Godwin Austen)	8,611	Karakoram	July 31, 1954
3. Kanchenjunga	8,597	Himalayas	May 25, 1955
4. Lhotse	8,511	Himalayas	May 18, 1956
5. Makalu I	8,481	Himalayas	May 15, 1955
6. Dhaulagiri I	8,167	Himalayas	May 13, 1960
7. Mansalu I	8,156	Himalayas	May 9, 1956
8. Chollyo	8,153	Himalayas	Oct. 19, 1954
9. Nanga Parbat	8,124	Himalayas	July 3, 1953
10. Annapurna I	8,091	Himalayas	June 3, 1950

Mountains	Height in Metres	Range	Date of First Ascent
11. Gasherbrum I	8,068	Karakoram	July 5, 1958
12. Broad Peak I	8,047	Karakoram	June 9, 1957
13. Gasherbrum II	8,034	Karakoram	July 7, 1956
14. Shisha Pangma (Gosainthan)	8,014	Himalayas	May 2, 1964
15. Gasherbrum III	7,952	Karakoram	Aug. 11, 1975

Types of World Agriculture

Viticulture: The cultivation of the vine for production of grapes and wine.

Pisciculture: The breeding, rearing and transplantation of fish by artificial means.

Sericulture: The raising of silk worms for the production of raw silk.

Horticulture: To grow flower front, vegetables on small plots.

Apiculture: Bee keeping on a commercial scale for the sale of honey.

Floriculture: The cultivation of flowers or flowering plants.

Mariculture: Sea farming, or the cultivation of marine plants and animals for commercial purposes.

Olericulture: The cultivation of vegetables and kitchen herbs.

Famous Straits of the World

Strait	Between	Country
Malacca Strait	Andaman Sea and South China Sea	Indonesia
Palk Strait	Mannar and Bay of Bengal	India-Sri Lanka
Magellan Strait	Pacific and South Atlantic Ocean	Chile
Dover Strait	English Channel and North Sea	England-France
Berring Strait	Berring Sea and Chukasi Sea	Alaska-Russia
Sugaroo Strait	Japan Sea and Pacific Ocean	Japan
Sunda Strait	Java and Indian Ocean	Indonesia
Gibralter Strait	Mediterranean Sea and Atlantic Ocean	Spain
Harmuj Strait	Persia and Bay of Oman	Oman-Iran
Hudson Strait	Bay of Hudson and Atlantic Ocean	Canada

World's Famous Official Documents

White Paper: India; **Orange Book:** Netherlands; **Yellow Book:** France; **Green Book:** Italy and Iran; **White Book:** Portugal, China and Germany; **Grey Book:** Japan and Belgium.

Famous Newspapers of the World

Newspaper	Place of Publishing	Language
Daily News	New York (America)	English
Guardian	London (Britain)	English
Pravada	Moscow (Russia)	Russian
Al-Ahram	Cairo (Egypt)	Arabic
Merdeca	Jakarta (Indonesia)	Indonesian
Times	London (Britain)	English
People's Daily	Beijing (China)	Chinese
New Statesman	Britain	English
Daily Mirror	Britain	English
Hindu, Hindustan Times, Times of India, Tribune, Statesman, Indian Express, Economic Times	India	English
Hindustan, Nav Bharat Times, Rashtriya Sahara, Dainik Jagaran, Punjab Kesari	India	Hindi

Important Boundary Lines

Boundary Line	Countries
Hindenberg Line	Germany-Poland
Maginot Line	France and Germany
Mannerhein Line	Russia-Finland
Mc Mahon Line	India and China
Order Niesse Line	Germany-Poland
Radcliff Line	India-Pakistan
Seigfrid Line	Germany-France
Durand Line	Pakistan and Afghanistan
17th Parallel	The line which defined the boundary between North Vietnam and South Vietnam before the two were united.
38th Parallel	North Korea and South Korea
49th Parallel	U.S.A. and Canada

10 Largest Countries

In Area

Rank	Country	Area (sq. km)
1.	Russia	1,70,75,000
2.	Canada	99,76,186
3.	China	95,96,960
4.	United States	93,72,614
5.	Brazil	85,11,965
6.	Australia	76,82,300
7.	India	32,87,263
8.	Argentina	27,76,654
9.	Kazakhstan	27,17,300
10.	Algeria	23,81,741

In Population (million)

Rank	Country	Population (2021)
1.	China	1,398
2.	India	1,339
3.	USA	335
4.	Indonesia	275
5.	Pakistan	238
6.	Nigeria	219
7.	Brazil	213
8.	Bangladesh	164
9.	Russia	142
10.	Japan	125

10 Smallest Countries

In Area

Rank	Country	Area (sq. km)
1.	Vatican City	0.44
2.	Monaco	1.95
3.	Nauru	21.00
4.	Tuvalu	26.00
5.	San Marino	62.00
6.	Liechtenstein	160.00
7.	Marshall Islands	181.00
8.	St. Kitts-Nevis	269.00
9.	Maldives	298.00
10.	Malta	316.00

In Population

Rank	Country	Population (2021)
1.	Vatican City	1,000
2.	Nauru	9,770
3.	Tuvalu	11,448
4.	Palau	21,613
5.	Monaco	31,223
6.	San Marino	34,467
7.	Liechtenstein	39,425
8.	St. Kitts-Nevis	54,149
9.	Dominica	74,584
10.	Marshall Islands	78,831

Signals/Signs and Meaning

Signal/Sign	*Meaning*
Red Triangle	Family Planning
Red Cross	Medical Help
Red Light	Danger, 'Stop' for the movement of vehicles
Green Light	Go
Olive Branch	Peace
White Pigeon or Dove	Peace
Black Strip on Arm	(i) Opposition (ii) Sorrow
Black Flag	Opposition
Red Flag	(i) Danger (ii) Revolution
White Flag	Treaty or Surrender
Yellow Flag	Vehicles with patients of contagious diseases
Two Bones across with a Skull	Danger of electricity
Half mast flown Flag	National mourning
Lotus	Sign of civilization and culture
Wheel (Chakra)	Sign of Progress
A blind folded woman with scale in hand	Sign of Justice
Reversed flown	National calamity flag

National Emblems of Important Countries

Country	*National Emblem*
America	Golden Rod
Australia	Kangaroo
Ireland	Shamrock
Italy	White Lily
Israel	Candelabrum
Iran	Rose
Canada	White Lily
Great Britain	Rose
Chile	Candor and Huemul
Germany	Corn Flower
Japan	Chrysanthemum
Zimbabwe	Zimbabwe Bird
Denmark	Beach
Turkey	Crescent and Star
The Netherlands	Lion
New Zealand	Kiwi, Fern Southern Cross
Norway	Lion
Nepal	Kukri
Pakistan	Crescent
Poland	Eagle
France	Lily
Belgium	Lion
Bangladesh	Water Lily
Mongolia	The Soyombo
Russia	Double headed eagle
Lebanon	Cedar Tree
Sudan	Secretary Bird
Syria	Eagle
India	Lioned Capital

Region wise Population

Region	*Population (2021)*	*World Share (in percentage)*
Asia	4,584,249,616	59.1%
Africa	1,375,397,882	17.4%
Europe	747,142,309	9.8%
Latin America and the Caribbean	651,321,069	8.4%
Northern America	373,076,833	4.8%
Oceania	41,663,096	0.5%

International Date Line

It roughly corresponds to 180°E or W meridian of longitude which falls on the opposite side of the Greenwich meridian and the date changes by one day (i.e. 24 hours), as this line is crossed. On crossing this line from east to west a day is added, and a day is subtracted on crossing it from west to east.

* * * * *

4. UNITED NATIONS ORGANISATION

- **Origin:** UN Charter was signed by 50 members on June 26, 1945. It officially came into existence on October 24, 1945.
- **UN Charter:** The Charter is the Constitution of the UNO and contains its aims and objectives and rules and regulations for its functioning.
- **Aims and Objectives:** They are security, welfare and human rights.
- **Headquarters:** New York.
- **Flag:** The flag is light blue in colour, and emblazoned in white, in its centre is the UN symbol—a polar map of world embraced by twin olive branches open at the top.
- **Official Languages:** The official languages of the UN are: English, French, Chinese, Russian, Arabic and Spanish. However, working languages are English & French only.
- **Main Organs of the UNO:** There are six main organs:
  1. **General Assembly:** It consists of representative of all members of the UN. Each member country has only one vote. It meets once a year and passes UN Budget.
  2. **Security Council:** It is the Executive body of the UN and is mainly responsible for maintaining international peace and security. It has 15 members, 5 of which (USA, UK, France, Russia and China) are permanent members. The 10 non-permanent members are elected by General Assembly for two-year term and are not eligible for immediate re-election.
  3. **Economic and Social Council:** It has 54 members elected by General Assembly.
  4. **Trusteeship Council:** It looks after interest of the people in areas not yet independent and leads them towards self-government.
  5. **International Court of Justice:** It has 15 judges, no two of whom may be nationals of the same state. They are elected by General Assembly and Security Council for a term of 9 years. The Court elects its President and Vice-President for a 3-year term.
  6. **Secretariat:** It is the Secretariat of the UN and is headed by the Secretary General.

Years Observed by United Nations Organisation

1967: International Tourism Year
1968: Human Rights Year
1970: International Education Year
1972: International Book Year
1973: Copernicus Year
1974: World Population Year
1975: International Women's Year
1979: International Year of the Child
1981: International Year of Disabled
1983: World Communication Year
1985: International Youth Year
1986: International Year of Peace
1987: International Year of Shelter for the Homeless
1990: International Literacy Year
1992: International Space Year
1993: International Year for World's Indigenous People
1994: International Year of Family

1995: International Year of Tolerance
1996: International Year for Eradication of Poverty
1998: Human Rights Year
1999: Year of Older Persons
2000: Year of the Culture of Peace
2001: International Year of Volunteer
2002: International Year of Eco-tourism
2003: International Year of Fresh Water
2004: International Rice Year
2005: International Year of Sports and Physical Education
2006: International Year of Deserts & Desertification
2008: International Year of Potato
2009: International Year of Astronomy
2010: International Year of Bio-diversity
2011: International Year of Forest
2012: International Year of Cooperatives
2013: International Year of Water Cooperation
2014: International Year of Family Farming
2015: International Year of Soil
2016: International Year of Pulses
2017: International Year of Sustainable Tourism for Development
2019: International Year of Indigenous Languages
2020: International Year of Plant Health
2021: International Year of Peace and Trust
2022: International Year of Artisanal Fisheries and Aquaculture
2023: International Year of Millets
2024: International Year of Camelids
2025: International Year of Glaciers Preservation; International Year of Quantum Science and Technology; International Year of Cooperatives; International Year of Peace and Trust.

- **Present Membership:** At present 193 countries are members of the UNO. South Sudan is the latest entrant to this world organisation.

Famous International Organisations, Headquarters and Year of Establishment

International Organisations	*Headquarters*	*Year of Establishment*
United Nations Organisations (U.N.O.)	New York	1945
International Monetary Fund (I.M.F.)	Washington	1945
World Health Organisation (W.H.O.)	Geneva	1948
Food & Agricultural Organisation (FAO)	Rome	1945
International Labour Organisation (ILO)	Geneva	1919
UNESCO	Paris	1946
International Court of Justice	The Hague	1945
Universal Postal Union (UPU)	Berne	1874
International Civil Aviation Organisation (ICAO)	Montreal	1947
UNIDO	Vienna	1966
International Atomic Energy Agency (IAEA)	Vienna	1957
International Finance Corporation (IFC)	Washington	1956
United Nations Development Programme (UNDP)	New York	1965
UNICEF	New York	1946
International Maritime Organisation (IMO)	London	1948
World Meteorological Organisation (WMO)	Geneva	1950
International Telecommunication Union (ITU)	Geneva	1865

International Organisations	*Headquarters*	*Year of Establishment*
Arab League	Cairo	1945
Commonwealth of Nations	London	1931
World Trade Organisation (WTO)	Geneva	1995
International Development Association (IDA)	Washington D.C.	1960
International Bank for Reconstruction and Development (IBRD)	Washington D.C.	1944
World Intellectual Property Organisation (WIPO)	Geneva	1967
Organisation of Islamic Conference (OIC)	Jeddah (Saudi Arabia)	1969
Red Cross	Geneva	1863
Interpol	Lyons	1923
Asian Development Bank (ADB)	Manila	1966
North Atlantic Treaty Organisation (NATO)	Brussels	1949
Association of South East Asian Nations (ASEAN)	Jakarta	1967
South Asian Association for Regional Cooperation (SAARC)	Kathmandu	1985
Asia-Pacific Economic Cooperation (APEC)	Singapore	1989
Organisation for Economic Cooperation and Development (OECD)	Paris	1961
Organisation of Petroleum Exporting Countries (OPEC)	Vienna	1960
Commonwealth of Independent States (CIS)	Minsk, Belarus	1991
International Olympic Committee (IOC)	Switzerland	1894
European Union (EU)	Brussels	Changed form of EEC Established in 1958
Amnesty International (AI)	London	1961
Shanghai Cooperation Organisation (SCO)	Beijing	2001

* * * * *

5. INDIAN CONSTITUTION & POLITY

INDIAN CONSTITUTION

India, as a sovereign state, has its own Constitution. The Indian Constitution has undergone a lengthy process over the years before its formal compositions. In fact, a number of legal developments contributed a lot in this direction. These developments, now acknowledged as the process of the constitutional development, are quite significant and these developments paved the way for the creation of an ideal constitution by a Constituent Assembly following a rigorous exercise.

CONSTITUENT ASSEMBLY

In accordance with the recommendation of the Cabinet Mission, which consisted of Lord Pethick-Lawrence, Sir Stafford Cripps and A.V. Alexander and which visited India in March 1946, the Constituent Assembly of India was elected by the Provincial Assemblies in July 1946. It had 389 members in all, including 93 representatives of Indian Princely States.

The important Committees of the Constituent Assembly were:

(*a*) **Union Powers Committee:** It had 9 members. Shri Jawaharlal Nehru was its Chairman;

(*b*) **Committee on Fundamental Rights and Minorities:** It had 54 members. Sardar Vallabhbhai Patel was its Chairman;

(*c*) **Steering Committee:** It had 3 members. Dr. K.M. Munshi (Chairman); Shri Gopalswamy Ayyangar and Shri Bishwanath Das;

(*d*) **Provincial Constitution Committee:** 25 members. Sardar Patel as Chairman;

(*e*) **Committee on Union Constitution:** 15 members. Pandit Nehru as Chairman.

The first session of the Assembly was held in New Delhi on December 9, 1946. It was attended by 207 members. Sachchidanand Sinha, as the oldest member of the Constituent Assembly, was elected provisional chairman of the session. However on December 11, 1946, Dr. Rajendra Prasad was elected as the Permanent Chairman of the Constituent Assembly.

THE LONG JOURNEY

- Demand for a Constituent Assembly composed of the people of India officially asserted by the Congress for the first time in 1935.
- Cripps' proposals of 1942 accepted this demand.
- The election for Indian Constituent Assembly held in 1946 according to the Cabinet Mission plan.
- First meeting of the Constituent Assembly for undivided India held on December 9, 1946.
- On 26 July, 1947, separate Constituent Assembly for Pakistan created.
- The sovereign Constituent Assembly for the Dominion of India (*i.e.,* excluding Pakistan) met for the first time on 14 August, 1947.
- Members of the Constituent Assembly indirectly elected.
- The electoral college consisted of members of the Provincial Legislative Assemblies (Lower Houses only).

- Each Province and each Indian State or group of States allotted seats in the Constituent Assembly proportional to their respective population (roughly in the ratio of one to a million).
- In all, provinces to elect 292 members and Indian states 93.
- Principle of Communal Electorate valid for election to the Constituent Assembly (Muslims, Sikhs, General).
- Method of election—proportional representation with single transferable vote.
- As the result of partition, membership of the CA reduced to 299.
- Constitution of India declared passed on 26th November, 1949.
- On 26th November, 1949, 284 members appended their signature to the Constitution.
- Drafting Committee of the Constituent Assembly chaired by Dr. Ambedkar.
- The Constitution underwent three readings before finalisation.
- Provisions relating to citizenship, elections, provisional parliament, temporary and transitional provisions came into effect on November 26, 1949.
- The Date of Commencement of Indian Constitution fixed for 26th January 1950.

Indian Constitution is a comprehensive document and it is the lengthiest written Constitution in the World.

The Preamble of the Constitution: "We the people of India, having solemnly resolved to Constitute India into a Sovereign, Socialist, Secular Democratic Republic and to secure to all its citizen."

Justice: Social, economic and political.

Liberty: Of thought, expression, belief, faith and worship.

Equality: Of status and of opportunity, and to promote among them all.

Fraternity: Assuring the dignity of the individual and the unity and integrity of the nation. In our Constituent Assembly, this twenty-sixth day of November, 1949, do hereby adopt, enact and give to ourselves this constitution."

SCHEDULES TO THE CONSTITUTION

The Constitution of India originally contained only eight schedules. Presently there are 12 schedules in the constitution.

First Schedule: It consists the list of the States and Union territories. ***Second Schedule:*** This Schedule is related to salary and allowances of the President, Governors, Speaker, Supreme Court and High Court Judges etc. ***Third Schedule:*** Contains forms of oath and affirmation. ***Fourth Schedule:*** Contains allocation of seats to each State and Union territory in the Council of States. ***Fifth Schedule:*** Provides for administration and control of scheduled areas and scheduled tribes. ***Sixth Schedule:*** Provides for administration of Tribal Areas in Assam, Meghalaya and Mizoram. ***Seventh Schedule:*** Distribution of powers and functions between the centre and state governments under three lists. ***Eighth Schedule:*** The languages recognised by Parliament. ***Ninth Schedule:*** It contains laws passed by the Union or States which cannot be taken to courts. ***Tenth Schedule:*** Provisions as to disqualification on the ground of political defection. ***Eleventh Schedule:*** Provisions regarding powers, authority etc. of Panchayati Raj institutions. ***Twelfth Schedule:*** Provisions regarding powers, authority etc. of Municipalities etc.

Foreign Sources of Indian Constitution

Foreign Sources	*Subject*
Britain	Parliamentary system, collective responsibilities of Cabinet
America	Fundamental right, Citizenship, Independent Judiciary, Judicial review
Canada	Division of powers
Ireland	Directive principles
Germany	Emergency provisions
Russia	Fundamental duties
Australia	Concurrent list

THE SUPREME COURT

The Supreme Court of India consists of the Chief Justice and other Judges whose number is prescribed by the Parliament from time to time. In 1950 there was a Chief Justice and there were 7 Judges. But the number of Judges continued increasing as per the need. The Supreme Court, at present, consists of the Chief Justice and 33 Judges.

The Chief Justice and other Judges of the Supreme Court are appointed by the President of India. For appointing the Chief Justice of India, the other Judges of the Supreme or High Courts may be consulted. Usually, the senior-most Judge in the Supreme Court is appointed as the Chief Justice. For the appointment of other Judges of the Supreme Court, the Chief Justice has to be consulted. Usually, the Chief Justice himself consults a collegium of the four senior-most Judges, and all of them need to agree for any candidate to be recommended for the appointment of a judge.

A person can be appointed as a Judge of the Supreme Court only if he/she:

I. is a citizen of India;

II. must have been at least a Judge of a High Court or of two or more such Courts in succession for at least five years; or

III. must have been an advocate of a High Court or of two or more such Courts in succession for at least ten years; or

IV. is, in the opinion of the President, a distinguished jurist.

Judges of the Supreme Court hold office till they attain the age of 65 years. But they may be removed from office by an order of the President, passed after an address by each House of Parliament supported by a special majority on the ground of proved misbehaviour or incapacity.

The Jurisdiction and Powers of the Supreme Court

The Supreme Court of India is a powerful judiciary. The Constitution of India has defined its jurisdiction and powers in detail, it has Original. Appellate and Advisory Jurisdictions Besides these jurisdictions, it has a few other important functions.

(*i*) Original Jurisdiction: The Supreme Court alone has the authority to hear directly certain cases. These are:

(*a*) Disputes between the Union government and one or more State governments,

(*b*) Disputes between two or more States,

(*c*) Disputes between the Government of India and one or more States on the one side and one or more States on the other side.

(*ii*) Appellate Jurisdiction: The power of a superior or higher court to hear and decide appeals against the judgment of the lower court is called appellate jurisdiction. The Supreme Court is a court of appeal for constitutional, civil and criminal cases. It can hear appeals against the judgments of the High Courts. It also has the power to review its own judgment. It may in its own discretion grant special lease to appeal against any judgment or order delivered or passed by any court or tribunal within the territory of India.

Moreover, an Appeal may come to the Supreme Court in any criminal case, if the High Court certifies that the case is fit for appeal to the Supreme Court. The special appellate power has become a handy weapon in the hands of the Court to review the decisions pertaining to elections and Labour and Industrial Tribunals.

(*iii*) Advisory Jurisdiction: The Supreme Court has a special advisory jurisdiction in matters which may specifically be referred to it by the President of India. If at any time, it appears to the President that a question of law or fact has arisen or is likely to arise, which is of such public importance that it is urgent to obtain the opinion of the Supreme Court on it, he/she may refer it to the Supreme Court. The Supreme Court may, after such hearing as it thinks fit, report to the President its opinion thereon. The report or the opinion of the Supreme Court is of course, not binding on the President. Similarly, there is no compulsion for the Court to give its advice.

(*iii*) eligible for election as a member of Rajya Sabha;

(*iv*) should not hold any office of profit;

(*v*) should not be a member of parliament; and

(*vi*) should not be of unsound mind.

Vice-President holds office for 5 years and can be removed from office earlier through a resolution passed by a two-third majority of Rajya Sabha agreed to by the Lok Sabha.

The Presiding Officer

Vice-President is the ex-officio chairman of Rajya Sabha and presides over the sessions of the Upper House. He performs all the duties of the President when the office of the President falls vacant due to the death, resignation or absence of the President. He draws a fix salary per month in his capacity of being the Chairman of the Rajya Sabha.

COUNCIL OF MINISTERS AND PRIME MINISTER

The Constitution of India provides for a parliamentary system of government under which the President is only a constitutional ruler and the real power is exercised by the Council of Ministers, headed by the Prime Minister. The members of the Council of Ministers hold office during the pleasure of the President but actually they stay in office as long as they enjoy the confidence of the majority in the Lok Sabha. As per the Constitution, the Council of Ministers is only an advisory body to assist the President but in reality, it enjoys extensive powers. Constitutionally, the executive authority has been vested in the President but in reality, these powers are exercised by the Prime Minister and the Council of Ministers.

PRIME MINISTER

The Prime Minister is the leader of the majority party in the Parliament and the President cannot exercise his discretion in the appointment of the Prime Minister. He stays in office till the majority of the members of Lok Sabha has confidence in him. He occupies an important position in relation to the Council of Ministers. He recommends the names of the persons to be included in the Council of Ministers. He allocates portfolios among them and can ask any minister to tender resignation. He can drop a minister while reshuffling the ministry. He coordinates the administration of various departments. He is the chief link between the President and the Council. He is the leader of the majority party and so, he has a great influence on the Parliament and the party. The Prime Minister enjoys such extensive powers as have been described as the virtual ruler of the country.

FUNDAMENTAL RIGHTS

Following fundamental rights are enjoyed by every Indian citizen, irrespective of caste, colour, creed and sex:

1. **Right to Equality:** No special privileges, no distinction on grounds of religion, caste, creed and sex.
2. **Right to Freedom:** The right to freedom of expression and speech, the right to choose one's own profession, the right to reside in any part of the Indian Union.
3. **Right to Freedom to Religion:** Except when it is in the interest of public order, morality, health or other conditions, everybody has the right to profess, practice and propagate his religion freely.
4. **Cultural and Educational Rights:** The Constitution provides that every community can run its own institutions to preserve its own culture and language.
5. **Right against Exploitation:** Traffic in human beings and forced labour and the employment of children under 14 years in factories or mines, are punishable offences.
6. **Rights to Constitutional Remedies:** When a citizen finds that any of his fundamental rights has been encroached upon, he can move the Supreme Court, which has been empowered to safeguard the fundamental rights of a citizen (Article 32).

Jurisdiction and Seat of High Courts

Name	*Year*	*Territorial Jurisdiction*	*Seat*
Allahabad	1866	Uttar Pradesh	Prayagraj (Bench at Lucknow)
Andhra Pradesh	2019	Andhra Pradesh	Amaravati
Bombay	1862	Maharashtra, Goa, Dadar and Nagar Haveli and Daman and Diu	Mumbai (Benches at Nagpur, Panaji and Sambhaji Nagar)
Calcutta	1862	West Bengal and Andaman & Nicobar Islands	Kolkata (Circuit Benches has at Shri Vijaya Puram and Jalpaiguri)
Chhattisgarh	2000	Chhattisgarh	Bilaspur
Delhi	1966	Delhi	Delhi
Gauhati	1948	Assam, Nagaland, Mizoram and Arunachal Pradesh	Guwahati (Benches at Kohima, Aizawl and Itanagar)
Gujarat	1960	Gujarat	Ahmedabad
Himachal Pradesh	1971	Himachal Pradesh	Shimla
Jammu & Kashmir and Ladakh	1928	Jammu & Kashmir, Ladakh	Srinagar and Jammu
Jharkhand	2000	Jharkhand	Ranchi
Karnataka	1884	Karnataka	Bengaluru (Circuit Benches at Dharwar and Gulbarga)
Kerala	1958	Kerala & Lakshadweep Islands	Kochi
Madhya Pradesh	1956	Madhya Pradesh	Jabalpur (Benches at Gwalior and Indore)
Madras	1862	Tamil Nadu & Puducherry	Chennai (Bench at Madurai)
Orissa	1948	Odisha	Cuttack
Patna	1916	Bihar	Patna
Punjab and Haryana	1966	Punjab, Haryana and Chandigarh	Chandigarh
Rajasthan	1949	Rajasthan	Jodhpur (Bench at Jaipur)
Sikkim	1975	Sikkim	Gangtok
Uttarakhand	2000	Uttarakhand	Nainital
Tripura	2013	Tripura	Agartala
Meghalaya	2013	Meghalaya	Shillong
Manipur	2013	Manipur	Imphal
Telangana	2019	Telangana	Hyderabad

FUNDAMENTAL DUTIES

The fundamental duties for the Indian citizens have been incorporated in the Constitution through the Constitution (42nd) Amendment Act, 1976. These duties are:

(*i*) to abide by the Constitution and respect its ideals and institutions, the National Flag and the National Anthem;

(*ii*) to cherish and follow the noble deeds which inspired our national struggle for freedom;

(*iii*) to uphold and protect the sovereignty, unity and integrity of India;

(*iv*) to defend the country and render national service when called upon to do so;

(*v*) to promote harmony and the spirit of common brotherhood amongst all the people transcending religious, regional or sectional diversities and to renounce practices derogatory to the dignity of women;

(*vi*) to value and preserve the rich heritage of our composite culture;

(*vii*) to protect and improve natural environment including forests, lakes, rivers and wildlife, and to have compassion for living creatures;

(*viii*) to develop the scientific temper, humanism and the spirit of inquiry and reform;

(*ix*) to safeguard public property and to abjure violence;

(*x*) to strive towards excellence in all spheres of individual and collective activity so that the nation constantly rises to higher levels of endeavour and achievement.

(*xi*) who is parent or guardian to provide opportunities for education to his child or, as the case may be, ward between age of six and fourteen years.

DIRECTIVE PRINCIPLES OF STATE POLICY

The Directive Principles of State Policy are contained in Article 36 to 51 in Part IV of the constitutions. Directive principles are not enforceable through courts. Main aim of Directive principles is to provide social and economic base of a genuine democracy.

Some Important Directive Principles:

- Provisions for adequate means of livelihood for all citizens (Art. 39).
- Right to work (Art. 41).
- Right to human condition of work and maternity relief (Art. 42).
- Right to a living wage and condition of work ensuring decent standard of life of worker (Art. 43).
- Common Civil Code (Art. 44).
- Prohibit consumption of liquor (Art. 47).
- Prevent slaughter of useful cattle (Art. 48).
- Organise Panchayati Raj (Art. 40).
- Separate the judiciary from the executive (Art. 50).
- Protect and maintain places of historic monuments (Art. 49).
- International peace (Art. 51).

Voting Age: The voting age in the election to the Lok Sabha and State Legislative Assemblies has been reduced from 21 to 18 years by the Constitution (61st) Amendment Act, 1989.

GOVERNOR

The Governor is appointed by the President and holds office during the pleasure of the President. Apart from the power to appoint the council of ministers, if the governor finds that the government of state cannot be carried on in accordance with the provisions of the constitution (Art. 356), he may send his report to the President who may assume to himself the functions of the government of the state. (This is popularly known as 'President's Rule').

THE ATTORNEY GENERAL OF INDIA

The Attorney General of India is the first law officer of the Government of India. Though he is not a member of cabinet he has the right to speak in the

House of Parliament, but he has no right to vote. The Attorney General of India shall be appointed by the President and shall hold office during his pleasure.

His duty shall be to give advice on such legal matter from time to time as may be referred to him by the President.

COMPTROLLER & AUDITOR GENERAL OF INDIA (CAG)

The Comptroller and Auditor General of India is guardian of the public purse and it is his duty to see that not a *paisa* is spent out of consolidated fund of India or of a state without the authority of the appropriate legislature. He is appointed by President of India.

Status

- Appointed by the President.
- A person with long administrative experience & knowledge of accounts is appointed.
- Holds office for 6 yrs or till 65 yrs of age.
- The President can remove him only on the recommendation of the 2 houses of Parliament (as in case of judge of Supreme Court).

UNION PUBLIC SERVICE COMMISSION (U.P.S.C.)

The UPSC has one chairman and nine members. The members as well as the chairman are appointed by the President. Roughly, one half of the members of UPSC should be persons who have held important offices under the central or the state government for at least 10 years. They retire after 6 years. The chairman or a member of the UPSC can be removed from the office by the President but after referring the case to the supreme Court, which, after holding enquiry, recommends for the same. The functions of the UPSC are:

(*i*) to conduct examination for appointment to the services of the Union;

(*ii*) to advise the government on the methods of recruitment; and

(*iii*) to advise the government on disciplinary method affecting a person who is serving under the government of India.

INTER-STATE COUNCILS

Article 263 provides for inter-state councils. The power of the President to set up Inter-State Councils not only for advising upon disputes but also for investigating and discussing subjects in which some or all of the states, or the Union and one or more of the states have common interest.

STAFF SELECTION COMMISSION

The Union Government has constituted the Staff Selection Commission for recruitment to non-technical Group C and some of Group B posts in the central departments and in subordinate offices. The administrative Reforms Commission had recommended the setting up of such a Commission.

* * * * *

6. PLANNING IN INDIA

The need for planning was felt in India even before independence. A National Planning Committee was set up by the Indian National Congress as early as 1938. The Planning Commission was set up in 1950. It is an advisory body engaged in the task of meaningful national planning. The main objectives of India's Economic Planning are as follows : (*i*) securing an increase in National Income; (*ii*) achieving a planned rate of investment within a given period to bring the actual investment as a proportion of national income to a higher level; (*iii*) reducing inequality in the distribution of income and wealth; (*iv*) providing additional employment; (*v*) adopting measures to increase agricultural production, manufacturing capacity for producers and a favourable balance of payments.

Five Year Plans in India

Plans	Period	Investment (₹ Crore)	Objectives
First Plan	April 1, 1951–March 31, 1956	1,960	Priority to agriculture, electricity and irrigation.
Second Plan	April 1, 1956–March 31, 1961	4,672	Development of basic and heavy industries.
Third Plan	April 1, 1961–March 31, 1966	8,577	Long term development of India's economy.
Annual Plan	April 1, 1966–March 31, 1967	2,137	
Annual Plan	April 1, 1967–March 31, 1968	2,205	
Annual Plan	April 1, 1968–March 31, 1969	2,283	
Fourth Plan	April 1, 1969–March 31, 1974	15,779	Enlarge the income of rural population and supply of goods of mass consumption.
Fifth Plan	April 1, 1974–March 31, 1979	39,426	Attain increased self reliance and employment avenues.
Annual Plan	April 1, 1979–March 31, 1980	12,176	
Sixth Plan	April 1, 1980–March 31, 1985	1,09,292	Removal of unemployment
Seventh Plan	April 1, 1985–March 31, 1990	2,18,730	Food work and productivity were the basic priorities.
Eighth Plan	April, 1992–March 31, 1997	4,95,670	Raising employment
Ninth Plan	April 1, 1997–March 31, 2002	9,41,041	Agriculture and rural development
Tenth Plan	April 1, 2002–March 31, 2007	14,91,610	Growth rate 7.8 percent per annum.
Eleventh Plan	April 1, 2007–March 31, 2012	36,44,718	Literacy, Employment, Rural development & Transport development.
Twelfth Plan	April 1, 2012–March 31, 2017	43,30,000	Long term development of India's economy.

INDIA'S AMBITIOUS 15-YEAR VISION PLAN

Niti Aayog has come forward with a draft 15-year vision plan to catapult the country's economy to more than three times as compared to the present day. The new plan is set to replace the centralised five-year plans the country has been following for decades.

The new plan is accompanied by shorter sub-plans—a seven-year strategy for 2017-24, and a three-year 'Action Agenda' from 2017-18 to 2019-20. No less than 300 specific action points covering a wide range of sectors have been drawn up as part of the 15 year vision.

The salient features of 15-year vision plan are:

- India aims to more than triple the size of its economy in 15 years with gross domestic product (GDP) expected to rise to ₹ 469 lakh crores from ₹ 137 lakh crore in 2015-16. Per capita GDP is expected to rise by three times to ₹ 3,14,667 in 2015-2016.
- NITI Aayog plans to work closely with staes to boost infrastructure and services, including regions that require special attention. The gov-ernment made a big push for Goods and Services Tax (GST), urging the state governments to speed up the legislation of state GST bills.
- India's urban population is expected to increase by 22 crores by 2031. The plan is likely to lay emphasis on urban development, taking a note from China's elaborate long-term development agenda.
- The plan envisages a central body for overseeing the implemention of sustainable development goals. Specific goals will cover clean water, removing hunger, climate efforts, responsible consumption, clean energy, quality educaiton, reduced inequality and gender equality, among others.
- The NITI Aayog will work as a "collaborative federal body whose strength is in its ideas, rather than in administrative or financial control."

NITI AAYOG

The National Institution for Transforming India, also called NITI Aayog, was formed via a resolution of the Union Cabinet on January 1, 2015. NITI Aayog is the premier policy 'Think Tank' of the Government of India, providing both directional and policy inputs. While designing strategic and long term policies and programmes for the Government of India, NITI Aayog also provides relevant technical advice to the Centre and States. At the core of NITI Aayog's creation are two hubs - *Team India Hub* and the *Knowledge and Innovation Hub*. The Team India Hub leads the engagement of states with the Central government, while the Knowledge and Innovation Hub builds NITI's think-tank capabilities. These hubs reflect the two key tasks of the Aayog.

FINANCE COMMISSION

Article 280 of the Constitution provides for the appointment of a finance commission every five year. President appoints chairman and members of this commission. Finance commission are to recommend to President the basis for the distribution of the net proceeds of taxes between the centre and the states and the principles which should govern the grants-in-aid to be given to the states out of the consolidated funds of India.

NATIONAL DEVELOPMENT COUNCIL

The National Development Council, set-up in 1952, consists of representatives of the Central Government as well as the State governments. It is the supreme body insofar as planning is concerned and it determines policies, issues guidelines, reviews working of the plan and finally approves the plan. The Council consists of the Prime Minister (Chairman), all Union Cabinet Ministers, Chief Ministers of all States and Union Territories and the Vice Chairman and members of the NITI Aayog. For matters relating to Plans and planning, the Union Minister of Planning is responsible to the Parliament.

RESERVE BANK OF INDIA

It is the Central Bank of the country. The Reserve Bank of India was established in 1935 with a capital of ₹ 5 crore. This capital of ₹ 5 crore was divided into 5 lakh equity shares of ₹ 100 each. In the beginning the ownership of almost all the share capital was with the non-government shareholders. In order to prevent the centralisation of the equity shares in the hands of a few people, **the Reserve Bank of India was nationalised on January 1, 1949.**

Establishment Years of Major Financial Institutions of India

• Imperial Bank of India	1921
• Reserve Bank of India (Nationalisation of RBI took place on January 1, 1949)	April 1, 1935
• Industrial Finance Corporation of India	1948
• State Bank of India	July 1, 1955
• Unit Trust of India	Feb. 1, 1964
• Bifurcation of UTI (UTI-I & UTI-II)	Feb. 2003
• IDBI	July 1964
• NABARD	July 12, 1982
• IRBI (Now it has been renamed a IIBIL since March 6, 1997)	March 20, 1985
• SIDBI	1990
• EXIM Bank	January 1, 1982
• National Housing Bank	July 1988
• Life Insurance Corporation (LIC)	September 1956
• General Insurance Corporation (GIC)	November 1972
• Regional Rural Banks	Oct. 2, 1975
• Technology Development & Information Co. of India Ltd.	1989
• Infrastructure Leasing & Financial Services Ltd.	1988
• Housing Development Finance Corporation Ltd. (HDFC)	1977

* * * * *

7. GENERAL SCIENCE

INVENTIONS AND DISCOVERIES

Important Inventions

Name of Invention	*Inventor*	*Nationality*	*Year*
Aeroplane	Orville & Wilbur Wright	U.S.A.	1903
Ball-Point Pen	John J. Loud	U.S.A.	1888
Barometer	Evangelista Torricelli	Italy	1644
Bicycle	Kirkpatrick Macmillan	Britain	1839-40
Bifocal Lens	Benjamin Franklin	U.S.A.	1780
Car (Petrol)	Karl Benz	Germany	1888
Celluloid	Alexander Parkes	Britain	1861
Cinema	Nicolas & Jean Lumiere	France	1895
Clock (mechanical)	I-Hsing & Liang Ling-Tsan	China	725
Diesel Engine	Rudolf Diesel	Germany	1895
Dynamo	Hypolite Pixii	France	1832
Electric Lamp	Thomas Alva Edison	U.S.A.	1879
Electric Motor (DC)	Zenobe Gramme	Belgium	1873
Electric Motor (AC)	Nikola Tesla	U.S.A.	1888
Electro-magnet	William Sturgeon	Britain	1824
Electronic Computer	Dr. Alan M. Turing	Britain	1943
Film (moving outlines)	Louis Prince	France	1885
Film (musical sound)	Dr. Le de Forest	U.S.A.	1923
Fountain Pen	Lewis E. Waterman	U.S.A.	1884
Gramophone	Thomas Alva Edison	U.S.A.	1878
Helicopter	Etienne Oehmichen	France	1924
Jet Engine	Sir Frank Whittle	Britain	1937
Laser	Charles H. Townes	U.S.A.	1960
Lift (Mechanical)	Elisha G. Otis	U.S.A.	1852
Locomotive	Richard Trevithick	Britain	1804
Machine Gun	James Puckle	Britain	1718
Microphone	Alexander Graham Bell	U.S.A.	1876
Microscope	Z. Janssen	Netherlands	1590
Motor Cycle	G. Daimler	Germany	1885
Photography (on film)	John Carbutt	U.S.A.	1888
Printing Press	Johann Gutenberg	Germany	c.1455
Razor (safety)	King C. Gillette	U.S.A.	1895
Refrigerator	James Harrison & Alexander Catlin	U.S.A.	1850

Name of Invention	Inventor	Nationality	Year
Safety Pin	Walter Hunt	U.S.A.	1849
Sewing machine	Barthelemy Thimmonnier	France	1829
Ship (steam)	J.C. Perier	France	1775
Ship (turbine)	Hon. Sir C. Parsons	Britain	1894
Skyscraper	W. Le Baron Jenny	U.S.A.	1882
Slide Rule	William Oughtred	Britain	1621
Steam Engine (condenser)	James Watt	Britain	1765
Steel Production	Henry Bessemer	Britain	1855
Steel (stainless)	Harry Brearley	Britain	1913
Submarine	David Bushnell	U.S.A.	1776
Tank	Sir Ernest Swinton	Britain	1914
Telegraph	M. Lammond	France	1787
Telegraph Code	Samuel F.B. Morse	U.S.A.	1837
Telephone (perfected)	Alexander Graham Bell	U.S.A.	1876
Television (mechanical)	John Logie Baird	Britain	1926
Television (electronic)	P.T. Farnsworth	U.S.A.	1927
Thermometer	Galileo Galilei	Italy	1593
Transformer	Michael Faraday	Britain	1831
Transistor	Bardeen, Shockley & Brattain	U.S.A.	1948
Washing Machine (elec.)	Hurley Machine Co.	U.S.A.	1907
Zip-Fastener	W.L. Judson	U.S.A.	1891

Important Discoveries

Discovery	Discoverer	Nationality	Year
Aluminium	Hans Christian Oerstedt	Denmark	1827
Atomic number	Henry Moseley	England	1913
Atomic structure of matter	John Dalton	England	1803
Chlorine	C.W. Scheele	Sweden	1774
Electromagnetic induction	Michael Faraday	England	1831
Electromagnetic waves	Heinrich Hertz	Germany	1886
Electromagnetism	Hans Christian Oersted	Denmark	1920
Electron	Sir Joseph Thomson	England	1897
General theory of relativity	Albert Einstein	Switzerland	1915
Hydrogen	Henry Cavendish	England	1766
Law of electric conduction	Georg Ohm	Germany	1827
Law of electromagnetism	Andre Ampere	France	1826
Law of falling bodies	Galileo	Italy	1590
Laws of gravitation & motion	Isaac Newton	England	1687
Laws of planetary motion	Johannes Kepler	Germany	1609-19
Magnesium	Sir Humphry Davy	England	1808
Neptune (Planet)	Johann Galle	Germany	1846
Neutron	James Chadwick	England	1932
Nickel	Axel Cronstedt	Sweden	1751
Nitrogen	Daniel Rutherford	England	1772

Discovery	Discoverer	Nationality	Year
Oxygen	Joseph Priestly C.W. Scheele	England Sweden	1772
Ozone	Christian Schonbein	Germany	1839
Pluto (Planet)	Clyde Tombaugh	U.S.A	1930
Plutonium	G.T. Seaborg	U.S.A	1940
Proton	Ernest Rutherford	England	1919
Quantum Theory	Max Planck	Germany	1900
Radioactivity	Antoine Bacquerel	France	1896
Radium	Pierre & Marie Curie	France	1898
Silicon	Jons Berzelius	Sweden	1824
Special theory of relativity	Albert Einstein	Switzerland	1905
Sun as centre of solar system	Copernicus	Poland	1543
Uranium	Martin Klaproth	Germany	1789
Uranus (Planet)	William Herschel	England	1781
X-rays	Wilhelm Roentgen	Germany	1895

Geographical Explorations/Discoveries

Place	Explorer/Discoverer	Nationality	Year
America	Christopher Columbus	Italy	1492
Hawaii Islands (Sandwich Islands)	Captain James Cook	England	1778
Newfoundland	John Cabot	England	1497
New Zealand	Abel Janszoon Tasman	Holland	1642
North Pole	Robert Peary	USA	1909
Sea Route to India (via Cape of Good Hope)	Vasco da Gama	Portugal	1498
South Pole	Roald Amundsen	Norway	1911

Scientific Instruments

Name of Instrument	Used for
Altimeter	measuring altitude
Ammeter	measuring strength of an electric current
Anemometer	measuring the velocity of wind
Audiometer	measuring level of hearing
Barometer	measuring atmospheric pressure
Callipers	measuring the internal and external diameters of tubes
Calorimeter	measuring quantity of heat
Compass	finding out direction
Dynamo	converting mechanical energy into electrical energy
Eudiometer	measuring volume changes during chemical reactions between gases
Galvanometer	detecting and determining the strength of small electric currents
Hydrometer	measuring specific gravity of a liquid
Hygrometer	measuring the humidity in the atmosphere
Lactometer	measuring the purity of milk
Manometer	measuring the gaseous pressure
Micrometer	measuring minute distances, angles, etc.

Name of Instrument	Used for
Microscope	seeing magnified view of very small objects
Periscope	with the help of this instrument an observer in a submarine can see what is going on the surface of the sea
Photometer	measuring intensity of light from distant stars
Pyrometer	measuring high temperatures
Radar	detecting and finding the presence and location of moving objects like aircraft, missile, etc.
Radiometer	measuring the emission of radiant energy
Rain Gauge	measuring the amount of rainfall
Seismograph	measuring and recording the intensity and origin of earthquake shocks
Sextant	measuring altitude and angular distances between two objects or heavenly bodies
Spectrometer	measuring the refractive indices
Spherometer	measuring the curvature of spherical objects/surface
Sphygmomanometer	measuring blood pressure
Stethoscope	ascertaining the condition of heart and lungs by listening to their function
Stroboscope	viewing objects that are moving rapidly with a periodic motion as if they were at rest
Tachometer	measuring the rate of revolution or angular speed of a revolving shaft
Telescope	viewing magnified images of distant objects
Theodolite	measuring the horizontal and vertical angles
Thermocouple	measuring the temperature inside furnaces and jet engines
Thermometer	measuring human body temperature
Thermostat	regulating constant temperature
Ultrasonoscope	measuring utrasonic sounds
Viscometer	measuring the viscosity of a fluid
Voltmeter	measuring potential difference between two points.

Diseases and the Parts of Body they Affect

Disease	Part of body affected
AIDS	Immune system of body
Arthritis	Inflammation of joints
Asthma	Lungs
Cataract	Eyes
Conjunctivitis	Eyes
Diabetes	Pancreas
Diphtheria	Throat
Glaucoma	Eyes
Eczema	Skin
Goitre	Front of the neck (due to enlargement of thyroid gland)
Gout	Joints of bone

Disease	Part of body affected
Jaundice	Liver
Meningitis	Brain or spinal cord
Pleurisy	Pleura (inflammation of)
Polio	motor neurons
Pneumonia	Lungs
Pyorrhoea	Sockets of teeth
Tuberculosis	Lungs
Typhoid	Intestine
Malaria	Spleen
Leukaemia	Blood
Rickets	Bones

8. SPACE RESEARCH

First in Space

First creator of rules regarding space research	—	Isaac Newton
First artificial satellite launched in space	—	Sputnik-1 (1957)
First living being sent in space	—	Louika (a dog)
Firstever manned spacecraft	—	Vostok-I
First man in space	—	Yuri Gagarin, U.S.S.R. (1961)
First woman in space	—	Valentina Tereshkova, U.S.S.R. (June 1963)
First man who moved in space out of the spacecraft	—	Alexi Livonov, U.S.S.R. (June 1965)
First person to land on moon	—	Neil Armstrong, America (21st July, 1969)
First fourwheeled carriage without human being on moon	—	Leunokhev-I, U.S.S.R. (1970)
First space lab in orbit	—	Skylab (America, 1973)
First space shuttle	—	Columbia (America, 1981)
First Indian (man) in space	—	Squadron leader—Rakesh Sharma (13th April, 1984)
First Indian (Woman) in space	—	Kalpana Chawla (19th Nov., 1997)
First American woman in space	—	Sailyride (1983)
First spacecraft on Mars	—	Pathfinder (6 July, 1997)
First woman who lead spacecraft	—	Allin Collis (America)
First spacecraft without man	—	Shenzoo, China (20th Nov. 1999)

Indian Space Programme : At a Glance

Satellite	*Date*	*Type*	*Launch Vehicle*	*Result*
Aryabhatta	19-04-75	Scientific	Cosmos	successful
Bhaskara I	07-06-79	Geosurvey	Cosmos	successful
Rohini	10-08-79	Geosurvey	S.L.V.3	unsuccessful
Rohini D-1	18-07-80	Geosurvey	S.L.V.3	successful
Rohini	31-05-81	Scientific	S.L.V.3	successful
Apple	19-06-81	Communication	Ariane	successful
Bhaskara II	20-11-81	Geosurvey	Cosonos	successful
INSAT-1A	10-04-82	Multipurpose	Delta	unsuccessful
Rohini	17-04-83	Scientific	S.L.V.3	successful
INSAT-1B	30-08-83	Multipurpose	Space Shuttle	successful
SROSS I	24-03-87	Technical	ASLV-D1	unsuccessful
IRS-1A	17-03-88	Remote sensing	Vostok	successful
INSAT-1D	12-06-90	Multipurpose	Delta	successful

Satellite	Date	Type	Launch Vehicle	Result
IRS-1B	29-08-91	Remote sensing	Vostok	successful
IRS-ID	29-09-97	Remote sensing	PSLV	successful
INSAT-3C	24-01-2002	Communication	Ariane-4	successful
CARTOSAT-2	10-01-2007	Communication	PSLV-C7	successful
INSAT-4CR	02-09-2007	Communication	GSLV-F04	successful
CARTOSAT-2A	28-04-2008	Communication	PSLV-C9	successful
Chandrayaan-I	22-10-2008	Maping and Scientific	PSLV-C11	successful
Oceansat-2	24-09-2009	Remote Sensing	PSLV-C14	successful
CARTOSAT-2B	12-07-2010	Communication	PSLV-C15	successful
Megha-Tropiques	12-10-2011	Maping and Scientific	PSLV-C18	successful
Spot-6	09-09-2012	Remote Sensing	PSLV-C21	successful
SARAL	25-02-2013	Scientific	PSLV-C20	successful
GSAT-7	30-08-2013	Defence	Ariane-5	successful
MOM	5-11-2013	Mapping	PSLV-C25	successful
GSAT-14	05-01-2014	Communication	GSLV-D5	successful
IRNSS-1B	04-04-2014	Mapping and Scientific	PSLV-C24	successful
Spot-7	30-06-2014	Remote Sensing	PSLV-C23	successful
GSAT-16	07-12-2014	Communication	Ariane-5	successful
IRNSS-1D	28-03-2015	Mapping and Scientific	PSLV-C27	successful
GSAT-6	27-08-2015	Communication	GSLV-D6	successful
Astrosat	28-09-2015	Mapping and Scientific	PSLV-C30	successful
GSAT-15	11-11-2015	Communication	Ariane-5	successful
TELEOS-1 & others	16-12-2015	Mapping and Scientific	PSLV-C29	successful
IRNSS-1E	20-01-2016	Mapping and Scientific	PSLV-C31	successful
IRNSS-1F	10-03-2016	Mapping and Scientific	PSLV-C32	successful
IRNSS-1G	28-04-2016	Mapping and Scientific	PSLV-C33	successful
CARTOSAT-2 & others	22-06-2016	Mapping and Scientific	PSLV-C34	successful
INSAT-3DR	08-09-2016	Meteorology	GSLV-F05	successful
SCATSAT-1 & others	26-09-2016	Multipurpose	PSLV-C35	successful
CARTOSAT-2 & 103	15-02-2017	Multipurpose	PSLV-C37	successful
GSAT-9	06-05-2017	Communications	GSLVMK-II	successful
GSAT-19	05-06-2017	Communications	GSLVMK-III-DI	successful
CARTOSAT-2E	23-06-2017	Earth Sciences	PSLV-C38	successful
GSAT-17	29-06-2017	Communications	Ariane-5 ECA	successful
GSAT-7A	19-12-2018	Military Satellite	GSLV-MKII-F11	successful
KalamSAT-V2	23-01-2019	Student Satellite	PSLV-C44	successful
Chandrayaan-2	22-07-2019	Lunar Exploration	GSLV-MKIII MO1	—
Cartosat-3	27-11-2019	Earth Imaging Satellite	PSLV-C47	successful
GSAT-30	17-01-2020	Communication	Ariane-5	successful
E0S-01	07-11-2020	Earth Observation	PSLV-C49	successful
Amezonia & 19 others	28-02-2021	Communication	PSLV-C51	successful
E0S-04	14-02-2022	Radar Imaging	PSLV-C52	successful
TelEOS-02 and LUMILITE-4	22-04-2023	Multipurpose	PSLV-C55	successful
Chandrayaan-3	14-07-2023	Lunar Exploration	LVM3M4	successful
Aditya-L1	02-09-2023	Solar Energy Observation	PSLV-C57	successful
XPoSAT	01-01-2024	Earth Observation	PSLV-C58	successful
INSAT-3DS	17-02-2024	Meteorological	GSLV-F14	successful
EOS-08	16-08-2024	Earth Observation	SSLV-D3	successful
Proba-3	05-12-2024	Earth Observation	PSLV-C59	successful
NVS-02	29-01-2025	Navigation	GSLV-F15	successful

* * * * *

9. INDIAN HISTORY

Famous Sites of Indus Valley Civilization

Name of Site	Year of Excavation	River/ Sea coast	Discoverer
Harappa (Montgomery–Pakistan)	1921	Ravi River	Dayaram Sahney
Mohanjodaro (Larkana–Pakistan)	1922	Indus River	Rakhal Das Banerjee
Chanhudaro (Sindh–Pakistan)	1931	Indus River	N.G. Mazumdar
Alamgir pur (Meerut – U.P.)	1952-55	Hindan River	Yagyadatta Sharma
Ropar (Punjab)	1953	Sutlej River	Yagyadatta Sharma
Rangpur (Kathiabar–Gujarat)	1953	Bhabar River	Madho Swaroop Vatsa, Rang Nath Rao
Kotdigi (Sindh–Pakistan)	1953	Indus River	Fazal Ahmed Khan
Lothal (Ahmedabad–Gujarat)	1954	Bhogwa River	Rang Nath Rao
Kalibanga (Ganganagar–Rajasthan)	1961	Ghaggar	Brajwasi Lal
Surkotara (Kutch–Gujarat)	1967	Ghaggar River	Ravindra Singh Vishta
Banawali (Hissar–Haryana)	1973	Ghaggar River	Ravindra Singh Vishta
Balakote	1979	Arabian Sea	George F. Dales
Dhaulavira (Gujarat)	1963-68	—	J.P. Joshi
	1990-91	—	Dr. R.S. Vishta

Wellknown Quotations

"Swarajya is My Birthright"	— Bal Gangadhar Tilak
"Give me blood, I shall give you freedom"	— Netajee Subhash Chandra Bose
"Inqalab Zindabad"	— Bhagat Singh
Saare Jahan Se Achcha, Hindustan Hamara"	— Dr. Mohammed Iqbal
"Dilli Chalo"	— Subhash Chandra Bose
"Sarfaroshi ki tamanna, Ab Hamare Dil Mein Hai."	— Ram Prasad Bismil
"I am socialist by nature".	— Jawahar Lal Nehru
"Go to Vedas"	— Swami Dayanand
"Aaram Haram Hai"	— Jawahar Lal Nehru
"Jai Jawan, Jai Kisan"	— Lal Bahadur Shastri
"Jai Jawan, Jai Kisan, Jai Vigyan"	— Atal Bihari Vajpayee
"Speak less, work more"	— Sanjay Gandhi
"Vijayee Vishwa Tiranga Pyara"	— Shyam Lal Gupta

"Quit India"	— Mahatma Gandhi
"Hindi, Hindu, Hindustan"	— Bharendu Harishchandra
"Purna Swarajya"	— Jawahar Lal Nehru
"Every lathi blow inflicted on my body will prove a nail in British coffin"	— Lala Lajpat Rai
"Jai Hind"	— Subhash Chandra Bose
"Do or die"	— Mahatma Gandhi
"Who lives if India dies"	— Jawahar Lal Nehru
"Vande Mataram"	— Bankim Chandra Chatterjee
"Jana Gana Mana Adhinayaka Jai Hai"	—Rabindranath Tagore
"Hate sin, not the sinner."	— Mahatma Gandhi
"Service of the people is the service of God"	— Swami Vivekananda
"Truth and non-violence are my God."	— Mahatma Gandhi

Battles and Wars in India

War	Year	Result
Battle of Kalinga	(261 B.C.)	Ashoka defeated the king of Kalinga
Second battle of Tarain	(1192 A.D.)	Muhammad Gori defeated Prithviraj Chauhan
First battle of Panipat	(1526 A.D.)	Babar defeated Ibrahim Lodi
Battle of Khanwa	(1527 A.D.)	Babar defeated Rana Sanga
Battle of Chausa	(1539 A.D.)	Shershah Suri defeated Humayun and became ruler of Delhi
Second Battle of Panipat	(1556 A.D.)	Akbar defeated Hemu
Battle of Talikota	(1565 A.D.)	Allied forces of Bijapur, Bidar, Golkunda and Ahamadnagar defeated the King of Vijay Nagar
Battle of Haldighati	(1576 A.D.)	Some historian say that this battle was indecisive but some say that Rana Pratap was defeated by Akbar.
Battle of Palasey	(1757 A.D.)	British forces defeated Nawab of Bengal Sirajudoulla
Battle of Wandiwash	(1760 A.D.)	British forces defeated the French
Third battle of Panipat	(1761 A.D.)	Maratha were defeated by Ahmad Shah Abadali
Battle of Buxar	(1764 A.D.)	British forces defeated the combined forces of Mir Quasim, Shah Alam Mughal empire and Awadh's Nawab
Third Anglo-Maratha War	(1792 A.D.)	Maratha were conclusively defeated
Fourth Anglo-Mysore War	(1799 A.D.)	Tipu Sultan died fighting the British forces
Second Anglo-Sikh War	(1848 A.D.)	British forces annexed Punjab from Sikh rulers
Indo-China War	(1962 A.D.)	China attacked India unilaterally and annexed some area
Indo-Pak War	(1965 A.D.)	Pakistan attacked India but had to suffer severe setbacks
Indo-Pak War	(1971 A.D.)	Pak declared war against India.

* * * * *

10. WORLD GEOGRAPHY

Earth: The earth constitutes land, water and air. Land is made up of rocks and soil. It is distributed in continents and islands. The water found in oceans, seas, lakes, etc. occupies about 2/3 of the earth's surface. The earth is surrounded by a cover of air, called atmosphere, which extends up to several hundred kilometres above its surface.

Shape: In ancient times people believed that the earth was flat in shape. Greek philosopher Pythagoras (6th century BC) was the first person to declare that the earth was round. After careful measurement, the scientists have found that the earth is slightly oblate (flattened at poles) and not exactly round.

Motions: The earth has two motions: *(i) Rotation:* Earth makes a complete round on its axis once each 24 hours (more exactly 23 hours, 56 minutes and 4.09 seconds). It causes days and night on the earth. *(ii) Revolution:* The earth makes a complete round of the Sun in one year. This revolution of earth produces alternate seasons.

Some Facts: **(1)** Equal Day and Night — March 21 and September 23. **(2)** Longest Day — June 21. **(3)** Shortest Day — December 22. **(4)** The sunlight takes eight minutes in travelling from the Sun to the Earth. **(5)** Average speed of the earth in orbit ---- 66,600 miles (107,220 km) per hour. **(6)** Earth's equatorial diameter is about 7926 miles (12,756 km). **(7)** Water (oceans, seas, lakes and rivers) occupies nearly 75 per cent of the surface of the earth. **(8)** Earth's average distance from the Moon — 2,38,857 miles (3,84,400 km). **(9)** Earth's average distance from the Sun — 93 million miles (149.4 million km).

Greenwich Time: It is the local time of the Greenwich observatory in London on 0° meridian. Greenwich time is international standard time.

International Date Line: Half way round the earth from the Greenwich is International Date Line on 180° longitude. It runs down mid-Pacific. It is one day earlier on the east of this line than it is on the west of the line. When it is Monday east of the line, it is Tuesday west of the line.

Zones: On the basis of temperature and distribution of solar heat on the surface of the earth, the earth has been divided into five zones: (1) Torrid Zone, (2) North Temperate Zone, (3) South Temperate Zone, (4) Arctic Zone, and (5) Antarctic Zone.

Continents: Large land masses forming large geographical divisions are called continents. There are seven continents: (1) Asia (29.5%), (2) Africa (20%), (3) Europe (6.5%), (4) North America (16.3%), (5) South America (11.8%), (6) Australia (5.2%), and (7) Antarctica (9.6%).

Highest Mountain Peaks: (1) Everest (Asia-8848 metres), (2) Aconcagua (South America-6960 metres), (3) Mckinley (North America-6194 metres), (4) Kilimanjaro (Africa-5895 metres), (5) Elbrus (Europe-5642 metres), (6) Vinson Massif (Antarctica-5140 metres), (7) Kosciusko (Australia-2228 metres).

Largest Oceans: (1) Pacific Ocean (The largest, covers almost 1/3 of the earth's total area, and the deepest about 6.8 miles at Mariana Trench in western Pacific); (2) Atlantic Ocean, and (3) Indian Ocean. Other seas and gulfs are — the Mediterranean Sea, South China Sea, Bering Sea, Caribbean Sea, East China Sea, Sea of Japan, North Sea, Baltic Sea, Hudson Bay and Gulf of Mexico.

Longest Rivers: (1) Nile (6650 km-Africa), (2) Amazon (6570 km-South America), (3) Mississippi-Missouri (5970 km-North America), (4) Yangtze Kiang (5470 km-Asia), (5) Ob Irtysh (5150 km-Europe), (6) Congo (4666 km-Africa).

Highest Waterfalls: (1) Angel (807 m-Venezuela), (2) Mongefossen (774 m-Norway), (3) Kukenaam (610 m-Venezuela), (4) Ribbon (491 m-USA), (5) King George VI (487 m-Guyana), (6) Upper Yosemite (435 m-USA).

Great Deserts: (1) Sahara (94 lakh sq km-North Africa), (2) Libyan (11.65 lakh sq km-North Africa), (3) Australian (16 lakh sq km-Australia), (4) Gobi (13 lakh sq km-Mongolia), (5) Great Victoria (6,47,000 sq km-Australia), (6) Syrian (5,20,000 sq km Arabia), (7) Arabian (23,30,000 sq km Arabia).

Largest Islands: (1) Greenland (21,75,600 sq km) (2) New Guinea (7,77,000 sq km), (3) Borneo (7,25,545 sq km), (4) Malagasy (5,90,000 sq km), (5) Baffin Island (4,76,070 sq km).

Major Producers of Crops, Minerals and Industrial goods

Coal	China, USA, India, Australia, Indonesia, Russia
Cocoa	Cote d'Ivaire, Ghana, Indonesia, Nigeria
Coffee	Brazil, Vietnam, Columbia, Indonesia
Copper	Chile, Peru, China, USA
Cotton	China, India, USA, Pakistan, Brazil
Gold	China, Australia, Russia, USA, Canada
Grapes	China, Italy, USA, France, Spain
Iron ore	Australia, Brazil, China, India
Jute	India, Bangladesh, China
Manganese	South Africa, China, Australia
Petroleum	Russia, Saudi Arabia, USA, Iraq
Rice	China, India, Indonesia, Bangladesh
Rubber	Thailand, Indonesia, Malaysia, Vietnam, India
Silk	China, India, Uzbekistan, Thailand
Silver	Mexico, Peru, China, Chili
Steel	China, Japan, India, USA
Tea	China, India, Kenya, Sri Lanka
Wheat	China, India, USA, France, Russia
Diamond	Russia, Australia, Congo, Botswana
Tobacco	China, Brazil, India, USA, Indonesia

The Highest, Biggest and Longest in the World

Airport	*Largest*	King Fahd International Airport, Dammon (Saudi Arabia)
Animal	*Tallest*	Giraffe (Average height 6.09 m)
	Largest & Heaviest	Blue Whale (190 tonnes)
	Longest recorded	Boot lace Worm (55 m)
	Fastest	Cheetah (Approximately 100 km/hr)
Bay	*With max. shore line*	Hudson Bay (Canada: 12268 km)
	With maximum area	Bay of Bengal (India: 217 million hc)
Building	*Tallest*	Burj Khalifa in Dubai (818 meter)
Canal	*Big ship (longest)*	Suez Canal (160 km) Busiest Kiel Canal (North Sea)
Church	*Largest*	Basilica of St. Peter (Vatican City Rome–Area 23000 sq. m.)
Continent	*biggest*	Asia (31,845,872 km^2)
	Smallest	Australia Mainland (Area 76,17,930 km^2)

Country,	*Largest in Population*	China (over 139.7 crore)
	Largest in Area	Russia (17,098,242 sq. km)
	With largest electorate	India (over 90 crores)
	Smallest independent	State of Vatican City (0.44 km^2)
Delta	*Largest*	Sundarban's Ganga-Brahmaputra delta (1,05,000 sq. km)
Epic	*Longest*	Mahabharata
Film	*Most Oscars*	Ben Hur (11 Oscars—1959); Titanic (11 Oscars—1998); The Lord of Rings : The Return of the King (11 Oscars—2003).
Island	*Biggest*	Greenland (2,175,600 sq km)
Lake	*Largest*	Caspian Sea (Azerbaijan, Russia, Iran border: 37.18 lakh km^2)
	Deepest	Baikal (Siberia)
	Largest (fresh water)	Superior Lake (USA—Canada border: 82,350 km^2)
Mountain	*Highest peak*	Mt. Everest (8848 m; Nepal)
	Highest range	Himalayas, Asia (upto 4200 m)
	Greatest mountain range	Himalaya-Karakoram (96 out of 109 peaks over 7315 m are here)
Ocean	*Largest and Deepest*	The Pacific (Area: 166,240,000 km^2; Depth: 10,924 m)
Planet	*Biggest*	Jupiter (equatorial diameter 142984 km)
	Brightest, hottest and nearest to Earth	Venus
	Nearest to Sun	Mercury
Plateau	*Highest*	Tibetan Plateau (Central Asia: 4900 m)
Platform	*Longest (rail)*	Shri Siddharoodha Swamiji Railway Station, Hubballi, Karnataka (India)
Religion	*Oldest*	Hinduism
Religion	*Largest*	Christianity
Rivers	*Longest*	(i) Nile (6650 km) (ii) Amazon (6437 km)
Star	*Brightest*	Sirius A (also called Dog Star)
Swimming course	*Longest recognised*	English Channel
Tunnel	*Longest (railway)*	Gotthard Base Rail Tunnel (Switzerland; 57.1 km)
	Largest (road)	Laerdal, Norway (24.51 km)
Wall	*Longest*	Great Wall of China (main length 3460 km; branches length 2860 km)
Waterfall	*Highest*	Salto-Angel (in Venezuela on a branch of river Carrao, 807 m.)

Capital & Currencies

Country	Capital	Currency
* Afghanistan	Kabul	Afghani
* Albania	Tirana	Lek
* Algeria	Algiers	Dinar
* Angola	Luanda	New Kwanza
* Argentina	Buenos Aires	Peso
* Armenia	Yeravan	Dram
* Australia	Canberra	Dollar
* Austria	Vienna	Euro
* Azerbaijan	Baku	Manat
* Bahrain	Manama	Dinar
* Bangladesh	Dhaka	Taka
* Barbados	Bridgetown	Dollar
* Belarus	Minsk	Ruble
* Belgium	Brussels	Euro
* Benin	Porto Novo	Franc
* Bhutan	Thimphu	Ngultrum[1]
* Bolivia	La paz	Dollar
* Botswana	Gaborone	Pula
* Brazil	Brasilia	Real
* Bosnia Herzegovina	Sarajevo	Dinar
* Bulgaria	Sofia	Lev
* Cambodia	Phnom-Penh	Riel
* Canada	Ottawa	Dollar
* Chile	Santiago	Peso
* China	Beijing	Yuan
* Colombia	Bogota	Peso
* Congo	Brazzaville	Franc
* Croatia	Zagreb	Kuna
* Cuba	Havana	Peso
* Cyprus	Nicosia	Euro
* Czech Republic	Prague	Koruna
* Denmark	Copenhagen	Krone
* Ecuador	Quito	Sucre
* Egypt	Cairo	Pound
* Estonia	Tallinn	Euro
* Ethiopia	Addis Ababa	Birr
* Fiji	Suva	Dollar
* Finland	Helsinki	Euro
* France	Paris	Euro
* Georgia	Tbilisi	Lari
* Germany	Berlin	Euro
* Ghana	Accra	Cedi
* Greece	Athens	Euro
* Guatemala	Guatemala City	Quetzal
* Guyana	George Town	Dollar
* Hungary	Budapest	Forint
* Iceland	Reykjavik	Krona
* India	New Delhi	Rupee
* Indonesia	Jakarta	Rupiah
* Iran	Teheran	Rial
* Iraq	Baghdad	Dinar
* Ireland	Dublin	Euro
* Israel	Jerusalem	Shekel
* Italy	Rome	Euro
* Jamaica	Kingston	Dollar
* Japan	Tokyo	Yen
* Jordan	Amman	Dinar
* Kazakhstan	Akmola	Tenge
* Kenya	Nairobi	Shilling
* Korea (S)	Seoul	Won
* Korea (N)	Pyongyang	Won
* Kyrgyzstan	Bishkek	Som
* Kuwait	Kuwait City	Dinar
* Laos	Vientiane	Kip
* Latvia	Riga	Euro
* Lebanon	Beirut	Pound
* Liberia	Monrovia	Dollar
* Libya	Tripoli	Dinar
* Lithuania	Vilnius	Litas
* Luxembourg	Luxembourg	Euro
* Macedonia	Skopje	Dinar
* Malawi	Lilongwe	Kwacha
* Malaysia	Kuala Lumpur	Ringgit
* Maldives	Male	Rufiyaa
* Mali	Bamako	Franc
* Mauritius	Port Louis	Rupee
* Mexico	Mexico City	Peso
* Moldavia	Chisinau	Leu
* Mongolia	Ulan Bator	Tugrik
* Morocco	Rabat	Dirham
* Mozambique	Maputo	Metical
* Myanmar	Nay Pyi Taw	Kyat
* Namibia	Winohoek	Dollar
* Nepal	Kathmandu	Rupee
* Netherlands	Amsterdam	Euro
* New Zealand	Wellington	Dollar
* Nigeria	Abuja	Naira
* Norway	Oslo	Krone
* Oman	Muscat	Rial
* Pakistan	Islamabad	Rupee

Country	Capital	Currency
∗ Panama	Panama City	Balboa
∗ Peru	Lima	New Sole
∗ Philippines	Manila	Peso
∗ Poland	Warsaw	Zloty
∗ Portugal	Lisbon	Euro
∗ Qatar	Doha	Riyal
∗ Romania	Bucharest	Leu
∗ Russia	Moscow	Ruble
∗ Saudi Arabia	Riyadh	Rial
∗ Senegal	Dakar	Franc
∗ Slovakia	Bratislava	Euro
∗ Spain	Madrid	Euro
∗ Sri Lanka	Colombo	Rupee
∗ Sudan	Khartoum	Dinar
∗ Suriname	Paramaribo	Guilder
∗ Sweden	Stockholm	Krona
∗ Switzerland	Berne	Swiss Francs
∗ Syria	Damascus	Pound
∗ South Africa	Capetown (Legislative) Pretoria *(Administrative)*	Rand

Country	Capital	Currency
∗ Tadzhikistan	Dushanbe	Ruble
∗ Taiwan	Taipei	Dollar
∗ Tanzania	Dodoma	Shilling
∗ Thailand	Bangkok	Baht
∗ Tunisia	Tunis	Dinar
∗ Turkiye	Ankara	Lira
∗ Turkmania	Ashikabad	Manat
∗ Uganda	Kampala	Shilling
∗ Ukraine	Kiev	Hyrvnia
∗ United Arab Emirates	Abu Dhabi	Dirham
∗ U.K.	London	Pound Sterling
∗ U.S.A.	Washington	Dollar
∗ Uruguay	Montevideo	Peso
∗ Uzbekistan	Tashkent	Som
∗ Venezuela	Caracas	Bolivar
∗ Vietnam	Hanoi	Dong
∗ Yemen	Sana'a	Rial
∗ Zimbabwe	Harare	Dollar
∗ Congo (Democratic Republic)	Kinshasa	Franc
∗ Zambia	Lusaka	Kwacha

First in the World

First Chinese visitor to India	Fahien
First foreign invader of India	Alexander, the Great (Greek)
First person to climb Mt. Everest	Tenzing Norgay (India) and Edmund Hillary (New Zealand) (1953)
First atom bomb dropped at	Hiroshima (Japan)
First man in the space	Yuri Gagarin (former USSR)
First woman in the space	Valentina Tereshkova (former USSR)
First person to walk in the space	Alexei Leonov (former USSR)
First person to land on the moon	Neil Armstrong (USA)
First and the only woman to have climbed Mt. Everest twice	Santosh Yadav (Indian; May 12, 1992; May 10, 1993)
First person on Mt. Everest without oxygen	Phu Dorjee (Indian; May 9, 1984)
First person to climb Mt. Everest twice	Nawang Gombu
First President of the USA	George Washington
First woman Prime Minister	Sirimavo Bandaranaike (Sri Lanka)
First person to swim across English Channel	Mathew Webb
First woman to swim across English Channel	Gertrude Caroline Ederle
First woman to climb Mt. Everest	Junko Tabei (Japan)
First woman to climb Mt. Everest alone and without oxygen supplies	Alison Hargreaves (Briton: May 13, 1995)

First Aeroplane to fly around the world without refuelling	Voyager (Dec. 1986)
First test-tube Baby	Louise Brown (UK; 1978)
First all-talking Film	Jaz Singer (1927)
First Secretary-General of the UN	Trygve Lie (Norway: 1946-53)
First woman President of the UN General Assembly	Vijayalakshmi Pandit (India: 1953)
First woman to reach North Pole	Ann Bancroft (1986)
First person to reach North Pole	Robert Peary
First person to reach South Pole	Amundsen (1911)
First woman to command Spacecraft in space	Ellin Collins

Popular Names

Popular Name	*Real Name*
Badshah Khan	Abdul Ghaffar Khan
Bapu, Father of Nation	M.K. Gandhi
Bard of Avon	William Shakespeare
Chachaji *or* Panditji	Jawaharlal Nehru
Desert Fox	Gen. Rommel (Germany)
Desh Bandhu	C.R. Das
Father of English Poetry	Geoffrey Chaucer
Fuhrer	Adolf Hitler
Grand Old Man of India	Dadabhai Naoroji
Grand Old Man of Britain	W.E. Gladstone
Gurudev	Rabindra Nath Tagore
Guruji	M.S. Golwalkar
Grand Commoner	Pitt, the younger
Iron Man of India	Sardar Patel
Lady with the Lamp	Florence Nightingale
Lal, Bal, Pal	Lala Lajpat Rai, Bal Gangadhar Tilak, Bipin Chandra Pal
Li-Kwan	Pearl Buck
Little Corporal *or* Man of Destiny	Napoleon Bonaparte
Lokmanya	Bal Gangadhar Tilak
Lok Nayak	Jayaprakash Narain
Mahamana	Pt. Madan Mohan Malaviya
Maid of Orleans	Joan of Arc
Maiden Queen	Queen Elizabeth I
Man of Blood and Iron	Prince Bismark
Netaji	Subhash Chandra Bose
Nightingale of India	Sarojini Naidu
Priyadarshini	Indira Gandhi
Punjab Kesari	Lala Lajpat Rai
Wizard of the North	Walter Scott

Geographical Surnames

Geographical Surname	*Real Name*
Bengal's Sorrow	Damodar River
Blue Mountains	Nilgiri Hills
China's Sorrow	Hwang-Ho
City of Palaces	Kolkata
City of Skyscrapers *or* Empire City	New York
City of Dreaming Spires	Oxford
Cockpit of Europe	Belgium
Dark Continent	Africa
Emerald Isle	Ireland
Eternal City	Rome
Forbidden City	Lhasa (Tibet)
Gateway of India	Mumbai
Gate of Tears	Strait of Bab-el-mandab
Gift of the Nile	Egypt
Granite City	Aberdeen (Scotland)
Hermit Kingdom	Korea
Holy Land	Jerusalem (Israel)
Island of Pearls	Bahrain (Persian Gulf)
Island of Cloves	Zanzibar
Key to the Mediterranean	Gibraltar
Land of Five Rivers	Punjab
Land of Golden Pagoda	Myanmar (Burma)
Land of Kangaroo	Australia
Land of Maple Leaf/Lillies	Canada
Land of Midnight Sun	Norway
Land of Morning Calm	Korea
Land of the Rising Sun	Japan
Land of Thousand Lakes	Finland
Land of Thunderbolt	Bhutan
Land of the White Elephants	Thailand
Manchester of the Orient	Osaka (Japan)
Pearl of the Antilles *or* Sugar Bowl of the World	Cuba
Pink City	Jaipur
Playground of Europe	Switzerland
Queen of the Adriatic	Venice (Italy)
Roof of the World	Pamirs
Sick Man of Europe	Turkey
Venice of the North	Stockholm (Sweden)
Windy City	Chicago
Whiteman's Grave	Guinea Coast of Africa
World's Loneliest Island	Tristan de Cunha

Book	Author
Arthashastra	Kautilya
A Suitable Boy	Vikram Seth
Bhagwat Gita	Ved Vyas
Chidambara	Sumitranandan Pant
Devdas	Sarat Chandra Chatterjee
Diwan-i-Ghalib	Mirza Ghalib
Discovery of India	Jawaharlal Nehru
Essays on Gita	Aurobindo Ghosh
Eternal India	Indira Gandhi
Faces of Everest	Major H.P.S. Ahluwalia
Ganadevata	Tarashankar Bandopadhyaya
Geet Govind	Jaya Dev
Geetanjali	R.N. Tagore
Glimpses of World History	Jawaharlal Nehru
Godaan	Prem Chand
Gul-e-Nagma	Firaq Gorakhpuri
Gunahon ka Devta	Dharmveer Bharti
Harsh Charita	Bana Bhatta
Hindu View of Life	S. Radhakrishnan
Idols	Sunil Gavaskar
India Divided	Dr. Rajendra Prasad
The Judgement	Kuldip Nayyar
Juhi ki Kali	Surya Kant Tripathi 'Nirala'
Justice of Peace ke Aansu	Janardan Prasad Singh
Chand ka Munh Terha Hai	Muktibodh
Kapalkundala	Bankim Chandra Chatterjee
Kadambari	Bana Bhatta
Kagaz Te Kanwas	Amrita Pritam
Kamayani	Jai Shankar Prasad
Kitni Nawon	S.H. Vatsyayan
Kumar Sambhav	Kalidas
Mahabharata	Ved Vyas

Book	Author
Malgudi Days	R.K. Narayan
Manvini Bhavai	Pannalal Patel
Mati Matal	Gopi Nath Mohanty
Meghdoot	Kalidas
Meri Ekyavan Kavitain	Atal Bihari Vajpayee
Meri Sansadiya Yatra	Atal Bihari Vajpayee
Mritunjaya	B.K. Bhattacharya
Mudrarakshasa	Vishakhadatta
My Experiments with Truth	M.K. Gandhi
My Own Boswell	M. Hidayatullah
My Presidential Years	R. Venkataraman
Nisheeth	Uma Shankar Joshi
'No, Sir'	P.G. Mavlankar
One Day Wonders	Sunil Gavaskar
Panchtantra	Vishnu Sharma
Passage to England	Nirad C. Chaudhuri
Prison Diary	Jaya Prakash Narayan
Raghuvansha	Kalidas
Rajtarangini	Kalhana
Ramayana	Balmiki
Ramcharit Manas	Tulsidas
Rukh Te Rishi	Harbhajan Singh
Satyarth Prakash	Swami Dayanand
Sur Sagar	Surdas
The Guide	R.K. Narayan
The Insider	P.V. Narasimharao
The Post Office — *Dak Ghar*	Rabindra Nath Tagore
The God of Small Things	Arundhati Roy
Urvashi	Ram Dhari Singh 'Dinkar'
Yama	Mahadevi Verma
My Country : My Life (Autobiography)	L.K. Advani
The Test of My Life	Yuvraj Singh
Twenty Years in a Decade	Shah Rukh Khan

IMPORTANT BOOKS WRITTEN IN JAIL

Book	Author
My Experiments with Truth	Mahatma Gandhi
Glimpses of World History	Jawaharlal Nehru
Discovery of India	
Gita Rahasya	Lokmanya Bal Gangadhar Tilak

Book	Author
Pilgrim's Progress	John Bunyan
Bible (in German language)	Martin Luther
Les Miserables	Victor Hugo
Long Walk to Freedom	Nelson Mandela

11. FIRST IN INDIA

First in India

Nobel Prize for Literature (1913)	Rabindra Nath Tagore
Nobel Prize for Physics (1929)	C.V. Raman
Nobel Prize for Peace (1979)	Mother Teresa
Nobel Prize for Economics (1998)	Amartya Sen
Special Oscar award winner (1992)	Satyajit Ray
First and the last Indian Governor-General of free India	C. Rajagopalachari
Woman Governor of the State	Smt. Sarojini Naidu
Indian Commander-in-Chief	General K.M. Cariappa
Woman Chief Minister of a State	Smt. Sucheta Kripalani
Woman President of United Nations General Assembly (1954)	Smt. Vijaylakshmi Pandit
President of International Court of Justice	Dr. Nagendra Singh
Woman to swim across the English Channel	Ms. Aarti Saha
Miss Universe	Miss Sushmita Sen
Miss World	Reita Faria
Indian to swim across the English Channel	Mihir Sen
Field Marshal	S.H.F.J. Manekshaw
Indian recipient of Victoria Cross	Khudadad Khan
Indian to conquer Mt. Everest	Sherpa Tenzing, May 29, 1953
Indian male cosmonaut (1984)	Rakesh Sharma
Indian female cosmonaut	Kalpana Chawla (19 Nov., 1997)
Woman to climb Mt. Everest	Miss Bachendri Pal, May 23, 1984
Woman to get Olympic Medal	Karnam Malleswari
Indian to address the UN General Assembly in Hindi	Atal Bihari Vajpayee
Newspaper	Bengal Gazette, Jan 27, 1780
Postage Stamp issued	In 1852
Telegraph line laid	In 1851, Kolkata; Diamond Harbour
Railways run	April 16, 1853; Bombay-Thana
Electric Train run	1925: Bombay-Kurla
Atomic Power Station	Tarapore (Maharashtra)
Passenger-cum-cargo ship made in India	Harshavardhan
Satellite	Aryabhatta (1975)
Rocket	Rohini (1967)
Atomic Reactor	Apsara (1956)
Climb Everest without oxygen	Phu Dorjee (1987)
First film (movie)	Raja Harishchandra (1913)
First film (talkie)	Alam Ara (1931)
Metro Railway	Kolkata Metro Railway

Test-tube baby, scientifically documented	Born on August 6, 1986 at K.E.M. Hospital, Mumbai
TV Centre	At Delhi
Indian to get an Oscar	Bhanu Athaiya
Woman pilot in IAF	Ms Harita Kaur Deol
Cellular Phone	Kolkata, August 1, 1995
Women president of Indian National Congress	Smt. Annie Besant
President of Indian National Congress	W.C. Banerjee (1885)
Indian who passed in I.C.S. Examination	Satendra Nath Tagore
Woman chief justice of High Court	Lila Saith (Himachal Pradesh)
Woman Foreign Secretary	Chokila Iyyar

First Important Officials of India

The Governor-General of free India	Lord Mountbatten
President	Dr. Rajendra Prasad
President (Female)	Pratibha Patil
Vice-President	Dr. S. Radhakrishnan
Prime Minister	Jawahar Lal Nehru
Prime Minister (Female)	Indira Gandhi
Deputy Prime Minister	Sardar Vallabhbhai Patel
Chief Justice	Harilal J. Kania
First Female Judge in Supreme Court	Smt. Meera Sahib Fatima Bibi
Speaker, Lok Sabha	Ganesh Vasudeo Mawlankar
Woman Speaker of Lok Sabha	Meira Kumar
Chief Election Commissioner	Sukumar Sen
Chief of Defence Staff (CDS)	General Bipin Rawat
Female Minister	Raj Kumari Amrit Kaur (Health Minister)
Female Governor	Sarojini Naidu (U.P.)
Female Chief Minister	Sucheta Kripalani (U.P. 1963)
Finance Commissioner	K.C. Niyogi
Leader of Opposition in Lok Sabha (Recognised)	Y.V. Chavan (Congress)
Leader of Opposition in Rajya Sabha (Recognised)	Kamalapati Tripathi (Congress)

Highest, Biggest, Largest & Longest in India

Award for Gallantry, highest	Param Vir Chakra
Award, highest civilian	Bharat Ratna
Bank, with largest number of branches	State Bank of India
Road Bridge, Longest	Bhupen Hazarika Setu, Across Lohit River (9.15 km)
Cattle fair, largest	Sonepur (Bihar)
Cellular Phone, First	Kolkata, August 1, 1995
City, Most Populous	Mumbai
Corridor, Longest	Rameshwaram Temple corridor (4,000 ft.)
Desert, Largest	Thar (Rajasthan)
Dam, Longest	Hirakud Dam (Odisha)

Delta, Largest	Sunderban's Delta
Dome, Largest	Gol Gumbaj (Bijapur)
Dam, Highest	Tihri Dam 261 m. (855 ft.)
Gateway, Highest	Buland Darwaja at Fatehpur Sikri (176 ft.)
Lake, Largest (Fresh water)	Wular Lake (Kashmir)
Literacy, Highest	Kerala (94%)
Museum, Largest	Indian Museum (Kolkata)
Mosque, Biggest	Jama Masjid (Delhi)
Peak, Highest	K-2 (Pak-Occupied Kashmir)
Platform, Longest	Shree Siddharoodha Swamiji Railway Station Hubballi, Karnataka (1507 m. long)
Railway Bridge, Longest	Vembanad Bridge, Kerala (4.6 km)
River, Longest	The Ganges (2525 Km)
Rainfall, Highest (annual mean)	Mowsynram near Cherrapunji (1178 cm)
Road, Longest	NH-44 (3,745 km)
Road-Rail Longest Bridge	Bogibeel bridge, Assam (4.94 km)
State, (Largest population)	Uttar Pradesh
State, Largest (in area)	Rajasthan
State, with maximum forest cover	Madhya Pradesh
State, with maximum density of population	Bihar
Tunnel, Longest (Road)	Dr. Shyama Prasad Mukherjee Tunnel (9.28 kms, J & K)
Tunnel, Longest (Railway)	T-50 Tunnel, Khari-Sumber section (12.77 kms) Jammu & Kashmir.
Minar, Highest	Qutub Minar (Delhi, 72.5 m.)
Waterfall, Highest	Kunchikal Waterfall (Karnataka: 455 m.)
Zoo, Largest	Arignar Anna Zoological Park, Chennai, Tamil Nadu

Table of Precedence

1. President
2. Vice-President
3. Prime Minister
4. Governors of States within their respective states
5. Former Presidents

5A. Deputy Prime Minister

6. Chief Justice of India, Speaker of Lok Sabha
7. Cabinet Ministers of the Union, Chief Ministers of States within their respective States, Deputy Chairman NITI Aayog, Former Prime Ministers. Leaders of opposition in Rajya Sabha and Lok Sabha

7A. Holders of the Bharat Ratna Decoration

8. Ambassadors Extraordinary and Plenipotentiary and High Commissioners of Commonwealth Countries accredited to India, Chief Ministers of States outside their respective States, Governors of States outside their respective states.
9. Judges of the Supreme Court

9A. Chairperson Union Public Service Commission, Chief Election Commissioner, Comptroller & Auditor-General of India.

10. Deputy Chairman Rajya Sabha, Deputy Chief Minister of States, Deputy Speaker Lok Sabha, Members of the NITI Aayog, Minister of State of the Union and Other Minister in the Ministry of Defence.

* * * * *

12. CULTURAL ACTIVITIES

AKADEMIES

There are three akademies for promotion of creative art.

1. **Lalit Kala Akademi, New Delhi:** Established in 1954, the Lalit Kala Akademi strives for the popularisation of Indian art within the country and in various countries of the world through exhibitions, publications, workshops and camps. Every three year it organises the Triennale India, an international exhibition. It publishes research papers on Indian arts. Besides organising seminars, it honours eminent artists. The Akademi has set up regional centres called Rashtriya Lalit Kala Kendras at Lucknow, Kolkata, Chennai and Bhubaneswar and a small office at Mumbai.
2. **Sangeet Natak Akademi, New Delhi:** The Sangeet Natak Akademi, set-up in 1953, aims at the promotion and development of dance, drama and music. It holds seminars and festivals, presents awards to the eminent artists and extends financial assistance to traditional teachers and scholarships to students. It also operates a scheme of exchange of troupes.
3. **Sahitya Akademi, New Delhi:** The Sahitya Akademi, established in 1954, has the main functions of development of Indian letters, setting up high literary standards, translation of literary works of one Indian language into other Indian languages, publication of books on history of literature and criticism, bibliographies and reference books. The Akademy has regional offices at Mumbai, Kolkata, Bengaluru and Chennai.
4. **National School of Drama:** It is one of the top theatre training institutes in the world and only one of its kind in India. It was set up in 1959 under Sangeet Natak Akademi but was later made autonomous organisation in 1975.

SCULPTURE

Archaeological Survey of India, set up in 1861, is responsible for preservation and maintenance of sculptures and historical monuments and manages a number of archaeological museums.

National Archives of India, established in 1891, it is the official custodian of all non-current records of permanent value of the Government of India and its predecessor bodies.

MUSEUMS

They are repositories of the cultural heritage and conserve and preserve historical technical and other materials against decay and transmit them to posterity as records of history.

MUSIC

Main Schools of Classical Music: There are two main schools of classical music, namely, the Hindustani and the Carnatic. The Hindustani school of classical music is in vogue in north-western India, eastern India and northern parts of the South India.

Musical Instruments: They are: Tabla, Mridangam, Pakhawaj, Chandai, Dholak, Veena, Sitar, Sarod, Gootuvadhyam, Sarangi, Flute, Nadaswaram, Shehnai, Shringi and Turahi.

DANCE

India has a very rich tradition of tribal, folk and classical dances.

Classical Dance

Dance	State	Famous Artists
Bharat Natyam	Tamil Nadu	Yamini Krishnamurthy, Rukmini Devi Arundale, Swapna Sundari, Sonal Mansingh, Vaijanti Mala, Mrinalini Sarabhai, Chandralekha, Indrani, Ram Gopal, Bal Saraswati
Kathakali	Kerala	Gopinath, K.K. Nayar, Kunju-Kurup, T.K. Chandu
Kuchipudi	Andhra Pradesh	Sapna Sundari, Raja Reddy, Shobha Nayar, Radha Reddy, Vedantam Satyanarayan, Vimpanti Chinna Satyam.
Kathak	North India	Birju Maharaj, Gopi Krishna, Shambhu Maharaj, Sitara Devi, Vishnu Sharma, Durga Lal, Shobhana Narayan
Odissi	Odisha	Kelucharan Mahapatra, Indrani Rehman, Madhavi Mudgal, Protima Bedi, Samyukta Panigrahi, Sonal Mansingh, Debudas
Manipuri	Manipur	Uday Shankar, Bipin Singh, Suryamukhi, Darohra Jhaveri

Famous Folk-Dance

State/(UT)	Folk Dance
Andhra Pradesh	Dandari, Banjara
Assam	Bihu, Keli Gopal, Sataria
Bihar	Chhau, Magahi, Durga dance
W. Bengal	Kirtan, Kalatri, Asweabadh, Brita, Kalidance
Chhattisgarh	Saila, Karama, Bhagoria
Gujarat	Garba, Rasalila, Tippani, Dandia,
Haryana	Damyal, Lahoor
Himachal Pradesh	Dussehra dance, Hikat, Notio
Jammu & Kashmir	Dumhal
Jharkhand	Jhau, Ghumakudia, Jadur, Sarhul, Soharai, Karama, Vaima, Loojhari, Jat-Jatin, Vidayat
Karnataka	Yakshagan, Dolu Kunitha
Kerala	Mohini Attam, Padayuni
Madhya Pradesh	Lota Nritya, Jawara
Maharashtra	Tamasha, Dahi Handi, Gof, Deepak Dindi
Manipur	Dhol Cholam
Meghalaya	Nongakarem
Nagaland	Bamboo dance
Odisha	Chhau, Maya Shabari, Dalachai
Punjab	Gidda, Bhangra, Panihari
Rajasthan	Thumar, Kathaputali, Tera Tali
Tamil Nadu	Terukalathu, Kabalatam, Kargam, Pulivesham
Tripura	Hazagiri
Uttar Pradesh	Rasalila, Nautanki, Thali, Dhurang, Jhumela, Huraka, Bol.
Uttarakhand	Kajari, Karan
Goa	Dhode Modini

Musical Instruments and Artists

Musical Instrument	Artists	Musical Instrument	Artists
Flute	Hari Prasad Chaurasia, Panna Lal Ghosh, T.R. Mahalingam, N. Ramani, Vijaya Raghava Rao	Sitar	Pandit Ravishankar, Vilayat Khan
		Santur	Shiv Kumar Sharma
		Rudraveena	Zia Mohiuddin Dagar
Tabla	Allah Rakha, Gudai Maharaj, Latif Khan, Zakir Hussain	Pakhawaj	Govind Rao, Anokhe Lal, Kanthi Maharaj
		Mridanga	Palghat R. Raghu, U.S. Burman
Violin	Lalgudi Jayaraman, L. Subramaniam, M.S. Gopal Krishnan, S. Subrahmaniam, V.G. Jog, N. Rajan	Harmonium	Purushottam Walawakar, M. Dhaulpuri
		Guitar	Pt. Vishnu Mohan Bhatt, Brij Bhushan Kalra
Shehnai	Bismilla Khan, Imrat Khan Ali Akbar	Ghatam	T.H. Vinayakaram
Sarod	Khan, Amjad Ali Khan, Alauddin Khan, Saren Rani, Brij Narayan	Janjira	V. Nagarajan
		Symphony	Jubin Mehta

Major Wild Life Sanctuary in India

India is rich in flora and fauna. However, due to increasing population and industrial and commercial activities, there has been acute pressure on forests. The Government has taken several steps to check the sharp fall in the number of these species. Among the measures are declaration of certain habitats as national parks and sanctuaries. 106 national parks and 573 sanctuaries have been established till March 2025, important ones being given below:

Assam: Kaziranga National Park (know for one-horn Rhinoceroses); Manas Sanctuary.

Jharkhand: Hazaribagh National Park; Betla Tiger Reserve Palamau.

Gujarat: Valvadar National Park, Bhavnagar; Marine National Park, Gir Forests.

Himachal Pradesh: Rohla National Park; Motichur Sanctuary.

Jammu & Kashmir: Dachigam Sanctuary.

Karnataka: Bandipur National Park; Bannargheta National Park, Bangalore; Nagorhole National Park, Coorg; Ranganthitto Bird Sanctuary.

Kerala: Eravikulam Rajmallay National Park, Idduki; Periyar Game Sanctuary.

Madhya Pradesh: Kanha National Park; Bandhavgarh National Park, Shahdol; Shivpuri National Park.

Maharashtra: Taloba National Park, Chandrapur; Panch National Park, Nagpur; Borivali National Park, Mumbai; Nawagaon National Park, Bandara; Melghat National Park.

Manipur: Keibul Lamjao National Park.

Odisha: Simlipal, Tiger Sanctuary.

Rajasthan: Sariska Sanctuary; Ghana Bird Sanctuary, Ranthambhor Sanctuary.

Sikkim: Khangchandzenda National Park, Gangtok.

Tamil Nadu: Vedanthangal Bird Sanctuary; Guindy National Park, Chennai; Mudumalai Sanctuary; Kalakad-Munden Thurai Reserve.

Uttar Pradesh: Chandraprabha Sanctuary; Dudhwa National Park, Lakhimpur.

West Bengal: Jaldapara Sanctuary; Sunderbans.

Uttarakhand: Corbett National Park; Nainital.

* * * * *

13. AWARDS

NATIONAL AWARDS

★ **Bharat Ratna:** This is India's highest civilian award. It is given for exceptional work on art, literature, science and recognition of public service of the highest order. Government servants are not eligible for it.

★ **Padma Vibhushan:** The **Padma Vibhushan** is the second-highest civilian award of the Republic of India, preceded by Bharat Ratna and followed by Padma Bhushan. Instituted on 2 January 1954, the award is given for "exceptional and distinguished service", without distinction of race, occupation, position, or sex. The award criteria include "service in any field including service rendered by Government servants" including doctors and scientists, but excludes those working with the public sector undertakings.

During 1 May and 15 September of every year, the recommendations for the award are submitted to the Padma Awards Committee, constituted by the Prime Minister of India. The recommendations are received from all the state and the union territory governments, the Ministries of the Government of India, the Bharat Ratna and previous Padma Vibhushan award recipients, the Institutes of Excellence, the Ministers, the Chief Ministers and the Governors of State, and the Members of Parliament including private individuals. The committee later submits their recommendations to the Prime Minister and the President of India for the further approval. The award recipients are announced on Republic Day.

★ **Padma Bhushan:** The **Padma Bhushan** is the third-highest civilian award in the Republic of India, after the Bharat Ratna and the Padma Vibhushan, but coming before the Padma Shri. It is announced on the occasion of Republic Day of India every year. It is conferred by the President of India at a function held at Rashtrapati Bhavan sometime around March or April. The award was established on 2 January 1954 by the president of India. It is awarded to recognize distinguished service of a high order to the nation, in any field.

★ **Padma Shri: Padma Shri** (also Padmashree) is the fourth highest civilian award in the Republic of India, after the Bharat Ratna, the Padma Vibhushan and the Padma Bhushan. Awarded by the Government of India, it is announced every year on India's Republic Day.

Padma Awards were instituted in 1954 to be awarded to citizens of India in recognition of their distinguished contribution in various spheres of activity including the Arts, Education, Industry, Literature, Science, Sports, Medicine, Social Service and Public Affairs. It has also been awarded to some distinguished individuals who were not citizens of India but did contribute in various ways to India.

The selection criteria have been criticized in some quarters with the claim that many highly deserving artists have been left out in order to favor certain individuals.

On its obverse, the words "Padma", meaning lotus in Sanskrit, and "Shri", a Sanskrit-derived honorific equivalent to 'Mr.' or 'Ms.', appear in Devanagari above and below a lotus flower. The geometrical pattern on either side is in burnished bronze. All embossing is in white gold.

GALLANTRY AWARDS

★ **Param Vir Chakra:** The highest award for bravery or some daring and pre-eminent act of valour or self-sacrifice in the presence of the enemy, whether on land, at sea or in the air.

★ **Mahavir Chakra:** It is the second highest decoration and is awarded for acts of conspicuous gallantry in the presence of the enemy, whether on land, at sea or in the air.

★ **Vir Chakra:** It is the third in order of awards given for acts of gallantry in the presence of enemy, whether on land, at sea or in the air.

★ **Ashok Chakra:** This medal is awarded for the most conspicuous bravery or some daring or pre-eminent act of valour or self-sacrifice on land, at sea or in the air but not in the presence of enemy.

★ **Vishishta Sewa Medal:** It is awarded to personnel of all the three Services in class I, II and III in recognition of distinguished service of the "most exceptional" and "exceptional" and a "high" order respectively. Prefixes *Parma* and *Ati* are added before first two categories of medals respectively.

★ **Jeewan Raksha Padak:** Awarded for meritorious acts or a series of acts of a human nature displayed in saving life from drowning, fire and rescue operations in mines etc.

National Sports Awards

★ **Major Dhyan Chand Khel Ratna Award:** The scheme was launched in the year 1991-92 with the objective of honouring sportspersons to enhance their general status and to give them greater dignity and place of honour in society. Under this scheme, an amount of ₹ 25 lakh is given as award for the most spectacular and outstanding performance by a sportsperson over a period of four years immediately preceding the year in which award is to be given.

★ **Dronacharya Award:** Dronacharya Award is an award presented by ministry of youth Affairs and Sports, Government of India for excellence in sports coaching. The Dronacharya (Lifetime) awardees gets ₹ 15 lakh and Dronacharya (Regular) awardees gets ₹ 10 lakh a bronze statuette of Dronacharya and scroll of honour. The award was instituted in 1985.

★ **Arjuna Award:** The Arjuna Awards are given by the ministry of youth Affairs and sports, government of India to recognize outstanding achievement in National sports. Instituted in 1961 the award carries a cash prize of 15,00,000 a bronze statue of Arjuna and a scroll.

★ **Arjuna Award (Lifetime):** Arjuna Award (Lifetime) is India's highest award for lifetime achievement in sports and games, given by the ministry of youth Affairs and sports, government of India. The award is initiated in 2002. The award carries a cash prize of ₹ 10,00,000 a plaque and a scroll of honour.

★ **Maulana Abul Kalam Azad Trophy:** This trophy was instituted in 1956-57. The top overall performing university in the inter-university tournaments is given the Maulana Abul Kalam Azad (MAKA) Trophy, which is a rolling trophy. A small replica of the MAKA Trophy is also awarded for retention by the university. In addition, the university also gets a cash prize of ₹ 15 lakh. The second and third best universities also receive cash awards amounting to ₹ 5 lakh and ₹ 3 lakh respectively.

Other Awards

★ **Jnanpith Award:** Awarded to outstanding authors of creative literature in any of the Indian languages recognised by the Constitution of India. It was sponsored by the Bharatiya Jnanpith a culturo-literary society founded in 1944 by Shanti Prasad Jain, an eminent industrialist.

★ **Sahitya Akademi Award:** It is awarded for outstanding literary works and comprises a cash prize of ₹ 1,00,000 in each of the 22 languages mentioned in the Eighth schedule of the Constitution and Rajasthani and English that it supports and a copper plaque.

★ **Saraswati Samman:** The award is given by K.K. Birla Foundation to an outstanding author for his literary work in any Indian language mentioned in the Eighth Schedule of the Constitution and published during the last 10 years.

★ **Dada Saheb Phalke Award:** The prestigious Dada Saheb Phalke Award is given to the persons for outstanding contribution to the growth and development of Indian cinema. First presented in 1969, the award was introduced by the government of India to commemorate Dadasaheb Phalke's contribution to Indian Cinema. Phalke, who is popularly known as and often regarded as a the Father of Indian Cinema was an Indian film-maker who directed India's first-length feature film, Raja Harishchandra. The first recipient of the award was actress Devika Rani, who was honoured at the 17th National film Awards.

★ **Indira Gandhi Award:** The award has been instituted for promoting national integration and understanding amongst the religious groups, communities and ethnic groups of India.

★ **Gujar Mal Modi Award:** The award carries ₹ 2.01 lakh as cash prize, apart from a silver shield and a scroll and is given to the best scientist of the year who makes an outstanding contribution to research resulting in new innovative technology.

★ **Vachaspati Puraskar:** K.K. Birla Foundation's prestigious Vachaspati Puraskar carries a cash award of ₹ 1,50,000 for outstanding Sanskrit works published during the last ten years.

★ **Bhartendu Harishchandra Awards:** The Bhartendu Harishchandra Awards were instituted in 1983, by the Ministry of Information and Broadcasting for original Hindi writing on any subject in mass communications like journalism, publication, advertising, broadcasting films, etc.

★ **Kabir Samman:** The award is conferred annually on a person of literature of very high order on the basis of his or her superb creativity and consistent commitment to the most recent and latest trends of literary creation in any of the Indian languages. The award carries ₹ 3 lakh and a letter of citation.

INTERNATIONAL AWARDS

★ **Nobel Prizes:** The most prestigious award in the world is supported by the Nobel Foundation of US. This award was set up in 1900 under the will to Alfred Bernhard Nobel (1833-96). Alfred Nobel was an unmarried. Swedish scientist and chemical engineer who discovered Nitroglycerin ($C_3H_5N_3O_9$) and its use in the manufacture of dynamite in 1966. The interest accrued on the fortune left by him is divided annually among the persons who have made outstanding contribution in science, literature, peace and economics. Swedes found out about the prizes only after his death in 1896. When they read his will in which he had donated the annual income from his fortune to support the awards. In his will he ordered that 'the most worthy shall receive the prize, whether he is Scandinavian or not. This led to his criticism as being unpatriotic for not reserving the prizes only for Swedes.

Nobel Foundation's Prize Awarding Bodies

(*i*) The Royal Swedish Academy of Sciences, awards the Nobel prize in Physics and Chemistry.
(*ii*) The Nobel Assembly of Karolinska Chirugical Institute. Sweden, awards the Nobel Prize in Medicine and Physiology.
(*iii*) The Swedish Academy awards the Prize in Literature.
(*iv*) The Committee of the Norwegian Parliament awards the Prize for Peace.
(*v*) The Bank of Sweden awards the Nobel Prize in Economics.

★ **Ramon Magsaysay Award:** The Raman Magsaysay Award, named after a Philippines President, who died in an air crash in 1957, is given annually to Asian nationals or institutions who have made worthy contributions to public service, community leadership, journalism, literature and the creative arts and international understanding. It carries a gold medal, a certificate and US$ 50,000. It is awarded on August 31, every year.

- **Pulitzer Prize:** Instituted in 1970 and named after the US publisher Joseph Pulitzer (1847-1911). It is conferred annually in the United States for accomplishment in journalism, literature and music under the management to the Pulitzer Prize Board at Columbia University.
- **Man Booker Prize:** Instituted in 1968, it is the highest literary award set up by the Booker Company and the British Publishers Association along the lines of the Pultizer Prize, of USA, worth £ 20,000 (1992). The Booker Prize has only been shared in 1974 and 1992. Since 2002, it has been known as the **'Man Booker Prize'**, reflecting the sponsorship by an investment company, the Man Group plc. The winner receives £ 50,000 and both the winner and the shorlisted authors are guaranteed a world wide readership plus a dramatic increase in book sales.
- **Oscar Awards:** The annual Oscar presentation has been held since 1929. After three-quarters of a century of recognizing excellence in cinema achievement, the annual presentation of the Oscars has become the Academy of Motion Picture Arts and Sciences' most famous activity.
- **Kalinga Award:** The award given for popularisation of science is an international award conferred annually by the United Nations Educational, Scientific and Cultural Organisation (UNESCO) to a person with a distinguished career of service in the interpretation of science and research to the public. The award was instituted in 1952 at the initiative of Mr Biju Patnaik the founder of the Kalinga Foundation Trust in Odisha.
- **Grammy Award:** The Grammy Foundation was established in 1989 to cultivate an awareness, appreciation and advancement of the contribution of recorded music American culture from the and technical legends of the past to the still unimagined musical breakthroughs of the future generations of the music professionals. The Grammy Foundation works in partnership with its founder, the Recording Academy, to bring national attention to important issues such as the value and impact of music and arts education and the urgency of preserving our rich cultural legacy.

Highest Honours of Some Countries

Country	Highest Honour	Country	Highest Honour
India	Bharat Ratna	Britain	Member of British Empire, Victoria Cross
Pakistan	Nishan-e-Pakistan		
Kuwait	Mubarak-Al-kabir Medal	Japan	Order of Moulovenice Sun
Saudi Arabia	Shah Abdul Aziz Medal	Denmark	Order of Diana Brog
Argentina	The Order of Sona Martin	France	Legend of Honour
Nicaragua	Augusto-Caesar Sandino Order	America	Presidential Medal of Freedom
Vietnam	The order of the Golden Star	Germany	Pore Lee Merit Iron Cross
Hungary	The Order of Banner	The Netherlands	Netherlands Lion

✱✱✱✱✱

14. COMPUTER

The computer is the system of that electronic device through which various informations are processed on the basis of a definite set of instructions called program and mathematical (numerical) and non-mathematical both types of informations are processed. The first mechanical computer was composed or fabricated by Blaise Pascal in 1642 and it is called Pascalene. But in 1833, Charles Babbage first time conceived an automatic calculator or computer. Charles Babbage is called the father of modern computer. Herman made an electronic tabulating machine based on punch cards which operates automatically. In 1937, first mechanical computer mark-I was fabricated by Howard Akeen. The most outstanding contribution in the development of modern computer goes to John Wan Newmaan who brought the 2nd revolution in the area of computer in 1951. He discovered EDVAC (Electronic Discrete Variable Automatic Computer) and utilised the stored program and the binary number system in the computer.

Functions of Computer

1. Collection and composition (input) of datas;
2. Storage of datas.
3. Processing of datas.
4. Retrieval or output of the proccessed informations and datas.

Units of Computer

1. Input unit.
2. Central processing unit–CPU.
3. External Memory unit.
4. Output unit.

The CPU of the computer is called brain of the computer and sometimes CPU is also called Micro Processor of the computer. The data is entered through the input unit in the computer and through the central processing unit with the help of External Memory Unit datas are arranged and processed. Ultimately by the output unit these datas or informations are issued or released.

Parts of Computer

- **Monitor :** The monitor of the computer is like a television in which the picture appears in the form of doted points on the screen and these are called pixcels.
- **Hard Disc and Floppy Disc :** The Hard Disc is the permanent disc in the computers while the Floppy Disc is the disc utilised when datas or informations are to be transferred from one computer to another.
- **Mouse :** The mouse of the computer is like the remote control of TV through which computer is directly regulated or controlled without utilising the key-board.
- **Printer :** The printer is a device which prints any documents or processed informations of the computer.

Some high level languages

1. **FORTRAN :** This language was developed for solving the mathematical formulae very quickly and conveniently.
2. **COBOL :** This language was developed for the commerical purposes. For the processing of this language a group of sentences is selected called paragraph and all paragraphs composed are called a section, while all sections composed are called a division.
3. **BASIC :** In basic a definite part of the prescribed instruction is only inserted in the computer.

4. **ALGOL :** This was basically fabricated and designed for the complex algebraic calculations.
5. **PASCAL :** It is an amplified and modified form of ALGOL.
6. **COMAL :** This computer language is used for the students of secondary level.
7. **LOGO :** This language is used for children and kids for drawing Graphic line diagrams.
8. **PROLOG :** This language is developed in 1973 in France and this language is used for Artificial Intelligence which is capable and equivalent to the logical program.
9. **FORTH :** This language was invented by Charles Mure which is frequently used in all types of the works in the computer.

Computer Virus

The computer virus is an electronic code which is used to abolish or erradicate the inclusive informations or programs of the computer. Some important computer viruses are Micheleanjalo, Dork Avangor, kilo, filip, Macmug, Scores, Casecade, Jeruslem, Date crime, Coloumbs crime, Internet virus, Pachcom, Pach EXE, COM-EXE, Marizuana, C-brain, bloody, Chenge Mungu and Desi etc.

Computer Networking

There are two types of networkings which are usually occur—Local Area Networking (LAN) and Wide Area Networking (WAN). By LAN all the computers of the same buildings are connected like the computers of university premises, computers of offices etc. By WAN all the comptuers of a large area are connected like the computers of all the offices of a city or town etc. In India a very large computer network namely INDONET has been installing through which all the main towns and cities has to be interlinked.

Computer Terminology

- **Bit :** The bit is a unit of measurement of the electronic data. One bit is either 0 or 1 but not both. On composing 8 bits, 1 byte is formed.
- **Bug :** The Bug is the error in the computer program or system and its eradication is called Debug.
- **Byte :** Total eight bits compose a byte. Thus 8 bits = 1 byte.
- **CD-ROM :** A CD like of music CD in which data can be stored substantially called CD-ROM. In a CD with comparison to floppy extremely more datas can be stored but one problem in it is that one time recorded data can not be deleted or modified.
- **Chip :** It is a thin slice on which by a special mechanism a circuit is designed which is normally made from Silicon.
- **Memory System :** The place where computer data and program are temporarily kept is called Memory system. Usually memory is implied from RAM.
- **Modem :** The device which converts digital signals into analogue signals and vice-versa is called Modem.
- **RAM :** It is Random Access Memory (a place) where datas to be processed are kept temporarily and it is unstable memory.
- **ROM :** It is Read Only Memory and it is stable or Non-valatile memory which doesn't ended after power off.
- **Scanner :** It is a device through which graphic image is transformed to digital image and the scanners are of usually two types one desktop and another hand operating.

Programing

Computers perform phenomenal feats of calculation, but they do not do so in a complicated way. They actually carry out very simple operations, such as addition and subtraction. They achieve their fantastic computing power by carrying out these operations at incredible speed.

The programme, or set of instructions for operating the computer, is therefore written as a sequence of very simple steps. (See box below) Several computer languages have been developed for different applications, including BASIC, COBOL, FORTRAN and PASCAL. Writing programmes is very skilled and time-consuming work. But for most typical computer applications ready-written programmes are available, called "packages".

* * * * *

15. SPORTS

Important Cups & Trophies

International

Cup/Trophy	Sport	Cup/Trophy	Sport
American Cup	Yacht Racing	*Walker Cup*	Golf
Ashes	Cricket	*Westchester Cup*	Polo
Benson and Hedges	Cricket	*Wightman Cup*	Lawn Tennis
Canada Cup	Golf	*World Cup*	Cricket
Colombo Cup	Football	*World Cup*	Hockey
Corbitton Cup	Table Tennis (Women)	*Reliance Cup*	Cricket
Davis Cup	Lawn Tennis	*Rothman's Trophy*	Cricket
Derby	Horse Race	*William's Cup*	Basketball
Grand National	Horse Streple Chase Race	*European Champions Cup*	Football
Jules Rimet Trophy	World Soccer Cup	*Eisenhower Cup*	Golf
King's Cup	Air Races	*Essande Champions Cup*	Hockey
Merdeka Cup	Football	*Rene Frank Trophy*	Hockey
Ryder Cup	Golf	*Grand Prix*	Table Tennis
Swaythling Cup	Table Tennis (Men)	*Edgbaston Cup*	Lawn Tennis
Thomas Cup	Badminton	*Grand Prix*	Lawn Tennis
Uber Cup	Badminton (Women)	*World Cup*	Weightlifting
U. Thant Cup	Tennis		

National

Cup/Trophy	Sport	Cup/Trophy	Sport
Agarwal Cup	Badminton	*C.K. Naidu Trophy*	Cricket
Agha Khan Cup	Hockey	*Chakola Gold Trophy*	Football
All India Women's Guru Nanak Championship	Hockey	*Divan Cup*	Badminton
Bandodkar Trophy	Football	*Deodhar Trophy*	Cricket
Bangalore Blues Challenge Cup	Basketball	*Duleep Trophy*	Cricket
Barna-Bellack Cup	Table Tennis	*D.C.M. Cup*	Football
Beighton Cup	Hockey	*Durand Cup*	Football
Bombay Gold Cup	Hockey	*Dhyan Chand Trophy*	Hockey
Burdwan Trophy	Weightlifting	*Dr. B.C. Roy Trophy*	Football (Junior)
Charminar Trophy	Atheletics	*Ezra Cup*	Polo
Chadha Cup	Badminton	*F.A. Cup*	Football
		G.D. Birla Trophy	Cricket
		Ghulam Ahmed Trophy	Cricket
		Gurmeet Trophy	Hockey

OLYMPIC GAMES

First of all these games were held by the Greeks in 776 B.C. on Mount Olympus in honour of the Greek God Zeus. In this way, the history of Olympic Games is about twenty eight hundred years old. These games continued to be held every four years until 394 A.D. When these games were stopped by a royal order of the emperor of Rome. The modern Olympic Games which started in Athens in 1896, are the result of the devotion and dedication of a French educator Baron Pierre de Coubertin and the first Olympic meet in the modern series was held in 1896 in Athens, the Capital of Greece. Since then, they are being held every four years except for breaks during world wars. The Olympic flag is white in colour with five coloured rings, each ring symbolic of a continent. Summer as well as winter Olympics are held in the same year.

ASIAN GAMES

After the Second World War, most of the Asian Countries gained independence. On the lines of Olympic Games, Asian Games were planned every four years. India hosted the first Asian Games in 1951.

COMMONWEALTH GAMES

The Commonwealth Games are held every four years, in the year in which Asian Games are held. All the Commonwealth Countries (former colonies of Britain) can take part in it. The first Commonwealth Games were held in 1930 at Hamilton (Canada).

CRICKET WORLD CUP

The first Cricket World Cup was organised in England in 1975. A separate women's Cricket World Cup has been held every 4 years since 1973. Australia is the winner of 2023 Cricket World Cup.

HOCKEY WORLD CUP

The first Hockey World Cup was organised in Barcelona (Spain) in 1971. Women's Hockey World Cup has been held since 1974.

FOOTBALL WORLD CUP

The Football World Cup is organised by FIFA (Federation of International Football Association). The World Cup is called 'Jules Rimet Cup' named after the name of FIFA President Jules Rimet. The first Football World Cup was organised in Uruguay in 1930.

Personalities Associated with Sports

- **Athletics:** Carl Lewis, Linford Christy, Ben Johnson, Calvin Smith, Edwin Moses, Sergei Bubka, Sebestian Coe, Florence Griffith Joyner, Rosa Mota, Harold Schmidt, Milkha Singh, P.T. Usha, Shiny Abraham, Vandana Rao, Jesse Owens, Jyotirmoy Sikdar.
- **Boxing:** Cassius Clay (Mohammad Ali), Joe Frazier, Mike Tyson, Larry Holmes, Frank Bruno, Henry Cooper, Archie Moore, Evander Holyfield, George Foreman.
- **Badminton:** Prakash Padukone, Syed Modi, Dinesh Khanna, Jamie Paulson, Nandu Natekar, Liem Swie King, Saina Nehwal, P.V. Sindhu.
- **Billiards:** Wilson Jones, Geet Sethi, Michael Ferreira, Pankaj Advani.
- **Chess:** Boris Spausky, Gary Kasparov, Anatoly Karpov, Victor Korchonoi, Vishwanathan Anand, Konern Humpy, Parveen Thipsay, Rohini Khadilkar.
- **Cricket:** Sunil Gavaskar, Bishen Singh Bedi, Kapil Dev, Mohd. Azharuddin, Sachin Tendulkar, G.R. Vishwanath, Lala Amarnath, Ajit Wadekar, B.S. Chandrashekhar, E.A.S. Prasanna, S. Venkatraghvan, Don Bradman, Richard Hadlee, Gary Sobers, Ian Botham, Vivian Richards, Clive Llyod, Dilip Sardesai, Charles Griffith, Imran Khan, Mushtaq Mohammad, Geoff Boycott, Tony Greg, Wasim Akram, Richie Benaud, Michael Holding, Greg Chappell, Javed Miandad, Vijay Manjrekar, M.A.K. Pataudi, S.M.H. Kirmani, Frank Worrell, Bill Lawry, Clive Rice, Mark Taylor, Joel Garner, Arjuna Ranatunga, Arvinda De'Silva, Saurav Ganguly,

Virat Kohli, M.S. Dhoni, Ajit Agarkar, Jacques Kallis, John Traicos, Brian Mcmillan, W.R. Hammond, Sanath Jaisurya.

- **Hockey:** Dhyan Chand, Ashok Kumar, Ajit Singh, Pargat Singh, Pritpal Singh, Zafar Iqbal, Shankar Laxman, Mervyn Fernandes, Mohammad Shahid, R. Charlesworth, Balbir Singh, Terry Walsh, Kishan Lal, Udlam Singh, Dhanraj Pillai.
- **Football:** Pele, Diego Maradona, Franz Beckenbour, Socrates, Raud Gullit, Garry Linekar, Emilo Butraguino, Coreca, P.C. Bannerji, Arunlal Ghosh, Chuni Goswami, Inder Singh, Davor Suker, Ronaldo, Rivaldo, Deschamps.
- **Tennis (Lawn):** Bjorn Borg, Jimmy Connors, John Mcenroe, Ivan Lendl, Pete Sampras, Billie Jean Kings, Chris Evert Lloyd, Martina Navratilova, Steffi Graf, Stefan Edberg, Andre Agassi, Michael Chang, Ramesh Krishnan, Boris Becker, Leander Paes, Ramanathan Krishnan, Zeeshan Ali, Vijay Amritraj, Anand Amritraj, Jaideep Mukherjee, Rod Laver, Roy Emerson, Naresh Kumar, Premjit Lall, John Newcombe, Martina Hingis, Arantxa Sanchez Vicario, Mary Pierce, Jana Novotna,Rozer Federer.
- **Golf:** Greg Norman, Jack Nikalus, Sandy Lyle, Seve Bellestros, Nick Faldo, Nick Price, Sher Ali, Jeeve Milkha Singh, S. Choudhary, R.K. Pitamber, Vikramjit Singh.
- **Gymnastics:** Nadia Comaneci, L. Latynina, V. Kaslavska, E. Szebo, W. Kim. Y. Ma, Y. Shrusunova, Daniela Silivas, A. Braglia, V. Chukarin, N. Andrianov, Sergi Kharkhov.
- **Swimming:** Arti Gupta, Arun Kumar Shaw, Baidyanath, Dawn Frazer, Mihir Sen, Aarti Saha, Mark Spitz.
- **Wrestling:** Dara Singh, Bhim Sen, Mukhtiar Singh, Sudesh Kumar, Chandagi Ram.

Stadia in Various Cities of India

- **Delhi:** Ambedkar Stadium, Arun Jaitley Stadium, Jawaharlal Nehru Stadium, Indira Gandhi Indoor Stadium, Shivaji Stadium, National Stadium.
- **Mumbai:** Brabourne Stadium, Wankhede Stadium.
- **Kolkata:** Eden Gardens, Salt Lake Stadium, Ranjit Stadium, Subhas Sarovar.
- **Chennai:** Nehru Stadium, Chidambaram Stadium, Chepauk.
- **Cuttack:** Barabati Stadium.
- **Kanpur:** Green Park.
- **Jamshedpur:** Keenan Stadium.
- **Nagpur:** Vidarbha CA Ground
- **Jaipur:** Swai Mansingh Stadium
- **Gwalior:** Roop Singh Stadium
- **Pune:** Nehru Stadium
- **Vadodara:** Moti Bagh Stadium
- **Patna:** Moin-ul-Haq Stadium
- **Hyderabad:** Lal Bahadur Stadium
- **Patiala:** Yaduvindra Stadium.
- **Bengaluru:** Chinnaswami Stadium.
- **Siliguri:** Kanchenjunga Stadium.
- **Faridabad:** Mayur Stadium.
- **Vishakhapatnam:** Indira Priyadarshini Stadium.

*****

MULTIPLE CHOICE QUESTIONS

GENERAL AWARENESS

1. The part of the Sun, which is visible during eclipses only, is known as
A. photosphere
B. chromosphere
C. corona
D. all the parts are visible with naked eye

2. Sphygmomanometer is used for
A. measuring the brain pulse of a patient
B. measuring the systolic and diastolic blood pressures of man
C. measuring the amount of blood in a human body
D. measuring the haemoglobin count in a human body

3. The most abundant gas in air is
A. nitrogen B. hydrogen
C. oxygen D. ozone

4. The most commonly found acid in nature is
A. hydrochloric acid B. sulphuric acid
C. lactic acid D. acetic acid

5. This bomb is used to destroy living beings but would not damage the buildings and other property
A. napalm bomb B. neutron bomb
C. hydrogen bomb D. None of the above

6. Electrical energy is measured in terms of units which are also termed as
A. KW B. KWH
C. WH D. KVAR

7. In cold countries, the radiator water of cars is mixed with glycerol. This is done to
A. increase the specific heat of water
B. reduce the freezing point of water
C. improve the engine efficiency
D. glycerol is not added in radiator water

8. If the Richter scale shows a value of 7.2, then the seismograph indicates
A. an earthquake of low intensity
B. an earthquake of very high intensity
C. an earthquake of moderate intensity
D. either A or C

9. The theory of origin of species is based primarily on
A. the process of biological evolution
B. the process of natural selection
C. the evolution of life from the oceans
D. the evolution of man from apes

10. Common coal used in our households is
A. Anthracite B. Bituminous coal
C. Lignite D. All of the above

11. Some recent findings on moon, which point out towards the possibility of settlement of man on moon, include
A. nil atmospheric gases
B. ice reserves on the poles
C. micro-organisms
D. None of the above

12. Viagra is a medicine for
A. treatment of AIDS
B. treatment of female fertility
C. treatment of male impotency
D. treatment of Lukaemia

13. Rickets is a disease which is caused by the deficiency of
A. Vitamin A B. Riboflavin
C. Vitamin C D. Vitamin D

14. When a ship enters waters of the sea from a river, then its level
A. rises as the sea water is saline and hence bouyancy force is more
B. decreases as ocean is a large mass of water
C. remains the same as water is the same for the river and the sea
D. None of the above

15. The major constituent of pearl is
A. calcium carbonate
B. calcium oxide and ammonium chloride
C. organic mass
D. calcium carbonate and silica

16. A healthy person needs ..... calories per day.
A. 2200 B. 2400
C. 2500 D. 1800

17. The value of one (marine) Naut is
A. 1951 metre per hour
B. 1852 metre per hour
C. 2305 metre per hour
D. 1860 metre per hour

18. Acid and base combine to form
A. salt and nitrogen
B. nitrogen and oxygen
C. salt and water
D. acid and alkali

19. Cellulose could be obtained from
A. wood and cotton B. silk and cotton
C. paper and silk D. wood and silk

20. ELISA test is done for the detection of
A. cancer B. AIDS
C. diabetes D. None of the above

21. Triple Antigen, prevents
A. small pox, malaria, whooping cough
B. tetanus, diphtheria, small pox
C. whooping cough, tetanus, polio
D. diphtheria, tetanus, whooping cough

22. A freely falling body
A. would fall towards the surface of the earth
B. would have no weight
C. would have one half of its original weight
D. None of the above

23. If the motor neurons of the spinal cord of a child are damaged, then he would develop the following disease.
A. Rickets B. Polio
C. Diphtheria D. Jaundice

24. Which one of the following is not a part of the balanced diet?
A. Vitamins B. Carbohydrate
C. Proteins D. Alcohol

25. Which statement is not correct in connection with human physiology?
A. The length of the small intestine is 7 metres and its diameter is 2.5 cm.
B. There are 639 muscles in a human body
C. An infant breathes 45 times per minute whereas a six year old child breathes 25 times per minute
D. The weight of the adult human brain is nearly 700 gms

26. The bottles of beer are not kept in the deep freezer because
A. beer is an alcohol which could burst under conditions of low temperature
B. alcohol could damage the deep freezer due to its corrosive action if the bottles break accidently
C. water content in beer gets converted into ice which expends (after change of state from water to ice) and this could lead to bursting of beer bottles
D. the low temperature could degrade the beer and hence, it may not good remain for consumption

27. Rocket works on the basis of
A. principle of conservation of momentum
B. principle of relativity
C. principle of conservation of mass
D. principle of conservation of energy

28. Which one of the following groups is more closely related from the viewpoint of taxonomy?
A. silverfish, starfish, cuttlefish
B. earthworm, seahorse, hookworm
C. housefly, dragonfly, butterfly
D. None of the above

29. Red blood corpuscles are produced in
A. liver B. spleen
C. bone marrow D. kidneys

30. The disease for which the first oral drug has been developed for treatment.
A. Cancer B. Pneumonid
C. Small pox D. Plauge

31. E-comm is a short form of
A. Engineering Commercial
B. Electronic Commercial
C. Electronic Commerce
D. None of the above

32. High AC voltages are used for transmitting electric power because
A. at high voltages, current is low and hence, losses are low

B. the transmission of power is quicker
C. the high voltages a consume lesser materials for transmission
D. None of the above

33. There is a hole in the boat through which, water is seeping into the boat. Just before the boat capsizes
A. water level would decrease
B. water level would increase
C. water level would remain the same
D. None of the above

34. During which month, the rate of rotation of the earth on its axis is the fastest?
A. December
B. May
C. the rate of rotation is fixed
D. It is fastest when the earth is closest to the Sun.

35. The time taken by the Sun rays to reach the earth is
A. 9 minutes B. 10 minutes
C. 7 minutes D. 8 minutes

36. The outer planets are
A. Moon, Earth, Mercury, Venus
B. Jupiter, Saturn, Uranus, Earth, Mars
C. Jupiter, Uranus, Saturn, Neptune
D. None of the above

37. According to the astrophysicists
A. the universe is mobile and expanding
B. the universe is heading for a collision with another universe
C. the universe is stationary
D. the doomsday of universe is near due to the formation of many new black holes

38. Which is popular as the White City?
A. New York B. Belgrade
C. Bangalore D. Bab-el-mandab

39. The national currency of Haiti is
A. Rupiah B. Gourde
C. Quetzal D. Dong

40. Which one is not a news agency of India?
A. UNI
B. PTI
C. Hindustan Samachar
D. Reuters

41. The abundant element of the earth's atmosphere is:
A. Oxygen B. nitrogen
C. hydrogen D. CO_2

42. The first talking movie of India was ..... and the first silent movie of India was .....
A. Aan, Aawara
B. Raja Harish Chandra, Alamara
C. Alamara, Raja Harish Chandra
D. Purana Mandir, Raja Harish Chandra

43. Hair becomes grey because
A. rays of the Sun force it to become grey
B. the quantity of melanin is reduced in human body with growing age
C. there is a lack of vitamins in the body due to growing age
D. None of the above

44. Salaries of Supreme Court judges are drawn from:
A. Law Ministry Grants
B. Consolidated Fund of India
C. Home Ministry Grants
D. Parliamentary Grants

45. The term "Paper-gold" is associated with
A. deficit budgeting
B. loans from the World Bank
C. Special Drawing Rights (SDRs) from the IMF
D. None of the above

46. TRAI refers to
A. Terresteral Remote Sensing Authority of India
B. Telecommunication Research Authority of India
C. Transport Regulatory Authority of India
D. Telecom Regulatory Authority of India

47. NSDL is an organisation in India which
A. provides security to depositors
B. accepts deposits from recognised bodies
C. provides data security for on-line computer systems
D. None of the above

48. The enzyme pepsin converts
A. proteins into peptones
B. fats to amino acids
C. carbohydrates to sugars
D. proteins to amino acids

49. Who among the following is not a winner of the PVC?
A. Bana Singh

B. Nirmal Jeet Singh Sekhon
C. Somnath Sharma
D. Shanti Swaroop Rana

50. Which one of the following pairs is not correct?
A. Narmada – Betul district
B. Krishna – near Mahabaleshwar
C. Chambal – near Mhow
D. Godavari – Nashik district

51. The Japanese art of flower arrangement is known as
A. Bonsai B. Ongami
C. Ikebota D. None of the above

52. The meaning of the Latin word *Vive Rex* is
A. Long live the king!
B. Let the Nation Live
C. A middle course
D. Nothing wrong here

53. The permanent station of India in Antarctica is known as
A. *Vikalp*
B. Antarctica India Station
C. *Maitri*
D. *Dakshin Yamunotri*

54. A man dies due to electrocution because
A. electric current passes through his body to earth which leads to sudden contraction and expansion of muscles (including heart muscles) and this, alongwith development of heat in the body, leads to heart failure.
B. there is no resistance offered by the body
C. the body allows the current to flow through the blood which cannot circulate any longer
D. None of the above

55. "Blue Dwarfs" are
A. members of the Russian circus
B. warriors of Mongolia
C. young stars of the universe
D. naval officers in the high seas

56. What is a fly leaf?
A. thin paper sheet for making packaging material
B. a blank page at the beginning or end of a book
C. a marker in a book
D. a sheet of paper next to the main title of the book

57. Who is associated with the theory of inheritance of acquired characters?
A. Spencer B. Mandeleev
C. Lamarck D. All of the above

58. Ligaments and tendons in the body are made up of
A. skeletal tissue B. muscular tissue
C. connective tissue D. epithelial tissue

59. A cell membrane is
A. completely permeable
B. impermeable
C. semi-permeable
D. None of the above

60. The tenure of the non-permanent members of the UN Security Council is
A. one year
B. three years
C. two years
D. there is no fixed tenure

61. Why proper earthing is necessary?
A. It reduces the consumption of electricity
B. It allows the current to flow through the earth wire and into the earth, thus protecting the person
C. It allows the appliance to operate efficiently
D. None of the above

62. Which one of the following items has not been included in the minimum needs programme?
A. unemployment allowance
B. rural water supply
C. rural electrification
D. adult education

63. This is not the principle organ of digestion and absorption in the human body.
A. small intestine B. stomach
C. large intestine D. Both A and B

64. Which are the two stars which appear as morning stars in the Eastern sky and evening stars in the Western sky?
A. Jupiter and Mars
B. Mars and Venus
C. Saturn and Mercury
D. Mercury and Venus

65. Which planet rotates on its axis from East to West?
A. Mercury B. Jupiter
C. Earth D. Venus

66. The chemical compound present in the stone of human kidney is
A. calcium phosphate B. calcium carbonate
C. silica D. calcium oxalate

67. Which one of the following diseases would be caused by bacterial infection?
A. tetanus B. rabies
C. cancer D. malaria

68. India On-line Limited is
A. an advertising agency
B. a reservation office
C. an information service
D. an internet services provider

69. CTBT is related to
A. economic sanctions imposed by the USA on India
B. the codename of Pokharan-II blasts
C. the nuclear test ban treaty which India is being forced to adhere to
D. codename of Pakistani nuclear arsenal

70. The disagreement between Lok Sabha and Rajya Sabha is solved by:
A. setting up Joint Select Committee
B. dissolving Lok Sabha
C. setting up adjudication committee
D. calling a joint session

71. The national anthem was written by ..... and was translated into English by .....
A. Bankim Chandra Chatterji, Aurobindo Ghosh
B. Rabindra Nath Tagore, Aurobindo Ghosh
C. Bankim Chandra Chatterji, Rabindra Nath Tagore
D. the national anthem was originally written in English and was translated later

72. The tear in human body is a solution of :
A. Sodium hydroxide and sodium chloride
B. Calcium bicarbonate and sodium chloride
C. Magnesium bicarbonate and sodium hydroxide
D. Sodium bicarbonate and Magnesium chloride

73. The drug seroxat is
A. a new medicine for treating the lepers.
B. a new medicine developed by British scientists and is used for the treatment of shyness and social phobia
C. is anti-AIDS therapy developed by France
D. is an antacid developed in India under guidance of WHO

74. What is "Bermuda Triangle" sometimes referred to as the "Grakeyard of ships", located?
A. in the South Pacific ocean
B. in the North Atlantic ocean
C. in the Indian ocean
D. in the Arctic ocean

75. The theory propounded by Nobel laurate Professor Amartya Sen–is commonly known as
A. The Famine Economics
B. The Theory of Economic Divide
C. The Amartya Sen Shift
D. The Amartya Sen Divide

76. Which is known as the Electronics City of India?
A. Tumkoor B. Secunderabad
C. Bhopal D. None of the above

77. The main objective behind the creation of concept of *Navratnas* in the public sector was
A. to increase the control of the PSUs over economy
B. to boost local manufacturing and exports in the core sectors
C. to improve the functional autonomy
D. to improve their image and efficiency by giving them high status

78. The North American seaport on the Pacific side is
A. Baltimore B. Boston
C. New York D. Seattle

79. The old name of Harare was
A. Sam B. Rhodesia
C. Salisbury D. Batavia

80. The famous Prince of Wales Museum is located in
A. Mumbai B. Kolkata
C. Vadodara D. Bangalore

81. Who invented Atom Bomb (Uranium Fission)?
A. A W Haffmann B. Otto Hahn
C. A Einstein D. None of the above

82. The first ever woman to go into space was
A. Kalpana Chawla
B. Valentina Tereshkova
C. Mary Pierce
D. None of the above

83. The highest mountain peak in India is
A. K-2 B. Everest
C. Kanchanjunga D. Makalu-I

84. The "Garden City" of England is
A. Portsmouth B. Manchester
C. Kent D. Warwickshire

85. *Habeas Corpus* is
A. an order of the International Court of Justice
B. a type of writ issued by a High Court or Supreme Court against illegal detention of a person.
C. the petition of a lawyer in the Supreme Court on behalf of his client for bail against the orders of any other court in India
D. None of the above

86. If impeachment motion is passed by the American Senate against the US President, he would have to
A. leave office and all his assets created by him during Presidency
B. leave office, lose his pensions, security cover and all those benefits that are accorded to a retired US President
C. jailed for five years and will not get any benefits.
D. retire honourably with all his benefits, compensations, assets and pensions remaining intact

87. Who appoints the non-permanent members of the UN Security Council?
A. the permanent members
B. the General Assembly
C. the International Court of Justice
D. None of the above

88. The Preamble of the Constitution was amended by:
A. 1st amendment B. 26th amendment
C. 42nd amendment D. 44th amendment

89. The only President to be elected twice is:
A. S. Radhakrishnan B. V.V. Giri
C. Rajendra Prasad D. N.S. Reddy

90. The official airline of Australia is
A. SIA B. Lufthansa
C. Modiluft D. None of the above

91. Which one of the following types of coal contains a higher percentage of carbon than the rest?
A. Bituminous Coal B. Lignite
C. Anthracite D. Peat

92. Ten Commandments were revealed by God to:
A. Abraham B. Moses
C. Jesus D. Peter

93. Kalinga in older days, is now known as:
A. Odisha B. Kohima
C. Karnataka D. Maharashtra

94. Bihu festival is celebrated in:
A. Gujarat B. Assam
C. Bihar D. West Bengal

95. Milk is an example of
A. gel B. emulsion
C. suspension D. mixture

96. The President can dissolve the Lok Sabha before expiry of its term, on the advice of:
A. Prime Minister
B. Speaker
C. Vice-President
D. Election Commissioner

97. In a landmark judgement, the Allahabad High Court ruled that
A. Capital Sentence is not to be imposed upon the rapists
B. pension is the fundamental right of the government employees
C. the Supreme Court should not be bothered for cases of financial compensation
D. None of the above

98. Tughlaq dynasty occupied Delhi throne after decline of:
A. Suri dynasty B. Slave dynasty
C. Lodhi dynasty D. Khilji dynasty

99. Governors of states are:
A. appointed by Chief Ministers
B. appointed by the President
C. elected by members of Legislative Assembly
D. elected by people

100. The partition of Bengal was carried out by:
A. Lord Curzon B. Lord Minto
C. Lord Canning D. Lord Ripon

101. The Air Force Day falls on
A. October 10 B. October 9
C. September 5 D. October 8

102. MAD stands for
A. Most Active Disease
B. Mica Aluminium Duo
C. Mutually Assured Death
D. Mutually Assured Destruction

103. "Disguised Unemployment" means
A. more persons employed for a job that only a few could accomplish
B. people without any technical jobs
C. woman without jobs in rural areas
D. employment of children in factories

104. In India, an active volcano is situated at
A. Lakshadweep
B. Chhotanagpur Plateau
C. Andaman and Nicobar
D. Malawa Plateau

105. The first country to establish trade relationships with India was
A. England B. France
C. Holland D. Portugal

106. Which has the highest share of electrical power generation in India?
A. thermal power
B. nuclear power
C. hydro-power
D. naphtha-based and gas-based power

107. The great ocean liner, known to be the best and luxurious during her times, sank in the year
A. 1902 B. 1912
C. 1908 D. 1889

108. Who among the following is known as the Indian Napoleon?
A. Chandra Gupta Maurya
B. Bindusar
C. Samudra Gupta
D. Harshvardhana

109. Time gap between two sessions of Parliament cannot exceed:
A. 3 months B. 6 months
C. 1 year D. no fixed gap

110. In which state, Panchayati Raj was introduced for the first time?
A. Bihar B. Punjab
C. Rajasthan D. Andhra Pradesh

111. Which one is not a national duty?
A. Respect the Constitution
B. Respect the President
C. Defend the country
D. Protect natural environment

112. Treaty of Seringapatam was signed between:
A. Tipu Sultan and Nawab of Hyderabad
B. Tipu Sultan and English
C. Tipu Sultan & Rani of Jhansi
D. Tipu Sultan and French

113. NHRC stands for
A. National Hydro Research Committee
B. National Handicapped Rahabilitation Council
C. National Human Rights Commission
D. None of the above

114. "Water water everywhere but not a drop to drink" who stated these lines in a poem?
A. John Milton
B. Samuel Taylor Coleridge
C. Lord Byron
D. P.B. Shelley

115. Rabindranath Tagore gave up his knighthood after:
A. Jallianwala Bagh Tragedy
B. Introduction of separate electorates
C. Bengal faminine
D. Bengal Partition

116. Which country is known as the land of golden wool?
A. India B. Turkey
C. Australia D. Myanmar

117. BIFR stands for
A. Bilateral and International Foreign Regulation
B. Board of Industrial Financial Resurrection

C. Board of Industrial and Financial Reconstruction
D. None of the above

118. Pinaca is a
A. drug for curing AIDS
B. multi-barrel rocket system
C. fighter aircraft developed by HAL
D. codename of the nuclear test operation carried out on May 11, 1998

119. Vice-President is ex-officio:
A. Member of Rajya Sabha
B. Chairman of Rajya Sabha
C. Member of Lok Sabha
D. Speaker of Lok Sabha

120. Vitamin C is not available in this food in sufficiently large quantities.
A. lemon B. tomato
C. cod liver oil D. fresh fruits

121. This book was not written in a jail
A. *Glimpses of World History* – J L Nehru
B. *The Bible* (German) – Martin Luther
C. *Les Miserables* – Victor Hugo
D. *Yama* – Mahadevi Verma

122. Who among the following can be removed from office through impeachment by Parliament?
A. Speaker of Lok Sabha
B. Prime Minister
C. President of India
D. Vice-President of India

123. The following is not the function of the liver.
A. to store excesssive sugar in the form of glycogen
B. the produce an antidote for neutralising poison
C. to manufacture red blood corpuscles
D. to purify the blood through bile

124. A fascist is a person whose views are extremely
A. left-winged B. rational
C. right-winged D. liberal

125. The famous mathematician and a professor of Astronomy designed this building in London
A. Westminister Abbey
B. St Paul's Cathedral
C. Stock Exchange
D. Tower of London

126. Which one of the following sounds cannot be heard by a human ear?
A. 30,000 vibrations per second
B. 10,000 vibrations per second
C. 1,000 vibrations per second
D. 300 vibrations per second

127. A weather balloon may not be inflated completely on the ground because
A. it cannot withstand the atmospheric pressure if inflated fully
B. if the balloon is inflated fully on ground, fuel consumption would be higher
C. the air inside the balloon expands as it rises and hence, the balloon could get burst
D. None of the above

128. Which one of the following vitamins is stored in the liver?
A. Vitamin C
B. Vitamin B_{12}
C. Vitamin A
D. Vitamin K and Vitamin A

129. All of the following are plant products except
A. silk B. cork
C. hemp D. linen

130. Which one of the following organs in the human body is known as "Adam's Apple"?
A. thyroid B. liver
C. thymus D. adrenal

131. Insecticides or medicines could be harmful
A. to the insects and weeds as they kill them instantaneously upon consumption
B. to the habitat as the environment could become polluted due to excessive usage of chemicals in our crop management processes
C. to the human beings and animals who consume the food adulterated by the insecticides and weedicides
D. to the transporters and movers of the crops who could inhale noxious fumes of insecticides and weedicides

132. Name the assassin of John Lennon
A. Art Buchwald
B. Lee Oswald
C. Mark David Chapman
D. None of the above

133. Which one of the following is not a sprinter?
A. Marion Jones
B. Florence Griffith Joyner
C. Ben Johnson
D. Susie O' Neill

134. Which of the following is called the "Gateway to the Pacific"?
A. Suez Canal B. Bering Sea
C. Panama Canal D. Gulf of Alaska

135. Which one of the following statements is true regarding the treaty on banning the land-mines?
A. the USA does not want to sign the CTBT
B. the treaty was kept open for signatures in Ottawa in December, 1997.
C. India has already signed it
D. A and B are true

136. Similipal Tiger reserve is situated in:
A. Madhya Pradesh B. Uttarakhand
C. Maharashtra D. Odisha

137. The famous Gandhian, who was also known as the "Frontier Gandhi," is
A. Liaqat Ali Khan
B. Yusuf Khan
C. Khan Abdul Ghaffar Khan
D. Abdul Wali Khan

138. Which one of the following is an alloy?
A. copper B. lanthanum
C. bronze D. uranium

139. World Environment Day is celebrated on
A. June 4 B. June 5
C. June 7 D. March 5

140. This country is the largest producer of cotton in the world.
A. India B. China
C. Egypt D. the USA

141. The quorum required to the Rajya Sabha is:
A. 100 B. 35
C. 25 D. 30

142. The temples of Khajuraho were built by
A. Chalukyas B. Pallavas
C. Rashtrakutas D. Chandelas

143. National Remote Sensing Agency (NRSA) is located at:
A. Hyderabad
B. Bengaluru
C. Thiruvananthapuram
D. Gadanki, near Tirupati

144. The clones for .... and .... have been developed.
A. man, cow B. crow, sheep
C. rat, cat D. sheep, rat

145. AWWA stands for
A. All Women Welfare Association
B. Army Wives Welfare Association
C. Airport Weather and Welfare Authority
D. None of the above

146. The popular book *The Gift of Time* by Jonathan Schell, deals with
A. the lewid affair of Bill Clinton and Monica Lewinsky
B. the elimination of nuclear weapons from the world
C. Indo-US relationships
D. the deteriorating environment in industrial America

147. How can a person move on a hard icy surface?
A. he should use roller skates
B. he should hop, sneeze, jump and step in the direction which is opposite to the direction of his required movement
C. he should hop, sneeze, jump and step in the direction in which the movement is required
D. he should skid on his knees and hands

148. The first conference of Non-Aligned Movement was held at:
A. The Hague
B. Moscow
C. Great Britain
D. Belgrade

149. Who is regarded as the founder of the scientific socialism?
A. Rousseau B. Karl Marx
C. Engles D. Lenin

150. Pyroclastics are
A. non-toxic gases
B. lava flows
C. fragments of hot rock and spattering lava
D. pollutant chemicals from a leather factory

151. Which one of the following is not a sedimentary rock?
A. slate B. limestone
C. clay D. sandstone

152. Oketa is
A. used to define human-induced climatic changes
B. used to describe increasing drought periods of high magnitudes
C. a unit to describe the prevailing cloudiness
D. None of the above

153. The following state produces the maximum quantities (85 percent) of raw silk in India
A. Kerala B. Jammu & Kashmir
C. Karnataka D. Tamil Nadu

154. Salal Hydro Electric Project is situated on the river
A. Beas B. Jhelum
C. Chenab D. Sutlej

155. Which is the largest island sea in the world?
A. Caribbean Sea B. Mediterranean Sea
C. Red Sea D. Beaufort Sea

156. What is the name of the bell used at the Lloyds in London?
A. The Great Bell B. The Charmer
C. The Tower Bell D. Lutine

157. What are "The Hagiographs?"
A. These are the poems written by Lord Byron
B. These are the holy writings of Jewish scriptures
C. These are the geographical lines representing same rainfall levels
D. None of the above

158. Which one of the following forms would provide the lowest protection?
A. Patent B. Trademark
C. Copyright D. Logo

159. The twenty-fifth State of India is
A. Goa B. Nagaland
C. Mizoram D. Delhi

160. What does the 17th Parallel line separate?
A. South and North America
B. North and South Korea
C. South and North Yemen
D. South and North Vietnam

161. Operation Flood-II, the prestigious milk products revolution of India, was initiated on
A. October 1, 1979 B. October 2, 1979
C. January 26, 1979 D. October 2, 1978

162. After World War I, the peace treaty was signed in:
A. Geneva B. Versailles
C. Paris D. Venice

163. Potassium chloride is given to the patient for
A. curing his bleeding gums
B. reducing his cholestrol level
C. reducing his blood pressure
D. alleviating his arthiritis pain

164. What is notation?
A. It is another word for "Mutually Assured Destruction"
B. It is the Latin deformation of the phrase "to swim"
C. It is a term used to denote the growth of illeterate masses
D. None of the above

165. The hideout of Adolf Hitler in the mountains was
A. Stuttgart B. Heidelberg
C. Berchtesgaden D. Both A and C

166. Who stated, "Where wealth accumulates decay?"
A. J M Keynes B. Adam Smith
C. Frederic Engels D. Oliver Goldsmith

167. Who was the national leader who wrote History of India on the walls of the Andaman Cellular Jail?
A. Ambedkar B. Vir Savarkar
C. Nandlal Bose D. Jyotiba Phule

168. The USA does not possess the following space shuttle
A. Columbia B. Atlantis
C. Challenger D. Discovery

169. The term "White Elephant" is used to denote
A. very bright and white item
B. very costly and expensive item
C. an item or a head that is very costly to maintain
D. an item or a head that is a part of the national economic budget of a country

170. Kolar Gold Mines are in this state.
A. Karnataka B. Bihar
C. Odisha D. Madhya Pradesh

21	22	23	24	25	26	27	28	29	30
D	B	B	D	D	C	A	C	C	C
31	32	33	34	35	36	37	38	39	40
C	A	A	C	D	C	A	B	B	D
41	42	43	44	45	46	47	48	49	50
B	C	B	B	C	D	A	A	D	A
51	52	53	54	55	56	57	58	59	60
D	A	C	A	C	B	C	A	C	C
61	62	63	64	65	66	67	68	69	70
B	A	C	B	D	D	A	C	C	D
71	72	73	74	75	76	77	78	79	80
B	B	B	B	C	D	C	D	C	A
81	82	83	84	85	86	87	88	89	90
B	B	A	C	B	B	B	C	C	D
91	92	93	94	95	96	97	98	99	100
C	B	A	B	B	A	B	D	B	A
101	102	103	104	105	106	107	108	109	110
D	D	A	C	D	A	B	C	B	C
111	112	113	114	115	116	117	118	119	120
B	B	C	B	A	C	C	B	B	C
121	122	123	124	125	126	127	128	129	130
D	C	D	C	B	A	C	C	A	A
131	132	133	134	135	136	137	138	139	140
C	C	D	C	D	D	C	C	B	B
141	142	143	144	145	146	147	148	149	150
C	D	A	D	B	B	B	D	B	C
151	152	153	154	155	156	157	158	159	160
A	C	C	C	B	D	B	A	A	D
161	162	163	164	165	166	167	168	169	170
B	B	C	B	C	D	B	C	C	A
171	172	173	174	175	176	177	178	179	180
B	D	A	D	A	C	C	C	D	C
181	182	183	184	185	186	187	188	189	190
A	A	D	B	D	A	D	D	D	B
191	192	193	194	195	196	197	198	199	200
C	B	C	A	B	A	D	B	D	A

SPORTS

1. The first winning stroke in Lawn Tennis gives the player:

A. 2 points B. 1 point
C. 10 points D. 15 points

2. Which of the following game is played for stipulated period of 70 minutes?

A. Hockey B. Football
C. Rugby D. Basketball

3. 'Merdeka cup' is associated with:

A. Golf
B. Football
C. Squash
D. Hockey

4. Arjuna Award has been instituted for outstanding contribution in the field of

A. Social Service

B. Games and Sports
C. Literature
D. Art and Music

5. Murugappa Gold Cup is associated with:
A. Football B. Polo
C. Hockey D. Bridge

6. Jimmy Connors and Geoff Boycott are related with following games respectively:
A. Tennis, Football B. Tennis, Cricket
C. Chess, Cricket D. Football, Hockey

7. The winner of the Golden Boot Award at the World Cup Soccer tournament organised in Yokohama was .... and he scored ...... goals.
A. Zinedine Zidane, four
B. Davor Suker, six
C. Ronaldo, eight
D. None of the above

8. Number of players in a team of Water polo is:
A. 7 B. 5
C. 9 D. 11

9. The term 'Steeple Chase' is associated with which of the following games
A. Polo B. Tennis
C. Horse Racing D. Cricket

10. Who is known as Father of India's "White Revolution" and "Operation Flood"?
A. Dr. Verghese Kurien
B. J.B. Kripalani
C. Baba Amte
D. Har Gobind Khorana

11. The first Olympic games were revived by ..... in 1896 at Athens
A. Lord Welsley
B. Queen Elizabeth-I
C. Baron Piere de Cubertin
D. None of the above

12. The national game of the USA is
A. swimming B. baseball
C. athletics D. None of the above

13. Jules Rimmet Cup is associated with
A. hockey B. archery
C. football D. table tennis

14. The approximate weight of a cricket ball is
A. 5.25 Oz B. 6.30 Oz
C. 7.20 Oz D. 8.25 Oz

15. The number of players on each side in a basketball match is
A. 10 B. 6
C. 5 D. 8

16. The first woman in the history of US open Championship to have played 100 matches, is:
A. Martina Navaratilova
B. Chris Evert
C. Steffi Graf
D. Helena Sukova

17. Swaythling Cup is associated with
A. World Table Tennis Tournament (men)
B. World Table Tennis Tournament (university)
C. World Table Tennis tournament (women)
D. World Hockey Tournament (university)

18. Which one of the following is not a cricket - playing nation?
A. West Indies B. Zimbabwe
C. Kenya D. Columbia

19. The first recipient of Major Dhyan Chand Khel Ratna Award (1991-92) was:
A. Geet Sethi B. N Kunjurani Devi
C. V Anand D. P K Garg

20. The first Olympic Games were held at Olympia (Greece) in the year:
A. 300 BC B. 776 BC
C. 500 BC D. 394 AD

21. Which of the following is the National Game of Spain?
A. Bull fighting B. Baseball
C. Rugby D. Golf

22. 'Ashes' is the name of a series between ..... and ..... and it relates to .....
A. Pakistan, Australia, Hockey
B. India, England, Cricket
C. England, Australia, Cricket
D. New Zealand, Australia, Cricket

23. The term "Butterfly Stroke" is associated with
A. Kabaddi B. Wrestling
C. Polo D. Swimming

24. Neeraj Chopra is associated with which sports?
A. Javelin Throw B. Tennis
C. Hockey D. Football

25. 'Gambit' is a term normally associated with
A. Bridge B. Chess
C. Billiards D. Polo

26. 'Bunker' and 'Chukker' are the two terms associated with
A. Polo B. Rowing
C. Bungey Jumping D. Ice Hockey

27. A Lawn Tennis court measures
A. 78 feet by 28 feet
B. 79 feet by 29 feet
C. 76 feet by 26 feet
D. 70 feet by 24 feet

28. Who scored the fastest timing (in case of an under-13 swimmer) for crossing the English Channel?
A. Arati Saha
B. Uday Shenoy
C. Rihen Mehta
D. Rupali Ramdas Ropal

29. Which one of the following has been entrusted with the responsibility of training coaches in various disciplines of sports?
A. Tata Football Academy
B. Ministry of Human Resource Development
C. Netaji Subhash Institute of Sports
D. Lakshmibai National College of Physical Education

30. The term 'Tee' is associated with which of the following sports?
A. Table Tennis
B. Polo
C. Golf
D. Judo

31. 'Deodhar Trophy' is associated with which of the following games?
A. Hockey B. Cricket
C. Football D. Basketball

32. Who was the first deaf & dumb swimmer in the world to swim 30 km Gibralter strait?
A. Des Renford
B. Mihir Sen
C. Arti Pradhan
D. Taranath Shenoy

33. The height of the net in the centre of the tennis court is
A. 3 feet, 5 inches B. 3 feet, 2 inches
C. 2 feet, 8 inches D. 2 feet, 6 inches

34. 'Canon' is a sports term associated with the following game.
A. Billiards B. Volleyball
C. Shot-Put D. Table Tennis

35. The Himalayan Mountaineering Institute is located in
A. Leh B. Darjeeling
C. Kohima D. Dispur

36. The diameter of a golf hole is
A. 4.36 inches B. 4.50 inches
C. 5.63 inches D. 4.75 inches

37. The total distance of a Marathon Race is ..... miles and ..... yards.
A. 29, 388 B. 26, 380
C. 26, 385 D. 25, 372

38. The first woman, who won six gold medals in a single Olympics tournament, was
A. Evelyn Ashford
B. Florence Griffth Joyner
C. Kristin Otto
D. Susi Susanti

39. In which year on account of a decree issued by Roman Emperor the Olympic Games were ceased to be played?
A. 350 AD B. 394 AD
C. 300 BC D. 384 AD

40. Putney (UK) is a place most frequently associated with
A. swimming B. horse racing
C. boat rowing D. polo

41. Rafael Nadal is associated with which sports?
A. Tennis B. Badminton
C. Cricket D. None of the above

42. The term 'Finesse' is normally associated with this game.
A. Chess B. Bridge
C. Snooker D. Rowing

43. The following trophy is not associated with cricket.
A. Ranji Trophy
B. Rohintan Baria Trophy
C. Singer-Akai-Nidahas Trophy
D. Lady Rattan Tata Trophy

44. Tonya Harding is a controversial athlete and has been associated with the following game.
A. Rowing B. Table Tennis
C. Figure Skating D. Boxing

45. When and where the first Asian Games were held?
A. 1955, Seoul B. 1951, New Delhi
C. 1954, Manila D. 1970, Bangkok

46. Who among the following won Gold medal in Tokyo Olympics 2020?
A. Pradeep Verma
B. Mangal Singh
C. Neeraj Chopra
D. P.V. Sindhu

47. What is the measurement of a Golf Hole?
A. 3½ inch in diameter
B. 4½ inch in diameter
C. 7½ centimeter in diameter
D. 10 inch in diameter

48. The term 'Diamond' is associated with the game of:
A. Baseball B. Bridge
C. Basketball D. Billiards

49. K Sasikaran is well known as a
A. table tennis player B. swimmer
C. chess player D. football player

50. Who won men's single at the Australian Open 2025?
A. Jannik Sinner
B. Roger Federer
C. Stanislas Wawrinka
D. Alexander Zverev

ANSWERS

1	2	3	4	5	6	7	8	9	10
D	A	B	B	C	B	C	A	C	A
11	**12**	**13**	**14**	**15**	**16**	**17**	**18**	**19**	**20**
C	B	C	A	C	B	A	D	C	B
21	**22**	**23**	**24**	**25**	**26**	**27**	**28**	**29**	**30**
A	C	D	A	B	A	A	D	C	C
31	**32**	**33**	**34**	**35**	**36**	**37**	**38**	**39**	**40**
B	D	B	A	B	B	C	C	B	C
41	**42**	**43**	**44**	**45**	**46**	**47**	**48**	**49**	**50**
A	B	D	C	B	C	B	A	C	A

HONOURS AND AWARDS

1. In which of the following years 'Nobel Prizes' were instituted?
A. 1910 B. 1905
C. 1901 D. 1911

2. The writer who refused the Nobel Prize for Literature was:
A. Winston Churchill
B. Prem Chand
C. Jean Paul Sartre
D. None of the above

3. Which country awards the Noble Prize?
A. USA B. India
C. Russia D. Sweden

4. In which of the following years Arjuna Awards were instituted
A. 1951 B. 1971
C. 1961 D. 1965

5. National Awards for Popularising Science was instituted in the year
A. 1981 B. 1985
C. 1987 D. 1988

6. The Government of which state has instituted the 'Tansen Samman'?
A. Madhya Pradesh B. Uttar Pradesh
C. Gujarat D. Maharashtra

7. The Lifetime Achievement Award, instituted by DRDO, has been awarded to an eminent nuclear scientist. His name is
A. Dr A P J Abdul Kalam
B. Mr B D Nagchowdhary
C. Mr George Fernandes
D. Mr Mulayam Singh Yadav

8. Who returned the award of 'Sir' given by the British government in protest against the "Jallianwala Bagh Massacre" on April 13, 1919?
A. Prem Chand
B. Thomas Roe
C. Rabindra Nath Tagore
D. Dada Bhai Nauroji

9. Nobel Prize is not awarded in the following disciplines
A. Chemistry and Physics
B. Literature and Peace
C. Economics and Medicine
D. Geography and Space Research

10. In which year Nehru Award for International Understanding instituted
A. 1965 B. 1969
C. 1974 D. 1964

11. Which of the following Indians was awarded Legion D award, the highest civilian awards of France
A. Jawahar Lal Nehru B. Satyajit Ray
C. Mother Teresa D. Shahrukh Khan

12. 'Pulitzer' prizes are awarded to Americans for excellence in
A. Films B. Journalism
C. Medicine D. Social Work

13. C.V. Raman received Nobel Prize in the year
A. 1934 B. 1931
C. 1932 D. 1930

14. Saraswati Samman is awarded by
A. Government of India
B. Sahitya Academy
C. K.K. Birla Foundation
D. Lalit Kala Akademi

15. On which day every year National Awards for Teachers are announced?
A. August 15 B. September 5
C. November 19 D. November 14

16. The National Award given to the distinguished sportsmen/women in India is known as
A. Dronacharya Award
B. Param Vir Chakra
C. Arjun Award
D. Nehru Award

17. The prestigious Ramon Magsaysay Award was instituted in the memory of Mr Ramon Magsaysay who was
A. the Secretary – General of UN
B. the Commander of NATO in Europe
C. the President of the Philippines
D. the President of Cambodia

18. The Kalinga Prize is awarded by UNESCO but it was founded by an Indian. His name is
A. Biju Patnaik B. Sharad Pawar
C. C V Raman D. Piloo Modi

19. Who was the first Indian to receive the World Food Prize?
A. Dr. Verghese Kurien
B. Dr. Amrita Patel
C. Dr. M.S. Swaminathan
D. None of these

20. Jesse Owens Global award is given in the field of:
A. Literature B. Sports
C. Science D. Journalism

21. Nobel Alfred Bernhard after whom Nobel Prizes are given was:
A. Engineer B. Doctor
C. Chemist D. Pilot

22. Grammy Awards are given in the field of
A. painting B. architecture
C. music D. rock dance

23. The highest civilian award of India is
A. *Padma Vibhushan* B. *Padma Shri*
C. *Bharat Ratna* D. *Param Vir Chakra*

24. The highest military award of India is
A. Shaurya Chakra
B. Param Vishisht Sewa Medal
C. Param Vir Chakra
D. Kirti Chakra

25. The first ever B R Ambedkar National Award was given to
A. Baba Amte
B. T Shiv Shankar Pillai
C. International Red Cross
D. National Institute for Social Work and Social Sciences

26. 'Victory Medal' is awarded in:
A. UK B. USA
C. Russia D. France

27. Which one of the following is not a Shram Award
A. Shram Bhushan B. Shram Dev
C. Shram Devi D. Shram Vir

28. Dr Shanti Swaroop Bhatnagar Awards are given in any field of science by
A. Indian Council of Applied Economic Research
B. Defence Research and Development Organisation
C. National Institute for Social Work and Social Sciences
D. Tata Institute of Fundamental Research

29. Who is the winner of the Miss World-2025 contest?
A. Nadia Ferreira
B. Opal Suchata Chuangsri
C. Lalela Mswane
D. Toni-Ann Singh

30. First Miss World Competition was established by 'Miss World Incorporation' in the year
A. 1941 B. 1950
C. 1951 D. 1957

31. The size of an Olympic medal is ..... mm and thickness is ..... mm.
A. 50, 2.5 B. 60, 3.0
C. 60.5, 3.5 D. 55.2, 2.5

32. "Dhanwantari Award" is given in the field of
A. swimming B. Bharata Natyam
C. cinema D. medicine

33. Nobel Prizes are not given for which of the following fields?
A. Physics B. Chemistry
C. Music D. Peace

34. Which is the second Highest Civilian award in India?
A. Padam Vibushan B. Padam Shri
C. Bharat Ratna D. Ashok Chakra

35. Abel Prize is associated with:
A. Mathematics B. Film
C. Music D. Writing

36. The second highest gallantry award in India is:
A. Padam Bhushan B. Vir Chakra
C. Mahavir Chakra D. Ashok Chakra

37. 'Mubarak-Al-Kabir' medal is the highest honour of
A. Kuwait B. Iran
C. Afghanistan D. Iraq

38. Bharatendu Harish Chandra awards are given annually for:
A. best local self administration
B. showing kindness and generosity of unusual kind
C. promoting original writing in Hindi
D. None of the above

39. Who won the Man Booker Prize 2024 for 'Orbital'?
A. Samantha Harvey
B. Subhash Khot
C. Maryam Mirzakhani
D. Arthur Avila

40. Who has been selected for the prestigious Jnanpith award for the year 2024?
A. Alok Puranik
B. Vinod Kumar Shukla
C. Mrinal Pandey
D. Vishwanath Tiwari

41. Name the women sportsperson, who became the first Indian women to hold an honorary rank of Lieutenant Colonel in the countrys's defence forces.
A. Krishna Punia B. Saina Nehwal
C. Sania Mirza D. MC Mary Kom

42. Oscar award is related to
A. books
B. politics
C. European Community
D. films

43. Miss Universe award 2024 has been won by whom?
A. Victoria Kjaer Theilvig
B. Manya Singh
C. Olivia Yace
D. Shree Saini

44. Out of the Gallantry awards — PVSM, AVSM and VSM — the most exceptional medal is
A. PVSM
B. AVSM
C. VSM
D. All have equal recognition status

45. *Jeewan Raksha Padak* is awarded for
A. bravery in the battle front
B. fine display of vocal music skills
C. saving the life of human beings
D. None of the above

46. Who is not eligible for Bharat Ratna?
A. A government official
B. A sportsperson
C. A film actress
D. A Prime Minister

47. Jamnalal Bajaj award is given in the field of
I. Social Work
II. Fine Arts
III. Application of Science and Technology
IV. Literature
A. I and II B. I, II and III
C. II and IV D. I and III

48. In which year Indira Gandhi Peace Prize was instituted?
A. 1985 B. 1984
C. 1986 D. 1987

49. Borlaug Award was instituted for recognising outstanding contribution in the field of:
A. Ecology B. Medicine
C. Agriculture D. Journalism

50. Except Dr. Nelson Mandela, who is the other non-Indian so far honoured with Bharat Ratna
A. Dr. Julius Nyerere
B. Helen Hint
C. Hideki Yuka
D. Khan Abdul Ghaffar Khan

ANSWERS

1	2	3	4	5	6	7	8	9	10
C	C	D	C	C	A	B	C	D	D
11	**12**	**13**	**14**	**15**	**16**	**17**	**18**	**19**	**20**
B	B	D	C	B	C	C	A	C	B
21	**22**	**23**	**24**	**25**	**26**	**27**	**28**	**29**	**30**
C	C	C	C	D	B	B	C	B	C
31	**32**	**33**	**34**	**35**	**36**	**37**	**38**	**39**	**40**
B	D	C	A	A	C	A	C	A	B
41	**42**	**43**	**44**	**45**	**46**	**47**	**48**	**49**	**50**
D	D	A	A	C	A	D	C	C	D

BOOKS AND AUTHORS

1. The book "*The Insider*" is written by
A. Madhav Rao Scindia
B. Nana Patekar
C. Shobha De
D. P V Narasimha Rao

2. *India Wins Freedom* was written by
A. Dadabhai Nauroji
B. Ashfaqulla Khan
C. Sarojini Naidu
D. Maulana Abul Kalam Azad

3. *A Tale of Two Cities* is, in fact, the story of two famous cities. Those cities are
A. Paris and New York
B. London and New York
C. London and Paris
D. Stockholm and New York

4. *Ben Hur* was penned by
A. Lewis Wallace
B. Lord Byron
C. William Shakespeare
D. None of the above

5. *Panchatantra* was written by
A. R K Narayan B. R K Laxman
C. Vishnu Sharma D. None of the above

6. Arundhati Roy has been awarded the prestigious

A. Booker's Prize – 1997
B. Jnanpeeth Award – 1997
C. Sahitya Akademi Award – 1998
D. None of the above

7. Who wrote *Odyssey?*
A. George Orwell B. Homer
C. Dom Moraes D. None of the above

8. Which one of the following was not written by Shakespeare?
A. *As You Like It*
B. *Mcbeth*
C. *Hamlet*
D. *A Farewell to Arms*

9. Lewis Carol wrote a masterpiece. What is its name?
A. *Don Quixote*
B. *Alice in Wonderland*
C. *Adventures of Robinson Crusoe*
D. *Great Expectations*

10. The *Tamil Ramayana* is the work of
A. Tulsidas B. Jayangondar
C. Kambar D. Veda Vyas

11. In *Shrimad Bhagwat Geeta,* Lord Krishna teaches his disciple Arjuna to
A. rise to the occasion and fight with his near and dear ones
B. withdraw from the battlefield
C. do his duty and not to expect anything in return
D. attack the enemy in a planned and meticulous approach

12. Who wrote *Origin of Species?*
A. Charles Darwin
B. Alexander Flaming
C. G.B. Shaw
D. D.H. Lawrence

13. The poet and the well-known friend of Prithvi Raj Chauhan, who wrote *Prithvi Raj Raso,* was
A. Harisena B. Vishnu Datt
C. Chand Bardai D. None of the above

14. The first book was printed in India in the year 1561. Its name was
A. *The spiritual Compendium of the Christian Life*
B. *Aain-e-Akbari*
C. *Babur Nama*
D. *Ram Charit Manas*

15. The famous book *Runs and Ruins* was written by
A. Sir Donald Bradman
B. Sunil Gavaskar
C. Kapil Dev
D. Richard Hadlee

16. Adam Smith wrote the following famous book
A. The Wreck
B. Dr Zhivago
C. The Wealth of Nations
D. Tarzan of the Apes

17. H G Wells is known as a
A. poet
B. science-fiction writer
C. thriller-fiction writer
D. essay writer and critic

18. Tukaram wrote his devotional songs in this language
A. Urdu B. Gujarati
C. Hindi D. Marathi

19. Our ancient scholars and writers used this language for their social, religious and political books and works
A. Tamil
B. Sanskrit
C. Urdu
D. Hindi *(Devanagari)*

20. *Gora* is the hero of a book written by Rabindra Nath Tagore. What is the name of the book?
A. *Geetanjali* B. *Patanjali*
C. *Gora* D. *Twelfth Night*

21. Shylock is
A. the villain *in A Pound of Flesh* by William Shakespeare
B. an old Jew who is a famous hero of the Israeli nation
C. the hero of *Miranda,* written by William Shakespeare
D. the comic character of *Alice In the Wonderland* by Lewis Caroll

22. The following was a famous Hindi author and story-writer

A. Shobha De B. Aruna Asaf Ali
C. Mahadevi Verma D. Amrita Pritam

23. *Mudrarakshasa* was composed by
A. Vishakhadatta B. Bhavabhuti
C. Sivananda D. Jayadeva

24. *Razor's Edge* was written by
A. Toni Morrison
B. Saul Bellow
C. W Somerset Maugham
D. None of the above

25. *Sakharam Binder* is a famous play written by
A. Anil Barve B. Vijay Tendulkar
C. V S Naipaul D. Tasleema Nasreen

26. The major work of Sir Isaac Newton is
A. *Principia*
B. *Heritage*
C. *Human knowledge*
D. *I Dare*

27. The hero of *The Jungle Book,* written by Rudyard Kipling, is
A. the lion
B. Mowghuli
C. the father of Mowghuli
D. there is no hero

28. Who stated, "Peace hath her victories, no less renowned than war?"
A. Alfred Lord Tennyson
B. William Shakespeare
C. John Milton
D. None of the above

29. Macawber is a character who was created by
A. Thomas Hardy B. P G Wodehouse
C. Charles Dickens D. J W Von Goethe

30. *Pride and Prejudice* was written by
A. Anton Chekhov B. Maxim Gorky
C. Jane Austen D. Anthony West

31. *In the Afternoon Time* is the English translation of the autobiography of the famous poet, Harivansh Rai Bachchan. The autobiography was translated into English by
A. Vikram Seth B. Dr Rupert Snell
C. William Faulkner D. P D Tandon

32. Who is the author of the book *The Celestine Vision?*
A. Paul Hockins B. Salman Rushdie
C. Joseph Conrad D. James Redfield

33. The author of the famous book *Blue Mountain Revisited* is
A. Charles Kingsley
B. Virginia Woolf
C. Arthur Koestler
D. Peter Topkins

34. Homer was the great poet of the following language
A. Italian B. Greek
C. Arabic D. French

35. Hard Choices is a famous book written by :
A. Hillary Clinton
B. Barack Obama
C. Narendra Modi
D. Imran Khan

36. *Godaan* was written by Munshi Prem Chand and it depicts
A. the methodology for taking adequate care of the cows
B. exploitation of simple rural folk by the rich landlords of rural India
C. the mutiny of 1857 in which, Indians refused to bite the *Kartoos* made with cow beef
D. None of the above

37. Manu wrote a book during ancient times in which, he divided the Aryan society into four distinct classes. What was the name of the book?
A. *Arthashastra*
B. *Manusmriti*
C. *Moti Mahal*
D. *My Truth*

38. R. Venkataraman wrote *My Presidential Years.* What was the main theme of the book?
A. It described the aristocratic procedures being followed in the *Rashtrapati Bhawan* during his tenure as President
B. It described the power equations and ploys in the centre and in the states during his term
C. It described how he felt caged while he was President due to a load of procedures and formalities
D. It explained the machinations of the political party which was in power during his tenure as President

39. The hero of the play cried in the end, "Et Tu, Brute!" and died. Which is the play and who is the author?
A. The Wealth of Nations — Adam Smith
B. Mein Kempf — Adolf Hitler
C. Julius Caesar — William Shakespeare
D. None of the above

40. Don Veto Corleone was the undisputed king of the underworld in this novel. This masterpiece was also converted into a film in which Al Pacino played the role of the Don. What is the name of the novel and that of the author?
A. *A Farewell to Arms* — E Hemingway
B. *The Godfather* — Mario Puzo
C. *From Here to Eternity* — James Jones
D. *Dialogue with Death* — Arthur Koestler

41. *Gypsy Camp Vanishes Into the Blue* was a famous blockbuster movie made by the erstwhile USSR. The original story was written by a famous author. His name is
A. Leo Tolstoy
B. Anton Chekhov
C. Maxim Gorky
D. Leon Uris

42. The total number of *Puranas* written during the Vedic age is
A. 22 B. 9
C. 18 D. 25

43. Who wrote Monsoon Memories?
A. Jo Nesbo
B. Ratna
C. Renita D'Silva
D. Amartya Sen

44. 'Waiting for a Visa' is the autobiography of which of the following persons:
A. Indira Gandhi
B. Mahatma Gandhi
C. Jawaharlal Nehru
D. B.R. Ambedkar

45. According to *The Ramayana,* who received the last teaching lessons from the knowledgeable Ravana while he was on his death-bed?
A. Rama
B. Sugreeva
C. Laxmana
D. Both A and C

46. He was a German but he saved many a Jew from the cruel hands of the Nazis. A movie was made on this theme which won the coveted Oscar Prize. The book and the author are
A. *Operation Shylock* — Philip Roth
B. *Schindler's List* — Thomas Keneally
C. *The Rescue* — Joseph Conrad
D. *The Slave* — Isaac Bashevis Singer

47. He was the favourite assistant of Sherlock Holmes, the famous character created by Arthur Conan Doyle. His name is
A. Zhivago B. Watson
C. Hawkins D. Hector

48. He was a former member of British Parliament. He has written many hit fiction novels. One of his novels is
A. Shall We Tell the President?
B. The Rape of the Lock
C. Snow Country
D. Small Land

49. He wrote *Sharmili*, *Gaylord* and *Kati Patang*. His novels were written in Hindi and some of them have been converted into films also. His name is
A. Gita Mehta
B. B N Mullick
C. Nirad C Chaudhary
D. Gulshan Nanda

50. 'The Lives of Others' is written by..........
A. Neel Mukherjee
B. Charu Singh
C. R.D. Pradhan
D. Shivani Lohia

ANSWERS

1	2	3	4	5	6	7	8	9	10
D	D	C	A	C	A	B	D	B	C

11	12	13	14	15	16	17	18	19	20
C	A	C	A	B	C	B	D	B	C
21	**22**	**23**	**24**	**25**	**26**	**27**	**28**	**29**	**30**
A	C	A	C	B	A	B	C	C	C
31	**32**	**33**	**34**	**35**	**36**	**37**	**38**	**39**	**40**
B	D	D	B	A	B	B	C	C	B
41	**42**	**43**	**44**	**45**	**46**	**47**	**48**	**49**	**50**
C	C	C	D	C	B	B	A	D	A

ECONOMY, BUSINESS AND COMMERCE

1. Who is the Chairman of Island Development Authority?
A. President
B. Prime Minister
C. Finance Minister
D. Minister of Environment

2. World Economic Situation and Prospects Report is associated with:
A. IMF B. World Bank
C. United Nations D. WTO

3. The economies of the Oriental countries depend upon the growth or decline of
A. the American economy
B. the Japanese economy
C. the Korean economy
D. the Thai economy

4. The difference between the monetary policy and the fiscal policy is
A. fiscal policy tries to control aggregate demand through budgetary means whereas monetary policy controls the same through the quantity of money and the rate of interest
B. monetary policy is related to the money supply whereas the fiscal policy is related to the rate of interest
C. monetary policy is automatic whereas the fiscal policy is discretionary
D. both the policies are similar and have similar objectives

5. Which one of the following is a *Navratna* Company?
A. Delhi Vidyut Board
B. National Textiles Corporation
C. Mahanagar Telephone Nigam Ltd
D. Electronics Corporation of India Ltd

6. Which country holds the dubious distinction of becoming the biggest user of anti-dumping duty (ADD) since the Uruguay Round?
A. China B. Japan
C. US D. India

7. Find the odd city with the viewpoint of Indian Railways
A. Chittaranjan B. Chennai
C. Kapurthala D. Trombay

8. Which company released the slogan "Redefining the value of Rupee?"
A. Toshiba B. Samsung
C. Akai D. Panasonic

9. 'Shishu', 'Tarun' and 'Kishore' named enterprises are associated with:
A. SBI
B. IDBI
C. MUDRA Bank
D. NABARD

10. The major field of research of the Nobel laureate, Amartya Sen, is
A. mixed economy
B. welfare economics
C. the Amartya Sen Shift
D. capitalistic economy

11. GST has been implemented in:
A. 2014 B. 2015
C. 2016 D. 2017

12. Which one of the following is not a chief characteristic of FEMA?
A. Current account transactions are permitted unless there are RBI restrictions
B. Capital accounts transactions are permitted unless there are RBI transactions

C. Treatment for violations is harsh and is deemed to be a congnisable and non-bailable offence

D. Enforcement Directorate can arrest the accused in case of violations

13. The current market trends are

A. recession oriented

B. inflation oriented

C. recession oriented with inflation

D. boom oriented

14. Which of the following is not helpful in controlling money supply?

A. CRR

B. Bank Rate

C. Free Market Policy

D. Change in margin requirement

15. This company does not deal in consumer durables?

A. Samsung B. Akai

C. Godrej D. Nestle

16. Find the odd one out.

A. Lintas B. HTA

C. Contract D. LML

17. E-com does not require?

A. Internet connectivity

B. Technological inputs

C. Negotiations through E-mail

D. Knowledge about entertainment groups

18. Which one of the following is not an infrastructure related project?

A. Narmada Valley Project

B. North-South and East-West Corridors

C. Software exports

D. Railway modernisation

19. When the stock markets crash, then

A. stocks sell at lower prices than anticipated

B. scrips sell at higher prices than anticipated

C. the sellers are not very keen to sell in anticipation of sudden rise in values of stocks

D. None of the above

20. What is 'Dumping?'

A. It is the term given by the economists to excavation and digging activities of the MNCs that deal in earth moving equipment

B. It is the sale of the products and services by foreign nations and firms at very low prices so that they could find firm markets in India

C. It is the excessive supply of fast moving consumer goods by a developed country to an under-developed country

D. It is a series of measures taken by Government of India to facilitate international trade

21. Varishtha Pension Bima Yojna has been launched by

A. National Insurance Co.

B. LIC of India

C. Oriental Insurance Co.

D. United India Insurance Co.

22. Which company is the manufacturer of the product brand name 'Spectra?'

A. Telco B. Kinetic

C. LML D. None of the above

23. Who wrote the General Theory of Employment, Interest and Money?

A. Kaldor B. Marx

C. Keynes D. Marshall

24. Which one of the following is not an electronics products manufacturer?

A. Samsung B. Matsushita

C. Motorola D. Ford

25. World Economic Situation and Prospects Report is associated with—

A. IMF

B. World Bank

C. United Nations

D. WTO

26. What is the base year of newly introduced Consumer Price Index (CPI)?

A. 2000 B. 2004

C. 2012 D. 2011

27. The spirit of JIT is to

A. produce that much which could be sold and acquire that much of material inputs that could justify the sales

B. produce less but buy still lesser

C. collect orders from the markets and then produce

D. keep your inventory levels just equal to the market demand for the products

28. 'New Silk Route' is a rail route which links China with the European country—
A. France B. Germany
C. Italy D. Japan

29. Who among the following was first among the European nations to trade with India?
A. Britain B. Spain
C. Portugal D. France

30. GTX Extra is a brand name associated with
A. MRF B. HP
C. IOL D. Castrol

31. In India, the first bank of limited liability managed Indians and founded in 1881 was
A. Hindustan Commercial Bank
B. Oudh Commercial Bank
C. Punjab and Sind Bank
D. Bank of India

32. In the new millennium, the industries related to.....would be facing maximum growth rates?
A. manufacturing
B. FMCGs
C. information technology
D. consumer non-durables

33. Which one of the following items is not exported from India?
A. gold ornaments B. leather items
C. software products D. nuclear weapons

34. The stock value index of the registered companies of a stock exchange is known as
A. Nikkei B. Dow-Jones
C. Sensex D. None of the above

35. India has her only OTCEI in
A. Kolkata B. Indore
C. Mumbai D. New Delhi

36. Estimates of National Income in India are prepared by
A. Ministry of Finance
B. NITI Aayog
C. Reserve Bank of India
D. Central Statistical Organisation

37. If the Rupee becomes stronger vis-a-vis the US Dollar, then
A. exports would rise
B. imports would remain stagnant
C. exports would decline
D. None of the above

38. Which of the following is a subsidiary of RBI?
A. SIDBI
B. NABARD
C. National Housing Bank
D. All of the above

39. Which one of the following is not a core operation of L & T group?
A. Electricals
B. Construction Machinery
C. Shipping
D. Cement

40. The famous breakfast cereal Kellogg was started as .... during its early days of inception.
A. medicine
B. diet for patients in a nursing home
C. breakfast food for some top businessmen of the USA
D. diet enriching ingredient for the school-going children in Europe

41. Who observed, "as the population increases, the economic means of supporting that population do not grow in the same proportion?".
A. Goldsmith B. Malthus
C. Frederic Engels D. Adam Smith

42. The eminent Nobel Laureate–Amartya Sen is known for his research in
A. welfare economics
B. draughts and famines
C. poverty elimination
D. free market system of economy

43. Index 'Residex' is associated with:
A. Share Prices
B. Mutual Fund Prices
C. Land Prices
D. Price Inflation Index

44. The new industrial policy of India was announced in
A. 1996 B. 1991
C. 1997 D. 1998

45. If supply of onions is reduced, then
A. the demand would rise and the prices of the existing stocks would jump up
B. the demand would rise but prices would remain unaffected

C. the demand would fall as the users would avoid taking onions because of the fear of a sharp price rise
D. None of the above

46. How could the government break the vicious cycle of poverty among the poor masses?
A. By providing them with money
B. By providing them with opportunities of employment and entreprenenrship
C. By educating them about family planning
D. By getting loans for them from global financial agencies

47. WTO is dedicated to
A. liberal trade terms between the member nations
B. removal of all the trade protection procedures by all the member nations
C. agreements on patents of agricultural commodities like rice etc.
D. None of the above

48. Under which clause of Income Tax Act, taxpayer gets tax rebate on the premium paid for health insurance?
A. 80A B. 80C
C. 80D D. 80G

49. The basic objective of SIDBI is to
A. give more loans for infrastructure development to the corporate sector
B. grant loans to agricultural farmers for export of their commodities
C. solve the financial problems of small scale industries
D. assist IDBI and ICICI in the process of national industrial development

50. The major function of the Food Corporation of India is:
A. to control the demand side of foodgrains
B. to distribute high yielding variety seeds
C. to check the fluctuation in foodgrain price by controlling supply
D. to extend credit to farmers

ANSWERS

1	**2**	**3**	**4**	**5**	**6**	**7**	**8**	**9**	**10**
B	B	B	A	C	D	D	C	C	B
11	**12**	**13**	**14**	**15**	**16**	**17**	**18**	**19**	**20**
D	D	C	C	D	D	D	C	A	B
21	**22**	**23**	**24**	**25**	**26**	**27**	**28**	**29**	**30**
B	D	C	D	B	C	A	B	C	D
31	**32**	**33**	**34**	**35**	**36**	**37**	**38**	**39**	**40**
B	C	D	C	C	D	C	C	C	B
41	**42**	**43**	**44**	**45**	**46**	**47**	**48**	**49**	**50**
B	A	C	B	A	B	A	C	C	C

BANKING AND FINANCE

1. Which one of the following services is not provided by the mobile banking service?
A. Checking of balance of an account
B. Requesting for an accounts statement
C. Enquiring details of the fixed deposit
D. Asking for share prices of all the stocks at the BSE

2. Scheduled bank is that bank which is:
A. Nationalised
B. Not-nationalised
C. Based at foreign country
D. Included in the Second Schedule of R.B.I.

3. Grameen Bank and Micro Credit are asociated with:
A. Manmohan Singh B. Bill Gates
C. Md. Yunus D. Aung San Su Ki

4. ICICI Bank, prior to commencing its operations as a bank was a/an:
A. Market research group
B. Industrial finance corporation

C. Small-time player in consumer durables
D. Conduct for RRBs

5. If there is a capital flight from India:
A. Exchange rate of rupee will fall
B. Share prices will rise
C. Interest rate will fall
D. Exchange rate of rupee will rise

6. The headquarters of standard Chartered Bank are located at:
A. New York B. Hawai
C. London D. New Delhi

7. The term 'Orange Economy' is referred to:
A. Orange Farming
B. Creative Economy
C. Food Processing Industry
D. Silk Industry

8. India's first floating ATM has been launched in Kerala by
A. Canara Bank
B. Corporation Bank
C. HDFC Bank
D. State Bank of India

9. Which are the three international credit card companies?
A. Amex, Citibank, Master
B. Master, Amex, HSBC
C. Amex, Master, Visa
D. Visa, Citibank, Standard Chartered

10. Name the first bank in India to start using PKI (Public Key Infrastructure) based digital signatures for electronic fund transfer.
A. Bank of Punjab
B. Punjab National Bank
C. Canara Bank
D. Bank of Baroda

11. Federal Reserves is the Central Bank of...
A. Britain B. U.S.A.
C. Japan D. Canada

12. Capital market means
A. Mutual funds B. Money market
C. Direct taxes D. Securities market

13. The World Bank has given a go-ahead to India on the Baglihar Hydro-electric Project being build on the river:
A. Jhelum B. Sutlej
C. Chenab D. Beas

14. Which state has maximum branches of public sector commercial banks?
A. U.P. B. Maharashtra
C. Karnataka D. Gujarat

15. The "Adhoc Treasury Bill System" of meeting budget deficit in India was replaced by 'Ways and Means Advances System' which has come into force on:
A. March 31, 1997 B. April 1, 1996
C. April 1, 1997 D. None of these

16. Plastic money relates to:
A. Plastic currency B. Paper currency
C. ATM cards D. Credit cards

17. What is the minimum period for which banks may accept term deposits, according to RBI guidelines?
A. 15 days B. 30 days
C. 46 days D. 91 days

18. In the context of stock market, the abbreviation IPO stands for
A. Immediate Payment Order
B. Internal Policy Obligation
C. External Policy Obligation
D. Initial Public Offering

19. The Reserve Bank of India (RBI) keeps on modifying various rates/ratios to keep the flow of liquidity in the market in a balanced situation. Which of the following rates/ratios/indexes is not directly controlled by the RBI?
A. Cash Reserve Ratio (CRR)
B. Bank Rate
C. Repo Rate
D. Wholesale Price Index (WPI)

20. Which bank launched the first international credit card in India?
A. Hong Kong Bank B. Citibank
C. SBI D. Deutsche Bank

21. What is near money?
A. Money that is banked in nearby banks
B. Assets that are easily convertible into cash
C. Money held in local currency
D. Money that can be recalled easily

22. What is fiat money?
A. Money not backed by gold or any other valuable goods
B. Money issued by a government fiat
C. Money used to buy worthless assets
D. Assets that are easily convertible into cash

23. Which bank introduced the first Automatic Teller Machine (ATM) in India?
A. State Bank of India
B. Citibank
C. Bank of America
D. Hong Kong Bank

24. Bank of Rajasthan, belongs to which business family of India?
A. Hindujas B. Singhanias
C. Bangurs D. Modis

25. Which company launched the first electronic cash card in India?
A. Kotak Mahindra B. SBI
C. Bank of Baroda D. Escorts Finance

26. Where is the foreign exchange of India deposited?
A. Reserve Bank of India
B. State Bank of India
C. Both (A) and (B)
D. Union Finance Ministry

27. The apex institution in the field of industrial development banking in India is:
A. IFCI B. ICICI
C. LIC D. IDBI

28. Banking Sector will fall under which of the following sectors?
A. Agricultural Sector B. Service Sector
C. Manufacturing Sector D. Industrial Sector

29. Which of the following types of borrowings from the IMF has the softest servicing conditions?
A. Second Tranch Loan B. SAF
C. ESAF D. Oil facility

30. If the cash-reserve ratio is lowered by the Central Bank, what will be its effect on credit creation?
A. It will decrease credit creation
B. It will not decrease credit creation
C. It will increase credit creation
D. It will not change credit creation

31. "Conditionality" of an I.M.F. loan to a member country stands for:
A. Schedule of disbursement of loan instalments
B. Interest and repayment terms of the loan
C. The policy steps which the borrower country must take
D. An assessment of the credit-worthiness of the borrower

32. Credit is a:
A. Stock concept B. Flow concept
C. A stock-flow concept D. None of these

33. The IBRD aims at:
A. Promoting international monetary co-operation
B. Helping in reconstruction and development of economics
C. Helping children all over the world
D. Promoting the peaceful uses of atomic energy

34. People's Bank of India was founded in the year:
A. 1910 B. 1911
C. 1901 D. 1920

35. The RBI was established in the year:
A. 1935 B. 1936
C. 1940 D. 1945

36. Blank cheque is:
A. Without date
B. A cheque which has been signed and dated but in which the amount payable has not been filled in
C. Without signatures
D. None of the above

37. The United Commercial Bank was started by the Birlas in the year:
A. 1948 B. 1943
C. 1949 D. 1950

38. Financial Investment is:
A. Any investment
B. Investment which cannot be traded
C. Any investment which can be traded, such as shares, certificates of deposit, etc
D. None of the above

39. A Joint Account is:
A. A firm account
B. A bank account owned jointly by two or more people
C. A shop account
D. None of the above

40. The Foreign Investments Board was set up in the year:
A. 1960 B. 1968
C. 1969 D. 1970

41. The SBI floated its first Mutual Fund in the year:
A. 1987 B. 1988
C. 1989 D. 1990

42. Loan Shark is:
A. A person who lends money at a very high interest rate
B. Lending money at lower rates
C. Lending money without interest
D. None of the above

43. The IDBI started its operations in year:
A. 1964 B. 1965
C. 1966 D. 1967

44. Banking Companies Act was passed in the year:
A. 1947 B. 1948
C. 1949 D. 1950

45. Bearer Cheque is a cheque that is payable to:
A. A person whosoever present it to the banker
B. Only to the account person
C. Only to the account holder
D. None of the above

46. The Imperial Bank was converted to State Bank of India in the year:
A. 1950 B. 1955
C. 1956 D. 1957

47. The Unit Trust of India was launched in the year:
A. 1964 B. 1965
C. 1966 D. 1967

48. Treasury Bills are:
A. Taxes
B. Marketable financial bills of the central government
C. Acts
D. None of the above

49. CACS (Capital Adequacy, Asset Quality, Compliance and Systems) is a rating model used by RBI. This system is used by RBI to rate:
A. State run banks outside India
B. Foreign banks operating in India
C. Private banks in India
D. Co-operative banks

50. Name of the first Indian financial institution to be listed on the New York Stock Exchange (NYSE).
A. IFCI B. UTI
C. ICICI D. IDBI

ANSWERS

1	2	3	4	5	6	7	8	9	10
D	D	C	B	A	C	B	D	C	A
11	**12**	**13**	**14**	**15**	**16**	**17**	**18**	**19**	**20**
B	D	C	A	C	D	B	D	D	A
21	**22**	**23**	**24**	**25**	**26**	**27**	**28**	**29**	**30**
B	A	D	C	D	A	D	B	C	C
31	**32**	**33**	**34**	**35**	**36**	**37**	**38**	**39**	**40**
C	C	B	C	A	B	B	C	B	B
41	**42**	**43**	**44**	**45**	**46**	**47**	**48**	**49**	**50**
A	A	A	B	A	B	A	B	B	C

* * * * *